TURKEY, THE GREAT POWERS,
AND THE BAGDAD RAILWAY

THE MACMILLAN COMPANY
NEW YORK · BOSTON · CHICAGO · DALLAS
ATLANTA · SAN FRANCISCO

MACMILLAN & CO., Limited
LONDON · BOMBAY · CALCUTTA
MELBOURNE

THE MACMILLAN CO. OF CANADA, Ltd.
TORONTO

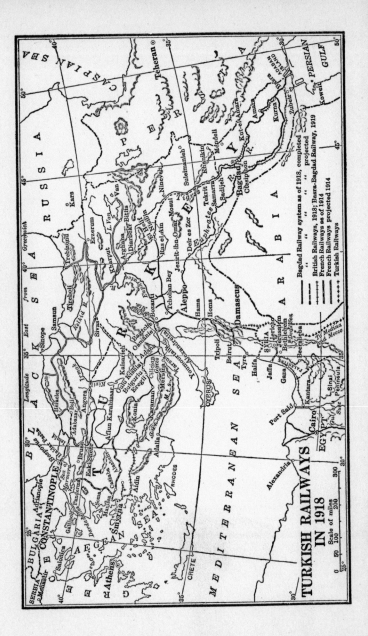

TURKISH RAILWAYS
IN 1918

Scale of miles
0 50 100 200 300

Bagdad Railway system as of 1918, completed
"   "   "   "   1918; Basra-Bagdad Railway, 1919
"   "   "   "   projected
French Railways as of 1914
French Railways projected 1914
Turkish Railways

Turkey, The Great Powers,
and
The Bagdad Railway

A Study in Imperialism

BY

EDWARD MEAD EARLE, Ph.D.

ASSISTANT PROFESSOR OF HISTORY IN
COLUMBIA UNIVERSITY

New York

THE MACMILLAN COMPANY

1923

COPYRIGHT, 1923,
BY THE MACMILLAN COMPANY.

Set up and electrotyped. Published July, 1923.

Press of
J. J. Little & Ives Company
New York, U. S. A.

"When the history of the latter part of the nineteenth century will come to be written, one event will be singled out above all others for its intrinsic importance and for its far-reaching results; namely, the conventions of 1899 and of 1902 between His Imperial Majesty the Sultan of Turkey and the German Company of the Anatolian Railways."— Charles Sarolea, *The Bagdad Railway and German Expansion as a Factor in European Politics* (Edinburgh, 1907), p. 3.

"The Turkish Government, I know, have been accused of being corrupt. I venture to submit that it has not been for want of encouragement from Europeans that the Turks have been corrupt. The sinister—I think it is not going too far to use that word—effect of European financiers on Turkey has had more to do with the misgovernment than any Turk, young or old."—Sir Mark Sykes, in the House of Commons, March 18, 1914.

PREFACE

THE Chester concessions and the Anglo-American controversy regarding the Mesopotamian oilfields are but two conspicuous instances of the rapid development of American activity in the Near East. Turkey, already an important market for American goods, gives promise of becoming a valuable source of raw materials for American factories and a fertile field for the investment of American capital. Thus American religious interests in the Holy Land, American educational interests in Anatolia and Syria, and American humanitarian interests in Armenia, are now supplemented by substantial American economic interests in the natural resources of Asia Minor. Political stability and economic progress in Turkey no longer are matters of indifference to business men and politicians in the United States; therefore the Eastern Question—so often a cause of war—assumes a new importance to Americans. This book will have served a useful purpose if—in discussing the conflicting political, cultural, and economic policies of the Great Powers in the Near East during the past three decades—it contributes to a sympathetic understanding of a very complicated problem and suggests to the reader some dangers which American statesmanship would do well to avoid. Students of history and international relations will find in the story of the Bagdad Railway a laboratory full of rich materials for an analysis of modern economic imperialism and its far-reaching consequences.

The assistance of many persons who have been intimately associated with the Bagdad Railway has enabled the author to examine records and documents not heretofore available to the historian. To these persons the author is glad to assign a large measure of any credit which may accrue to this book as an authoritative and definitive account of German railway enterprises in the Near East. He wishes especially to mention: Dr. Arthur von Gwinner, of the *Deutsche Bank,* president of the Anatolian and Bagdad Railway Companies; Dr. Karl Helfferich, formerly Imperial German Minister of Finance, erstwhile managing director of the *Deutsche Bank,* and at present a member of the Reichstag; Sir Henry Babington Smith, an associate of the late Sir Ernest Cassel, a director of the Bank of England, president of the National Bank of Turkey, and at one time representative of the British bondholders on the Ottoman Public Debt Administration; Djavid Bey, Ottoman Minister of Finance during the régime of the Young Turks, an economic expert at the first Lausanne Conference, and at present Turkish representative on the Ottoman Public Debt Administration; Mr. Ernest Rechnitzer, a banker of Paris and London, a competitor for the Bagdad Railway concession in 1898-1899; Rear Admiral Colby M. Chester, of the United States Navy (retired), beneficiary of the "Chester concessions."

Valuable assistance in the collection and preparation of material has been rendered, also, by the following persons, to whom the author expresses his grateful appreciation: Sir Charles P. Lucas, director, and Mr. Evans Lewin, librarian, of the Royal Colonial Institute; Sir John Cadman, director of His Majesty's Petroleum Department; Professor George Young, of the University of London, formerly attaché of the British embassy at Constantinople; Mr. Charles V. Sheehan, sub-manager in London of the National City Bank of New York; Mr. M. Zekeria, chief of the Turkish Information Service in the United

States; Mr. René A. Wormser, an American attorney who assisted the author in research work in Germany during the summer of 1922. Dr. Gottlieb Betz, of Columbia University, and Dr. John Mez, American correspondent of the *Frankfurter Zeitung,* have aided in the translation of important documents.

Professors Carlton J. H. Hayes and William R. Shepherd, of Columbia University, have been patient advisers and judicious critics of the author during the preparation of his manuscript. To them he owes much, as teachers who stimulated his interest in international relations, and as colleagues who cheerfully coöperate in any useful enterprise. Professor Parker Thomas Moon, of Columbia University, also has read the manuscript and offered many valuable suggestions.

EDWARD MEAD EARLE

Columbia University
　　June, 1923

CONTENTS

xii CONTENTS

CONTENTS

MAPS

TURKEY, THE GREAT POWERS,
AND THE BAGDAD RAILWAY

TURKEY, THE GREAT POWERS AND THE BAGDAD RAILWAY

A Study in Imperialism

CHAPTER I

AN ANCIENT TRADE ROUTE IS REVIVED

Many a glowing tale has been told of the great Commercial Revolution of the sixteenth century and of the consequent partial abandonment of the trans-Asiatic trade routes to India in favor of the newer routes by water around the Cape of Good Hope. It is sometimes overlooked, however, that a commercial revolution of the nineteenth century, occasioned by the adaptation of the steam engine to land and marine transportation, was of perhaps equal significance. Cheap carriage by the ocean greyhound instead of the stately clipper, by locomotive-drawn trains instead of stage-coach and caravan, made possible the extension of trade to the innermost and outermost parts of the earth and increased the volume of the world's commerce to undreamed of proportions. This latter commercial revolution led not only to the opening of new avenues of communication, but also to the regeneration of trade-routes which had been dormant or decayed for centuries. During the nineteenth century and the early part of the twentieth, the medieval trans-Asiatic highways to the East were rediscovered.

The first of these medieval trade-routes to be revived

by modern commerce was the so-called southern route. In the fifteenth century curious Oriental craft had brought their wares from eastern Asia across the Indian Ocean and up the Red Sea to some convenient port on the Egyptian shore; here their cargoes were trans-shipped *via* caravan to Alexandria and Cairo, marts of trade with the European cities of the Mediterranean. The completion of the Suez Canal, in 1869, transformed this route of medieval merchants into an avenue of modern transportation, incidentally realizing the dream of Portuguese and Spanish explorers of centuries before—a short, all-water route to the Indies. Less than forty years later the northern route of medieval commerce—from the "back doors" of China and India to the plains of European Russia— was opened to the twentieth-century locomotive. With the completion of the Trans-Siberian Railway in 1905 the old caravan trails were paralleled with steel rails. The Trans-Siberian system linked Moscow and Petrograd with Vladivostok and Pekin; the Trans-Caspian and Trans-Persian railways stretched almost to the mountain barrier of northern India; the Trans-Caucasian lines provided the link between the Caspian and Black Seas.

The heart of the central route of Eastern trade in the fifteenth century was the Mesopotamian Valley. Oriental sailing vessels brought commodities up the Persian Gulf to Basra and thence up the Shatt-el-Arab and the Tigris to Bagdad. At this point the route divided, one branch following the valley of the Tigris to a point north of Mosul and thence across the desert to Aleppo; another utilizing the valley of the Euphrates for a distance before striking across the desert to the ports of Syria; another crossing the mountains into Persia. From northern Mesopotamia and northern Syria caravans crossed Armenia and Anatolia to Constantinople. This historic highway—the last of the three great medieval trade-routes to be opened to modern transportation—was traversed by the Bagdad Railway. The locomotive provided a new short cut to the East.

That a commercial revolution of the nineteenth century should revive the old avenues of trade with the East was a matter of the utmost importance to all mankind. To the Western World the expansion of European commerce and the extension of Occidental civilization were incalculable, but certain, benefits. Statesmen and soldiers, merchants and missionaries alike might hail the new railways and steamship lines as entitled to a place among the foremost achievements of the age of steel and steam. To the East, also, closer contacts with the West held out high hopes for an economic and cultural renaissance of the former great civilizations of the Orient. Alas, however, the reopening of the medieval trade-routes served to create new arenas of imperial friction, to heighten existing international rivalries, and to widen the gulf of suspicion and hate already hindering cordial relationships between the peoples of Europe and the peoples of Asia. Economic rivalries, military alliances, national pride, strategic maneuvers, religious fanaticism, racial prejudices, secret diplomacy, predatory imperialism—these and other formidable obstacles blocked the road to peaceful progress and promoted wars and rumors of wars. The purchase of the Suez Canal by Disraeli was but the first step in the acquisition of Egypt, an imperial experiment which cost Great Britain thousands of lives, which more than once brought the empire to the verge of war with France, and which colored the whole character of British diplomacy in the Middle East for forty years. No sooner was the Trans-Siberian Railway completed than it involved Russia in a war with Japan. So it was destined to be with the Bagdad Railway. Itself a project of great promise for the economic and political regeneration of the Near East, it became the source of bitter international rivalries which contributed to the outbreak of the Great War. It is one of the tragedies of the nineteenth and twentieth centuries that the Trans-Siberian Railway, the Suez Canal, and the Bagdad Railway—potent instruments of civilization for the promotion of peaceful progress and material prosperity—could not have been constructed without occasioning imperial friction, political intrigues, military alliances, and armed conflict.

The geographical position of the Ottoman Empire, the enormous potential wealth of its dominions, and the political instability of the Sultan's Government contributed to make the Bagdad Railway one of the foremost imperial problems of the twentieth century. At the time of the Bagdad Railway concession of 1903 Turkey held dominion over the Asiatic threshold of Europe, Anatolia, and the European threshold of Asia, the Balkan Peninsula. Constantinople, the capital of the empire, was the economic and strategic center of gravity for the Black Sea and eastern Mediterranean basins. By possession of northern Syria and Mesopotamia, the Sultan controlled the "central route" of Eastern trade throughout its entire length from the borders of Austria-Hungary to the shores of the Persian Gulf. The contiguity of Ottoman territory to the Sinai Peninsula and to Persia held out the possibility of a Turkish attack on the Suez and trans-Persian routes to India and the Far East. In fact, the Sultan's dominions from Macedonia to southern Mesopotamia constituted a broad avenue of communication, an historic world highway, between the Occident and the Orient. To a strong nation, this position would have been a source of strength. To a weak nation it was a source of weakness. As Gibraltar and Suez and Panama were staked out by the empire-builders, so were Constantinople and Smyrna and Koweit. Strategically, the region traversed by the Bagdad Railway is one of the most important in the world.

Turkey-in-Asia, furthermore, was wealthy. It possessed vast resources of some of the most essential materials of modern industry: minerals, fuel, lubricants, abrasives. Its deposits of oil alone were enough to arouse the cupidity of the Great Powers. Irrigation, it was believed, would accomplish wonders in the revival of the ancient fertility of Mesopotamia. By the development of the country's latent agricultural wealth and the utilization of its industrial potentialities, it was anticipated that the Ottoman Empire would prove a valuable source of essential raw materials, a satisfactory market for finished products, and a rich field for the investment of capital. Economically, the territory served by the Bagdad Railway was one of the most important undeveloped regions of the world.

Neither the geographical position nor the economic wealth of the Ottoman Empire, however, need have been a cause for its exploitation by foreigners. Had the Sultan's Government been strong—powerful enough to present determined resistance to domestic rebellion and foreign intrigue—Turkey would not have been an imperial problem. But Abdul Hamid and his successors, the Young Turks, showed themselves incapable of governing a vast empire and a heterogeneous population. They were unable to resist the encroachments of foreigners on the administrative independence of their country or to defend its borders against foreign invasion. That the Ottoman Empire, under these circumstances, should fall a prey to the imperialism of the Western nations was to be expected. Its strategic importance was a "problem" of military and naval experts. Its wealth was an irresistible lure to investors. Its political instability was the excuse offered by European nations for intervening in the affairs of the empire on behalf of the financial interests of the business men or the strategic interests of the empire-builders. Diplomatically, then, the region traversed by the Bagdad Railway was an international "danger zone."

The problem of maintaining stable government in Turkey was complicated by the religious heritage of the Ottoman Empire. It was the homeland of the Jews, the birthplace of Christianity, the cradle of Mohammedanism. European crusaders had waged war to free the Holy Land from Moslem desecrators; the followers of the Prophet had shed their blood in defence of this sacred soil against infidel invaders; the sons of Israel looked forward to a revival of Jewish national life in this, their Zion. It is small wonder that Turkey-in-Asia was a great field for missions—Protestant missions to convert the Mohammedan to the teachings of Christ; Catholic missions to win over, as well, the schismatics; Orthodox missions to retain the loyalty of adherents to the Greek Church. Despite their cultural importance in the development of modern Turkey, the missions presented serious political problems to the Sultan. They hindered the development of Turkish nationalism by teaching foreign languages, by strengthening the separatist spirit of the religious minorities, and by introducing Occidental ideas and customs. They weakened the autocracy by idealizing the democratic institutions of the Western nations. They occasioned international complications, arising out of diplomatic protection of the missionaries themselves and the racial and religious minorities in whose interest the missions were maintained. In no country more than in Turkey have the emissaries of religion proved to be so valuable—however unwittingly —as advance pickets of imperialism.

Complicating and bewildering as the Near Eastern question always has been, the construction of the Anatolian and Bagdad Railways made it the more complicating and bewildering. The development of rail transportation in the Ottoman Empire was certain to raise a new crop of problems: the strategic problem of adjusting military preparations to meet new conditions; the economic problem of exploiting the great natural wealth of Turkey-in-Asia; the political problem of prescribing for a "Sick Man" who was determined to take iron as a tonic. These problems, of course, were international as well as Ottoman in their aspects. The economic and diplomatic advance of Germany in the Near East, the resurgent power of Turkey, the military coöperation between the Governments of the Kaiser and the Sultan were not matters which the other European powers were disposed to overlook. Russia, pursuing her time-honored policy, objected to any bolstering up of the Ottoman Empire. France looked with alarm upon the advent of another power in Turkish financial affairs and, in addition, was desirous of promoting the political ambitions of her ally, Russia. Great Britain became fearful of the safety of her communications with India and Egypt. Thus the Bagdad Railway overstepped the bounds of Turco-German relationships and became an international diplomatic problem. It was a concern of foreign offices as well as counting houses, of statesmen and soldiers as well as engineers and bankers.

The year 1888 ushered in an epoch of three decades during which two cross-currents were at work in Turkey. On the one hand, earnest efforts were made by Turks, old and young, to bring about the political and economic regeneration of their country. On the other, the steady growth of Balkan nationalism, the relentless pressure of European imperialism, and the devastation of the Great War gradually reduced to ruins the once great empire of Suleiman the Magnificent. The history of those three decades is concerned largely with the struggles of European capitalists to acquire profitable concessions in Asiatic Turkey and of European diplomatists to control the finances, the vital routes of communication, and even the administrative powers of the Ottoman Government. The coincidence between the economic motives of the investors and the political and strategical motives of the statesmen, made Turkey one of the world's foremost areas of imperial friction. Its territories and its natural wealth were "stakes of diplomacy" for which cabinets maneuvered on the diplomatic checkerboard and for which the flower of the world's manhood fought on the sands of Mesopotamia, the cliffs of Gallipoli, and the plains of Flanders. To tell the story of the Bagdad Railway is to emphasize perhaps the most important single factor in the history of Turkey during the last thirty eventful years.

CHAPTER II

BACKWARD TURKEY INVITES ECONOMIC EXPLOITATION

TURKISH SOVEREIGNTY IS A POLITE FORMALITY

The reign of Sultan Abdul Hamid II (1876-1909) began with a disastrous foreign war; it terminated in the turmoil of revolution. And during the intervening three decades of his régime the Ottoman Empire was forced to wage a fight for its very existence—a fight against disintegration from within and against dismemberment from without.

One of the principal problems of Abdul Hamid was the government of his vast empire in spite of domestic dissension and foreign interference. His subjects were a polyglot collection of peoples, bound together by few, if any, common ties, obedient to the Sultan's will only when overawed by military force. In Turkey-in-Asia alone, Turks, Arabs, Armenians, Kurds, Jews, Greeks combined to form a conglomerate population, professing a variety of religious faiths, speaking a diversity of languages and dialects, and adhering to their own peculiar social customs. Of these, the Armenians were receiving the sympathy, support, and encouragement of Russia; the Kurds were living by banditry, terrorizing peasants and traders alike; the Arabs were in open revolt.[1]

Nature seemed to make more difficult the task of bringing these dissentient peoples under subjection. The mountainous relief of the Anatolian plateau lent itself to the success of guerrilla bands against the gendarmerie; a high mountain barrier separated Anatolia, the homeland of the Turks, from the hills and deserts of Syria and Mesopotamia, the strongholds of the Arabs. The vast extent of the empire—it is as far from Constantinople to Mocha as it is from New York to San Francisco—still further complicated an already tangled problem, for there were not even the poorest means of communication. Under these circumstances the authority of the Sultan was as often disregarded as obeyed. To police the country from the Adriatic to the Indian Ocean, from the borders of Persia to the eastern coast of the Mediterranean, was a physical impossibility. Universal military service was enforced only in the less rebellious provinces. It was almost out of the question to mobilize the military strength of the empire for defence against foreign invasion or for the suppression of domestic insurrection. Efforts to build up effective administration from Constantinople were paralyzed by incompetent, insubordinate, and corrupt officials.[2]

To these problems of maintaining peace and order at home there was added the equally difficult problem of preventing the extension of foreign interference and control in Ottoman affairs. The integrity of Turkey already was seriously compromised by the hold which the Great Powers possessed on Turkish governmental functions. Under the Capitulations foreigners occupied a special and privileged position within the Ottoman Empire. Nationals of the European nations and the United States were practically exempt from taxation; they could be tried for civil and criminal offences only under the laws of their own country and in courts under the jurisdiction of their own diplomatic and consular officials; in fact, they enjoyed favors comparable to diplomatic immunity. By virtue of treaties with the Sultan the Powers exercised numerous extra-territorial rights in Turkey, such, for example, as the maintenance of their own postal systems.[3]

The finances of Turkey, furthermore, were under the control of the Ottoman Public Debt Administration, composed almost entirely of representatives of foreign bondholders and responsible only to them. The Council of Administration of the Public Debt—composed of one representative each from the United Kingdom, France, Germany, Austria-Hungary, Italy, and Turkey—had complete control of assessment, collection, and expenditure of certain designated revenues. In fact, it controlled Ottoman financial policy and exercised its control in the interest of European bankers and investors. Customs duties of the Sultan's dominions might be increased only with the consent of the Great Powers. Almost all administrative and financial questions in Turkey were directly or indirectly subject to the sanction of foreigners.[4]

European governments were not content to interfere in the affairs of the Ottoman Empire. They sought to destroy it. Their zeal in this latter respect was limited only by their jealousies as to who should become the heir of the Sick Man. Russia encouraged the Balkan and Transcaucasian peoples to resist Turkish domination; France acquired control of Tunis and built up a sphere of interest in Syria; Great Britain occupied Egypt; Italy cast longing glances at Tripoli and finally seized it; Greece fomented insurrection in Crete. Germany and Austria-Hungary sought to bring all of Turkey into the economic and political orbit of Central Europe. The Powers rendered lip-service to the sovereignty and the territorial integrity of the Ottoman Empire, but they never allowed their solemn professions to interfere with their imperial practices. At best Turkish sovereignty was a polite fiction—it was always a fiction, if not always polite.

The economic backwardness of Turkey emphasized the existing political confusion and instability. From one end of the empire to the other, it seemed, obstacle was piled on obstacle to prevent the modernizing of the nation. Brigandage made trade hazardous; there were almost no roads; the rivers of Anatolia and Cilicia were not navigable; the mineral resources of the country had been neglected; internal and foreign customs duties were the last straws to break the camel's back—business was taxed to death. Agriculture, the occupation of the great majority of the people, was in a state of stagnation. The absence of systems of drainage and irrigation made the countryside the victim of alternate floods and droughts. Methods of cultivation were archaic: the wooden plow, used by the Hittites centuries before, was among the most advanced types of agricultural implements in use in Anatolia and Syria; harvesting and threshing were performed in the most antiquated manner; fertilization and cultivation were practically unknown. Markets were inaccessible; the peasant could not dispose of a surplus if he had it; therefore, production was limited to the needs of the family, and the Turkish peasant acquired a widespread reputation for inherent laziness.

Industrially, the Ottoman Empire had back of it a great past. The fine and dainty fabrics of Mosul; the famous mosque lamps, wonder-art of the glass-workers of Mesopotamia; the master workmanship of the coppersmiths of Diarbekr; the tiles of Erzerum; the steel work and the enamels of Damascus—all of these had been far-famed articles of world commerce for centuries. But Turkey in the nineteenth and twentieth centuries was, industrially as well as politically, a "backward nation." Her manufactures were conducted under the time-honored handicraft system, which long since had been discarded by her European neighbors. In other words, Turkey had not experienced the Industrial Revolution which was the modern foundation of Western society and civilization. But Turkey was victimized by the Industrial Revolution. Her manufactures—with the exception of some luxuries of incomparable craftsmanship—produced by outworn methods, found it increasingly difficult to compete even in the markets of the Ottoman Empire with the cheaper machine-made goods of Europe. The pitiless competition of the industrialized West eliminated the cottage spinner and weaver, the town tailor and cobbler. And yet for Turkey to adopt European methods—to introduce the machine, the factory, and the factory town—was for a time impracticable. There was no mobile fund of capital for the purpose, and even Young Turks were not in a position to furnish the necessary technical skill. As for foreign capital and foreign directing genius, they could be obtained only under promises and guarantees which might still further jeopardize the independence of the Ottoman Empire.[5]

THE NATURAL WEALTH OF ASIATIC TURKEY OFFERS ALLURING OPPORTUNITIES

It was not because of a lack of natural resources that Turkey was a "backward nation." The Sultan's Asiatic dominions were rich in raw materials, in fuel, and in agricultural possibilities. Anatolia, for example, is a great storehouse of important metals. A fine quality of chrome ore is to be found in the region directly south of the Sea of Marmora and in Cilicia, constituting sources of supply which were sufficient to assure Turkey first position among the chrome-producing nations until 1900, when exports from Russia and Rhodesia offered serious competition.

There are valuable deposits of antimony in the vilayets of Brusa and Smyrna, as well as commercially profitable lead and zinc mines near Brusa, Ismid, and Konia. These metals, particularly chrome and antimony, are not only valuable for peace-time industry, but are almost indispensable in the manufacture of armor-plate, shells and shrapnel, guns, and armor-piercing projectiles.[6]

In the vicinity of Diarbekr there are mines, which, although not entirely surveyed, promise to yield large supplies of copper. Southern Anatolia is the world's greatest source of emery and other similar abrasives. The famous meerschaum mines near Eski Shehr enjoy practically a universal monopoly. Boracite, mercury, nickel, iron, manganese, sulphur, and other minerals are to be found in Anatolia, although there is some question of the commercial possibilities of the deposits.[7]

Although Anatolia is not ranked among the principal fuel-producing countries of the world, its coal deposits are not inconsiderable. Operation of the chief of the coalfields, in the vicinity of Heraclea, was begun in 1896 by a French corporation, *La Société française d'Héraclée,* which invested in the enterprise during the succeeding seven years more than a million francs. The venture proved to be profitable, for by 1910 the mines were producing in excess of half a million tons of coal annually. In addition to coal, Anatolia possesses large deposits of lignite which, mixed with coal, is suitable fuel for ships, locomotives, gasworks, and factories.[8]

Oil exists in large quantities in Mesopotamia and in smaller quantities in Syria. The deposits are said to be part of a vast petroliferous area stretching from the shores of the Caspian Sea to the coast of Burma. As early as 1871 a commission of experts visited the valleys of the Tigris and the Euphrates for the purpose of studying the possibility of immediate exploitation of the petroleum wells in that region. They reported that although there was a plentiful supply of petroleum of good quality, difficulties of transportation made it extremely doubtful if the Mesopotamian fields could compete with the Russian and American at that time. The oil supply was then being exploited on a small scale by the Arabs and proved to be of sufficient local importance, as well as of sufficient profit, to warrant its being taken over by the Ottoman Civil List, in 1888, as a government monopoly.[9]

In 1901 a favorable report by a German technical commission on Mesopotamian petroleum resources stated that the region was a veritable "lake of petroleum" of almost inexhaustible supply. It would be advisable, it was pointed out, to develop these oilfields if for no other purpose than to break the grip of the "omnipotent Standard," which, in combination with Russian interests, might speedily monopolize the world's supply.[10] Shortly afterward, Dr. Paul Rohrbach, a celebrated German publicist, visited the Mesopotamian valley and wrote that the district seemed to be "virtually soaked with bitumen, naphtha, and gaseous hydrocarbons." He was of the opinion that the oil resources of the region offered far greater opportunity for profitable development than had the Russian Transcaucasian fields.[11] In 1904 the *Deutsche Bank,* of Berlin, promoters of the Bagdad Railway, obtained the privilege of making a thorough survey of the oilfields of the Tigris and Euphrates valleys, with the option within one year of entering into a contract with the Ottoman Government for their exploitation.[12] Shortly thereafter Rear Admiral Colby M. Chester, of the United States Navy, became interested in the development of the oil industry in Asiatic Turkey.[13]

The Near East possesses not only mineral wealth but potential agricultural wealth as well. Mesopotamia, for example, gives promise of becoming one of the world's chief cotton-growing regions. In antiquity the Land of the Two Rivers was an important center of cotton production, and recent experiments have held out great inducements for a revival of cotton culture there. The climate of Mesopotamia is ideal for such a purpose. The length of the summer season is from six to seven months, with a constantly rising temperature, as contrasted with a shorter season and variable temperatures in America and Egypt. Frost is almost unknown. Rainfall is plentiful during the early part of the year and scarce, as it should be, during the growing period. The soil contains a good percentage of the essential phosphorus, potash, and nitrogen. It is believed that Mesopotamia can grow cotton as good as the best Egyptian and better than the best American product and at a considerably higher yield per acre.[14]

Extravagant prophecies have been made regarding the rôle of irrigation in bringing about an agricultural renaissance in Turkey-in-Asia. A writer in the Vienna *Zeit* of August 31, 1901, predicted that as soon as the economic effects of irrigation and of the Bagdad Railway should be fully realized, "Anatolia, northern Syria, Mesopotamia, and Irak together will export at least as much grain as all of Russia exports to-day." Dr. Rohrbach claimed that this probably would prove to be an exaggeration, but that certainly Mesopotamia would become one of the great granaries of the world.[15] Sir William Willcocks, the distinguished English engineer who had planned and supervised the construction of the famous irrigation works of the Nile, was no less enthusiastic about the prospects of Mesopotamia. "With the Euphrates and Tigris floods really controlled," he wrote, "the delta of the two rivers would attain a fertility of which history has no record; and we should see men coming from the West, as well as from the East, making the Plain of Shinar a rival of the land of Egypt. The flaming swords of inundation and drought would have been taken out of the hands of the offended Seraphim, and the Garden of Eden would have again been planted. . . . Speaking in less poetical language we might say that the value of every acre in the joint delta of the two rivers would be immediately trebled before the irrigation works were carried out, and again increased many fold more the day the works were completed. Every town and hamlet in the valley from Bagdad to Basra would find itself freed from the danger, expense, and intolerable nuisance of flooding, and the resurrection of this ancient land would have been an accomplished fact."[16]

Here in the Near East, then, was a great empire awaiting exploitation by Western capital and Western technical skill. No man could adequately predict its ultimate contributions in raw materials to Western industry, or accurately foretell its ultimate capacity in consumption of the products of Western factories, or confidently prophesy its final rôle in the promotion of Western commerce. But a trained and intelligent observer, surveying the situation at the opening of the twentieth century, could have said with a certain amount of assurance that there were two essential conditions to even a partial realization of the economic possibilities of the Ottoman Empire: the provision of adequate railway communications and the establishment of political security. The former of these conditions was met, in part, during the régime of Abdul Hamid and his successors, the Young Turks. The second, in spite of earnest efforts by loyal Ottomans, has not yet been satisfied.

Forces Are at Work for Regeneration

Probably there was no group of men more fully aware of the needs of Turkey than the members of the Ottoman Public Debt Administration. They were concerned, it is true, solely with obtaining prompt payment of interest and principal of Ottoman bonds and with improving Ottoman credit in European financial markets. But the accomplishment of this purpose, they realized, was altogether out of the question in the continued presence of political instability and economic stagnation. One must feed the goose which lays the golden eggs. They sought some means, therefore, of establishing domestic order in the Ottoman Empire, of lessening the constant danger of foreign invasion, and of providing a tonic for the economic life of the nation. All of these purposes, it was believed, would be served by the encouragement of railway construction in Turkey.

The interest and imagination of the Ottoman Public Debt Administration were stimulated by the plans of the eminent German railway engineer Wilhelm von Pressel, one of the Sultan's technical advisers. Von Pressel had established an international reputation because of his services in the construction of important railways in Switzerland and the Tyrol. In 1872 he was retained by the Ottoman Government to develop plans for railways in Turkey, and a few years later he assumed a prominent part in the construction of the trans-Balkan lines of the Oriental Railways Company. No one knew more than von Pressel of the railway problems of Turkey; few were more enthusiastic about the rôle which rail communications might play in a renaissance of the Near East.

Von Pressel foresaw the possibility of establishing a great system of Ottoman railways extending from the borders of Austria-Hungary to the shores of the Persian Gulf. In this manner the far-flung territories of the empire would be brought into communication with one another and with the capital, and an era would be begun of unprecedented development in agriculture, mining, and commerce. A market would be provided for the crops of the peasantry; the hinterland of the ports of Constantinople, Smyrna, Mersina, Alexandretta, and Basra would be opened up; heretofore inaccessible mineral resources would be exploited. Foreign commerce might be restored to the prosperity it had once enjoyed before the Commercial Revolution of the sixteenth century replaced the caravan routes of the Near East by the new sea routes to the Indies. Mesopotamia might be transformed into a veritable economic paradise. The railways also would insure political stability, for rapid mobilization and transportation of the gendarmerie to danger points would enable the Sultan's Government to suppress rebellions of the turbulent tribesmen of Kurdistan, Mesopotamia, and Arabia. Peace and prosperity were goals within easy reach, thought von Pressel, if Turkey could be provided with a comprehensive system of railways.[17]

To the Ottoman Public Debt Administration peace and prosperity were means to reaching another goal—a full treasury. Greater income for the Turkish farmer, miner, artisan, and trader would mean greater opportunities for the extension of tax levies. And the greater the tax receipts the greater would be the payments to the European bondholders and the greater the value of the bonds themselves. Obviously, railway construction would improve Turkish credit in the financial centers of the world. But, for the time, the Ottoman Government had at its disposal neither the capital nor the technical skill to carry into execution the plans for an ambitious program of railway building, and private enterprise showed no disposition to interest itself without substantial guarantees. It was under these circumstances, therefore, that the Ottoman Public Debt Administration recommended to the Sultan that certain revenues of his empire should be set aside for the payment of subsidies to railway companies.[18]

The Public Debt Administration were not unaware that

the payment of railway subsidies would materially increase the amount of the imperial debt and mortgage certain of the imperial revenues. But they were confident that railways would be a powerful stimulant to economic prosperity in Turkey and would ultimately increase the revenues of the Government by an amount in excess of the amount of the subsidies. They believed that generous initial expenditures in a worth-while enterprise might yield generous final returns. As an instance of this they could point to the development of sericulture in Turkey. Under the auspices of the Ottoman Public Debt Administration tens of thousands of dollars were expended in the reclamation of more than 130,000 acres of land and the planting thereon of over sixty million mulberry trees. As a result, the silk crop increased more than tenfold during the years 1890-1910, with a result that there was a corresponding increase in the 10% levy (or tithe) on agricultural products in the regions affected. If the Public Debt Administration were actuated by self-interest, at least it was intelligent and far-sighted self-interest.[19]

But Sultan Abdul Hamid was no less interested than foreign bondholders in the extension of railway construction in his empire. Railways could be utilized, he believed, to serve his dynastic and imperial ambitions. Effective transportation was essential to the solution of at least three vexatious political problems: first, the problem of exercising real, as well as nominal, authority over rebellious and indifferent subjects in Syria, Mesopotamia, Kurdistan, Arabia, and other outlying provinces; second, the problem of compelling these provinces, by military force if necessary, to contribute their share of blood and treasure to the defence of the empire;[20] third, the problem of perfecting a plan of mobilization for war, on whatever front it might be necessary to conduct hostilities. The maintenance of order, the enforcement of universal military service, the collection of taxes in all provinces of the empire, and defence against foreign invasion—all of these policies would be seriously handicapped, if not paralyzed, by the absence of adequate railway communications.

For strategic reasons, if for no other, Abdul Hamid would have especially favored the Bagdad Railway. For strategic reasons, also, he supplemented the Bagdad system with the famous Hedjaz Railway—from Damascus to the holy cities of Medina and Mecca—one of the achievements of which the wily old Sultan was most proud.[21] The completion of these two railways would have extended Turkish military power from the Black Sea to the Persian Gulf, from the Bosporus to the Persian Gulf. General von der Goltz epitomized their military importance in the following terms: "The great distance dividing the southern provinces from the rest of the empire was not the only difficulty in holding them in control; it made Turkey unable to concentrate her strength in case of great danger in the north. It must not be forgotten that the Osmanlie Empire in all former wars on the Danube and in the Balkans has only been able to utilize half her forces. Not only did the far-off provinces not contribute men, but, on the contrary, they necessitated strong reënforcements to prevent the danger of their being tempted into rebellion. This will be quite changed when the railroads to the Persian Gulf and the Red Sea are completed. The empire will then be rejuvenated and have renewed strength." [22] The General might have added that the new railways might conceivably be utilized for the transportation to the Sinai Peninsula of an army intended to threaten the Suez Canal and Egypt.[23]

The Ottoman Government made it plain from the very start that the Bagdad Railway, in particular, was intended to serve military, as well as purely economic, purposes. The concession of 1903 contained a number of explicit provisions regarding official commandeering of the lines for the objects of suppressing rebellion, conducting military maneuvers, or mobilizing in the event of war. Furthermore, the Ottoman military authorities insisted that strategic considerations be taken into account when the railway was constructed. For example, the sections of the Bagdad line from Adana to Aleppo were carried through the Amanus Mountains, in spite of formidable engineering difficulties and enormous expense, although the railway could have been carried along the Mediterranean coast with greater ease and economy. The latter course, however, would have exposed to the guns of a hostile fleet the jugular vein of Turkish rail communications. From an economic point of view the Amanus tunnels were the most expensive and most unremunerative part of the Bagdad Railway; strategically, they were indispensable. This point was emphasized in 1908, when the Ottoman General Staff refused to consider a proposal to divert the line from the mountain passes to the shore.[24]

One of the most frequent criticisms of Turkish railway enterprises in general, and of the Bagdad Railway in particular, is that they were military as well as economic in character. Such criticisms, however, must be discounted, for potentially every railway is of military value. And in the European countries few railways were constructed without frank consideration of their adaptability to military purposes in time of war. Railways, in fact, were one of the most important branches of Europe's "preparedness" for war. Which European nation, therefore, was in a position to cast a stone at Turkey for adopting this lesson from the civilized Occident? If the Ottoman Empire had a right to prepare for defence against invasion, it had the right to make that defence effective—at least until such time as its neighbors, Russia and Austria, should abandon military measures of potential menace to Turkey.

Germans and Turkish Nationalists contended that there was a certain amount of cant in the righteous indignation of the Powers that Turkey should become militaristic. Was Russia, they said, as much interested in the welfare of Turkey as she was angered at the active measures of the Sultan to prevent a Russian drive at Constantinople *via* the southern shore of the Black Sea? Was France as much concerned with the safety of Turkey as she was solicitous of the imperial interests of her ally? Was Great Britain engaged in preserving the peace of the Near East, or was she fearful of a stiffened Turkish defence of Mesopotamia or of a Turkish thrust at Egypt? [25] For the Sultan to have admitted that foreign powers had the right to dictate what measures he might or might not take for the defence of his territories would have been equivalent to a surrender of the last vestige of his sovereignty. Obviously this was an admission he could not afford to make.

Whatever else Abdul Hamid may have been, he was no fool. To assume that this shrewd and unscrupulous autocrat walked into a German trap when he granted the Bagdad Railway concession is naïve and absurd. Abdul Hamid was not in the habit of giving things away, if he could avoid it, without adequate compensation for himself and his empire. As Lord Curzon said, there was no axiom dearer to the Sultan's heart than that charity not only begins, but stays, at home. [26] Abdul Hamid knew that the granting of railway subsidies would mortgage his empire. He knew that mortgages have their disadvantages, not the least of which is foreclosure. But mortgages also have their advantages. Abdul Hamid granted extensive railway concessions, carrying with them heavy subsidies, because he hoped the new railways would strengthen his authority within the Ottoman Empire and improve the political position of Turkey in the Near East.

BIBLIOGRAPHICAL AND EXPLANATORY NOTES

[1] Count L. Ostrorog, *The Turkish Problem* (Paris, 1915, English translation, London, 1919), Chapter II; Leon Dominian, *The Frontiers of Language and Nationality in Europe* (London, 1917); V. Bérard, *Le Sultan, l'Islam, et les puissances* (Paris, 1907), pp. 15 *et seq.*; E. Fazy, *Les Turcs d'aujourd'hui* (Paris, 1898); A. Vamberry, *Das Türkenvolk* (Leipzig, 1885); A. Geiger, *Judaism and Islam* (London, 1899). Regarding Arab nationalism, in particular, *cf.* N. Azoury, *Le réveil de la nation arabe* (Paris, 1905); E. Jung, *Les puissances devant la révolte arabe* (Paris, 1906). A fascinating tale of the Arab separatist movement during the Great War is that of L. Thomas, "Lawrence: the Soul of the Arabian Revolution," in *Asia* (New York), April, May, June, 1920. *Cf.*, also, H. S. Philby, *The Heart of Arabia* (2 volumes, New York, 1923).

[2] There is a wealth of material upon the problems of the Ottoman Empire during the reign of Abdul Hamid. In particular, consult the following: A. Vamberry, *La Turquie d'aujourd'hui et d'avant quarante ans* (Paris, 1898); C. Hecquard, *La Turquie sous Abdul Hamid* (Paris, 1901); G. Dory, *Abdul Hamid Intime* (Paris, 1901); Sir Edwin Pears, *The Life of Abdul Hamid* (London, 1917); W. Miller, *The Ottoman Empire, 1801-1913* (Cambridge, 1913), Chapters XVI-XVIII; N. Verney and G. Dambmann, *Les puissances étrangères dans le Levant, en Syrie, et en Palestine* (Paris, 1900); Baron von Oppenheim, *Von Mittelmeer zum persischen Golfe* (2 volumes, Berlin, 1899-1900); Lavisse and Rambaud, *Histoire Générale* (12 volumes, 1894-1901), Volume XI, Chapter XV; Volume XII, Chapter XIV; R. Davey, *The Sultan and His Subjects* (London, 1897); V. Cardashian, *The Ottoman Empire of the Twentieth Century* (Albany, N. Y., 1908).

[3] The texts of the various treaties of capitulation may be found in G. E. Noradounghian (ed.), *Recueil d'actes internationaux de l'Empire ottoman, 1300-1902* (4 volumes, Paris, 1897-1903), Volume I, documents numbers 153, 170, 196, 201, etc., *ad lib.*, Volume II, numbers 499, 593, etc., *ad lib.;* also *Recueil des traités de la Porte ottomane avec les puissances étrangères, 1536-1901* (10 volumes, Paris, 1864-1901), *passim;* E. A. Van Dyck, *Report on the Capitulations of the Ottoman Empire,* Forty-seventh Congress, Special Session, Senate Executive Document No. 3, First Session, Senate Executive Document No. 87 (Washington, 1881-1882); G. Pelissie du Rausas, *Le régime des capitulations dans l'Empire ottoman* (2 volumes, Paris, 1902-1905); A. R. von Overbeck, *Die Kapitulationen des osmanischen Reiches* (Breslau, 1917); W. Lehman, *Die Kapitulationen* (Weimar, 1917); P. M.

Brown, *Foreigners in Turkey, Their Juridical Status* (Princeton, 1914).

⁴ For an account of the establishment, functions, and operation of the Ottoman Public Debt Administration, *cf.* George Young (ed.), *Corps de droit ottoman—Recueil des codes, lois, régle-ments, ordonnances, et actes les plus importants du droit in-térieur, et d'études sur le droit coutumier de l'Empire ottoman* (7 volumes, Oxford, 1905-1906), Volume V, Chapter LXXXV; A. Heidborn, *Manuel de droit public et administratif de l'Empire ottoman* (2 volumes, Vienna, 1912), Volume II; C. Morawitz, *Les finances de Turquie* (Paris, 1902); A. du Velay, *Essai sur l'histoire financière de la Turquie* (Paris, 1903), Parts V and VI; L. Delaygue, *Essai sur les finances ottomanes* (Paris, 1911).

⁵ There were a few factories erected in Turkey by foreign cap-italists, notably those of the Oriental Carpet Manufacturers, Ltd., the American Tobacco Company, and the *Deutsche-Levantischen Baumwollgesellschaft.* In general, however, the factory and the factory town were not common phenomena in Asiatic Turkey. An interesting account of the effects of the Industrial Revolu-tion upon economic conditions in Turkey is that of Talcott Williams, *Turkey a World Problem of Today* (Garden City, 1921), pp. 268 *et seq.*; W. S. Monroe, *Turkey and the Turks: an Account of the Lands, Peoples and Institutions of the Ottoman Empire* (London, 1909), Chapter X; M. J. Garnett, *Turkish Life in Town and Country* (London, 1904).

⁶ J. E. Spurr (ed.), *Political and Commercial Geology* (New York, 1921), pp. 109, 115-116, 172-173, 184-185; *Anatolia,* No. 17 in a series of handbooks published by the Historical Section of the Foreign Office (London, 1920), pp. 88-90.

⁷ Spurr, *op. cit.,* pp. 358-359; *Armenia and Kurdistan,* No. 62 of the Foreign Office Handbooks, p. 60; L. Dominian, "The Mineral Wealth of Asia Minor," in *The Near East,* May 26, 1916, p. 91; E. Banse, *Auf den Spuren der Bagdadbahn* (Weimar, 1913), pp. 140-145; L. de Launay, *La Géologie et les richesses minerales de l'Asie* (Paris, 1911); R. Fitzner, *Anatolien, Wirt-schaftsgeographie* (Berlin, 1902); P. Rohrbach, *Die wirtschaft-liche Bedeutung Westasiens* (Halle, 1902); G. Carles, *La Turquie économique* (Paris, 1906); E. Mygind, "Anatolien und seine wirtschaftliche Bedeutung," in *Die Balkan Revue,* Volume 4 (1917), pp. 1-6.

⁸ L. Dominian, "Fuel in Turkey: an Analysis of Coal Deposits," in *The Near East,* June 23, 1916, pp. 186-187; J. Kirsopp, "The Coal Resources of the Near East," *ibid.,* October 10, 1919, pp. 393-394.

⁹ F. Maunsell, "The Mesopotamian Petroleum Field," in the *Geographical Journal,* Volume IX (1897), pp. 523-532; L. Domi-

nian, "Fuel in Turkey: Petroleum," in *The Near East,* July 14, 1917; *Mesopotamia,* No. 63 of the Foreign Office Handbooks, pp. 34, 85-86; *Syria and Palestine,* No. 60 of the Foreign Office Handbooks, p. 111.

[10] *Parliamentary Papers,* 1921, Cmd. 675; *The Near East,* October 26, 1917, p. 516.

[11] *Die Bagdadbahn* (1903), pp. 26-28.

[12] *Parliamentary Papers,* 1921, Cmd. 675. For some reason or other this option was allowed to lapse.

[13] H. Woodhouse, "American Oil Claims in Turkey," in *Current History* (New York), Volume XV (1922), pp. 953-959.

[14] *Report of the Department of Agriculture in Mesopotamia, 1920* (Bagdad, 1921); *The Cultivation of Cotton in Mesopotamia* (Bagdad, 1922); "Cotton Growing in Mesopotamia," in the *Bulletin of the Imperial Institute,* Volume 18 (1920), pp. 73-82.

[15] Rohrbach, *op. cit.,* pp. 30-46.

[16] Quoted in *The Near East,* October 6, 1916, pp. 545-546. For an elaboration of the views of Sir William Willcocks see the following of his books and articles: *The Recreation of Chaldea* (Cairo, 1903); *The Irrigation of Mesopotamia* (London, 1905, and Constantinople, 1911); "Mesopotamia, Past, Present and Future," in the *Geographical Journal,* January, 1910, pp. 1-18. For further works on the economic resources of Turkey-in-Asia consult, also, the following: K. H. Müller, *Die wirtschaftliche Bedeutung der Bagdadbahn* (Hamburg, 1917); L. Blanckenhorn, *Syrien und die deutsche Arbeit* (Weimar, 1916); L. Schulmann, *Zur türkischen Agrarfrage* (Weimar, 1916); A. Ruppin, *Syrien als Wirtschaftsgebiet* (Berlin, 1917).

[17] W. von Pressel, *Les chemins de fer en Turquie d'Asie* (Zurich, 1902), pp. 4-5, 52-59, etc. *ad lib.* For statements of the importance of von Pressel in the development of railways in Turkey *cf.* André Chéradame, *La question d'Orient: la Macédoine, le chemin de fer de Bagdad* (Paris, 1903), pp. 25 *et seq.*; C. A. Schaefer, *Die Entwicklung der Bagdadbahnpolitik* (Weimar, 1916), p. 13.

[18] *Corps de droit ottoman,* Volume IV, pp. 62-64.

[19] Sir H. P. Caillard, Article "Turkey" in the *Encyclopedia Britannica,* eleventh edition, Volume 27, p. 439; *Reports of the Ottoman Public Debt* (London, 1884 *et seq.*), *passim.*

[20] In Turkey all Mussulmans over 20 years of age were liable to military service for a period of 20 years, 4 of which were with the colors in the regular army. Residents in the outlying territories, notably the Arabs and the Kurds, constantly avoided military service and went unpunished because of the inability of the Government to send punitive expeditions into these regions. Railways would have produced satisfactory bases of

operations for such expeditions and would have shortened their lines of communication. *The Statesman's Year Book,* 1903, pp. 1168-1170.

[21] The Hedjaz Railway was a great national enterprise which indicated the strength of Moslem feeling in Turkey and which proved the desire of the Ottoman Government to construct national railways as far as capital and technical skill could be obtained. So far as Abdul Hamid was concerned, the railway was an attempt to gain prestige for his claim to the Caliphate, as well as a move to strengthen his political position in Syria and the Hedjaz. In April, 1900, the Sultan announced to the Faithful his determination to construct a railway from Damascus to the holy cities of Medina and Mecca. An appeal was issued to Mohammedans the world over for funds to carry out the work. The Sultan headed the list with a subscription of about a quarter of a million dollars, and by 1904 over three and a half million dollars had been collected. The only compulsory contributions were the levies of 10% on the salary of every official in the civil and military service of the empire. It is estimated that the contributions eventually amounted to almost fifteen million dollars. The engineers in charge of the construction were Italians, although the great bulk of the work was done by the army and the peasantry. Nearly seven hundred thousand persons were employed on the construction work at one time or another, the non-Moslems being replaced as quickly as Mussulmans could be trained to take their places. On August 31, 1908, the thirty-second anniversary of the accession of Abdul Hamid, the railway was completed to Medina, where construction was halted temporarily because of the Young Turk Revolution and the international complications which followed it. *Corps de droit ottoman,* Volume IV, pp. 242-244; A. Hamilton, *Problems of the Middle East* (London, 1909), pp. 273-292; *Annual Register,* 1908, pp. 328-329.

[22] Quoted by Hamilton, *op. cit.,* pp. 274-275.

[23] *Via* the Bagdad Railway and the Syrian system Turkish troops could have been transported to a point less than 200 miles from Suez. A successful attack on the Canal, of course, would have severed British communications with the East. In addition, it would have given the Sultan an opportunity to attack, and assert his suzerainty over, Egypt. Dr. Rohrbach made a great point of this alleged menace to the British position in Egypt. *Cf. Die Bagdadbahn,* pp. 18-19; *German World Policies,* pp. 165-167. This program, however, would have been an altogether too ambitious one for the military strength of the Ottoman Empire, which had such far-flung frontiers to defend. In any event, British statesmen seemed to realize that the Sinai

Peninsula was a formidable natural defence against an attack on the Suez Canal and that such an expedition would be merely a pin-prick in the imperial flesh. *Parliamentary Debates, House of Lords,* fifth series, Volume 7 (1911), pp. 601 *et seq.* The termination in a fiasco of the Turkish drive of 1914-1915 against the Canal confirmed this prophecy.

[24] *Infra,* p. 83; Kurt Wiedenfeld, *Die deutsch-türkische Wirt-schaftsbeziehungen* (Leipzig, 1915), p. 23; *Report of the Bagdad Railway Company,* 1908, pp. 4-5.

[25] *Cf., e.g.,* K. Helfferich, *Die deutsche Türkenpolitik,* p. 22.

[26] *Persia and the Persian Question,* Volume I, p. 634.

CHAPTER III

GERMANS BECOME INTERESTED IN THE NEAR EAST

THE FIRST RAILS ARE LAID

During the summer of 1888 the Oriental Railways—from the Austrian frontier, across the Balkan Peninsula *via* Belgrade, Nish, Sofia, and Adrianople, to Constantinople—were opened to traffic. Connections with the railways of Austria-Hungary and other European countries placed the Ottoman capital in direct communication with Vienna, Paris, Berlin, and London (*via* Calais). The arrival at the Golden Horn, August 12, 1888, of the first through express from Paris and Vienna was made the occasion of great rejoicing in Constantinople and was generally hailed by the European press as marking the beginning of a new era in the history of the Ottoman Empire. To thoughtful Turks, however, it was apparent that the opening of satisfactory rail communications in European Turkey but emphasized the inadequacy of such communications in the Asiatic provinces. Anatolia, the homeland of the Turks, possessed only a few hundred kilometres of railways; the vast areas of Syria, Mesopotamia, and the Hedjaz possessed none at all. Almost immediately after the completion of the Oriental Railways, therefore, the Sultan, with the advice and assistance of the Ottoman Public Debt Administration, launched a program for the construction of an elaborate system of railway lines in Asiatic Turkey.[1]

The existing railways in Asia Minor were owned, in

1888, entirely by French and British financiers, with British capital decidedly in the predominance. The oldest and most important railway in Anatolia, the Smyrna-Aidin line—authorized in 1856, opened to traffic in 1866, and extended at various times until in 1888 it was 270 kilometres in length—was owned by an English company. British capitalists also owned the short, but valuable, Mersina-Adana Railway, in Cilicia, and held the lease of the Haidar Pasha-Ismid Railway. French interests were in control of the Smyrna-Cassaba Railway, which operated 168 kilometres of rails extending north and east from the port of Smyrna. It was not until the autumn of 1888 that Germans had any interest whatever in the railways of Asiatic Turkey.[2]

The first move of the Sultan in his plan to develop railway communication in his Asiatic provinces was to authorize important extensions to the existing railways of Anatolia. The French owners of the Smyrna-Cassaba line were granted a concession for a branch from Manissa to Soma, a distance of almost 100 kilometres, under substantial subsidies from the Ottoman Treasury. The British-controlled Smyrna-Aidin Railway was authorized to build extensions and branches totalling 240 kilometres, almost doubling the length of its line. A Franco-Belgian syndicate in October, 1888, received permission to construct a steam tramway from Jaffa, a port on the Mediterranean, to Jerusalem—an unpretentious line which proved to be the first of an important group of Syrian railways constructed by French and Belgian promoters. Shortly afterward the concession for a railway from Beirut to Damascus was awarded to French interests.[3]

But the great dream of Abdul Hamid was the great dream of Wilhelm von Pressel: the vision of a trunk line from the Bosporus to the Persian Gulf, which, in connection with the existing railways of Anatolia and the new railways of Syria, would link Constantinople with Smyrna, Aleppo, Damascus, Beirut, Mosul, and Bagdad. As early as 1886 the Ottoman Ministry of Public Works had suggested to the lessees of the Haidar Pasha-Ismid Railway that they undertake the extension of that line to Angora, with a view to an eventual extension to Bagdad. The proposal was renewed in 1888, with the understanding that the Sultan was prepared to pay a substantial subsidy to assure adequate returns on the capital to be invested. The lessees of the Haidar Pasha-Ismid line, however, were unable to interest investors in the enterprise and were compelled to withdraw altogether from railway projects in Turkey-in-Asia. Thereupon Sir Vincent Caillard, Chairman of the Ottoman Public Debt Administration, endeavored to form an Anglo-American syndicate to undertake the construction of a Constantinople-Bagdad railway, but he met with no success.[4]

The opportunity which British capitalists neglected German financiers seized. Dr. Alfred von Kaulla, of the *Württembergische Vereinsbank* of Stuttgart, who was in Constantinople selling Mauser rifles to the Ottoman Minister of War, became interested in the possibilities of railway development in Turkey. With the coöperation of Dr. George von Siemens, Managing Director of the *Deutsche Bank,* a German syndicate was formed to take over the existing railway from Haidar Pasha to Ismid and to construct an extension thereof to Angora. On October 6, 1888, this syndicate was awarded a concession for the railway to Angora and was given to understand that it was the intention of the Ottoman Government to extend that railway to Bagdad *via* Samsun, Sivas, and Diarbekr. The Sultan guaranteed the Angora line a minimum annual revenue of 15,000 francs per kilometre, for the payment of which he assigned to the Ottoman Public Debt Administration the taxes of certain districts through which the railway was to pass. Thus came into existence the Anatolian Railway Company (*La Société du Chemin de Fer Ottomane d'Anatolie*), the first of the German railway enterprises in Turkey.[5]

The German concessionaires were not slow to realize the possibilities of their concession. They elected Sir Vincent Caillard to the board of directors of their Company, in order that they might receive the enthusiastic coöperation of the Ottoman Public Debt Administration and in order that they might interest British capitalists in their project. With the assistance of Swiss bankers they incorporated at Zurich the *Bank für orientalischen Eisenbahnen,* which floated in the European securities markets the first Anatolian Railways loan of eighty million francs—more than one fourth of the loan being underwritten in England. Shortly thereafter this same financial group, under the leadership of the *Deutsche Bank,* acquired a controlling interest in more than 1500 kilometres of railways in the Balkan Peninsula, by purchasing the holdings of Baron Hirsch in the Oriental Railways Company. The *Bank für orientalischen Eisenbahnen* became a holding company for all of the *Deutsche Bank's* railway enterprises in the Near East.[6]

Under the direction of German engineers, in the meantime, construction of the Anatolian Railway proceeded at so rapid a rate that the 485 kilometres of rails were laid and trains were in operation to Angora by January, 1893. About the same time a German engineering commission, assisted by two technical experts representing the Ottoman Ministry of Public Works and by two Turkish army officers, submitted a report on their preliminary survey of the proposed railway to Bagdad. This was enthusiastically received by the Sultan, who reiterated his intention of constructing a line into Mesopotamia at the earliest practicable date.[7]

In 1887 there was no German capital represented in the railways of Asiatic Turkey. Five years later the *Deutsche Bank* and its collaborators controlled the railways of Turkey from the Austro-Hungarian border to Constantinople; they had constructed a line from the Asiatic shore of the Straits to Angora; they were projecting a railway from Angora across the hills of Anatolia into the Mesopotamian valley. In coöperation with the Austrian and German state railways they could establish through service from the Baltic to the Bosporus and, by ferry and railway, into hitherto inaccessible parts of Asia Minor. Almost overnight, as history goes, Turkey had become an important sphere of German economic interest. Thus was born the idea of a series of German-controlled railways from Berlin to Bagdad, from Hamburg to the Persian Gulf!

The Ottoman Government apparently was well pleased with the energetic action of the German concessionaires in the promotion of their railway enterprises in Turkey. In any event, a tangible evidence of appreciation was extended the Anatolian Railway Company by an imperial *iradé* of February 15, 1893, which authorized the construction of a branch line of 444 kilometres from Eski Shehr (a town about midway between Ismid and Angora) to Konia. The new line, like its predecessor, was guaranteed a minimum annual return of 15,000 francs per kilometre, payments to be made under the supervision of the Ottoman Public Debt Administration. The obvious advantages of developing the potentially rich regions of southern Anatolia, and of providing improved communication between Constantinople and the interior of Asia Minor, led the Anatolian Company to hasten construction, with the result that service to Konia was inaugurated in 1896.[8]

Simultaneously with the granting of the second Anatolian concession the Sultan authorized an important extension to the French-owned Smyrna-Cassaba Railway. The existing line was to be prolonged a distance of 252 kilometres from Alashehr to Afiun Karahissar, at which latter town a junction was to be effected with the Anatolian Railway. Another French company was awarded a concession for the construction of the Damascus-Homs-Aleppo railway, in Syria, under substantial financial guarantees from the Ottoman Treasury. It was said that these concessions to French financiers were "compensatory" in character and were granted upon the urgent representations of the French ambassador in Constantinople.[9]

Between 1896 and 1899 no further definite steps were taken to extend the Anatolian Railway beyond Angora, as had been provided by the original concession. In the latter year, however, largely because of Russian objections to the further development of railways in northern Asia Minor, the Sultan took under consideration the advisability of projecting and building, instead, a line from Konia to Bagdad *via* Aleppo and Mosul. Early in 1899 a German commission left Constantinople to make a thorough survey of the economic and strategic possibilities of such a line. Included in the commission were Dr. Mackensen, Director of the Prussian State Railways; Dr. von Kapp, Surveyor for the State Railways of Württemberg; Herr Stemrich, the German Consul-General at Constantinople; Major Morgen, German military attaché; representatives of the Ottoman Ministry of Public Works. It was this commission that finally decided upon the route of the Bagdad Railway.[10]

At the close of the nineteenth century, therefore, the sceptre of railway power in the Near East was passing from the hands of Frenchmen and Englishmen into the hands of Germans. In a period of about ten years the German-owned Anatolian Railway Company had constructed almost one thousand kilometres of railway lines in Asia Minor. A German mission was blazing a trail through Syria and Mesopotamia for the extension of the Anatolian Railway to the valley of the Tigris River and the head of the Persian Gulf. German prestige seemed to be in the ascendancy: the Directors of the Anatolian Company reported to the stockholders in 1897 that, "as in former years, our Company has concerned itself continuously with the development of trade, industry, and agriculture in the region served by the Railway. As a result our enterprise has enjoyed in every sense the wholehearted support and the powerful protection of His Majesty the Sultan. Our relationships with the Imperial Ottoman Government, the local authorities, and all classes of the people themselves are more cordial than ever." [11]

The system of railways thus founded had been conceived by a German railway genius; it had been constructed by German engineers with materials made by German workers in German factories; it had been financed by German bankers; it was being operated under the supervision of German directors. In the minds of nineteenth-century neo-mercantilists this was a matter for national pride. A Pan-German organ hailed the Anatolian Railways and the proposed Bagdad enterprise in glowing terms: "The idea of this railway was conceived by German intelligence; Germans made the preliminary studies; Germans overcame all the serious obstacles which stood in the way of its execution. We should be all the more pleased with this success because the Russians and the English busied themselves at the Golden Horn endeavoring to block the German project." [12]

THE TRADERS FOLLOW THE INVESTORS

The construction of the Anatolian Railways by German capitalists was accompanied by a considerable expansion of

German economic interests in the Near East. In 1889, for example, a group of Hamburg entrepreneurs established the *Deutsche Levante Linie,* which inaugurated a direct steamship service between Hamburg, Bremen, Antwerp, and Constantinople. It was the expectation of the owners of this line that the construction of the Anatolian railways would materially increase the volume of German trade with Turkey—an expectation which was justified by subsequent developments. In 1888, the year of the original railway concession to the *Deutsche Bank,* exports from Germany to Turkey were valued at 11,700,000 marks; by 1893, when the line was completed to Angora, they mounted to a valuation of 40,900,000 marks, an increase of about 350%. Imports into Germany from Turkey during the same period rose from 2,300,000 marks to 16,500,000 marks, showing an increase of over 700%. No small proportion of the phenomenal increase in the volume of German exports to Turkey can be attributed to the use of German materials on the Ismid-Angora railway. In any event, there was no further substantial development of this export trade between 1895 and 1900, although imports into Germany from Turkey reached the high figure of 28,900,000 marks at the close of the century.[13]

That German traders should follow German financiers into the Ottoman Empire was to be expected. The *Deutsche Bank*—sponsor of the Anatolian Railways—had been notably active in the promotion of German foreign commerce. From its very inception it had devoted itself energetically to the promotion of industrial and commercial activity abroad, thus carrying out the object announced in its charter "of fostering and facilitating commercial relations between Germany, other European countries, and oversea markets." By the establishment of foreign branches, by the liberal financing of import and export shipments, by the introduction of German bills of exchange in the four corners of the earth, and by other similar methods, this great bank was largely responsible for the emancipation of German traders from their former dependence upon British banking facilities. The Anatolian Railways concessions marked the initial efforts of the *Deutsche Bank* at Constantinople. What it had done elsewhere it could be expected to do in the interests of German business men operating in Turkey.[14]

The London *Times* of October 28, 1898, contained a significant review of the status of German enterprise in the Ottoman Empire during the decade immediately preceding. Whereas ten years before, the finance and trade of Turkey were practically monopolized by France and Great Britain, the Germans were now by far the most active group in Constantinople and in Asia Minor. Hundreds of German salesmen were traveling in Turkey, vigorously pushing their wares and studiously canvassing the markets to learn the wants of the people. The Krupp-owned Germania Shipbuilding Company was furnishing torpedoes to the Turkish navy; Ludwig Loewe and Company, of Berlin, was equipping the Sultan's military machine with small arms; Krupp, of Essen, was sharing with Armstrong the orders for artillery. German bicycles were replacing American-made machines. There was a noticeable increase of German trade with Palestine and Syria. In 1899 a group of German financiers founded the *Deutsche Palästina Bank,* which proceeded to establish branches at Beirut, Damascus, Gaza, Haifa, Jaffa, Jerusalem, Nablus, Nazareth, and Tripoli-in-Syria.

Promoters, bankers, traders, engineers, munitions manufacturers, ship-owners, and railway builders all were playing their parts in laying a substantial foundation for a further expansion of German economic interests in the Ottoman Empire.[15]

THE GERMAN GOVERNMENT BECOMES INTERESTED

In a sense, German diplomacy had paved the way for the Anatolian Railway concessions. For numerous reasons, which need not be discussed here, French and British influence at the Sublime Porte gradually declined during the decades of 1870-1890. British prestige, in particular, waned after the occupation of Egypt in 1882. The German ambassador at Constantinople during most of this period was Count Hatzfeld, an unusually shrewd diplomatist, who perceived the extraordinary opportunity which then existed to increase German prestige in the Near East. His place in the counsels of the Sultan became increasingly important, as he missed no chance to seize privileges surrendered by France or Great Britain.[16]

An instance of Count Hatzfeld's activity was the appointment of a German military mission to Turkey. Until 1870 there had been a French mission in Constantinople, with almost complete control over the training and equipment of the Ottoman army. At the outbreak of the Franco-German War, however, the mission was recalled because of the crying need for French officers at the front. After the termination of hostilities, and again after the collapse of the Turkish defence against Russia in 1877, the Sultan requested the reappointment of the mission, but the French Government politely declined the invitation. The German ambassador seized upon this neglected opportunity and, in 1883, persuaded Abdul Hamid to invite the Kaiser to designate a group of German officers to serve with the Ottoman General Staff.[17]

In command of the German military mission despatched to Turkey in response to this invitation was General von der Goltz. This brilliant officer—who, appropriately enough, was to die in the Caucasus campaign of 1916—remained in Turkey twelve years, reorganizing the Turkish army, forming a competent general staff, establishing a military academy for young officers, and formulating plans for an adequate system of reserves. So great was his success that he won the lasting respect of Turkish military and civil officials; time and time again he was invited to return to Turkey as military adviser extraordinary; in 1909 he answered the call of the Young Turks and lent his ripened judgment to the solution of their distracting problems; he was granted the coveted title of Pasha. The personal prestige of von der Goltz was of no small importance in brightening Germany's rising star in the Near East.[18]

Another event of first rate importance in the history of German ventures in the Ottoman Empire was the accession, in 1888, of Emperor William II. During the three decades of his reign the economic foundations of German imperialism were strengthened and broadened; the superstructure of German imperialism was both reared and destroyed. During his régime the German industrial revolution reached its height, and the empire, it seemed, became one enormous factory consuming great quantities of raw materials and producing a prodigious volume of manufactured commodities for the home and foreign markets. Simultaneously there was developed a German merchant marine which carried the imperial flag to the seven seas. A normal concomitant of this industrial and commercial progress was the expansion of political and economic interests abroad—renewed activity in the acquisition of a colonial empire; marked success in the further conquest of foreign markets; the creation of a great navy; the phenomenal increase of German investments in Turkey. It is no insignificant coincidence that German financiers received their first Ottoman railway concession in the year of the accession of William II and that the capture of Aleppo—ending once and for all the plan for a German-controlled railway from Berlin to Bagdad—occurred just a few days before his abdication.

From the first the Kaiser evinced a keen interest in the Ottoman Empire as a sphere in which his personal influence might be exerted on behalf of German economic expansion and German political prestige. He was quick to recognize the opportunities for German enterprise in a country where much went by favor, and where political influence could be effectually exerted for the furtherance of commercial interests. In one of a round of royal visits following his accession, the young Emperor, in November, 1889, paid his respects to the Sultan Abdul Hamid. Upon the arrival in the Bosporus of the imperial yacht *Hohenzollern,* the Kaiser and Kaiserin received an ostentatious welcome from the Sultan and cordial greetings from the diplomatic corps. It was suggested at the time that there was more than formal significance in this visit of the German sovereigns, coming, as it did, when prominent German financiers were engaged in constructing the first kilometres of an important Anatolian railway. This impression was confirmed when, shortly after the Emperor's return to the Fatherland, a favorable commercial treaty was negotiated by the German ambassador at Constantinople and ratified by the German and Ottoman Governments in 1890.[19]

The expansion of German economic interests and political prestige in the Ottoman Empire was not looked upon with favor by Bismarck. The Great Chancellor was primarily interested in isolating France on the continent and in avoiding commercial and colonial conflicts overseas. In particular he had no desire to become involved in the complicated Near Eastern question—toward which at various times he had expressed total indifference and contempt—for fear of a clash with Russian ambitions at Constantinople. He realized that German investments in

Turkey might lead to pressure on the German Government to adopt an imperial policy in Asia Minor, as, indeed, German investments in Africa had forced him to enter colonial competition in the Dark Continent.[20] When the *Deutsche Bank* first called the Chancellor's attention to its Anatolian enterprises, therefore, Bismarck frankly stated his misgivings about the situation. In a letter to Dr. von Siemens, Managing Director of the *Deutsche Bank,* dated at the Foreign Office, September 2, 1888, he wrote:[21]

"With reference to the inquiry of the *Deutsche Bank* of the 15 ultimo, I beg to reply that no diplomatic objections exist to an application for a concession for railway construction in Asia Minor.

The Imperial Embassy at Constantinople has been authorized to lend support to German applicants for such concessions—particularly to the designated representative of the *Deutsche Bank* in Constantinople—in their respective endeavors in this matter.

The Board of Directors in its inquiry has correctly given expression to the assumption that any official endorsement of its plans, in the present state of affairs, would neither extend beyond the life of the concession nor apply to the execution and operation of the enterprise. As a matter of fact, German entrepreneurs assume a risk in capital investments in railway construction in Anatolia—a risk which lies, first, in the difficulties encountered in the enforcement of the law in the East, and, second, in the increase of such difficulties through war or other complications.

The danger involved therein for German entrepreneurs must be assumed exclusively by the entrepreneurs, and the latter must not count upon the protection of the German Empire against eventualities connected with precarious enterprises in foreign countries." [22]

Bismarck disapproved of the visit of William II to Turkey in 1889. Failing to persuade the young Emperor to abandon the trip to Constantinople, the Chancellor did what he could to allay Russian suspicions of the purposes of the journey. Describing an interview which he had with the Tsar, in October, 1889, Bismarck wrote, in a memorandum recently taken from the files of the Foreign Office: "As to the approaching journey of the Kaiser to the Orient, I said that the reason for the visit to Constantinople lay only in the wish of our Majesties not to come home from Athens without having seen Constantinople; Germany had no political interests in the Black Sea and the Mediterranean; and it was accordingly impossible that the visit of our Majesties should take on a political complexion. The admission of Turkey into the Triple Alliance was not possible for us; we could not lay on the German people the obligation to fight Russia for the future of Bagdad." [23] In 1890, however, Prince Bismarck was dismissed, and the chief obstacle to the Emperor's Turkish policy was removed.

During the succeeding decade the German diplomatic and consular representatives in the Ottoman Empire rendered yeoman service in furthering investment, trade, and commerce by Germans in the Near East. It became proverbial among foreign business men in Turkey that no service was too menial, no request too exacting, to receive the courteous and efficient attention of the German governmental services. German consular officers were held up as models for others to pattern themselves after. The British Consul General at Constantinople, for example, informed British business men that his staff was at their disposal for any service designed to expedite British trade and investments in Turkey. "If," he wrote, "any merchant should come to this consulate and say, 'The German consulate gives such and such assistance to German traders, do the same for me,' his suggestion would be welcomed and, if possible, acted on at once." [24]

A judicious appointment served to reinforce the already

strong position of the Germans in Turkey. In 1897 Baron
von Wangenheim was replaced as ambassador to Constantinople by Baron Marschall von Bieberstein (1842–
1912), a former Secretary of State for Foreign Affairs.
Baron Marschall was one of the most capable of German
bureaucrats. The Kaiser was glad to have him at Constantinople because his training and experience made him
an admirable person for developing imperial interests
there; his political opponents considered his appointment
to the Sublime Porte a convenient method of removing
him from domestic politics. The new ambassador's political views were well known: he was a frank believer in a
world-policy for Germany; he was an ardent supporter of
colonialism, if not of Pan-Germanism; he was a bitter
opponent of Great Britain; he espoused the cause of a
strong political and economic alliance between the German
and Ottoman Empires. What Baron Marschall did he
did well. Occupying what appeared, at first, to be an
obscure post, he became the foremost of the Kaiser's
diplomatists and for fifteen years lent his powerful personality and his practical experience to the furthering of
German enterprise in Turkey.[25]

In 1898 William II made his second pilgrimage to the
Land of Promise. Every detail of this trip was arranged
with an eye to the theatrical: the enthusiastic reception at
Constantinople; the "personally conducted" Cook's tour
to the Holy Land; the triumphal entry into the Holy City
through a breach in the walls made by the infidel Turk;
the dedication of a Lutheran Church at Jerusalem; the
hoisting of the imperial standard on Mount Zion; the gift
of hallowed land to the Roman Catholic Church; the visit
to the grave of Saladin at Damascus and the speech by
which the Mohammedans of the world were assured of
the eternal friendship of the German Emperor.[26] The
dramatic aspects of the royal visit were not sufficient,

however, to obscure its practical purpose. It was generally supposed in western Europe that the Kaiser's trip to Turkey was closely connected with the application of the Anatolian Railways for the proposed Bagdad Railway concessions.[27] But little objection was raised by the British and French press. Paris laughed at the obvious absurdity of a Cook's tour for a crowned head and his entourage; London took comfort in the discomfiture which the incident would cause Russia. But there was no talk then of a great Teutonic conspiracy to spread a "net" from Hamburg to the Persian Gulf.[28]

The true significance of this royal pilgrimage of 1898 cannot be appreciated without some reference to its background of contemporary events. For the preceding four years the Ottoman Government had permitted, if not actually incited, a series of ruthless massacres of Christians in Macedonia and Armenia. European public opinion was unanimous in condemnation of the intolerance, brutality, and corruption of Abdul Hamid's régime; the very name of the "Red Sultan" was anathema. Under these circumstances any demonstration of friendship and respect for the Turkish sovereign would be considered flagrant flaunting of public morality.[29] By Abdul Hamid, on the other hand, it would be welcomed as needed support in time of trouble. With the Kaiser the exigencies of practical politics triumphed!

It was appropriate, furthermore, that the year 1898 should be marked by some definite step forward in German imperialist progress in Turkey, for during that year notable advances had been made by German imperialism in other fields. On March 5 there was forcibly wrung from China a century-long lease of Kiao-chau and of certain privileges in the Shantung Peninsula, thus assuring to German enterprise a prominent position in the Far East. Two weeks later was passed the great German naval law of 1898, laying the foundation of a fleet that later was to challenge British supremacy of the seas. German diplomacy had developed interests in eastern Asia; it was developing interests on the seas and in western Asia; it had abandoned a purely Continental policy. No further signs were needed that a new era was dawning in German foreign affairs—unless, perhaps, it be mentioned that the great Prince Bismarck quietly passed away at Friedrichsruh on July 30 of that momentous year!

GERMAN ECONOMIC INTERESTS MAKE FOR NEAR EASTERN IMPERIALISM

Bismarck's policy of aloofness in the Near East, however desirable it may have been from the political point of view, could not have appealed to those statesmen and soldiers and business men who believed that diplomatic policies should be determined in large part by the economic situation of the German Empire. The interest of William II in Turkey was enthusiastically supported by all those who sought to have German foreign affairs conducted with full recognition of the needs of industrialized Germany in raw materials and foodstuffs, of the importance of richer and more numerous foreign markets for the products of German factories, and of the exigencies of economic, as well as military, preparation for war. The great natural wealth of the Ottoman Empire in valuable raw materials, the possibilities of developing the Near East as a market for manufactured articles, and the geographical situation of Turkey all help to explain why the economic exploitation of the Sultan's dominions was a matter of more vital concern to Germany than to any other European power. To make this clear it will be necessary to digress, for a time, to consider the nature of the imperial problems of an industrial state and, in particular, the problems of industrial Germany.

Under modern conditions the needs of an industrial state are imperious. Such a state is dependent for its very existence upon an uninterrupted supply of foodstuffs for the workers of its cities and of raw materials for the machines of its factories. As its population increases—unless it be one of those few fortunate nations which, like the United States, are practically self-sufficient—its importations of foodstuffs mount higher and higher. As its industries expand, the demand for raw materials becomes greater and more diversified—cotton, rubber, copper, nitrates, petroleum come to be considered the very life-blood of the nation's industry. It is considered one of the functions of the government of an industrial state—whether that government be autocratic and dynastic or representative and democratic—to interest itself in securing and conserving sources of these essential commodities, as well as to defend and maintain the routes of communication by which they are transported to the domestic market. The securing of sources of raw materials may involve the acquisition of a colonial empire; it may require the establishment of a protectorate over, or a "sphere of interest" in, an economically backward or a politically weak nation; or it may necessitate nothing more than the maintenance of friendly relations with other states. Protection of vital routes of communication may demand the construction of a fleet of battleships; it may be the *raison d'être* for a large standing army; it may necessitate only diplomatic support of capitalists in their foreign investments. Methods will be dictated by circumstances, but the impulse usually is the same.[30]

The German Empire was an industrial state, and its needs were imperious. In the face of a rapidly increasing population the nation became more and more dependent upon importations of foreign foodstuffs. Herculean efforts were made to keep agricultural production abreast of the domestic demand for grain: transient laborers were imported from Russia and Italy to replace those German peasants who had migrated to the industrial cities; machinery was introduced and scientific methods were applied; high protective tariffs were imposed upon imported foodstuffs to stimulate production within the empire. These measures, however, were insufficient to meet the situation; the greatest intensive development of the agricultural resources of the nation could not forestall the necessity of feeding some ten millions of Germans on foreign grain.[31]

German manufacturers, as well, were unable to obtain from domestic sources the necessary raw materials for their industrial plants. Many essential commodities were not produced at all in Germany and in only insignificant quantities in the colonies. Some German industries were almost wholly dependent upon foreign sources of supply for their raw materials. The most striking example of this was the textile manufactures, which had to obtain from abroad more than nine tenths of their raw cotton, jute, silk, and similar essential supplies.[32] Interruption of the flow of these or other indispensable goods would have brought upon German industrial centers the same paralysis which afflicted the British cotton manufactures during the American Civil War.

The German Empire had to pay for its imported foodstuffs and raw materials with the products of its mines and factories, with the services of its citizens and its ships, with the use of its surplus funds, or capital.[33] The development of a German export trade was the natural outcome of the development of German industry. And as German industries expanded, the demand for imported raw materials increased, thus rendering more necessary the extension of the export trade. The German industrial revolution of the late nineteenth century was at once the cause and the effect of the growing dependence of German economic prosperity upon foreign markets.[34]

But foreign commerce is not concerned with the sale of manufactured articles only. In its export trade, German industry was closely allied with German shipping and German finance. The services rendered German trade by the German merchant marine need not be reiterated; they are sufficiently well known. The relationship between the policies of German industry and the policies of German finance was no less important. The export of goods by German factories was supplemented by the so-called "export of capital" by German banks. Sometimes the German trader followed the German investor; sometimes the investor followed the trader. But whichever the order, the services rendered by the investor were to develop the purchasing power and the prosperity of the market, as well as to oil the mechanism of international exchange.[35] The industrial export policy and the financial export policy went hand in hand. Certainly this was the case in the Near East.

The German Empire depended for its welfare, if not for its existence, upon an uninterrupted supply of food for its workers and of raw materials for its machines. But this supply, in turn, was conditional upon the maintenance and development of a thriving export trade. The allies of this export trade were a great merchant marine and a vigorous policy of international finance and investment. Thus the nation which in 1871 was economically almost self-sufficient, by 1900 had extended its interests to the four corners of the earth. This could not have been without its effects upon German international policy. "The strength of the nation," said Prince von Bülow, "rejuvenated by the political reorganization, as it grew, burst the bounds of its old home, and its policy was dictated by new interests and needs. In proportion as our national life has become international, the policy of the German Empire has become international. . . . Industry, commerce, and the shipping trade have transformed the old industrial life of Germany into one of international industry, and this has also carried the Empire in political matters beyond the limits which Prince Bismarck set to German statecraft." [36]

From the German point of view, the call to German imperialism was clearly urgent, but the resources of German imperialism were seriously limited. The colonial ventures of the Empire had culminated in no outstanding successes and in some outstanding failures. Entering the lists late, the Germans had found the spoils of colonial rivalry almost completely appropriated by those other knights errant of white civilization, French, British, and Russian empire-builders. The few African and Asiatic territories which the Germans did succeed in acquiring were extensive in size, but unpromising in many other respects. With the exception of German East Africa the colonies were comparatively poor in the valuable raw materials so much desired by the factories of the mother country; they were unimportant as producers of foodstuffs. Attempts to induce Germans to settle in these overseas possessions were singularly unsuccessful. On the other hand, colonial enterprises had involved the empire in enormous expenditures aggregating over a billion marks; had precipitated a series of wars and military expeditions costing the nation thousands of lives and creating a host of international misunderstandings; had won for Germans widespread notoriety as poor colonizers, as tactless and autocratic officials, as ruthless overlords of the natives. It was no wonder that the German people seemed to be thoroughly discouraged and discontented with their colonial ventures.

However, even had the German colonies been richer

than they were, they, alone, could not have solved the imperial problem of an industrialized Germany. German colonial trade was possessed of the same inherent weakness as German overseas commerce—it would be dependent, in the event of a general European war, upon British sea power. German industry could be effectually crippled by interruption of the flow of essential raw materials, such as cotton and copper, or by the cutting of communications with her foreign markets. It was questionable whether the German navy could be relied upon to keep the seas open.

Blockades, furthermore, exist not only in time of war, but in time of peace as well. European nations were surrounded by tariff barriers which seriously restricted the development of international trade and served to promote a system of national economic exclusiveness—a condition of affairs which harmonized only too well with the existing colossal military establishments. In this respect, of course, Germany was more sinner than sinned against. But in such an age it behooved every nation to build its industries, as well as its armies, with some view to the contingencies of war.

German statesmen and economists were by no means backward in understanding the situation. Although they had no disposition to overlook the development of the merchant marine and the navy, they believed this was not enough. They sought to build up in Central Europe a system of economic alliances, as they previously had effected a formidable military alliance. Thus might Germany and her allies become an economically self-sufficient unit, freed from dependence upon British sea power.[37] And into this alliance could be incorporated the Near East!

Beyond the Bosporus lay a country rich in oils and metals; a country capable of supplying German textile mills with cotton of superior quality; a country which in ancient times was fabulously wealthy in agricultural products; a country which gave promise of developing into a rich market for western commodities. Communication with this wonderland was to be established by a German-controlled railway upon which service could be maintained in time of war, as in time of peace, without the aid of naval power. What greater inducements could have been offered to German imperialists, living in an imperialist world? Turkey was destined to fall within the economic orbit of an industrialized Germany!

A distinguished German publicist said in 1903, "From the German point of view, it would be unparalleled stupidity if we did not most energetically do our part to acquire a share in the revival of the ancient civilization of Mesopotamia, Syria, and Babylonia. What we do not do others will surely do—be they British, French, or Russian; and the increased economic advantage which, through the Bagdad Railway, will accrue to us in the Nearer East would otherwise not only fail to be ours, but would serve to strengthen our rivals in diplomacy and business." [38] Some years later, in the midst of the Great War, an American writer expressed much the same point of view: "Hemmed in on the west by Great Britain and France and on the east by Russia, born too late to extend their political sovereignty over vast colonial domains, and unable (if only for lack of coaling stations) to develop sea power greater than that of their rivals, nothing was more natural than the German and Austro-Hungarian conception of a *Drang nach Osten* through the Balkan Peninsula, over the bridge of Constantinople, into the markets of Asia. The geographical position of the Central European states made as inevitable a penetration policy into the Balkans and Turkey as the geographical position of England made inevitable the development of an overseas empire." [39] Karl

Helfferich has said that "it was neither accident nor deliberate purpose, as much as it was the course of German economic development, which led Germany to take an active interest in Turkey." [40]

BIBLIOGRAPHICAL AND EXPLANATORY NOTES

[1] *The Annual Register,* 1888, pp. 44, 310.

[2] Good general statements of the transportation problem of Turkey during the two decades 1880-1900 are Verney and Dambmann, *op. cit.,* Part III; J. Courau, *La locomotive en Turquie d'Asie* (Brussels, 1895), pp. 18-47; *Corps de droit ottoman,* Volume IV, pp. 117 *et seq.*

[3] *Corps de droit ottoman,* Volume IV, pp. 202-223, 237-242, etc.

[4] *Bulletin de la Chambre de Commerce française de Constantinople,* August 31, 1888, p. 10; September 30, 1888, p. 31. *Cf.,* also a prospectus issued by a banker, Mr. W. J. Alt, "Heads of a Convention for the extension of the Haidar Pasha-Ismid Railway" (London, 1886), a copy of which was loaned to the author by Mr. Ernest Rechnitzer.

[5] The story of these negotiations is well told in a new book by Dr. Karl Helfferich, *Georg von Siemens—ein Lebensbild* (Leipzig, 1923), the proofs of which I have had the privilege of reading. For an official copy of the convention and by-laws of the Anatolian Railway Company (*Firman Impérial de concession et statuts de la Société du Chemin de Fer Ottomane d'Anatolie,* Constantinople, 1889), I am indebted to Dr. Arthur von Gwinner, of the *Deutsche Bank. Cf.,* also, *Administration de la dette publique ottomane—Rapport sur les opérations de l'année 1888* (Constantinople, 1889); *Report of the Anatolian Railway Company,* 1889, pp. 1-2; *Corps de droit ottoman,* Volume IV, pp. 120-142.

[6] Helfferich, *op. cit.,* Part V; A. P. Brüning, *Die Entwicklung des ausländischen, speciell des überseeischen deutschen Bankwesens* (Berlin, 1907), pp. 14 *et seq.*; *Report of the Anatolian Railway Company,* 1889, p. 3; *Report of the Deutsche Bank,* 1892, p. 4, 1890, p. 4.

[7] *Report of the Anatolian Railway Company,* 1891, p. 20, 1892, pp. 16, 23.

[8] *Actes de la concession du chemin de fer Eski Shehr-Konia* (Constantinople, 1893); *Report of the Anatolian Railway Company,* 1896, pp. 4, 9.

[9] *Corps de droit ottoman,* Volume IV, pp. 191-197. The junction of the two systems at Afiun Karahissar did not immediately

materialize. The distance from that town to Constantinople is longer by sixty-six kilometres than the distance to Smyrna; the latter port, therefore, is the better natural outlet for the products of Anatolia. This diversion of traffic to Smyrna the Anatolia Railway sought to avoid, it is said, by granting discriminatory rates in favor of through freight to Constantinople over its own lines. A rate war ensued between the Anatolian and Smyrna-Cassaba systems, and neither was willing to permit an actual joining of the tracks at Afiun Karahissar, with the result that for years the rails of the two roads lay a comparatively few yards apart. This absurd situation, so obviously detrimental to the interests of the two roads, was remedied by an agreement of 1899. *Infra*, pp. 59-60. *Cf.*, also R. LeCoq, *Un chemin de fer en Asie Mineure* (Paris, 1907), pp. 23-24; *Report of the Anatolian Railway Company*, 1899, p. 3.

[10] A summary of the report of the Commission is to be found in *Diplomatic and Consular Reports*, No. 3140 (London, 1903), pp. 26 *et seq.* A statement of its membership and purposes is given in the *Report of the Anatolian Railway Company*, 1899, p. 9.

[11] *Report of the Anatolian Railway Company*, 1897, p. 3.

[12] *Alldeutsche Blätter*, December 17, 1899. It should be borne in mind, however, that until the Bagdad Railway concession was granted French financiers held the lead in the number of kilometres of railway in operation or contracted for. The situation in 1898 was as follows:

British Kiloms.	*French* Kiloms.	*German* Kiloms.
Smyrna-Aidin... 373	Smyrna - Cassaba 512	Haidar Pasha-Ismid 91
Mersina-Adana.. 67	Jaffa - Jerusalem 87	Ismid-Angora. 485
Total 440	Beirut - Damascus 247	Eski Shehr-Konia 444
	Damascus-Aleppo 420	Total 1,020
	Total 1,266	

All of the British and German lines were in operation in 1898, whereas the French Syrian Railways were only partially completed.

[13] *Statistisches Handbuch für das deutsche Reich*, Volume 2, pp. 506, 510; *Diplomatic and Consular Reports*, No. 2950 (1902),

pp. 5, 23; *Turkey in Europe,* No. 16 of the Foreign Office Handbooks, pp. 86-87.

[14] J. Riesser, *Die deutschen Grossbanken und ihre Konzentration im Zusammenhang mit der Entwicklung der Gesamtwirtschaft in Deutschland* (third edition, Jena, 1909) ; translated into English and published as Senate Document No. 593, Sixty-first Congress, Second Session, 1911. References here given are to the translation. In this connection *cf.* "The Oversea and Foreign Business of the German Credit Banks," pp. 420 *et seq.*

[15] *Syria and Palestine,* p. 126; *The Times,* October 28, 1898, August 2 and 16, 1899.

[16] Karl Helfferich, *Die deutsche Türkenpolitik* (Berlin, 1921), pp. 10 *et seq.*; J. A. R. Marriot, *The Eastern Question* (Oxford, 1917), pp. 347 *et seq.*

[17] L. Ostrorog, *The Turkish Problem* (London, 1919), pp. 52-53; E. Dutemple, *En Turquie d'Asie* (Paris, 1883), pp. 131 *et seq.*

[18] For a biographical account of General von der Goltz (1843-1916) *cf.* F. W. Wile, *Men Around the Kaiser* (Philadelphia, 1913), Chapter XXVI. Bismarck consented to the appointment of von der Goltz's military mission—which was not in accord with his general Eastern policy—as a sort of insurance against the possibility that chauvinism, Pan-Slavism, and anti-German elements in Russia should gain the ascendancy at the court of the Tsar. In such an event it might be possible to utilize Turkish bayonets and Turkish artillery, especially if they had been trained by Prussian officers. *Memoirs of Prince Hohenlohe-Schillingsfürst* (English translation, New York, 1906), Volume II, p. 268.

[19] *Recueil d'actes internationaux de l'Empire Ottoman,* Volume IV (1903), Document No. 960.

[20] Mary E. Townsend, *Origins of Modern German Colonialism* (New York, 1921), Chapters V-VII; Prince Bismarck, *Reflections and Reminiscences* (New York, 1899), Volume II, pp. 233 *et seq.*

[21] For this letter, hitherto unpublished, I am indebted to Dr. Karl Helfferich, son-in-law of the late George von Siemens.

[22] The italics are mine.

[23] *Die grosse Politik der europäischen Kabinette, 1871-1914* (Berlin, 1922 *et seq.*), Volume VI, pp. 360-361. (A compilation of documents from the files of the Foreign Office, edited by a non-partisan commission appointed by the Government of the German Republic.) Of Bismarck's policy in the Near East the Ex-Kaiser writes, "Bismarck spoke quite disdainfully of Turkey, of the men in high position there, and of conditions in that land. I thought I might inspire him in part with essentially more

favorable opinions, but my efforts were of little avail . . . Prince Bismarck was never favorably inclined toward Turkey and never agreed with me in my Turkish policy." W. von Hohenzollern, *My Memoirs, 1878-1918* (New York, 1922), p. 27.

[24] *Diplomatic and Consular Reports,* No. 2950 (1902), p. 20.

[25] For information regarding the appointment of Baron Marschall to Constantinople the author is indebted to Dr. Arthur von Gwinner, who believes that the Baron was being sentenced to political exile when he was detailed to the Sublime Porte, but that his opponents overlooked the possibilities of the embassy at the Ottoman capital. Wile, *op. cit.,* Chapter XVIII, gives a short biographical account of Baron Marschall.

[26] *Cf.* E. Lamy, "La France du Levant: Voyage de l'Empereur Guillaume II," in *Revue des deux mondes,* Volume 150 (1898), pp. 880-911, Volume 151 (1899), pp. 315-348; E. Lewin, *The German Road to the East* (New York, 1917), pp. 105 *et seq.*; C. S. Hurgronje, *The Holy War, Made in Germany* (New York, 1915), pp. 70-71; *The All Highest Goes to Jerusalem,* being an English translation of a series of articles published in *Le Rire* (Paris) during 1898 (New York, 1917). In Germany the royal pilgrimage was intended to be taken seriously. Herr Heine, of the Munich *Simplicissimus,* was convicted of *lèse majesté* and imprisoned for six months for having published humorous cartoons of the Kaiser and his party on their travels. *The Annual Register,* 1898, pp. 255-258.

[27] The author found some difference of opinion in Germany regarding the connection between the Kaiser's visit and the pending Anatolian and Bagdad concessions. Dr. von Gwinner denies that there was any such purpose behind the Emperor's trip to the East—or, at least, if there was, that it was unsolicited by the promoters and not looked upon with favor by them. Dr. Helfferich, on the other hand, is convinced that His Majesty was directly concerned with the desirability of obtaining additional railway concessions for German financiers. The Kaiser himself agrees with Dr. Helfferich. *Cf., My Memoirs, 1878-1918,* p. 86.

[28] *Cf.* foreign correspondence in *The Times* (London), October 25, 1898, and days immediately thereafter.

[29] For an analysis of this situation see *The Manchester Guardian,* July 31, 1899, which took the stand that "for no sort of mercantile gain would a nation be justified in making friendly advances to the blood-stained tyrant of Armenia."

[30] In this connection see Leonard Woolf, *Economic Imperialism* (London and New York, 1920), Chapter I; Ramsay Muir, *The Expansion of Europe* (New York, 1917), Chapter I; J. E. Spurr (editor), *Political and Commercial Geology* (New York, 1920), Chapter XXXII, entitled "Who Owns the Earth?"; Aspi-

Fleurimont, "La Question du coton," in *Questions diplomatiques et coloniales,* Volume 15 (1903), pp. 429-432; J. A. B. Scherer, *Cotton as a World Power* (New York, 1922). In addition, for the wider aspects of imperialism, consult H. N. Brailsford, *The War of Steel and Gold* (New edition, London, 1915), Chapter II; F. C. Howe, *Why War?* (New York, 1916), *passim*; Walter Lippman, *The Stakes of Diplomacy* (New York, 1915); J. A. Hobson, *Imperialism: A Study* (London, 1902).

[21] W. H. Dawson, *The Evolution of Modern Germany* (New York, 1908), Chapter XII. P. Rohrbach, *Deutschland unter den Weltvölkern,* p. 17.

[22] Riesser, *op. cit.,* pp. 110, 121.

[23] It should be remarked here that the author is not unaware of the fallacy of speaking of "German trade" and "German industry." He is cognizant of the fact that trade takes place not between countries, but between individuals. If he anthropomorphizes the German Empire for the purposes of this description, it is not because of either ignorance or malice, but for convenience.

[24] For further consideration of German economic progress during the late nineteenth century see: Dawson, *op. cit.,* Chapters III, IV, XII, XVI; E. D. Howard, *The Cause and Extent of the Recent Industrial Progress of Germany* (New York, 1907); T. B. Veblen, *Imperial Germany and the Industrial Revolution* (New York, 1915); W. H. Dawson, *Industrial Germany* (London, 1913); Karl Helfferich, *Germany's Economic Progress and National Wealth* (New York, 1913); G. Blondel, *L'Essor industriel et commercial du peuple allemand* (Paris, 1900).

[25] Paul Dehn, *Weltwirtschaftliche Neubildungen* (Berlin, 1904), *passim.*

[26] Bernhard von Bülow, *Imperial Germany* (English translation, New York, 1914), pp. 17, 18-20.

[27] The extent of German economic control of central and eastern Europe before the War is indicated by Mr. J. M. Keynes, in his book *The Economic Consequences of the Peace* (New York, 1920), pp. 17-18: "Germany not only furnished these countries with trade, but in the case of some of them supplied a great part of the capital needed for their own development. Of Germany's pre-war foreign investments, amounting in all to about six and a half billion dollars, not far short of two and a half billions was invested in Russia, Austria-Hungary, Bulgaria, Rumania, and Turkey. And by the system of 'peaceful penetration' she gave these countries not only capital, but what they needed hardly less, organization. The whole of Europe east of the Rhine thus fell into the German industrial orbit, and its economic life was adjusted accordingly." A frank German ad-

mission of a policy of a self-sufficient Central Europe is the work of Friedrich Naumann, *Mittel-Europa,* translated into English by C. M. Meredith and published under the title *Central Europe* (New York, 1917). See, especially, Chapters IV-VII. *Cf.,* also, Ernst zu Reventlow, *Deutschlands auswärtige Politik* (3rd revised edition, Berlin, 1916), pp. 336 *et seq*; K. H. Müller, *Die Bedeutung der Bagdadbahn* (Hamburg, 1916), p. 29.

[88] Paul Rohrbach, *Die Bagdadbahn* (Berlin, 1903), p. 16.

[89] H. A. Gibbons, *The Reconstruction of Poland and the Near East* (New York, 1917), pp. 57-58. The author is not in agreement with either Dr. Rohrbach or Dr. Gibbons. He certainly would hesitate to call any imperialist policy "inevitable."

[40] *Die deutsche Türkenpolitik,* p. 8.

CHAPTER IV

THE SULTAN MORTGAGES HIS EMPIRE

THE GERMANS OVERCOME COMPETITION

During 1898 and 1899 the Ottoman Ministry of Public Works received many applications for permission to construct a railway to Bagdad. Whatever may have been thought later of the financial prospects of the Bagdad Railway there was no scarcity then of promoters who were willing and anxious to undertake its construction. It was not because of lack of competition that the *Deutsche Bank* finally was awarded the all-important concession.

In 1898, for example, an Austro-Russian syndicate proposed the building of a railway from Tripoli-in-Syria to an unspecified port on the Persian Gulf, with branches to Bagdad and Khanikin. The sponsor of the project was Count Vladimir I. Kapnist, a brother of the Russian ambassador at Vienna and an influential person at the Tsar's court. Count Kapnist had the support of Pobêdonostsev, the famous Procurator of the Holy Synod, who was an avowed Pan-Slavist and an enthusiastic promoter of Russian colonization in Asia Minor.[1] The Sultan instructed his Minister of Public Works to study the Kapnist plan and submit a report. The Austro-Russian syndicate, however, made no further progress at Constantinople. The Sublime Porte obviously was opposed to any expansion of Russian influence in Turkey—a point of view which received the encouragement of the British and German ambassadors. Furthermore, in Russia itself there was opposition to Count Kapnist's project. Count Witte, Im-

58

perial Minister of Finance, and foremost political opponent
of Pobêdonostsev, emphasized the strategic menace to
Russia of improved railway transportation in Turkey and
sturdily maintained that Russian capital and technical
skill should be kept at home for the development of Russian railways and industry. By the spring of 1899 the
Kapnist plan had been shelved.[2]

In the meantime French bankers had become interested
in the possibilities of constructing a railway from the
Mediterranean to the Persian Gulf, utilizing the existing
railways in Syria as the nucleus of an elaborate system.
Their spokesman was M. Cotard, an engineer on the staff
of the Smyrna-Cassaba Railway. This project was possessed of such strong financial and political support at
Constantinople that the *Deutsche Bank* considered it best
to negotiate for a merger with the French interests involved.[3] Accordingly conversations were held at Berlin
early in 1899 between the *Deutsche Bank* and the Anatolian Railway Company, on the one hand, and the Imperial Ottoman Bank and the Smyrna-Cassaba Railway,
representing French interests, on the other. The result
was an important agreement of May 6, 1899, the chief
provisions of which were as follows:[4]

1. The *Deutsche Bank* admitted the Imperial Ottoman
Bank to participation in the proposed Bagdad Railway Company. German and French bankers were to be equally represented in ownership and control, each to be assigned 40%
of the capital stock, the remaining 20% to be offered to
Turkish investors. If British, or other capital were subsequently interested in the Company, the share of the new
participants was to be taken from the German and French
holdings in equal proportions.

2. A *modus vivendi* was arrived at between the Anatolian
and Smyrna-Cassaba Railways. The prevailing rate-war was
to be stopped; a joint commission was to be appointed to

agree upon a uniform tariff for the two companies; a junction of the two lines was to be effected and maintained at Afiun Karahissar for reciprocal through traffic.

3. In order to assure the faithful execution of the agreement between the Anatolian and Cassaba railways, each of the companies was to designate two of its directors to sit on the board of the other.[5]

4. French proposals for the construction of a Euphrates Valley railway were to be withdrawn.

5. The French and German bankers were to use their best offices with their respective governments to secure united diplomatic support for the claims of the *Deutsche Bank* to prior consideration in the award of the Bagdad Railway concession.

This agreement temporarily removed all French opposition to the Bagdad Railway. M. Constans, the French ambassador at Constantinople, joined Baron Marschall von Bieberstein in cordial support of the new "Franco-German syndicate." [6]

Competition had arisen, however, from a third source. During the summer of 1899 British bankers, represented in Constantinople by Mr. E. Rechnitzer, petitioned for the right to construct a railway from Alexandretta to Bagdad and the Persian Gulf. The terms offered by the British financiers were considered more liberal than any heretofore proposed,[7] and they were endorsed by the Ministry of Public Works. Mr. Rechnitzer enlisted the aid of Mahmoud Pasha, a brother-in-law of the Sultan. He secured the assistance of Sir Nicholas O'Connor, the British ambassador. He attended to the niceties of Oriental business by sending the Sultan and his aids costly presents.[8] He engineered an effective press campaign in Great Britain to arouse interest in his project. Just how much success Mr. Rechnitzer's plan might have achieved on its own merits is an open question. It definitely col-

lapsed, however, in October, 1899, when the outbreak of
the Boer War diverted British attention and energies from
the Near East to South Africa.[9]   It was under these circumstances that the Sultan, on November 27, 1899,
announced his decision to award to the *Deutsche Bank* the
concession for a railway from Konia to Bagdad and the
Persian Gulf.[10]

The success of the Germans was not unexpected. They
had a strong claim to the concession, for, in 1888 and
again in 1893, the Sultan had assured the Anatolian Railway Company that it should have priority in the construction of any railway to Bagdad. On the strength of that
assurance, the Anatolian Company had conducted expensive surveys of the proposed line.[11]   After a short period
of sharp competition for the concession in 1899, the
Deutsche Bank group was left in sole possession of the
field—the Russian promoters had withdrawn because of
lack of support at home; the French financiers had accepted a share in the German company in preference to
sole responsibility for the enterprise; the British proposals
had lost support when the Boer difficulty temporarily ob-
scured all other issues. The diplomatic situation, furthermore, was distinctly favorable to the German claims. The
Fashoda Affair and the serious Anglo-Russian rivalry in
the Middle East had served to put Russia, France, and
Great Britain at sixes and sevens, leaving Germans practically a free hand in the development of their interests
in Asia Minor.

Aside from these purely temporary advantages, however,
there were excellent reasons, from the Ottoman point of
view, for awarding the Bagdad Railway concessions to the
German Anatolian Railway Company. The usual explana-
tions—that the soft, sweet-sounding flattery of William II
overcame the shrewdness of Abdul Hamid; that Baron
Marschall von Bieberstein dominated the entire diplomatic

situation at the Porte ; that the German military mission exerted a powerful influence in the final result—are more obvious than convincing. These were all contributing factors in the success of the Germans, but they were not determining factors. The reasons for the award of the concession to the *Deutsche Bank* were partly economic, partly strategic, partly political.

The Germans alone submitted proposals which met the demands of the Public Debt Administration and the Ottoman Government. They proposed to extend the existing Anatolian Railway from Konia, across the mountains into Cilicia and Syria, down the valley of the Tigris to Bagdad and Basra and the Persian Gulf. The railway which they had in mind would reach from one end of Asiatic Turkey to the other ; in connection with the railways of southern Anatolia and of Syria, it would provide continuous railway communication between Constantinople and Smyrna in the north and west, with Aleppo, Damascus, Beirut, Mecca, and Mosul in the south and east. There were serious technical and financial difficulties in the construction of such a railway, it is true, but there were political and economic considerations which warranted the expenditure of whatever effort and funds might be necessary to carry the line to completion.

On the other hand, the groups other than the Germans proposed the construction of a trans-Mesopotamian railway which did not come up to specifications. They submitted plans calling for the building of a line from some Mediterranean port—such as Alexandretta or Tripoli-in-Syria—down the Euphrates valley to the Persian Gulf.[12] Such a line would have had obvious advantages, from the point of view of the concessionaires, over the projected German railway. The cost of construction would have been materially less, for it would have been unnecessary to build the costly sections across the Taurus and

Amanus mountains. The prospects of immediate earning power were better, for the railway would have been able to take over some of the caravan trade from Arabia to the Syrian coast and from Mesopotamia to Aleppo. From the Ottoman point of view, however, the proposal was altogether unsatisfactory. The railway would have developed the southern provinces of the empire without connecting them with Anatolia, the homeland of the Turks themselves and the heart of the Sultan's dominions. It might have promoted a separatist movement among the Arabs. Its termini on the Mediterranean and the Persian Gulf could have been controlled by the guns of a foreign fleet. From every standpoint—economic, political, strategic—the acceptance of such a proposal was out of the question.

Even had all other things been equal, it is probable that the German bankers would have been given preference in the award of the concession. The Turkish Government was determined that the Anatolian lines should be made the nucleus of the proposed railway system for the empire. That being the case, no purpose, other than the promotion of confusion, would have been served by awarding the Bagdad plum to interests other than those which controlled the Anatolian Railway Company. This reasoning was fortified by the fact that the Company had made an enviable record in its dealings with the Ottoman Ministry of Public Works. The existing lines were well constructed and were being operated in a manner entirely satisfactory to the Ottoman Government and to the peasantry and business men of Anatolia. And M. Huguenin, Assistant General Manager of the Anatolian system, announced that his Company would observe a similar policy in the construction and operation of the proposed Bagdad Railway. "We are determined," he said, "to build a model line such as exists nowhere in Turkey, able in all respects to undertake efficiently an international service involving high speeds over the whole line." [13]

From the political point of view, too, there were reasons for giving preference to German capitalists. Abdul Hamid was seeking moral and material assistance for the promotion of his favorite doctrine of Pan-Islamism. He sought to foster this movement, which looked toward the unification of Islamic communities for resistance to Christian European domination over the Moslem world. As Caliph of the Mohammedan world, Abdul Hamid placed himself at the head of those defenders of the faith who had been propagating the idea that Mussulmans everywhere must resist further Christian encroachment and aggression, be it political, economic, religious, cultural. That the Sultan's primary motives were religious is doubtful. Apparently he believed that the Pan-Islamic movement could be utilized to the greater glory of his dynasty and his empire. As the tsars of Russia had utilized their position as head of the Orthodox Church for the purpose of strengthening the power of the autocracy, so Abdul Hamid proposed to exploit his position as Caliph for purposes of personal and dynastic aggrandizement. [14]

In awarding the Bagdad Railway concession, which was of such considerable economic and political importance, it was essential to choose the nationals of a power which would be sympathetic toward Pan-Islamism. Would it be Russia, whose tsars had set fires in Afghanistan, sought to destroy the independence of Persia, and threatened all of the Middle East? Would it be Great Britain, whose professional imperialists were holding in subjection more than sixty million Mohammedans in India alone? Would it be France, whose soldiers controlled the destinies of millions of Mussulmans in Algeria and Tunis? These nations could have no feeling for Pan-Islamism other than fear and hatred, [15] for it threatened their dominion over their Moslem colonies. Germany, however, had everything to gain and nothing to lose in lending support to Abdul Hamid's Pan-Islamic program. She had practically no Mohammedan subjects and therefore had no reason to fear Moslem discontent. She had imperial interests which might be served by the revolt of Islam against Christian domination.[16]

Turkish patriots, as well as Moslem fanatics, would have preferred to see Germans favored in the award of economic concessions in the Ottoman Empire. The Germans came to Turkey with clean hands. Their Government had never despoiled the Ottoman Empire of territory and appeared to have no interests which could not be as well served by the strengthening of Turkey as by its destruction. On the other hand, Russia, traditional enemy of the Turks, sought, as the keystone of her foreign policy, to acquire Constantinople and the Straits. France, by virtue of her protectorate over Catholics in the lands of the Sultan, sought to maintain special privileges for herself in Syria and the Holy Land. Great Britain held Egypt, a nominal Turkish dependency, and was fomenting trouble for the Sultan in the region of the Persian Gulf.[17] Germany, it appeared, was the only sincere and disinterested friend of the Ottoman Empire!

The rising prestige of Germany in the Near East and the rapid expansion of German economic interests in Turkey, however, did not, during these crucial years of 1898-1900, arouse the fear or the cupidity of other European powers. Russia, it is true, objected for strategic reasons to the construction of the proposed Bagdad Railway via the so-called "northern" or trans-Armenian route from Angora. But when the Tsar was assured by the Black Sea Basin Agreement that a southern route from Konia would be substituted, M. Zinoviev, the Russian minister at Constantinople, withdrew his formal diplomatic protest.[18]   The French Government adopted a policy of benevolent neutrality toward the claims of the *Deutsche Bank* for the concession, on the ground that the Imperial Ottoman Bank, representing powerful financial interests in Paris, was to be given a substantial participation in the proposed Bagdad Railway Company.   The pact of May 6, 1899, between the German and French promoters satisfied even M. Delcassé![19]

In Great Britain, likewise, there was the friendliest feeling toward the German proposals.   When the Kaiser made his second visit to the Near East in 1898 the London *Times* said: "In this country we can have nothing but good wishes for the success of the Emperor's journey and for any plans of German commercial expansion which may be connected with it.   Some of us may perhaps be tempted to regret lost opportunities for our own influence and our own trade in the Ottoman dominions.   But we can honestly say that if we were not to have these good things for ourselves, there are no hands we would rather see them in than in German hands."[20]   *The Morning Post* of August 24, 1899, expressed the hope that no rivalry over the Bagdad Railway would prejudice the good relations between Great Britain and Germany.   "So long as there is an efficient railway from Haidar Pasha to Bagdad, and so long as the door there is open, it should not really matter who makes the tunnels or pays the porters.   If it should be necessary to insist on an open door, the Foreign Office will probably see to it; while if it should happen to be, as usual, asleep, there are always means of poking it up.   As a matter of general politics it may not be at all a bad thing to give Germany a strong reason for defending the integrity of Turkey and for resisting aggression on Asia Minor from the North."

Sympathetic consideration of German expansion in the Near East was not confined to the press.   Cecil Rhodes,

great apostle of British imperialism, visited Germany in
the spring of 1899 and came away from Berlin favorably
disposed toward the Bagdad Railway and none the less
pleased with the Kaiser's apparent enthusiasm for the
Cape-to-Cairo plan. In November of the same year
William II paid a royal visit to England. It was then that
Joseph Chamberlain, Secretary for the Colonies, learned
the details of German plans in the Ottoman Empire, but, so
far from being alarmed, he publicly announced his belief in
the desirability of an Anglo-German entente. The almost
simultaneous announcement of the award of the preliminary Bagdad Railway concession met with a favorable
reception from the British press.[21]

At the same time, however, less cordial sentiments
were expressed toward Russia and France. There was
general agreement among the London newspapers regarding at least one desirable feature of the Bagdad
Railway enterprise: the discomfiture it would be certain to
cause the Tsar in his imperial ambitions in the Near East.
The Globe characterized as "impudence" the desire of
Russia to regard Asiatic Turkey as "a second Manchuria." [22] No love was being lost, either, on France.
The Daily Mail of November 9, 1899, said: "The French
have succeeded in wholly convincing John Bull that they
are his inveterate enemies. England has long hesitated
between France and Germany. But she has always respected German character, while she has gradually come
to feel scorn for France. Nothing in the nature of an
entente cordiale can exist between England and her nearest neighbor. France has neither courage nor political
sense."

The Bagdad Railway Concession Is Granted

It was almost three years after the Sultan's preliminary
announcement of the Bagdad concession that the imperial

decree was issued. During the interval the German technical commission was completing its survey of the line; details of the concession were being arranged between Zihni Pasha, Minister of Public Works, and Dr. Kurt Zander, General Manager of the Anatolian Railway Company; Dr. von Siemens was working out plans for the financing of the enterprise. Finally, on March 18, 1902, an imperial *iradé* of Abdul Hamid II definitely awarded the Bagdad Railway concession to the Anatolian Railway Company.[23]

The Constantinople despatches announcing the Sultan's award met with a varied reception. In Germany, of course, there was general satisfaction and, in some quarters, jubilation. The Kaiser telegraphed his personal thanks to the Sultan. In Vienna, the semi-official *Fremdenblatt* expressed the opinion that "the construction of the railway would be an event of the greatest economic and political importance and would materially strengthen Turkey's power of resistance."[24] M. Delcassé, French Minister of Foreign Affairs, interpolated in the Chamber, informed the Deputies that, whether one liked it or not, the convention was a *fait accompli* which France must accept, particularly because French capitalists were associated with the German concessionaires in the enterprise.[25] The Russian Government was silent at the time, although two months before M. Witte had informed the press that he saw no reason for granting financial assistance or diplomatic acquiescence to a possible competitor of Russian trans-Asiatic railways.[26]

In England there was very little opposition, but much friendly comment, on the German plans. Earl Percy expressed the hope that Great Britain would do nothing to interfere with the construction of the Bagdad Railway. "Germany," he told the House of Commons, "is doing for Turkey what we have been doing for Persia, for the social improvement and material welfare of native races; and in the struggle between the Slavonic policy of compelling stagnation and the Teutonic policy of spreading the blessings and enlightenment of civilization, the victory will lie with those nations which are striving, selfishly or unselfishly, consciously or unconsciously, to fulfil the high aims which Providence has entrusted to the imperial races of Christendom." Lord Cranborne, Under-Secretary for Foreign Affairs, announced that, although the Government had every intention of maintaining the *status quo* in the Persian Gulf, it would not otherwise interfere in the project for a German-owned trans-Mesopotamian railway. Lord Lansdowne, Secretary for Foreign Affairs, informed the French and German ambassadors at London that His Britannic Majesty's Government would not oppose the Bagdad enterprise, particularly if British capital were invited to participate in its consummation.[27] This was taken as a definite promise, for English financiers already had been asked to take a share in the Bagdad Railway Company by purchase, *pro rata,* of portions of the holdings of the German and French interests.[28]

Although there was a noticeable lack of unanimity in European diplomatic circles, little or no reason existed in 1902 to believe that any determined resistance would be made to the consummation of the plans for the construction of the Bagdad Railway. The chief difficulties of the concessionaires seemed to be not political, but financial and administrative. The year 1902 was one of economic depression; in Germany, in particular, industrial and financial conditions were distinctly unfavorable for the flotation of a large bond issue such as would be required to raise funds for the construction of the Bagdad Railway. Certain of the minor provisions of the convention of 1902, furthermore, were unsatisfactory to the financiers of the project. The concession for the lines beyond Konia had been granted to the Anatolian Railway Company without privilege of assignment to any other corporation. This meant that any participation of outside capital in the new Bagdad Railway would, of necessity, involve participation in the profits of the Anatolian lines already in operation—a prospect by no means pleasing to the original promoters. Furthermore, there was some question as to the advisability of placing under a single administrative head all of the line and branches from Constantinople to the Gulf.[29]

It was because of these difficulties, financial and administrative, that the *Deutsche Bank* marked time until March 5, 1903, when a revised Bagdad Railway convention was executed and plans were perfected for the financing of the first section of the line. It is to this Great Charter of the Berlin-to-Bagdad plan that we now must turn our attention.[30]

The definitive convention of 1903 provided that the existing Anatolian lines were to continue in the possession of their owners; the construction and operation of the new railway beyond Konia was to be vested—without right of cession, transfer, or assignment—in a new corporation, the Bagdad Railway Company. This new company was incorporated under Turkish law on March 5, 1903, with a capital stock of fifteen million francs, of which the Anatolian Railway Company subscribed ten per cent. Continued Turco-German control of the railway enterprise was assured by a provision of the charter that of the eleven members of the Board of Directors, three should be appointed by the directors of the Anatolian Railway Company, and at least three others should be Ottoman subjects.[31]

It was apparent that the Ottoman Government expected big things of the German concessionaires and their French associates. The new convention provided, first, for the construction of a great trunk line from Konia, southeastern terminus of the existing Anatolian Railways, to the Persian Gulf. This was to be the Bagdad Railway proper, but the concession carried with it, also, the privilege of constructing important branches in Syria and Mesopotamia. With all its proposed tributary lines completed, the Railway would stretch from the Bosporus to the Persian Gulf and from the Mediterranean to the frontiers of Persia. Second, it was stipulated that the Anatolian Railway Company should effect any necessary improvements on its lines to make possible the early initiation of a weekly express service between Constantinople and Aleppo and the operation of fortnightly express trains to Bagdad and the Persian Gulf as soon as the lines should be completed. The Anatolian concessions were extended for a period of ninety-nine years from 1903 to make them coincident with the new concession. The concessionaires were obliged to make all improvements and to complete all new construction by 1911, it being understood, however, that this time limit might be extended in the event of delays by the Government in the execution of the financial arrangements or in the event of *force majeure*— the latter specifically including, not only a European war, but any radical change in the financial situation in Germany, England, or France.[32]

THE LOCOMOTIVE IS TO SUPPLANT THE CAMEL

The Bagdad Railway was to revive the "central route" of medieval trade—to traverse one of the world's historic highways. It was to bring back to Anatolia, Syria, and Mesopotamia some of the prosperity and prestige which they had enjoyed before the explorations of the Portuguese and Spaniards had opened the new sea routes to the Indies.[33]

The starting point of the new railway was to be Konia. This town of 44,000 inhabitants, situated high in the Anatolian plateau, was a landmark in the Near East. It was once the capital of the Seljuk Turks and during its heyday had been a crossroads of the caravan routes of Asia Minor. Along one of these old routes to the northwest ran the Anatolian Railway, with which the Bagdad line was to be linked. From Konia the new railway was to cross the Anatolian table-lands, at an average altitude of 3500 feet, passing through the towns of Karaman and Eregli. Just beyond the latter town are the foothills of the Taurus, the first of the mountain barriers between Asia Minor and the Mesopotamian valley. In crossing the Taurus range the railway was to pass through the famous Cilician Gates, down the eastern slope into the fertile Cilician plain. At Adana, center of the trade of this region, a junction was to be effected with the existing railway to Mersina, a small port on the Mediterranean.[34]

Formidable engineering difficulties faced the succeeding stretch of the railway. Beyond Adana stood the second mountain barrier of the Amanus range, through which there was no natural pass, and it was apparent that costly blasting and tunneling would be required before the hills could be pierced.[35] Once beyond the mountains the railway could be carried quickly to Aleppo, a city of 128,000, "the emporium of northern Syria," and a meeting place for the Mesopotamian, Syrian, and Anatolian trade-routes. At this point connections were to be established with the important railways of Syria, providing direct communication with Hama, Homs, Tripoli-in-Syria, Beirut, Damascus, Jaffa, and Jerusalem. In fact, enthusiastic Syrians have prophesied that when all projected transcontinental railways are completed in Europe, Asia, and Africa, Aleppo will become "the crossroads of the

world"—a junction point for rail communication between
Berlin and Bagdad, Calais and Calcutta, Bordeaux and
Bombay, Moscow and Mecca, Constantinople and Cairo
and Cape Town.[36] Seventy miles away from Aleppo,
along one of the few good wagon roads in Turkey, lay the
important Mediterranean port of Alexandretta. Leaving
Aleppo, the Bagdad Railway was to turn east, crossing a
desert country, to Nisibin and to Mosul, on the Tigris.
From this sector of the railway it was proposed to construct several short spurs into the Armenian foothills, as
well as a longer branch from Nisibin to Diarbekr and
Kharput.

The city of Mosul is the northern gateway to the Mesopotamian valley, the "Land of the Two Rivers." In medieval times it was a center of caravan routes between
Persia, Mesopotamia, Syria, and Anatolia, and once was
famed for its textile manufactures, which produced a
cloth named after the city, "muslin." It is located on the
site of a suburb of the ancient city of Nineveh and guards
a high pass leading through the mountains into Armenia.
In 1903 it had a population of 61,000 and bade fair, after
the completion of the Bagdad Railway, to regain some
of its lost lustre. South and southeast of Mosul flows
the Tigris River all the way to the Persian Gulf. Along
the valley of this river was to run the new railway, through
the towns of Tekrit, Samarra, and Sadijeh, to Bagdad.[37]

In 1903 the splendor of the ancient city of Bagdad was
very much dimmed. Although it still was the center of
an important caravan trade with Persia, Arabia, and Syria,
its prosperity was but a name compared with the riches
which the city had enjoyed before the commercial revolution of the sixteenth century. The population of 145,000—
in part nomad—was to a large extent dependent upon the
important export trade in dates and cereals, amounting, in
1902, to almost £1,000,000. All told, the trade of Bagdad

was valued at about £2,500,000 annually. Whether the shadow of the former great Bagdad could be transformed into a living thing was an open question.[38]

Five hundred miles south of Bagdad is the Persian Gulf,[39] the proposed terminus of the Bagdad Railway. About sixty miles north of the Gulf, located on the Shatt-el-Arab—the confluence of the Tigris and Euphrates Rivers—is the port of Basra, the outlet for the trade of Bagdad. Communication between these two Mesopotamian cities was carried on, in 1903, by means of a weekly steamer service operated by the English firm of Lynch Brothers, under the name "The Euphrates and Tigris Steam Navigation Company, Ltd." The Lynch Brothers—typical British imperial pathfinders—had established themselves at Basra during the decade 1840-1850 and had succeeded during the following half-century in securing a practical monopoly of the river trade from Bagdad to the Persian Gulf. The absence of effective competition and the hesitancy of the Turkish Government to grant permission for the operation of additional steamers were responsible for a totally inadequate service. It was not uncommon for freight to stand on the wharves at Bagdad and Basra for three months or more awaiting transportation. Under these circumstances it was to be expected that freight charges would be exorbitant; it cost more to transfer cargoes from Bagdad to Basra than from Basra to London. The advent of the Bagdad Railway promised great things for the trade of lower Mesopotamia and Persia.[40]

It was the aim of the Turkish Government and the concessionaires not only to compete with the river trade of the Tigris, but to develop the Euphrates valley as well, there being no steamer service on the latter river. With this in mind, it was decided to divert the railway beyond Bagdad from the Tigris to the Euphrates and down the valley to Basra. For a time Basra was to mark the terminus of the railway; the concession made provision, however, for the eventual construction of a branch "from Zubeir to a point on the Persian Gulf to be agreed upon between the Imperial Ottoman Government and the concessionaires." [41]

Of considerable importance was a proposed branch line from Sadijeh, on the Tigris, to Khanikin, on the Persian frontier. This railway, it was believed, would take the place of the existing caravan route from Bagdad to Khanikin and thence to Teheran. The annual value of British trade alone transported *via* this route was estimated at about three quarters of a million pounds sterling.[42]

The Bagdad Railway, as thus projected, was one of the really great enterprises of an era of dazzling railway construction. Here was a transcontinental line stretching some twenty-five hundred miles from Constantinople, on the Bosporus, to Basra, on the Shatt-el-Arab—a project greater in magnitude than the Santa Fé line from Chicago to Los Angeles or the Union Pacific Railway from Omaha to San Francisco.[43] It was a promise of the rejuvenation of three of the most important parts of the Ottoman Empire—eastern Anatolia, northern Syria, and Mesopotamia. It was to open to twentieth-century steel trains a fifteenth-century caravan route. It was to replace the camel with the locomotive.

THE SULTAN LOOSENS THE PURSE-STRINGS

There are special and peculiar problems connected with the construction of railways in the economically backward areas of the world. In well populated regions, such as western Europe, railways have been built to accommodate existing traffic; in sparsely populated regions, such as eastern Russia and western United States, they have been constructed chiefly to create new traffic. In the economically advanced countries of the world the railway has been the result of civilization; in the backward countries it has been the outpost of civilization. A new railway in an un-developed region is obliged at the outset to concern itself mainly with the upbuilding of the territory through which it runs, in order to assure abundant traffic for the future; during this period its receipts are rarely, if ever, adequate to meet the costs of operation. Private capital cannot be expected to assume alone the risk and burden thus in-volved, but the public service which the railway renders during this critical time justifies the government in sub-sidizing the enterprise until it can become self-supporting. The granting of state subventions has been a common practice of the nineteenth and twentieth centuries. China time and time again has pledged national revenues in support of railway construction; the Latin-American coun-tries have been conspicuous exemplars of the same prac-tice; more than half of the railways of Russia were constructed with government funds.[44]

There was every reason to believe that the Bagdad Rail-way would be built with some system of state guarantees. Almost every railway in Asiatic Turkey at one time or another had been the recipient of a government subvention, and the proposed trans-Mesopotamian railway faced many more obstacles than had faced any then in operation. The provinces through which the Bagdad Railway was to pass were sparsely settled and were too backward, economically, to warrant the construction of a railway for the accommo-dation of existing traffic;[45] the German technical com-mission of 1899 had pointed out that the estimated gross operating revenue for some years would be entirely inade-quate to pay the expenses of running trains even if there should be an unlooked for volume of passenger and mail service to India. In time, it was believed, improved transportation and greater political security would induce immigration and produce wide-spread economic prosperity in the provinces of Anatolia, Syria, and Mesopotamia, thus assuring financial independence to the railway.[46]   During the interim, however, a state guarantee appeared to be necessary.

Under the terms of the convention of 1903, the Turkish Government undertook partially to finance the construction of the Bagdad Railway.   For each kilometre of the line built the Government agreed to issue to the Company the sum of 275,000 francs, nominal value, in Imperial Ottoman bonds, to be secured by a first mortgage on the railway and its properties.[47]   The payment of interest and sinking fund on these bonds was to be guaranteed by the assignment to the Public Debt Administration for this purpose of the revenues of certain of the districts through which the railway was to pass.   For the purpose of financing the first section of two hundred kilometres beyond Konia, there was delivered to the Company on March 5, 1903, an issue of fifty-four million francs of "Imperial Ottoman Bagdad Railway Four Per Cent Bonds, First Series." [48]   Similar payment for the construction of subsequent sections was to be made the subject of further agreement between the Government and the concessionaires.

In addition to supplying in this manner the actual funds for the building of the railway, the Ottoman Government guaranteed gross operating receipts of forty-five hundred francs annually for each kilometre of the line open to traffic.   If the receipts failed to reach that sum, the Government was to reimburse the Company for the deficiency.   If the receipts amounted to more than forty-five hundred francs per kilometre in any given year, the excess over that amount to ten thousand francs was to belong to the Government; any excess over and above ten thousand francs was to be divided sixty per cent to the Government, forty per cent to the Railway. The Government also agreed to reimburse the Company, in thirty annual payments of three hundred fifty thousand francs, for such improvements as might be necessary to prepare the Anatolian Railways for the initiation of a through express service to the Persian Gulf and, furthermore, to subsidize that express service at the rate of three hundred fifty thousand francs annually from the date of the completion of the main line to Aleppo.[49]

Closely connected with these financial guarantees were grants of public lands. Lands owned by the Government and needed for right-of-way were transferred to the concessionaires free of any charge. Additional land required for construction purposes might be occupied without rental as well as worked by the Company for sand and gravel. Wood and timber necessary for the construction and operation of the railway might be cut from State-owned forests without compensation. The concessionaires were permitted to operate mines within a zone twenty kilometres each side of the line, subject to such regulations as might be laid down by the Ministry of Public Works. As a public utility, the railway was granted the right of expropriation of such privately owned land as might be essential for the right-of-way, as well as quarries, gravel-pits, or other properties necessary for purposes of construction. The Company was authorized, also, to conduct researches for objects of art and antiquity along the route of the railway![50]

In the foregoing respects the Bagdad Railway Convention was by no means revolutionary in character. In issuing its bonds for the purpose of financing railway construction, in pledging public revenues as a guarantee of traffic receipts, in granting public lands for right-of-way, the Imperial Ottoman Government was following well-established precedents of the nineteenth century. The United States, for example, had adopted similar measures to encourage the building of transcontinental railways. To cite a single instance, Congress granted the promoters of the Union Pacific system a right-of-way through the public domain, twenty sections of land on each side of each mile of the railway, and a loan of bonds of the United States to an amount of fifty million dollars. Between 1850 and 1873 alone the Government transferred to the railways some thirty-five million acres of public lands, an area in excess of that of the State of New York.[51]

In certain other respects, however, the Bagdad Railway Convention was radical and far-reaching in its innovations. Worthy of first mention among its unusual provisions is the sweeping tax exemption granted the concessionaires by *Article 8:* "Manufactured material for the permanent way and materials, iron, wood, coal, engines, cars and coaches, and other stores necessary for the initial establishment as well as the enlargement and development of the railway and everything pertaining thereto which the concessionaires shall purchase in the empire or import from abroad shall be exempt from all domestic taxes and customs duties. The exemption from customs duties shall also be granted the coal necessary for the operation of the road, imported abroad by the concessionaires, until the gross receipts of the line and its branches reach 15,500 francs per kilometre. Likewise, during the entire period of the concession the land, capital, and revenue of the railway and everything appertaining thereto shall not be taxed; neither shall any stamp duty be charged on the present Convention or on the Specifications annexed thereto, the additional conventions, or any subsequent instruments; nor on the issue of Government bonds; nor on the amounts collected by the concessionaires on account of the guarantee for working expenses; nor shall any duty be levied on their stock, preferred stock and bonds, or on the bonds which the Imperial Ottoman Government shall issue to the concessionaires." Thus the Bagdad Railway not only was assured of a subsidy constituting a preferred claim on certain taxes collected from the Turkish peasantry, but, in addition, was exempted from the payment of important contributions to the national revenue. The extent to which such an arrangement would confound confusion will be clear if one will recall that many other restrictions on the collection and disbursement of public funds were vested in the Ottoman Public Debt Administration.[52]

Incidental to the railway, the Bagdad Company was granted other valuable concessions. The corporation was given permission to establish and operate tile and brick works along the line of the railway. For the direct and indirect use of the railway and its subsidiary enterprises the Company was authorized to establish hydro-electric stations for the generation of light and power. The erection of necessary warehouses and depots was permitted as essential to the proper operation of the railway. The Anatolian Railway was empowered to provide for satisfactory ferry service between Constantinople and Haidar Pasha, in order to insure direct sleeping-car service from Europe to Asia and to provide other facilities for through traffic. All of these subsidiary projects were to enjoy the same exemption from taxation as the railway itself.[53]

The concessionaires were granted the right of constructing at Bagdad, Basra, and at the terminus on the Persian Gulf modern port facilities, including "all necessary arrangements for bringing ships alongside the quay and for the loading, unloading, and warehousing of goods." During the period of the construction of the railway the Company was granted rights of navigation on the Tigris,

the Euphrates, and the Shatt-el-Arab for the transportation of materials and supplies necessary to the building
and operation of the main line and its branches.[54] These
river and harbor concessions aroused the fear and the
rage of the Lynch Brothers, who, as we shall see, were to
be among the leaders of British opposition to the Bagdad
Railway.[55]

These, then, were the outstanding economic provisions
of the Bagdad Railway Convention of 1903. The Imperial Ottoman Government assumed the cost of the construction of the railway and, in addition, guaranteed a
certain minimum annual return on each kilometre in operation. It pledged for these purposes the taxes of the
districts through which the railway was to pass, and it de-
puted the Ottoman Public Debt Administration to collect
these revenues and supervise payments to the concessionaires. As additional compensation to the Company
it made large grants of public lands and conceded valuable
privileges indirectly connected with the construction of
the railway. In this manner the Sultan mortgaged his
empire. But mortgages have their purposes, and Abdul
Hamid hoped for big things from the Bagdad Railway.

SOME TURKISH RIGHTS ARE SAFEGUARDED

As mortgagor the Sultan was certain to insist upon
the recognition and protection of certain rights. To assure
observance by the concessionaires of their obligations under
the convention, supervision over construction, operation,
and maintenance of the railway was vested in the Ministry
of Public Works, represented by two Imperial Railway
Commissioners. As a guarantee of good faith the Company was obliged to deposit with a Constantinople bank a
bond of £30,000, subject to release only upon the completion of the entire line. The Ottoman Government was

determined, also, that the concession, far-reaching as were its implications, should not lead to additional extra-territorial rights, or "capitulations," in favor of foreign powers. The concessionaires were forbidden to contract for the transportation of foreign mails, or to perform other services for the foreign post offices in Turkey, without the formal approval of the Ottoman Government. It was specified, also, that, inasmuch as the Anatolian and the Bagdad Railway Companies were Ottoman joint-stock corporations, all disputes and differences between the Government and the Companies, or between the Companies and private persons, "arising as a result of the execution or interpretation of the present Convention and the Specifications attached thereto, shall be carried before the competent Ottoman courts." It was further provided that the concessionaires "must correspond with the State Departments in Turkish, which is the official language of the Imperial Ottoman Government!" [56]

The Government was sincere in its determination that the railway should become a powerful instrument in the economic development of the backward provinces of the empire. A significant clause specified that the section between Bagdad and Basra should not be placed in operation before the section between Konia and Bagdad should have been opened to traffic, although immediate operation of trains on the former section would have enabled the Company to compete with the valuable trade of the Lynch Brothers on the Tigris. The traffic between Bagdad and Basra would have been profitable and would thus have decreased by a considerable figure the total subsidies the Treasury might be obliged to pay for railway operation. It was of more immediate concern to the Turkish Government, however, that southern Mesopotamia should be connected by an economic and political link with the rest of the Sultan's dominions. Elaborate regulations were laid down regarding a minimum train service which the Company was required to supply, and it was specified in this connection that Turkish mails, together with postal employees and officials, should be transported without charge and under such other conditions as the Government might stipulate. To forestall discriminatory treatment of passengers and shippers maximum rates were prescribed for all classes of traffic, including express, insurance, and similar supplementary services; it was decreed that "all rates, whether they be general, special, proportional, or differential, are applicable to all travelers and consignors without distinction"; the concessionaires were "formally prohibited from entering into any special contract with the object of granting reductions of the charges specified in its tariffs." [57] This last provision was of the utmost importance, as it enabled Germans and Turks alike to point to the railway as an outstanding example of the economic "open door."

One of the chief interests of the Turkish Government in the construction of the Bagdad Railway was the possibility of its utilization for military purposes. In time of peace for purposes of maneuvers or the suppression of rebellion, in time of war for purposes of mobilization, the Company was required, upon requisition of the military authorities, to place at the disposal of the Government its "entire rolling stock, or such as might be necessary, for the transportation of officers and men of the army, navy, police or gendarmerie, together with any or all equipment." The Government undertook to maintain order along the line and to construct such fortifications as it might consider necessary to defend the railway against invading armies, and the Company was obliged to expend, under the direction of the Minister of War, a total of four million francs for the construction of military stations. To give effect to all of these provisions, a special military convention was to be drawn up and approved by the Company and the Minister of War.[58]

Upon the expiration of the concession all rights of the concessionaires in the railway, port works, and other subsidiary enterprises were to revert, free of all debt and liability, to the Imperial Government. In the meantime, a semblance of Turkish nationality was to be assured the enterprise by the stipulation that the railway employees and officials should wear the fez and such uniform as might be approved by the Government. It was contemplated, also, that within five years after the opening of each section to traffic the whole of the operating staff, except the higher officials, should be composed exclusively of Ottoman subjects.[59]

Appended to the Bagdad Railway Convention was a secret agreement binding the Company not to encourage or instal foreign settlements or colonies in the vicinity of the Anatolian or Bagdad Railways.[60] Although the Sultan had mortgaged his empire, at least he was determined to retain possession![61]

BIBLIOGRAPHICAL AND EXPLANATORY NOTES

[1] On this point *cf.* M. Solovieff, *La Terre Sainte et la société impériale de Palestine* (Petrograd, 1892). The society there referred to was said to be liberally patronized by the Tsar and other members of the imperial family.

[2] For details of the Kapnist plan see *The Times* (London), December 17, 1898; *The Euphrates Valley Railway*—a prospectus (London, 1899).

[3] In a memorandum of June 10, 1899, to the Sultan, Dr. Kurt Zander, General Manager of the Anatolian Railway Company, said that, in accordance with the wishes of the Sultan—and "to avoid all obstacles and avert every possibility of opposition"— his Company sought to arrive at a satisfactory understanding with the Smyrna-Aidin and Smyrna-Cassaba railways. All proposals to the Smyrna-Aidin Company, however, "met with evasive answers, which finally resulted in a termination of nego-

tiations." *Cf.*, also, E. Aublé, *Bagdad—son chemin de fer, son importance, son avenir* (Paris, 1917), pp. 9 *et seq.*

[4] For a copy of the text of this agreement the author is indebted to Mr. E. Rechnitzer. Summaries were published in *The Times,* August 10, 1899; *Le Temps* (Paris), August 15, 1899; *Corps de droit ottoman,* Volume IV, pp. 155-156.

[5] In June, 1899, the Anatolian Railway Company elected to its Board of Directors M. L. Rambert, of the Imperial Ottoman Bank, and in June, 1900, M. Gaston Auboyneau, of the same institution. The new directors replaced Mr. George Henry Maxwell Batten, of London, and Sir Edward F. G. Law, of the Ottoman Public Debt Administration. The refusal of the Smyrna-Aidin line to come to a working agreement with the Anatolian Company thus removed the last British directors from the board of the latter. *Cf. Reports of the Anatolian Railway Company,* 1898-1900, *passim.*

[6] A letter from Mr. E. Rechnitzer to the Sultan, dated August 16, 1899, accuses M. Constans of having publicly referred to the "accord" between French and German interests in Turkish railways. Dr. Karl Helfferich states that the agreement between the two railway companies was supplemented by a gentlemen's agreement between the two ambassadors. *Die Vorgeschichte des Weltkrieges* (Berlin, 1919), p. 127. This would seem to be confirmed by André Chéradame, *op. cit.,* pp. 48 *et seq.*

[7] The proposals previously made called for an absolute guarantee of several thousands of francs income per kilometre per annum. Mr. Rechnitzer's plan called for "an annual guarantee of 15,000 francs in gross receipts per kilometre, the said guarantee to be paid exclusively out of the excess of the tithes of the *vilayets* through which the railway is to pass; it being understood that in the event that the excess of such tithes be not sufficient to defray the kilometric guarantee, the concessionaire shall have no redress against the Imperial Government on account of the insufficiency." Memorandum of May 14, 1899, from Mr. Rechnitzer's files. Although this plan had the great advantage of requiring no immediate payments from the Ottoman Treasury, it probably would have cost Turkey more in the long run, for the guarantee specified was excessively high. Compare with provisions of the Bagdad Railway concession of March, 1903, *infra.* Mr. Rechnitzer also asked for extensive port privileges in Alexandretta and in the port to be determined on the Persian Gulf. The chief features of the plan were outlined in a pamphlet published in London, July 29, 1899, entitled *The Euphrates Valley Railway.*

[8] Mr. Rechnitzer now has in his possession a beautiful watch—inlaid with a map of the Ottoman Empire, in precious stones,

showing the route of the proposed Euphrates Valley Railway—
which he presented to Abdul Hamid in 1899. He repurchased it
at a public auction held in Paris after the Young Turk revolution of 1909.

[9] In a letter dated September 30, 1922, to the author Mr. Rechnitzer outlines the situation as follows: "My offer being much
more favorable than that of the Germans, it seemed likely in
August, 1899, that it would be accepted. Unfortunately the
Transvaal War broke out in the autumn of that year, and the
German Emperor, a few days after the declaration of war, spe-
cially came to London to ask our Government to give him a
free hand in Turkey. It appears that there was an interview
between the Emperor and Mr. Joseph Chamberlain, who was
more interested in Cecil Rhodes' scheme in Africa than in my
scheme in Turkey. As a consequence Sir Nicholas O'Connor
was instructed to inform the Turkish Government that the
British Government's support was withdrawn from my offers."
It is only fair to add, however, that there may have been other
factors in the situation. *The Financial News* (London), of
August 17, 1899, intimated that Mr. Rechnitzer's proposal did
not have sufficiently strong financial backing; that it was more
Austrian than British; that the support of the British Government was more formal than whole-hearted.

[10] *Report of the Anatolian Railway Company*, 1899, pp. 9-10;
The Annual Register, 1899, p. 292. Simultaneously the Sultan
granted the *Deutsche Bank* group a concession for the construction of port and terminal facilities at Haidar Pasha, across the
Straits from Constantinople. Sweeping privileges were granted
for the building of docks, stations, sidings, and quays to a subsidiary of the Anatolian Railway, the Haidar Pasha Port Company. The latter company completed a handsome station and
terminal at Haidar Pasha in 1902, the year before the definitive
Bagdad Railway concession. Furthermore, it entered into close
coöperation with the Mahsoussie Steamship Company, a Gov-
ernment-owned company operating a ferry service between Constantinople and the Asiatic side of the Straits; in this manner
adequate service was assured passengers and freight from European to Asiatic points. The text of the concession is to be
found in *Corps de droit ottoman*, Volume III, pp. 342-351. *Cf.,*
also, *Report of the Anatolian Railway Company*, 1902, p. 8.

[11] *Supra*, pp. 31-34.

[12] The single exception was Mr. Rechnitzer's plan, which provided that within five years of the award of the concession, the
Sultan might require the construction of a spur from Alexandretta to Konia, on terms to be agreed upon between the Government and the concessionaire. The chief feature of Mr. Rech-

nitzer's plan, however, unquestionably was the railway from Alexandretta to the Persian Gulf—*i.e.*, the Syrian and Mesopotamian, not the Anatolian and Cilician, sections. Furthermore, there were political objectives connected with the Rechnitzer proposal which, however attractive to British imperialists, could not have been regarded with equanimity by the Sultan. The following are typical quotations from Mr. Rechnitzer's prospectus: "It has long been the object of English statesmen to consolidate the position of England in the Persian Gulf, where British interests (both political and commercial) are now paramount. With a railway in this region controlled by British interests . . . a very strong foothold would accrue to British influence" (p. 12). Among the advantages of the proposed railway are listed the following (pp. 17-18): "It will place under British control two important ports, one on the Mediterranean and the other on the Persian Gulf; it will strengthen British influence in Turkey and in the Persian Gulf, and indirectly, in Persia and Afghanistan; it will afford England powerful means of exercising her influence over the territory of Central Persia, and of establishing new commercial enterprises over an enormous area of unexploited country of exceptional wealth."

[23] Quoted by A. D. C. Russell, "The Bagdad Railway," in *The Fortnightly Review,* Volume 235 (1921), p. 312. *Cf.,* also, *Corps de droit ottoman,* Volume IV, pp. 153 *et seq.*

[24] Pan-Islamism started as a religious and cultural revival but rapidly took on political and economic significance. Later, in connection with Turkish nationalism (see *infra,* Chapter IX), it became a serious international problem. A short, popular discussion of the rise of Pan-Islamism is Lothrop Stoddard's *The New World of Islam* (New York, 1921), Chapters I, II, V. *Cf.,* also, *Mohammedan History,* No. 57 of the Foreign Office Handbooks (London, 1920), Part I; G. Charmes, *L'avenir de la Turquie: le pan-islamisme* (Paris, 1883); A. J. Toynbee, *Nationality and the War* (London, 1915), pp. 399-411, and *Turkey: a Past and a Future* (New York, 1917); Tekin Alp, *Türkismus und Pantürkismus* (Weimar, 1915); C. Snouck Hurgronje, *The Holy War, "Made in Germany"* (New York, 1917). Regarding Abdul Hamid's place in the Pan-Islamic movement *cf. Mohammedan History,* pp. 42-46.

[25] Great Britain, characteristically enough, took steps to protect her interests by reviving the Arabian caliphate—*i.e.,* by supporting the claims of the Sherif of Mecca to the caliphate.

[26] *Infra,* pp. 127-128.

[27] Regarding British activities in Koweit, *cf. infra,* pp. 197-198.

[28] *Infra,* p. 149.

[29] *Infra,* pp. 155-157; Chéradame, *op. cit.,* pp. 267 *et seq.;* K.

Helfferich, *Die Vorgeschichte des Weltkrieges* (Berlin, 1919), pp. 124 *et seq.*

[20] *The Times*, October 28, 1898

[21] *Annual Register*, 1899, pp. 289-291; *Parliamentary Debates, House of Commons,* Volume 120 (1903), p. 1247, Volume 126 (1903), p. 108; W. von Hohenzollern, *My Memoirs, 1887-1918,* pp. 84-86, 101-103.

[22] *The Globe*, August 10, 1899. *Cf.,* also, *The Morning Herald,* August 10, 1899, and *The Westminster Gazette,* August 11, 1899.

[23] No attempt is made here to analyze the convention of March 18, 1902 (which had been preceded by a draft convention of January 8, 1902), as it was superseded by the convention of March 5, 1903. *Cf. infra,* pp. 70-71, 77-84. The text of the convention of 1902 is to be found as an appendix to R. LeCoq, *Un chemin de fer en Asie Mineure* (Paris, 1907). George von Siemens (1839-1901) did not live to see the consummation of his great plans for the development of Turkish railways. After his death in 1901 his work was taken up by his successor as Managing Director of the *Deutsche Bank,* Dr. Arthur von Gwinner. For a short account of the life of von Siemens see an obituary by Professor J. Riesser, in *Bank-Archiv,* No. 2, November, 1901. The work of von Siemens in the development of German economic enterprises in the Near East is told in a biography by his son-in-law, Dr. Karl Helfferich, *Georg von Siemens* (Leipzig, 1923).

[24] *The Times*, January 25, 1902.

[25] *Journal officiel, Débats parlementaires, Chambre des députés,* 1902, pp. 1468 *et seq.*

[26] *The Times*, January 25, 1902.

[27] *Parliamentary Debates, House of Commons,* Volume 101, pp. 129, 597, 628, 669, Volume 120 (1903), p. 1371.

[28] *Report of the Anatolian Railway Company,* 1901, p. 17; *The Times,* January 25, 1902.

[29] *Annual Register,* 1902, pp. 290-291; *Report of the Bagdad Railway Company,* 1904, p. 7.

[30] *La Société Impériale Ottomane du Chemin de Fer de Bagdad-Firman, Convention, Cahier des Charges, Statuts,* in French and Turkish (Constantinople, 1905); translated into English in *Parliamentary Papers,* No. Cd. 5635, Volume CIII (1911), No. 1. Where references are here given to the convention itself, no preceding identifying word will be given, the citation being merely, *e.g., Article I.* The *Statuts* will be referred to as "By-Laws" and the *Cahier des Charges* as "Specifications."

[31] Turco-German control of the Board of Directors was not inconsistent with the agreement of 1899 between the *Deutsche Bank* and the Imperial Ottoman Bank, which assured French

interests only 40% of the shares of the Bagdad Railway Company. For details of the organization of the Company see the *Report of the Anatolian Railway Company*, 1903, pp. 4-7; *By-Laws, passim.*

[32] *Articles 1-4, 7, 12, 37-39; Specifications,* Article 30.

[33] In this connection see Sir W. M. Ramsay, *The Historical Geography of Asia Minor* (London, 1890); D. G. Hogarth, *The Nearer East* (London, 1902); Jastrow, *op. cit.,* Chapter II; Sir C. W. Wilson, *Murray's Handbook for Asia Minor* (London, 1895 and 1900); R. Fitzner, *Anatolien-Wirtschaftsgeographie* (Berlin, 1902); F. Dernburg, *Auf deutscher Bahn in Kleinasien* (Berlin, 1892). Good general accounts of the regions through which the Bagdad Railway was to run are: Baron E. von der Goltz, *Reisebilder aus dem griechisch-türkischen Orient* (Halle, 1902); R. Oberhummer and H. Zimmerer, *Durch Syrien und Kleinasien* (Berlin, 1899); E. Banse, *Die Türkei; eine moderne Geographie* (Berlin, 1916); Sir Mark Sykes, *The Caliph's Last Heritage—A Short History of the Turkish Empire* (London, 1915), Part 2, Chapters II and IV. A well-informed article describing the projected route of the Bagdad railway is one by a member of the German technical commission, "Die anatolischen Eisenbahnen und ihre Fortsetzung bis zum persischen Golf," in *Archiv für Eisenbahnwesen,* Volume 26 (1903), pp. 75-90.

[34] For a description of the line from Konia to Adana, including an historical sketch of the principal towns served by the railway, *cf.* Karl Baedeker, *Konstantinopel und das westliche Kleinasien* (Leipzig, 1905), pp. 156-172, and *Konstantinopel, Balkanstaaten, Kleinasien, Archipel, Cypern* (second edition, Leipzig, 1914), pp. 270-306, generously supplied with excellent maps.

[35] A popular account of the engineering difficulties facing the construction of the railway from Adana to Aleppo is to be found in *The Scientific American,* supplement, Volume 51 (1901), pp. 21248-21249.

[36] *Cf.* W. H. Hall (of the Syrian Protestant College in Beirut), *The Near East* (New York, 1920), particularly an interesting map, p. 174. According to the convention of 1903, Article 1, Aleppo was to be connected with the main line by a branch from Tel-Habesh, but in 1910 the route was changed, on petition of the inhabitants, to include Aleppo as a station on the Bagdad line itself. *Report of the Bagdad Railway Company,* 1910, p. 8. Statistics regarding the population of Aleppo and other cities along the line are taken, unless otherwise indicated, from the *Statesman's Year Book,* 1903, *passim.*

[37] *Article 38;* "The Trade of the Mesopotamian Valley," in *Commerce Reports,* No. 280 (Washington, 1912), pp. 1050-1065, and No. 256 (1913), pp. 350-358; Karl Baedeker, *Palestine and*

Syria, with the chief routes through Mesopotamia and Babylonia (fourth edition, Leipzig, 1906), pp. 351-411.

[38] Valentine Chirol, *The Middle Eastern Question, or Some Political Problems of Indian Defence* (New York, 1903), pp. 179-182.

[39] This is the distance by the Tigris and the Shatt-el-Arab; as the crow flies, the distance is about 150 miles shorter.

[40] Regarding the Lynch Brothers see David Fraser, *The Short Cut to India* (London, 1909), pp. 42 *et seq.; Mesopotamia,* p. 30; *The Near East,* August 11, 1916, p. 358; *infra,* pp. 190-191.

[41] *Article 1,* which describes in detail the route of the Bagdad Railway and its branches.

[42] Chirol, *op. cit.,* p. 179; *Supplement to Daily Consular and Trade Reports,* Annual Series (Washington, 1915).

[43] The distances on the Bagdad Railway may be estimated as follows:

Haidar Pasha to Ismid............	91	kilometres
Ismid to Eski Shehr..............	174	"
Eski Shehr to Konia..............	444	"
Konia to Basra...................	2,264	"
Branch lines, about...............	800	"
Total	3,773	kilometres,

or approximately 2,400 miles. This does not include the section of the Anatolian Railway from Eski Shehr to Angora, a distance of 311 kilometres, or 194 miles additional. The Atchison, Topeka and Santa Fé Railway from Chicago to Los Angeles is 2,246 miles in length. The distance from Chicago to San Francisco *via* the Chicago and Northwestern-Union Pacific system is 2,261 miles. *Official Guide of the Railways of the United States* October, 1921, pp. 679, 825.

[44] *Cf., e.g.,* T. W. Overlach, *Foreign Financial Control in China* (New York, 1919), *passim; La Gaceta Oficial* of the Republic of Cuba for the years 1911 and 1912, regarding the *Ferrocarril de la Costa Norte de Cuba;* the *Statesman's Year Book,* 1903, p. 1044.

[45] The average population per square mile in eastern Anatolia was 27, in northern Syria 31, in Mesopotamia 13.

[46] *Diplomatic and Consular Reports,* 1903, No. 3140, pp. 26-27; Sir William Willcocks, *The Recreation of Chaldea* (Cairo, 1903).

[47] This financial assistance was granted at the rate of 11,000 francs per kilometre, payable annually throughout the ninety-nine years of the concession. The obligation was capitalized and met by the issue of 4% bonds as here described.

[48] *Bagdad Railway Loan Contract,* March 5, 1903. M. Léon Berger, President of the Ottoman Public Debt Administration, and a French citizen, was one of the signatories of this document. The bonds of the loan were issued in denominations of 500 francs, 408 marks, 20 pounds sterling, 22 pounds Turkish, and 245 Dutch florins, in order to facilitate their sale in the international securities markets. The *Deutsche Bank* was made fiscal agent for all transactions in connection with the loan, with the single qualification that it was to appoint as its Paris agent the Imperial Ottoman Bank, representing the French interests in the enterprise. The syndicate apparently made a profit of over 2,500,000 francs on the transaction, as the bonds were delivered to the concessionaires, under *Article 35* of the Convention, valued at 81½% of par but were sold at 86.40.

[49] *Articles 35* and *37.*

[50] *Articles 6, 10, 22, 27.*

[51] *Cf.* W. A. Dunning, *Reconstruction, Political and Economic, 1865-1877* (New York, 1907), pp. 145, 227; H. V. Poor, *Manual of the Railroads of the United States* (New York, 1869), pp. xlvi-xlvii.

[52] *Supra,* p. 11.

[53] *Articles 13, 24, 25, 33; Specifications,* Article 4.

[54] *Articles 9* and *23.*

[55] *Infra,* pp. 190-191.

[56] *Articles 5, 18, 29, 34.*

[57] *Article 29; Specifications,* Articles 21, 24, 25, 29, 30.

[58] *Articles 15, 26, 45; Specifications,* Article 26.

[59] *Articles 20* and *21.* Another sop to Turkish pride was *Article 46,* which required the Company to contribute annually to the Constantinople Poorhouse the sum of £500.

[60] *The Times,* March 14, 1903, contained a report of this secret appendix. A denial was issued by the Berlin *National Zeitung* of March 18, 1903, but the existence of the supplementary agreement was confirmed by Dr. von Gwinner in 1909 (*op. cit.,* p. 1092). Djavid Bey, in a memorandum to the author, has stated that the Ottoman Government considered this appendix of the utmost importance.

[61] A proviso of the concession of 1903 was that the *Deutsche Bank* was to float an Ottoman Four Per Cent Loan of March, 1903, to an amount of about $10,000,000. *Parliamentary Papers,* 1920, No. Cmd. 964, pp. 57-58.

CHAPTER V

PEACEFUL PENETRATION PROGRESSES

The Financiers Get Their First Profits

The convention of March, 1903, marked the beginning, not the end, of the work of the promoters of the Bagdad Railway. Ahead of Dr. von Gwinner[1] and his associates lay all sorts of obstacles, some of which proved to be insurmountable. There were the financial difficulties and risks attendant upon the task of borrowing and expending the funds for the construction of the railway—estimated at about one hundred million dollars. There were the technical difficulties of constructing a line across obstinate mountain barriers and inhospitable desert plains. There were the political difficulties of retaining the friendship of notoriously fickle Ottoman ministers and of preventing diplomatic opposition on the part of foreign powers. Events proved that this was to be a thorny path indeed— a path which was to lead through political intrigue, diplomatic bargaining, a Turkish revolution, and a world war.

The concessionaires began work in a manner indicative of a determination to succeed in spite of all obstacles. The Bagdad Railway Company was incorporated in Constantinople, March, 1903, under the joint auspices of the *Deutsche Bank* and the Imperial Ottoman Bank, as provided by their mutual agreement of 1899. Almost immediately an invitation was extended to British capitalists to participate in the enterprise. Three-cornered negotiations were conducted by German, French, and British bankers— under the watchful eyes of their respective foreign offices—

to arrive at some satisfactory plan for internationalization
of the railway. An agreement was reached by the financiers
by which British capital was to share equally in ownership
and control with the German and the French, but the
hostile attitude of the English press and the disapproval
of the Balfour Government led to the abandonment of
the proposed tripartite syndicate.[2]

Failing to secure British coöperation, the concessionaires
proceeded to finance the Bagdad Railway by other means.
Ten per cent of the stock of the Company was subscribed
by the Ottoman Government, ten per cent by the Anatolian
Railway Company, and the remainder by an international
syndicate headed by the *Deutsche Bank*. The Board of
Directors was enlarged to twenty-seven members, as follows: eight Germans, chosen by the *Deutsche Bank;* three
Germans elected by the Anatolian Railway Company;
eight Frenchmen designated by the Imperial Ottoman
Bank; four Ottomans; two Swiss; one Austrian; and one
Italian.[3] The control of the Bagdad Railway Company
thus remained in Turco-German hands, but French and
other interests were too well represented to justify the
criticism that the railway was a purely German enterprise
secretly coöperating with the German Foreign Office. In
fact, in 1903 Mr. Balfour and Lord Lansdowne were as
much alarmed by the possibility of pernicious French activities in the line as they were disturbed by the predominantly German character of the scheme.[4] Baron von
Schoen, one-time German Foreign Secretary, described the
Bagdad Railway as "an Ottoman enterprise which has an
international character under German guidance."[5]

The great resources of the *Deutsche Bank* were now
brought into play to provide the funds for the construction
of the first section of the railway. The necessary capital
was to be secured, it will be recalled,[6] by the sale of an
issue of Imperial Ottoman Bagdad Railway Bonds amount-

ing to 54,000,000 francs. With comparatively little difficulty the German share of the loan was subscribed, but the allotment of the Imperial Ottoman Bank and its associates was not so easily disposed of, because of the decision of the French Government to exclude the Bagdad Railway Bonds from the Bourse. Nevertheless, the entire loan was successfully underwritten, and by November, 1903, preparations had been completed for the construction of the line from Konia to Bulgurlu, a distance of 200 kilometres.[7]

Building of the railway went forward with great rapidity, and the rails reached Bulgurlu by early autumn, 1904. On October 25, the Sultan's birthday, this first section of the Bagdad Railway was opened to traffic with pompous ceremonies. And well might the concessionaires have celebrated! Not only had they passed the first milestone of their great task, but they had made a comfortable profit on their operations. By numerous economies the Bagdad Railway Company had saved 3,697,000 francs of the 54,000,000 francs allowed by the Ottoman Government to defray the costs of construction. The commissions of the bankers in underwriting the bond issue, it was said, raised the total profit on the first section of the railway—before a single train had been operated—to about 6,000,000 francs.[8] This surplus, however, was not all available for distribution among the concessionaires. A reserve fund of almost 4,000,000 francs was established to provide for the subsequent construction of the costly sections across the Taurus and Amanus mountains. The promoters had to be reimbursed for preliminary expenditures, such as the expensive surveying of the entire line from Konia to the Persian Gulf. Included in these "out of pocket" payments was a large item for *backshish*—gratuities to Ottoman dignitaries. "Nobody," said Dr. von Gwinner, "having done business in Turkey ignores the fact that *backshish* on the Bosporus ruled supreme and was hitherto an absolute condition of any contract. We had to pay in proportion to the importance of a business of some £20,000,-000." [9] Djavid Bey informs the author that the item of *backshish* must have amounted to almost £100,000, "for during the Hamidian régime friendship between sovereigns was not enough to bring about the granting of a concession."

Within nineteen months after the Turkish Government had issued its bonds to cover the cost of the project, the first section of the Bagdad Railway, from Konia to Bulgurlu, had been completed. The success of the concessionaires in this part of the enterprise might have been taken as a criterion of rapid progress with the further construction of the line to the Persian Gulf. Such an expectation, however, would have been premature. Beyond Bulgurlu lay the Taurus mountains and innumerable engineering difficulties which could be overcome only after the expenditure of considerable time and money. The Turkish Government, furthermore, was in no position to issue additional bonds to the amount of fifty or sixty millions francs to cover the costs of constructing the second section of the line. Interest and sinking fund charges on the first issue of Bagdad Railway bonds were a serious drain on the treasury; additional charges of a like character could be met only by an increase of the customs revenues of the Empire. Such an increase could not be effected, however, except by international agreement, because under existing treaties between Turkey and the Great Powers all import duties were fixed at eight per cent *ad valorem*.[10]

In 1903, coincident with the first issue of bonds for the Bagdad Railway, the Ottoman Government had requested permission to increase these duties to eleven per cent but had been unable to obtain the consent of the interested nations. It was not until 1906, after prolonged and irritating negotiations, that the Powers agreed to a three per cent increase, effective in July of the following year. Even then, however, the higher duties were assented to under a number of restrictions which rendered difficult the diversion of the increased revenue to the payment of railway guarantees; elaborate regulations were incorporated in the treaties prescribing expensive reform of the government of Macedonia and costly readjustments in the customs administration.[11]

By 1908, nevertheless, Turkish fiscal affairs were in a sufficiently satisfactory state to enable the Government to conclude arrangements for the construction of succeeding sections of the Bagdad Railway. On June 2 of that year an imperial *iradé* was granted authorizing the extension of the line from Bulgurlu to Aleppo and thence eastward to El Helif (near Nisibin), a distance of some eight hundred and forty kilometres. The completion of this portion of the line would bring the railway to a point about eleven hundred miles from Constantinople and only a little over seven hundred miles from Basra. Arrangements were effected for the immediate issue of the Imperial Ottoman Bagdad Railway Four Per Cent Loans, Second and Third Series, to an amount of one hundred and eight million and one hundred and nineteen million francs respectively, to provide the capital necessary for the building of the railway. Interest and sinking fund payments on these loans were guaranteed from the surplus of net revenues accruing to the Imperial Government from the Ottoman Public Debt. In case of emergency, certain taxes (notably the cattle tax) of the vilayets of Konia, Adana, and Aleppo were pledged for this purpose.[12]

Only a month after the conclusion of this convention the Near East was thrown into a state of turmoil as a result of the outbreak of the first of the Young Turk revolutions. Under these circumstances it appeared inexpedient to the Bagdad Railway Company to push construction of its line until such time as a reasonable degree of security should be restored. It was not until December, 1909, therefore, after the deposition of Abdul Hamid, that good friend of German enterprise in Turkey, that a construction company was formed to build the railway across the Taurus and Amanus mountains. During the autumn of the same year a Franco-German syndicate underwrote the second and third series of Bagdad Railway loans, thereby providing the necessary funds for the work.[13]

The Bankers' Interests Become More Extensive

The years 1904 to 1909 were lean years, judged by actual progress in the laying of rails from Bulgurlu to Bagdad and Basra. Nevertheless, they were years characterized, on the part of the investors interested in the consummation of the great enterprise, by every possible activity to prepare the way for eventual success on a grand scale. In the spring of 1906, for example, Dr. Karl Helfferich was appointed assistant general manager of the Anatolian Railways, and one year later was elected a managing director of the *Deutsche Bank* with general supervision over all of the Bank's railway enterprises in the Near East. The appointment of Dr. Helfferich—who, although he was only thirty-four years of age, had achieved an international reputation—aroused widespread comment and turned out to be an event of first-rate importance in the history of the Bagdad Railway. As a young professor of political science in the University of Berlin, Dr. Helfferich won general recognition as an unusually able economist. He was persuaded to enter the Government service in 1901 and became assistant secretary in the Colonial Department of the Ministry of Foreign Affairs. He was known to be in the good graces of the Emperor and of Prince von Bülow, and it was said that he became their chief adviser on Near Eastern affairs.[14] The choice of such a distinguished person as directing genius of the Anatolian and Bagdad Railways gave renewed confidence in Germany that the Bagdad plan would succeed. In Great Britain the appointment was, considered an ominous sign that a very real connection existed between the economic enterprises of the *Deutsche Bank* and the Near Eastern activities of the German Foreign Office.[15]

In 1907 the Anatolian Railway Company, under a contract with the Turkish Government, completed arrangements for the irrigation of the desert plain southeast of Konia. It was planned to water artificially about one hundred and fifty thousand acres of arid land, thus rendering the region independent of weather conditions. The effects of such an improvement would be far-reaching. Much idle land would be made available for profitable farming, and the yield of soil already under cultivation would be developed materially. Increased production might lead to a surplus of agricultural products for export, and the greater purchasing power of a prosperous Anatolian farming class would stimulate import trade. Agriculture, commerce, and manufacturing alike, therefore, could be served. The Anatolian Railway Company issued some 135,000 new shares of stock to defray its part of the expenses, hoping to be richly compensated by increased traffic on the railway. The Imperial Ottoman Treasury issued £800,000 of Konia Irrigation Bonds, an outlay which it hoped to offset by increased taxes from the Konia district, by rentals and sales of irrigated lands, and by decreased guarantees to this section of the railway.[16]

A number of German banks, meanwhile, were pushing their financial operations in the Near East. The success

of the *Deutsche Palästina Bank* [17] encouraged the formation of other similar institutions. The *Nationalbank für
Deutschland,* in 1904, founded the *Banque d'Orient,* with
offices in Hamburg, Athens, Constantinople, Salonica, and
Smyrna. The following year the *Dresdner Bank,* in
coöperation with other large Austro-German financial institutions, inaugurated the important *Deutsche Orientbank,*
with a capital stock of sixteen million marks. This latter
bank took over the Hamburg and Constantinople offices of
the *Banque d'Orient* and established a large number of
branches of its own, including those at Alexandria, Cairo,
and Smyrna. The *Deutsche Orientbank* became an active
promoter of industrial enterprises in Asiatic Turkey; for
example, in 1908 it organized *La Société pour Enterprises
Electriques en Orient,* a company which proceeded to take
over the surface railways as well as the electric light and
power concession of Constantinople. In 1908 the *Deutsche
Bank* itself formally opened an office in Constantinople
for the transaction of a general banking business.[18]

The entry of these German banks into the Near Eastern
field was of no small importance to the British and French
financial institutions already there. The German bankers
allowed liberal rates of interest on time and check deposits
and permitted reasonable overdrafts at low rates. These
practices were in sharp contrast with the rigid regulations
of the older-established banks. The *Deutsche Bank* undertook to collect claims of local merchants against the Turkish Government; through its influence in the Government
departments it cut red tape and secured payments which
otherwise might have been delayed for years. Constantinople business men welcomed their emancipation from
the ultra-conservative methods of the older institutions,
and it was not long before a very thriving business was
being transacted by the German banks and their agencies
in the Near East.[19] Here was a high-powered bomb to

disturb the quiet which heretofore had ruled in the banking community of Constantinople and of Asiatic Turkey. Germans were disturbing the financial, as well as the commercial and industrial, *status quo* in the Near East!

The advance of the German banks in Turkey was almost certain to be the first step in a more general industrial and commercial penetration. This will be the more readily understood if one recalls the close coöperation which characterized the relationships between the German banks and the business interests of the empire. This coöperation—which amounted, in effect, to financial interdependence—was one of the striking features of the German economic advance in the generation before the Great War. It strengthened German industrial enterprises at home and promoted German trade and investments abroad. If a great business needed capital, the banks furnished the necessary funds by the purchase of securities which made them at once creditors and copartners in that business. Sooner or later this connection would find expression in the appointment of a representative of the bank on the supervisory council of the industrial enterprise; occasionally a "captain of industry" would be elected to the board of directors of the bank. Although this procedure of interlocking directorates was not unique to Germany—it was an established practice in the United States, certainly—there was no country in which these alliances were so far-reaching, or in which financial power was so centrally controlled, as in the German Empire. In Germany finance and industry were wedded—permanently united for better or for worse.[20]

Of this alliance of banking and business the *Deutsche Bank,* chief promoter of the Bagdad Railway, was a shining example. Its industrial connections were too numerous to catalogue. It enjoyed intimate financial relations with hundreds of companies engaged in every important branch of manufacturing in Germany; it was represented on the directorates of the North German Lloyd and Hamburg-American steamship lines; it was the organizer of and chief stockholder in the German Petroleum Company. It was the owner of a number of overseas banking corporations stretching their activities from South America on the west to China on the east. The officers of the *Deutsche Bank* firmly believed that the export of capital and the export of commodities should go hand in hand. The other banks associated in the Bagdad Railway enterprise likewise were closely affiliated with important industrial enterprises. For example, the *Dresdner Bank* held the vice-chairmanship of Ludwig Loewe & Company, prominent manufacturers of munitions, and the chairmanship of the Orenstein Koppel Company, manufacturers of railway supplies. The *Bank für Handel und Industrie* possessed interests in the *Allgemeine Elektrizitäts-Gesellschaft,* the German General Electric Company. A still further evidence of this close association of financial and industrial interests was furnished in January, 1905, when the chief German banks entered into a "community of interests" with August Thyssen and Hugo Stinnes, the steel and coal barons of Germany.[21]

If German business men were likely to be interested in the economic development of Asia Minor, what was the nature of this interest?

BROADER BUSINESS INTERESTS DEVELOP

Speaking to the Reichstag in March, 1908, Baron von Schoen, Foreign Secretary of the Empire, explained a few of the opportunities which the Bagdad Railway opened to German industry and commerce. "The advantages," he said, "which accrue to Germany from this great enterprise, conceived on a grand scale, are obvious. In the first place, there arises the prospect of considerable participation of German industry in the furnishing of rails, rolling stock, and other railway materials. Furthermore, German engineers, German construction workers, and German contractors are very likely to find remunerative occupation in the construction of the railway. Finally, it is certain that with the rising civilization and the higher standard of living of the inhabitants of the country, a new market will be made available. That this territory will be opened up not merely for us, but also for other nations, we can allow without envy. . . . What we have in view is the development of regions that seem to be worth developing; we wish to coöperate in awakening from a sleep of a thousand years an ancient flourishing civilized region, thereby creating a new market for ourselves and others." [22]

This same idea had been advanced by others on other occasions. The *Alldeutsche Blätter* of December 17, 1899, had prophesied that the construction of the railway by a German-controlled syndicate would result in the purchase of some eighty million dollars' worth of German products and that, once completed, the railway would open to German business an enormous and wealthy market. Lord Ellenborough, speaking in the House of Lords of the United Kingdom, on May 5, 1903, expressed the opinion that "the capital disbursed in constructing the railway would be largely spent on German steel industries, and on salaries to German engineers and German surveyors, so that even if the railway, as a railway, were a failure, it would not be a total loss to Germany." [23] The British Consul General at Constantinople pointed out, in 1903, that, in addition to all of the aforementioned advantages, there would be innumerable special opportunities for the remunerative investment of German capital in the regions traversed by the railway. [24]

Events seemed to establish the wisdom of these expressions of opinion. Rails for the Bagdad line were ordered in Germany from the Steel Syndicate (*Stahlwerksverband*). Transportation of materials from Europe to the Near East was arranged for through German steamship companies. German engineers were given the executive positions in the construction and operation of the railway. Important subsidiary companies were formed for the construction of port and terminal facilities, for the building of irrigation works, and for other purposes incidental to the railway proper. German banks established branches on the ground in order to take advantage of other opportunities for the profitable investment of surplus funds.[25]

There was much evidence, however, to indicate that the preëminently German character of the railway was not preserved. An English observer, after a trip over the Anatolian lines in 1908, wrote that he noted a great predominance of Turkish, Greek, and Italian employees over the Germans. "The fact is," he maintained, "that the people who run the line, though Germans, care first for their own pockets and next for Germany. They buy or employ what is cheapest and most suitable and do not care a finger-snap for the origin of an article or a servant. Patriotism occupies a small place in the calculations of promoters. The tendency to deal with the Fatherland must always be strong, but it is founded chiefly on the fact that the German knows the goods available in his own country better than the goods of other countries and that credit and banking facilities are more easily obtained at home. The master impulse in every German engaged in business in Turkey, as in business men of every other nationality, is to make money for himself as soon as possible." This same observer pointed out that there was an astonishing absence of German employees in even the more responsible positions of the Anatolian Railway and that the great majority of the unskilled laborers were Italians.[26]

Ultra-patriotic Germans, furthermore, denounced Dr. von Gwinner and his associates for not making the Bagdad Railway an exclusively Teutonic enterprise. A speaker at a Berlin branch of the Pan German League had this to say of the situation: "The Bagdad Railway, which in its origins was entirely German, has, thanks to the criminal negligence of the *Deutsche Bank,* become almost wholly French. The German schools along the line of the Railway, which were established by von Siemens, have fallen into decay. The officials of the Railway speak French. The ordinary language for transacting the business of the Railway is French, although the French share of the capital is only thirty per cent. The German engineers may as well be called home to-day as to-morrow." [27]

Nevertheless, the rapid expansion of German financial interests in the Near East and the established policy of the German banks to encourage and assist export trade were factors in a remarkable development of German trade in the Ottoman Empire, as will be indicated by the following table:[28]

Year	Exports from Turkey to Germany—Marks	Imports to Turkey from Germany—Marks
1900	30,400,000	34,400,000
1901	30,000,000	37,500,000
1902	36,500,000	43,300,000
1903	37,700,000	50,200,000
1904	43,500,000	75,300,000
1905	51,600,000	71,000,000
1906	55,000,000	68,200,000
1907	55,100,000	81,500,000
1908	47,600,000	64,000,000
1909	57,300,000	78,900,000
1910	67,400,000	104,900,000
1911	70,100,000	112,800,000

This table eloquently describes the nature of the advance of German economic interests in Turkey. It does not, however, tell the whole story. Was this advance the result of a general increase of prosperity in the Ottoman Empire in which the Germans shared in common with other traders? Or was the increase in German trade out of proportion to the progress of other nationals—perhaps at the expense of the French and British? The following tables will help answer these questions: [29]

EXPORTS FROM TURKEY

Year	To United Kingdom Marks	To France Marks	To Italy Marks	To Austria Hungary Marks
1900.....	118,760,000	86,220,000	22,520,000	35,220,000
1901.....	122,000,000	....	26,120,000	31,540,000
1902.....	130,520,000	83,040,000	28,980,000	35,580,000
1903.....	127,400,000	81,200,000	38,120,000	39,900,000
1904.....	122,760,000	73,120,000	31,300,000	39,120,000
1905.....	118,960,000	80,780,000	42,240,000	37,640,000
1906.....	129,440,000	91,600,000	45,100,000	39,300,000
1907.....	136,600,000	95,320,000	50,480,000	34,640,000
1908.....	109,220,000	70,760,000	44,580,000	34,360,000
1909.....	109,320,000	79,000,000	59,080,000	36,600,000
1910.....	100,660,000	77,000,000	48,000,000	43,340,000

IMPORTS TO TURKEY

Year	From United Kingdom Marks	From France Marks	From Italy Marks	From Austria Hungary Marks
1900.....	102,920,000	29,800,000	29,720,000	53,440,000
1901.....	128,220,000	37,880,000	43,800,000	57,100,000
1902.....	123,980,000	37,200,000	40,400,000	61,380,000
1903.....	114,020,000	36,640,000	45,360,000	65,120,000
1904.....	151,960,000	40,880,000	53,280,000	77,600,000
1905.....	139,300,000	42,420,000	57,200,000	76,660,000
1906.....	167,040,000	47,300,000	70,900,000	92,620,000
1907.....	147,380,000	46,380,000	63,040,000	89,920,000
1908.....	145,260,000	51,600,000	58,700,000	69,240,000
1909.....	156,280,000	54,600,000	67,740,000	77,040,000
1910.....	177,160,000	58,400,000	94,000,000	107,300,000

Certain important conclusions may be drawn from these statistics:

1. British trade continued during the decade 1900-1910 to dominate the Near Eastern market. With total imports and exports in the latter year of over 277,000,000 marks it was in no immediate danger of being outstripped by its nearest rivals—a German trade of about 172,000,000 marks and an Austro-Hungarian trade of about 150,000,-000 marks.

2. France, whose Near Eastern trade in 1900 had proudly held a position second only to that of the United Kingdom, was being obliged to accept a less prominent place in the economic life of the Ottoman Empire. During the first ten years of the new century French merchants obviously were being outmaneuvered by Germans, Austro-Hungarians, and Italians. In spite of a total increase of 17% in exports and imports between France and Turkey it was apparent that French trade was not keeping the pace; during the same period Austro-Hungarian trade showed an increased valuation of 81%, German trade of 166%.

3. Although it continued to dominate the Near Eastern market, British commerce, likewise, was losing ground. Between 1900 and 1910 it showed an increase of only 25% as compared with the Italian record of 172% during the same period. During the decade British exports, although showing an increased valuation, fell off from 35% to 22½% of the total import trade of Turkey; for the same period German exports achieved not only an absolute gain of almost eighty million marks, but also a relative increase from 2½% to 11½% of the whole.

4. The advance of German trade was not equal to the advance of Italian trade in the Ottoman Empire during the same period. This explains, in part, the rapidly increasing political interest of Italy in the Near East and

seems to set at rest the notion that the Germans acquired a stranglehold on exports and imports from and to Turkey.

5. Looking at the question from a purely political standpoint, one's attention is struck by the fact that commercial laurels in the Ottoman Empire were going to the nationals of the Triple Alliance powers. Economically, Turkey was leaning toward the Central Powers. Few international alliances are not based upon coincidence of economic interests; it appeared that a solid foundation was being laid for the eventual affiliation of Turkey with the Triple Alliance.

SEA COMMUNICATIONS ARE ESTABLISHED

Exports and imports, however, are not the only items which enter into the international balance sheet. As has been so amply demonstrated in the experience of the British Empire, ocean freights may constitute one of the chief items in the prosperity of a nation which lives upon commerce with other nations. It was not surprising, therefore, that upon the heels of German banks and German merchants in the Near East closely followed those other great promoters of German economic expansion, the steamship companies. The success of the *Deutsche Levante Linie,* established in 1889,[30] indicated that there was room for additional service between German ports and the cities of the Aegean and the Mediterranean. Accordingly, in 1905, the Atlas Line, of Bremen, inaugurated a regular service from the Baltic to Turkish ports. One line was to ply between Bremen and Smyrna, with Rotterdam, Malta, Piraeus, Salonica, and Constantinople as ports of call. Another of this same company's lines was to carry freight and passengers from Bremen to the Syrian city of Beirut. During the same year the North German Lloyd was responsible for the formation of the

Deutsche Mittelmeer Levante Linie, providing service between Marseilles and Genoa and Smyrna, Constantinople, Odessa, and Batum.[31] The considerable increase of trade between Germany and Turkey made a very real place for these lines, especially in the transportation of such commodities as could not be expected to bear the heavy charges of transportation by rail through the Balkans and overland to German cities. These lines were put into operation to provide for a traffic already in existence and waiting for them.

Such was not the case, however, with the establishment of German steamship service to the Persian Gulf. Here British trade had been dominant for centuries. The German railway invasion had not as yet reached Mesopotamia, and German trade in this region was negligible. The establishment of a German steamship service to Basra would be equivalent to the throwing out of an advance guard and reconnaissance expedition on behalf of German trade. Incidentally it would mean the destruction of the practical monopoly which had been enjoyed by the British in the trade of Irak. It was considered of no slight importance, therefore, when, in April of 1906, the Hamburg-American Line announced its intention of establishing a regular service between European ports and the Persian Gulf. An office of the Company was immediately opened at Basra, and in August the first German steamer, with a German cargo, made its way up the Shatt-el-Arab. Soon afterward the Hamburg-American Line inaugurated, also, a service between British ports and Mesopotamia, and it provided a regular schedule of sailing dates, a luxury to which merchants doing business in the Near East had not heretofore been accustomed. With the aid of a government subsidy the German company cut freight rates in half. This rude disturbance of the *status quo* in the shipping of the Persian Gulf dealt a severe blow to British companies engaged in the carrying trade between European ports and Mesopotamia. After a futile rate war the British lines, represented by Lord Inchcape, came to an agreement, in 1913, with their German competitors, ending a rivalry which had been the cause of considerable concern on the part of their respective foreign offices.[32]

In order to coöperate with the attempts of Germans to have a share in the trade of the Mesopotamian valley, the German Government established a consulate at Bagdad in 1908. The services of this consulate, supplementing the pioneer work of the Hamburg-American Line, had immediate results in the development of commercial relationships with the Land of the Two Rivers. The value of exports from Basra to Germany increased from about half a million dollars in 1906 to slightly in excess of a million dollars in 1913; German goods received at Basra during the same period increased from about half a million dollars to almost nine million dollars. Herr von Mutius, the German Consul at Bagdad, conducted an active campaign of education and propaganda, urging upon business men at home the importance of participating further in the development of the economic resources of the land of the Arabs.[33]

The establishment of steamship communication between Europe and Asiatic Turkey was welcomed by the Bagdad Railway Company. To widen the scope of usefulness—and, consequently, to increase the revenues—of the railway it was essential that every feeder for freight and passenger service be utilized. This was a consideration in the agreement with the Smyrna-Cassaba line and in the purchase, in 1906, of the Mersina-Tarsus-Adana Railway.[34] The establishment of connections with the former system developed a satisfactory volume of traffic with Smyrna. The acquisition of the latter line provided direct connections with the Mediterranean coast.

Nevertheless, the promoters of the Bagdad Railway were by no means satisfied with their terminal ports. Constantinople was at a disadvantage as compared with Smyrna in the trade of Anatolia. Smyrna was within reach of the Bagdad system only over the tracks of a French-owned line which might not always be in the hands of well-disposed owners. The prospects that the Railway soon would reach Basra were not very bright. Mersina was limited in its possibilities of development— shut off by the mountains from Anatolia, on the north, and Syria, on the south, it was the natural outlet only for the products of the Cilician plain.

The port which the company sought to bring under its control was Alexandretta, on the Mediterranean, seventy miles from Aleppo. Article 12 of the concession of 1903 assured preference to the Bagdad Railway Company in the award of a "possible extension to the sea at a point between Mersina and Tripoli-in-Syria." The construction of a branch from the main line to Alexandretta would provide the Railway with sea communications for the valuable trade of northern Syria and the northern Mesopotamian valley, then almost entirely dependent upon the caravan routes centering in Aleppo. Accordingly, negotiations were begun in the spring of 1911 looking toward the building of a branch line to Alexandretta and the construction of extensive port facilities at that harbor.

Serious financial difficulties were encountered, however, in the promotion of this plan. The Young Turk budget of 1910 had announced that no further railway concessions carrying guarantees would be granted. Even had the Government been disposed to depart from its avowed intention, it would have been unable to do so. Suffering from the usual malady of a young government—lack of funds—it was running into debt continually and finding it increasingly difficult to borrow money. Early in 1911 the Imperial Ottoman Treasury addressed a request to the Powers for permission to increase the customs duties from eleven to fourteen per cent *ad valorem*. Great Britain immediately announced its determination to veto the proposed revision of the revenues, unless the increase were granted with certain important qualifications. Sir Edward Grey informed the House of Commons, March 8: "I wish to see the new régime in Turkey strengthened. I wish to see them supplied with resources which will enable them to establish strong and just government in all parts of the Turkish Empire. I am aware that money is needed for these purposes, and I would willingly ask British trade to make sacrifices for these purposes. But if the money is to be used to promote railways which may be a source of doubtful advantage to British trade, and still more if the money is going to be used to promote railways which will take the place of communications which have been in the hands of British concessionaires [*i.e.,* the Lynch Brothers], then I say it will be impossible for us to agree to that increase of the customs duty until we are satisfied that British trade interests will be satisfactorily guarded." [35] This clear pronouncement of British policy made it plain that no increased Turkish customs revenues could be diverted to the proposed Alexandretta branch. It was even doubtful if further funds would be forthcoming for the construction of the main line beyond El Helif.

This complicated domestic and international situation led to the conventions of March 21, 1911, between the Imperial Ottoman Government and the Bagdad Railway Company. One of these conventions provided for the construction of a branch line of the Bagdad Railway from Osmanie, on the main line, to Alexandretta, but without kilometric guarantee or other subsidy from the Turkish Government. A second convention leased for a period of ninety-nine years to the Haidar Pasha Port Company the exclusive rights of constructing port and terminal facilities at Alexandretta—including quays, docks, warehouses, coal pockets, and elevators. As in the case of the Bagdad Railway itself, public lands were to be at the disposal of the concessionaires without charge, and private lands were to be subject to the law of expropriation if essential for the purposes of the Company. Within the limits of the port the Company was authorized to maintain a police force for the maintenance of order and the protection of its property.[36]

Because of the refusal of the Powers to permit an increase in the customs, the Turkish Government was unable to assign further revenues to the payment of railway guarantees. The Bagdad Railway Company thereupon agreed to proceed with the construction of the sections from El Helif to Bagdad without additional commitments from the Imperial Ottoman Treasury. The Company likewise renounced its right to build the sections beyond Bagdad, including its concession for the construction of port works at Basra, with the proviso, however, that this section of the line, if constructed, be assigned to a Turkish company internationally owned and administered.[37] This surrender by the Bagdad Railway Company of its rights to the pledge of additional revenues by the Ottoman Treasury and its surrender of its hold on the sections of the railway beyond Bagdad are by far the most important provisions of the conventions of March 21, 1911.

German opinion, as a whole, considered these self-denying contracts of the Company an indication of the willingness of the *Deutsche Bank* and the German Government to go more than half way in removing diplomatic objections to the construction of the Bagdad Railway.[38] There were Englishmen, however, who felt that the conventions of 1911 were a mere gesture of conciliation; in their opinion the renunciation of these important rights was bait held out to win foreign diplomatic support and to induce the participation of foreign capital in the Railway and its subsidiary enterprises. Lord Curzon, for example, expressed to the House of Lords his belief that technical and financial difficulties made it impossible for the German bankers to proceed with the construction of the Bagdad line without the assistance of outside capital. He was firmly of the opinion that no railway stretching from the Bosporus to the Gulf could be financed by a single Power.[39]

The unsettled political conditions in Turkey, meanwhile, had delayed, but not halted, construction of the Bagdad Railway. The years 1910 and 1911 were marked by progress on the sections in the vicinity of Adana. From that Cilician city the railway was being laid westward to the Taurus Mountains, eventually to pass through the Great Gates and meet the tracks already laid to Bulgurlu. Eastward the line was being constructed in the direction of the Amanus mountains, although there seemed to be little chance for an early beginning of the costly tunneling of the barrier. During 1911 and 1912 attention was concentrated on the building of the sections east of Aleppo, which in 1912 reached the Euphrates River. The branch line to Alexandretta was completed and opened to traffic November 1, 1913.[40] Financial difficulties in the way of further construction of the main line were overcome in the latter part of 1913, when the *Deutsche Bank* disposed of its holdings in the Macedonian Railways and the Oriental Railways to an Austro-Hungarian syndicate. The funds thus obtained were re-invested in the Bagdad Railway, and the necessity was obviated for a further sale of securities on the open market.[41] In 1914 the Amanus tunnels were begun, a great steel bridge was thrown across the Euphrates, the sections east of Aleppo were constructed almost to Ras el Ain, in northern Mesopotamia. In addition, rails were laid from Bagdad north to Sadijeh, on the Tigris, before the outbreak of the Great War.[42]

Thus far we have considered the Bagdad Railway almost entirely as a business undertaking. In its inception, in fact, it was generally thus regarded throughout Europe. As time passed, however, the enterprise overstepped the bounds of purely economic interest and entered the arena of international diplomacy. The greatest usefulness of the Bagdad Railway was in the economic services it was capable of rendering the Ottoman Empire and, further, all mankind. Its widest significance is to be sought in the part it played in the development of German capitalistic imperialism. Its greatest menace was its consequent effects upon the relations between Turkey, Germany, and the other Great Powers of Europe. The succeeding chapters will deal with the political ramifications of the Bagdad enterprise.

BIBLIOGRAPHICAL AND EXPLANATORY NOTES

[1] Dr. Arthur von Gwinner (1856-   ) is one of the most distinguished of modern financiers. He was born, appropriately enough, at Frankfort-on-the-Main when that city was a center of international finance. His father, a lawyer, was an intimate friend of Schopenhauer and the latter's executor and biographer. In 1885 young Gwinner married a daughter of Philip Speyer and thus became a member of one of the famous families of bankers in Europe and America. For a time he conducted a private banking business in Berlin, but in 1894 he became an active director of the *Deutsche Bank*. Two years later he was sent to America to supervise the reorganization of the Northern Pacific Railway by its European creditors; and while he was in the United States, he formed lasting friendships with J. Pierpont Morgan and James J. Hill. In 1901 he succeeded Dr. von Siemens as the guiding spirit of the *Deutsche Bank,* which under his administration made even more remarkable progress than under his capable predecessor. As managing director of the *Deutsche Bank* he became president of the Anatolian and Bagdad

Railway Companies. It was in 1909 that Dr. von Gwinner's father received from the Kaiser the patent of hereditary nobility —an honor said to have been intended as much for the distinguished son as for the distinguished sire. Intellectually, Dr. von Gwinner is an international man: he quotes Dickens and Shakespeare and Molière, Goethe and Schiller and Lessing, with almost equal facility. His delightful personality stands out in all the Bagdad Railway negotiations.

[2] *Infra,* Chapter IX. The French bankers also shared in the ownership of the construction company. A. Géraud, "A New German Empire: the Story of the Bagdad Railway," in *The Nineteenth Century,* Volume 75 (1914), p. 967; *Report of the Bagdad Railway Company,* 1903, pp. 4, 8.

[3] Among the German members were Dr. von Gwinner; Dr. Karl Testa, representative of the German bondholders on the Ottoman Public Debt Administration; Dr. Alfred von Kaulla, a director of the *Württembergische Vereinsbank,* and original concessionaire of the Anatolian Railways; Dr. Karl Schrader, a member of the Reichstag; Dr. Kurt Zander, general manager of the Anatolian Railway Company. The directors nominated by the French interests were Count A. D'Arnoux, Director General, and M. Léon Berger, French member, of the Ottoman Public Debt Administration; MM. J. Deffes, G. Auboyneau, P. Naville, Pangiri Bey, and A. Vernes, of the Imperial Ottoman Bank, the last-named being vice-president of the Bagdad Railway Company; M. L. Chenut, a member of the Ottoman *Régie Générale de chemins de fer.* The Turkish members of the Board were Hamdy Bey, representative of the Ottoman bondholders on the Public Debt Administration; Hoene Effendi, under-secretary in the Ministry of Posts and Telegraphs; and two Constantinople bankers. The Swiss were Herr Abegg-Arter, president of the *Schweizerische Kreditanstalt,* of Zurich, and M. A. Turrettini, of *L'Union financière de Genève.* The Austrian was Herr Bauer, of the *Wiener Bankverein,* and the Italian was Carlo Esterle, of the Italian Edison Electric Company, of Milan. There were few important changes in the personnel of the Board of Directors between 1903 and 1914, perhaps the most notable being the election of Dr. Karl Helfferich, in 1906. *Cf. Reports of the Bagdad Railway Company,* 1903, *et seq.*

[4] *Cf. Parliamentary Debates, House of Commons,* fourth series, Volume 120 (1903), p. 1371. During the Great War a conspicuous German general complained that the Swiss in charge of the operation of the Railway was more interested in the commercial than in the strategic value of the line and did not coöperate with the military authorities. *Cf.* Field Marshal Liman von Sanders, *Fünf Jahre Türkei* (Berlin, 1919), p. 40.

[5] *Verhandlungen des Reichstages, Stenographische Berichte, XII Legislaturperiode, 1 Session,* Volume 231 (1908), p. 4253c.

[6] *Supra,* p. 77.

[7] Paul Imbert, "Le chemin de fer de Bagdad," in *Revue des deux mondes,* Volume 197 (1907), p. 672. The *Deutsche Bank,* with its capital and surplus of about $75,000,000, was the foremost of the German banks. Associated with it in the Bagdad Railway enterprise were a number of other financial institutions, including, it is said, the *Dresdner Bank* and the *Darmstädter Bank,* ranking second and fourth respectively among the great banks of the German Empire. Riesser, *op. cit.,* pp. 642-644.

[8] *Supra,* Chapter IV, Note 48; Fraser, *op. cit.,* pp. 48-49; Jastrow, *op. cit.,* p. 94; *Report of the Bagdad Railway Company,* 1904, p. 3; 1905, p. 4.

[9] Von Gwinner, *loc. cit.,* p. 1088.

[10] *Corps de droit ottoman,* Volume III, pp. 221-228.

[11] *Turkey in Europe,* pp. 128-129; *The Quarterly Review,* Volume 228 (1917), pp. 510-511; *Parliamentary Debates, House of Commons,* fourth series, Volume 159 (1906), pp. 1338, 1359; *ibid.,* Volume 162 (1906), p. 1419; Volume 178 (1907), p. 321; *ibid.,* fifth series, Volume 53 (1913), p. 368.

[12] *Société Impériale Ottomane du Chemin de fer de Bagdad— Convention Additionelle* (Constantinople, 1908); *Parliamentary Papers,* No. Cd. 5636, Volume CIII (1911); *Report of the Bagdad Railway Company,* 1908, pp. 4-5; 1909, p. 4; *Bagdad Railway Loan Contract, Second and Third Series,* June 2, 1908; *Report of the Deutsche Bank,* 1909, p. 12.

[13] *Report of the Deutsche Bank,* 1909, p. 12.

[14] *Report of the Bagdad Railway Company,* 1906, p. 4; K. Helfferich, *Die Vorgeschichte des Weltkrieges,* pp. 131-132; Dr. Helfferich's reputation was based largely upon his writings on two important subjects: the gold monetary standard; government promotion of foreign trade. *Cf. Germany and the Gold Standard* (London, 1896); *Beiträge zur Geschichte der deutschen Geldreform* (Leipzig, 1901). See the enthusiastic appreciation of Dr. Helfferich's services voiced by his associates of the *Deutsche Bank* upon the occasion of his appointment as Secretary of State for the Imperial Treasury, January, 1915. *Report of the Deutsche Bank,* 1915, pp. 11-12; *Report of the Bagdad Railway Company,* 1914, p. 8.

[15] *The Times,* October 25, 1905, commenting upon the proposed appointment of Helfferich.

[16] *Report of the Anatolian Railway Company,* 1907, p. 7; H. C. Woods, "The Bagdad Railway and Its Tributaries," in *The Geographical Journal,* Volume 50 (1917), pp. 32 *et seq.; Parliamentary Papers,* No. Cmd. 964 (1920). The irrigation system

thus planned was completed before the outbreak of the Great War. It justified the sanguine expectations of its promoters, for the agricultural yield of the irrigated lands increased from five to fifteen fold over the former production. In 1911 a similar irrigation project was gotten under way in Cilicia. *Diplomatic and Consular Reports*, No. 4835 (1911), pp. 18-19.

[17] *Cf. supra*, p. 37.

[18] Riesser, *op. cit.*, p. 454; *Report of the Dresdner Bank*, 1905, p. 6; *Diplomatic and Consular Reports*, No. 3553 (1905), p. 29; *Report of the Deutsche Bank*, 1908, p. 10. The Bagdad office of the *Deutsche Bank* was not established until 1914, just before the outbreak of the War. *Ibid.*, 1914, p. 9.

[19] The principal bank in Turkey before the War was the Imperial Ottoman Bank. This institution was owned by French and British capitalists, the French interest being predominant and in control. It was a quasi-public bank, founded in 1863, and enjoying since then a monopoly of bank-note issues. Its central office was at Constantinople, but it maintained a branch in practically every important city of Asiatic Turkey, including Smyrna, Jerusalem, Jaffa, Aleppo, Alexandretta, Beirut, Damascus, Basra, Bagdad, and Mosul. The capital stock of the Imperial Ottoman Bank was £10,000,000 sterling. A British bank of some importance was The Eastern Bank, Ltd., of which the Right Honorable Lord Balfour of Burleigh was chairman—the same Lord Balfour who was Secretary for Scotland in the ministry of his namesake, Arthur J. Balfour, in 1903, when the British Government quashed the participation of English capitalists in the Bagdad Railway. The head office of the Eastern Bank was in London, and it maintained branches in Basra and Bagdad, although its principal sphere of activity was India. Sir Ernest Cassell's National Bank of Turkey was not established until 1909. *Cf.* Caillard, *loc. cit.*, p. 439; weekly advertisements of these banks in *The Near East; Parliamentary Debates*, Index for 1903, p. v; *Turkey in Europe*, p. 36.

[20] D. S. Jordan, "The Interlocking Directorates of War," in *The World's Work*, July, 1913, p. 278; H. Hauser, *Les Méthodes Allemandes d'Expansion Économique*, seventh edition (Paris, 1917), *passim*; Riesser, *op. cit.*, pp. 366-367.

[21] Riesser, *op. cit.*, pp. 373-375, 432, 474, 745-746.

[22] *Verhandlungen des Reichstages, Stenographische Berichte, XII Legislaturperiode, 1 Session*, Volume 231 (1908), p. 4253c. The speech of the Secretary was followed by "Bravos" from the National Liberals.

[23] *Parliamentary Debates, House of Lords*, fourth series, Volume 121 (1903), p. 1340.

[24] *Diplomatic and Consular Reports*, No. 3140 (1903), p. 40.

[25] *Supra,* pp. 98-99, *Report of the Deutsche Bank,* 1909, p. 12; *Stenographische Berichte, XII Legislaturperiode, 2 Session,* Volume 260 (1910), p. 2181d, statement by Baron von Schoen.

[26] Fraser, *op. cit.,* pp. 16-17, 18-20. *Cf.,* also, *Report of the Bagdad Railway Company,* 1911, p. 4.

[27] *Staatsburger Zeitung* (Berlin), March 3, 1912.

[28] Compiled from the *Statistisches Jahrbuch für das deutsche Reich,* 1900-1914, as corrected for 1900-1905 according to the *Statistisches Handbuch für das deutsche Reich,* Volume 2, pp. 506-510. A remarkable increase of German exports to Turkey— an increase of 50%—is to be noted in the year 1904, during which the first section of the Bagdad Railway was constructed. Undoubtedly this increase is to be partially accounted for by the purchase in Germany of materials for right of way as well as rolling stock for the railway. This factor should not be over-estimated, however, as a glance at the following tables will show that imports into Turkey from other European countries during the same year likewise showed increases, without exception. The general falling off in trade during 1908 may be attributed, in part, at any rate, to the Young Turk Revolution of that year.

[29] Compiled from *Diplomatic and Consular Reports,* Nos. 2950 (1902), 3533 (1905), 4188 (1908), and 4835 (1910-1911).

[30] *Supra,* p. 36.

[31] *Diplomatic and Consular Reports,* No. 3533 (1905), p. 27; *Turkey in Europe,* pp. 86-87.

[32] *Mesopotamia,* pp. 99-101; Schaefer, *op. cit.,* p. 22. Regarding British interests in the Persian Gulf, *cf.,* a detailed statement by Lord Lansdowne to the House of Lords, May 5, 1903. *Parliamentary Debates, House of Lords,* fourth series, Volume 121 (1903), pp. 1347-1348.

[33] "Bagdad: Handelsbericht des kaiserlichen Konsulats für das Jahr 1908-1909," in *Deutsches Handels-Archiv,* 1910, part 2, pp. 27-35; also, "Bericht über den Handel in Basra und Bagdad für das Jahr 1910," *ibid.,* 1912, part 2, pp. 263-270; *Mesopotamia,* p. 108.

[34] *Cf. supra,* pp. 59-60; *Report of the Bagdad Railway Company,* 1906, p. 4, 1908, pp. 7-8; *Diplomatic and Consular Reports,* No. 3533 (1905), p. 29. The Mersina-Adana line was formally incorporated in the Bagdad system in 1908. *Cf. Deuxième convention additionelle à la convention du chemin de fer de Bagdad* (Constantinople, 1910).

[35] *Parliamentary Debates, House of Commons,* fifth series, Volume 22 (1911), pp. 1284-1285.

[36] *Quatrième convention additionelle à la convention du 5 Mars, 1903, relative au chemin de fer de Bagdad* (Constantinople, 1911).

H. F. B. Lynch (of the firm of Lynch Brothers), "The Bagdad Railway: the New Conventions," in the *Fortnightly Review*, new series, Volume 89 (1911), pp. 773-780. Mr. Lynch explains that his summary of the Alexandretta port concessions is based upon an authentic article appearing in *La Turquie*, a Constantinople newspaper, of March 21, 1911. *Diplomatic and Consular Reports*, No. 4835 (1911), p. 16; *The Times* (London), March 23, 1911.

[37] *Stenographische Berichte, XII Legislaturperiode, 2 Session*, Volume 266 (1911), pp. 5984c *et seq.; Troisième convention additionelle à la convention du 5 Mars, 1903, relative au chemin de fer de Bagdad* (Constantinople, 1911); *Parliamentary Debates, House of Common*, fifth series, Volume 23 (1911), pp. 582-583, statement by Sir Edward Grey.

[38] See speeches of Herr Scheidemann and Herr Bassermann before the Reichstag, March 30, 1911. *Stenographische Berichte, XII Legislaturperiode, 2 Session*, Volume 266 (1911), pp. 5980 *et seq.*

[39] *Parliamentary Debates, House of Lords,* fifth series, Volume 23 (1911), p. 589.

[40] D. Chatir, "L'État actuel du chemin de fer de Bagdad," in *Questions diplomatiques et coloniales*, Volume 36 (1913), pp. 279-281; *Report of the Bagdad Railway Company*, 1910, p. 4, 1911, p. 4, 1913, pp. 3-5, 1914, pp. 6-8.

[41] *Report of the Deutsche Bank*, 1913, pp. 11-12.

[42] *Report of the Bagdad Railway Company*, 1914, pp. 6-8. It was not until September, 1918, that the Amanus tunnels were completed, the first train being operated through to Aleppo just before the capture of that city by Lord Allenby's army. Von Sanders, *op. cit.*, p. 42.

CHAPTER VI

THE BAGDAD RAILWAY BECOMES AN IMPERIAL ENTERPRISE

POLITICAL INTERESTS COME TO THE FORE

It was asserted times without number that the Bagdad Railway was an independent financial enterprise, unconnected with the political aims of the German Government in Turkey and in no sense associated with an imperialist policy in the Near East. At the time the concession of 1903 was granted Dr. Rohrbach expressed the belief that political and diplomatic considerations were quite outside the plans and purposes of the promoters of the Railway.[1] Herr Bassermann, leader of the National Liberal Party, announced to the Reichstag that, although German capital was predominant in the Railway, there was no intent on the part of the owners or on the part of the Government to build with any political *arrière-pensée*. Baron von Schoen, Imperial Secretary for Foreign Affairs, reiterated this idea with emphasis. He pointed out that the Bagdad convention of 1903 was *not a treaty* between Germany and Turkey, *but a contract* between the Ottoman Government and the Anatolian Railway Company. He maintained that if the railway were considered, properly, as a purely economic enterprise, "all the fantastic schemes that are from time to time being attached to it would evaporate."[2] A British journalist wrote in 1913: "Gwinner, it may be assumed, is not building the Bagdad Railway for the purposes of the German General Staff. What chiefly keeps him awake of nights is how to extract dividends from it for the *Deutsche Bank* and how best to promote the golden opportunities which await the strategists of the German trading army in the Near East." [3]

The German Government, nevertheless, had been interested in the Bagdad plan almost from its inception. The visits of the Emperor to Constantinople and Palestine; the appointment of German military and consular officers to the technical commission which surveyed the line in 1899; the enthusiastic support of the German ambassador all contributed to the success of the enterprise. In fact, the German Government was almost too solicitous of the welfare of the concessionaires; assistance, it was said, bordered upon interference. During the early stages of the negotiations of 1898-1899 Dr. von Siemens complained that the German embassy was jeopardizing the success of the project by insisting that the issuance of the concessions should be considered a diplomatic, as well as a business, triumph. Dr. von Gwinner, also, was discontented with the tendency of the German Government to urge strategic, rather than purely economic, considerations. There was a widespread belief in Germany, as well as elsewhere in Europe, that the Imperial Foreign Office nurtured the Bagdad Railway and its affiliated enterprises with a full realization that "the skirmishes of the political advance guard are fought on financial ground, although the selection of the time and the enemy, as well as the manner in which these skirmishes are to be fought, depends upon those responsible for our foreign policy. Much more than ever before Germans will have to bear in mind that industrial contracts, commercial enterprises, and capital investments are conveying from one country to another not only capital and labor, but also political influence." [4]

Had the German Government been disposed to pursue a different policy in the Near East, had it refused to link its political power with the economic interests of its nationals, it would have been standing out against an accepted practice of the Great Powers. Lord Lansdowne, British Secretary of State for Foreign Affairs, informed the House of Lords, in May, 1903, that it was impossible for the Foreign Office to dissociate commercial and political interests. He doubted whether British success in the Middle and Far East could have been achieved without careful diplomatic promotion of British economic interests in those regions.[5] Through financial control Russia and Great Britain effectually throttled Persian reform and nationalist aspirations. The pioneer activities of French capital in Tunis and Morocco are outstanding instances of modern imperial procedure. Such also is the use by the Government of the French Republic of its power to deny listings on the Paris Bourse for the purpose of forcing political concessions—a procedure which a French banker described to the author as "a species of international blackmail."[6] A prominent historian and economist has described the Franco-Russian alliance as a "bankers' creation."[7] What other powers had been doing it was to be expected that Germany would do. The ownership and operation of the Bagdad Railway by a predominantly German company was an important factor in a notable expansion of German commercial and financial activities in the Near East. In an age of keen competition for economic influence in the so-called backward areas of the world, this growth of German interests in Turkey was almost certain to influence the diplomatic policy of Germany toward the Ottoman Empire. The political aspirations of the diplomatists were reënforced by the economic interests of the bankers.

Had the German Government not voluntarily taken the Bagdad enterprise under its wing, it might have been compelled to do so. Popular dissatisfaction with a "weak" policy toward investments in backward countries may force the hand of an unwilling government. Whether this dissatisfaction be spontaneous or created by an interested press or both, it is certain to be powerful, for there are few governments which can resist for long the clamor for vigorous fostering of the nation's interests and rights abroad. And there was no lack of popular enthusiasm in Germany for the Bagdad Railway. The fact that French capital had been invested in the undertaking was usually forgotten. The grand design came to be referred to, affectionately, as *unser Bagdad* and, somewhat flamboyantly, as the "B. B. B." (Berlin-Byzantium-Bagdad). German publicists of imperial inclinations contemplated the Railway with reverent amazement, as though hypnotized. The project speedily became an integral part of the national *Weltanschauung*—a means of enabling Germans to compete for the rich commerce of the Orient, to appropriate some of its enormous wealth, to develop some of its apparently boundless possibilities. As a branch of *Weltpolitik* it held out alluring inducements for the exercise of political influence in the East—an influence which would serve at once to discomfit the Continental rivals of Germany and to promote the *Drang nach Osten* of her Habsburg ally.

The political aims of the German Empire in Turkey, however, were not concerned with colonization or conquest. It was not proposed, for example, to encourage German colonization of the regions traversed by the Bagdad Railway. During the last two decades of the nineteenth century, it is true, attempts had been made to stimulate German settlements in Syria and Mesopotamia. But later, when the problem of German oversea migration had become less acute, all proposals for German colonization in the Near East were abandoned.[8]

The difficulties in the way of European settlement of

Asiatic Turkey were almost insurmountable. Mesopotamia is unbearably hot during the summer and is totally unfit for colonization by Europeans. During July and August the thermometer registers between 100 and 120 almost every day, and the heat is particularly oppressive because of the relatively high humidity. The total number of Europeans resident in Mesopotamia before the War was not in excess of 200, who were almost all missionaries, engineers, consuls, or archæologists. Palestine is more suitable as a place of residence, but the country is not particularly alluring; a few German agricultural colonies, chiefly Jewish, were established there, but they were comparatively unimportant in size, wealth, and political influence. In Anatolia the climate is tolerable, but not healthful for western Europeans. The plateau is subject to sudden and extreme changes in temperature in both winter and summer, and, consequently, pneumonia and malaria are almost epidemic among foreigners. To the German who was considering leaving the Fatherland to seek his fortune abroad, Mesopotamia, Syria, and Anatolia were by no means as attractive as Wisconsin, Minnesota, and the Dakotas. Turkey offered few inducements to compare with the lure of the United States or of South America.[9]

In addition to these natural difficulties, there existed the pronounced opposition of the Turks to foreign colonization of their homeland. This opposition was so deep-rooted that General von der Goltz warned his fellow countrymen not to migrate to the Near East if friendly relations were to be maintained with the Ottoman Empire. Paul Rohrbach said that colonization of Turkey-in-Asia by Europeans was quite out of the question. H. F. B. Lynch, of the English firm of Lynch Brothers, one of the most pronounced opponents of the Bagdad Railway, declared that fear of German settlement of Asia Minor was sheer nonsense, that no such plan was in contemplation by the promoters of the Bagdad enterprise, and that the reports of such intentions were the work of ignorant chauvinists. It will be recalled, also, that a secret annex to the concession of 1903 pledged the *Deutsche Bank* not to encourage German or other foreign immigration into Turkey.[10]

Germans denied, likewise, that they had any intention of utilizing the Bagdad Railway as a means of acquiring an exclusive sphere of economic interest in the Ottoman Empire. Attention was continually directed to Articles 24 and 25 of the Specifications of 1903, which decreed that rates must be applicable to all travelers and consignors without discrimination, and which prohibited the concessionaires from entering into any contract whatever with the object of granting preferential treatment to any one. Arthur von Gwinner, President of the Bagdad Railway, stated that his company had loyally abided by its announced policy of equality of treatment for all, regardless of nationality or other considerations, and he challenged the critics of the enterprise to cite a single instance in which the contrary had been the case. Dr. Rohrbach wrote, in 1903, that it was "unthinkable that Germans should seek to monopolize the territories of the Turkish Empire for the purposes of economic exploitation." Somewhat later he again stressed this point: "Germany's political attitude to Turkey is unlike that of all other European powers because, in all sincerity, we ask not a single foot of Turkish territory in Europe, Asia, or Africa, but have only the wish and the interest to find in Turkey—whether its domination be in future restricted to Asia or not—a market and a source of raw materials for our industry; and in this respect we advance no claim on other nations than that of the unconditional open door." Baron von Schoen pledged the Government to a policy of equal and unqualified opportunity for all in the regions to be opened up by the Railway.[11]

Furthermore, there is little reason to believe that the Germans had any intention of establishing a protectorate over Asiatic Turkey. Their determination to respect the territorial integrity of the Ottoman Empire was due, of course, not to magnanimity on their part as much as to expediency. Protectorates are expensive. For the same reason it may be doubted that there was any intention of maintaining an extensive military control over Turkey. German aims were to be served by the economic, military, and political renaissance of Turkey-in-Asia. A strong Turkey economically would be a Turkey so much the better able to increase the production of raw materials for the German market as well as to provide an ever more prosperous market for the products of German factories. A powerful Turkish military machine might strike some telling blows, in alliance with German arms, in a general European war; in the event of a Near Eastern conflict it might be utilized to menace the southern frontier of Russia or to strike at British communications with India. A politically strong Ottoman Empire might offer serious resistance to the Russian advance in the Middle East and might menace Britain's hold on her Mohammedan possessions.

On the other hand, a Turkey in subjection would be an unwilling producer and a poor customer. The occupation of Turkey by German armed forces would seriously deplete the ranks of the German armies on the Russian and French frontiers, and in time of war would confront the German General Staff with the additional problem of maintaining order in hostile Mohammedan territory. The conquering of Turkey would bring the German Empire into the ranks of European powers with Mohammedan subjects, thus exposing it to the menace, common to Great

Britain, France, and Russia, of a Pan-Islamic revival. For all of these reasons the obvious German policy was not only to respect the territorial integrity of Turkey, but to defend it against the encroachments of other powers. "Not a penny for a weak Turkey," said Rohrbach, "but for a strong Turkey everything we can give!" [12]

In its political aspects the Bagdad Railway was something more than a railway. It was one phase of the great diplomatic struggle for the predominance of power, one pawn in the great game between the Alliance and the Entente, one element of the Anglo-German rivalry on the seas. The development of closer relations, political and economic, between Germany and Turkey was in accord with the spirit of an era of universal preparedness—preparedness for pressing economic competition, preparedness for the expected great European war in which every nation would be obliged to fight for its very existence. Through control of the economic resources of the Ottoman Empire, German diplomacy sought to arrive at an *entente cordiale* or a formal military alliance with the Sultan. Through support of the chief Mohammedan power Germany might throw tempting "apples of discord" into the colonial empires of her chief European rivals, for Great Britain ruled about eighty-five million subject Mohammedans, Russia about seventeen million, France about fifteen million; but Germany possessed almost none.[13] Friedrich Naumann wrote in 1889, in connection with the Kaiser's pilgrimage to the Near East: "It is possible that the world war will break out before the disintegration of the Ottoman Empire. Then the Caliph of Constantinople will once more uplift the standard of the Holy War. The Sick Man will raise himself for the last time to shout to Egypt, the Soudan, East Africa, Persia, Afghanistan, and India, 'War against England.' It is not unimportant to know who will support him on his bed when he utters this cry." [14]

This menace to the British Empire was no more serious than another which was frankly espoused by certain supporters of the Bagdad plan—the possibility, even without a preponderance of naval power, of severing the communications of the empire in time of war. Dr. Rohrbach, for example, put it this way: "If it comes to war with England, it will be for Germany simply a question of life and death. The possibility that events may turn out favorably for us depends wholly and solely upon whether we can succeed in putting England herself in a precarious position. That cannot be done by a direct attack in the North Sea; all idea of invading England is purely chimerical. We must, therefore, seek other means which will enable us to strike England in a vulnerable spot. . . . England can be attacked and mortally wounded by land from Europe in only one place—Egypt. The loss of Egypt would mean not only the end of her dominion over the Suez Canal and of her communications with India and the Far East, but would probably entail, also, the loss of her possessions in Central and East Africa. We can never dream, however, of attacking Egypt until Turkey is mistress of a developed railway system in Asia Minor and Syria, and until, through the extension of the Anatolian Railway to Bagdad, she is in a position to withstand an attack by England upon Mesopotamia. . . . The stronger Turkey grows the more dangerous does she become for England." [15]

It is only fair to add, however, that Dr. Rohrbach was not an authorized spokesman of the German people, the German Government, or the Bagdad Railway Company. His views were personal and are to be given weight only in so far as they influenced or reflected public opinion in Germany; to estimate their importance by such a standard is no simple task. But whatever its true significance, Dr. Rohrbach's interest in the Bagdad Railway was certainly a source of great annoyance to Dr. von Gwinner, who was constantly called upon to explain irresponsible, provocative, and bombastic statements from Rohrbach's pen. It is well to recall that the writings of publicists are sometimes taken too seriously.[16]

It would have been foolhardy, nevertheless, to discard these possibilities as purely imaginary. Once the Bagdad Railway was constructed and its subsidiary enterprises developed, there would have existed the great temptation to utilize economic influence for the promotion of strategic and diplomatic purposes. In an era of intensive military and economic preparedness for war the observance of the niceties of international relationships is not always to be counted upon. In such circumstances the wishes of the business men—whether they were imperialistic or anti-imperialistic—may be over-ruled by the statesmen and the soldiers. The chance to strike telling blows at French prestige in the Levant; the opportunity to embarrass Russia by strengthening Turkey; the possibility of menacing the communications of the British Empire; the likelihood of recruiting Turkish military and economic strength in the cause of Germany,—these were alluring prospects for discomfiting the Entente rivals of the German Empire.

At the same time it should be mentioned that promotion of the Bagdad Railway would serve to weld firmer the Austro-German alliance. Austrian ambitions in the Near East centered in the Vienna-Salonica railway and were distinct from the Berlin-to-Bagdad plan of the Germans; nevertheless circumstances served to promote a community of interest. First, the routes of the railways through the Balkans coincided in part: the Austrian railway ran *via* Belgrade and Nish to Salonica; traffic "from Berlin to Bagdad" followed the same line to Nish, where it branched off to Sofia and Constantinople. Second,

Austrian, as well as German, trade would be carried over the Bagdad lines to the Orient, and Austrian industries would be able to secure raw materials from Anatolia and Mesopotamia. If the railway was to run from Berlin to Bagdad, it also was to run from Vienna to Bagdad. Third, similarly, German industry was to profit by the Austrian railway to Salonica, for it opened a new route to German commerce to the Aegean. "Germany's road to the Orient lay, literally as well as figuratively, across the Balkan Peninsula." [17] The *Drang nach Osten* was near to the hearts of both allies!

It was not without warning that the German nation permitted itself to be drawn into the imperial ramifications of the Bagdad Railway. Anti-imperialists sensed the dangers connected with such an ambitious project. Herr Scheidemann, leader of the Social Democrats in the Reichstag, for example, warned the German people that the railway was certain to raise increasingly troublesome international difficulties, and he expressed the fear that the German protagonists of the plan would come to emphasize more and more its political and military, rather than its economic and cultural, phases.[18] Karl Radek, also a Socialist, wrote that "The Bagdad Railway possessed great political significance from the very moment the plan was conceived." He prophesied that German economic penetration in Turkey would prove to be only the first step toward a formal military alliance, which, in turn, would heighten the fear and animosity of the Entente Powers. "The Bagdad Railway," he said, "constitutes the first great triumph of German capitalistic imperialism." [19] Business men and politicians of imperialist inclinations did not deny the charges of their pacifist opponents. Herr Bassermann, so far from deprecating a greater political influence in the Ottoman Empire, came to glory in it. Baron von Schoen qualified his earlier statements with the following enunciation of policy: "With reference to the attitude of the Imperial Government, it goes without saying that we are giving the enterprise our full interest and attention and will make every effort to further it." [20]

The political potentialities of the Bagdad Railway aroused the fear and opposition of the other European Powers. Exaggerated charges were made as to the intentions of the German promoters and the German Government, and there was a widespread feeling that there was something sinister about the plan. Professor Sarolea sounded a prophetic warning when he wrote, "The trans-Mesopotamian Railway . . . will play in the Near East the same ominous part which the Trans-Siberian played in the Far East; with this important difference, however, that whilst the Far Eastern conflict involved only one European Power and one Asiatic Power, the Near Eastern conflict, if it breaks out, must needs involve all the European powers, must force the whole Eastern Question to a crisis, and once begun, cannot be terminated until the map of Europe and Asia shall be reconstructed." [21]

RELIGIOUS AND CULTURAL INTERESTS REËNFORCE POLITICAL AND ECONOMIC MOTIVES

Along with economic and political motives for imperialist ventures there frequently goes a religious motive. That such should be the case in the Near East was to be expected because of the religious appeal of the Ottoman Empire as the homeland of the Jews, the birthplace of Christianity, the cradle of Mohammedanism. It was small wonder, then, that the Bagdad Railway, which promised to link Central European cities with the holy places of Syria and Palestine, should have been supported enthusiastically by German missionaries and other German Christians.

German Protestant missions were represented in the Holy Land as early as 1860, when the Kaiserswerth Deaconesses established themselves in Jerusalem. Shortly thereafter the *Jerusalems-Verein* began work in Jerusalem and Bethlehem, and about this same time, 1869, Lutheran missionaries calling themselves Templars settled near Jaffa. Under William II additional impetus was given to German religious activities in the Near East. The *Jerusalems-Verein*, which was taken under the special patronage of the Kaiserin Auguste Victoria, supported a Lutheran clergyman in Jerusalem and was responsible for the erection in the Holy City of the Church of the Redeemer. This same society rapidly spread its activities throughout all of Palestine, and in 1910 it dedicated the famous Kaiserin Auguste Victoria *Stiftung*,[22] erected on the Mount of Olives by the Hohenzollern family at a cost in excess of half a million dollars. The Evangelical Union, organized in 1896, established a large orphanage in Jerusalem, together with schools and related institutions, and proved to be a very useful auxiliary to the work of the Deaconesses in maintaining schools, dispensaries, and hospitals. Also in 1896 there was founded the *Deutsche Orient Mission*, which rendered its services particularly in Cilicia, and which kept up the interest of its supporters at home by the publication in Berlin of a monthly periodical, *Der Christliche Orient*. It was estimated that, during the early years of the twentieth century, the German Protestant societies maintained in Turkey-in-Asia about 450 missionaries and several hundred native assistants at a cost of hundreds of thousands of dollars. By 1910 the Germans occupied a conspicuous position in evangelical missions in the Near East.[23]

The German Catholics were no less zealous than their Protestant compatriots. Although for centuries Italian and French members of the Franciscan order had been preëminent in Catholic missions in Turkey, there was a marked tendency during the last decade of the nineteenth century and the first decade of the twentieth for German members of other religious orders to take an interest in the Near East. This may have been merely the result of a general increase in missionary activity connected with the increasing imperial activities of the German Government. It may have been due to the announced intention of the German Foreign Office to protect Christian missions and missionaries and to the vigorous fulfilment of that promise after the murder of two German Catholic priests in the Chinese province of Shantung. It may have been a natural consequence of the fact that the Prefect of the Propaganda from 1892-1902 was a famous German cardinal.[24] In any event, under the guiding ægis of the *Palästinaverein,* a society for the promotion of Catholic missions in the Holy Land, German Lazarists, Benedictines, and Carmelites established and maintained schools, hospitals, and dispensaries, as well as churches, in Syria and Palestine.[25]

Even Jewish religious interests in Palestine promoted Teutonic peaceful penetration in Turkey. As part of the Zionist activities of *L'Alliance Israelite Universelle,* agricultural colonies were founded by German Jews in the vicinity of Jaffa, Jerusalem, and Haifa. These colonists appeared to be proud of their German nationality and were an integral part of the German community in the Holy Land.[26]

The German Government had no intention of overlooking the political possibilities of this religious penetration. Promotion of missionary activities might be made to serve a twofold purpose: first, to win the support, in domestic politics, of those interested in the propagation of their faith in foreign lands—more particularly to hold the loyalty of the Catholic Centre party; second, to further one other means of strengthening the bonds between Germany and the Ottoman Empire.

An excellent illustration of the inter-relation among economic, political, and religious aspects of modern imperialism is to be found in the visit of William II to Turkey in 1898. On the morning of October 31—the anniversary of the posting of Luther's ninety-five theses at Wittenberg—the Emperor participated in the dedication of the Lutheran Church of the Redeemer in Jerusalem. During the afternoon of the same day he presented the supposed site of the Assumption of the Virgin Mary to the German Catholics of the Holy City, for the construction thereon of a Catholic memorial church, and he telegraphed the Pope expressing his hope that this might be but one step in a steady progress of Catholic Christianity in the Near East. The Kaiser likewise might have visited the German Jewish communities in the vicinity of Jerusalem, but perhaps he felt, as a French writer put it, that such a visit "between his devotions at Gethsemane and at Calvary would have created a public scandal." [27] Nevertheless he did not hesitate, a week later, at Damascus, to assure "three hundred million Mohammedans" that the German Emperor was their friend. Yet with all this pandering to religious interests—to the Protestants of Prussia, to the Catholics of South Germany, to his Moslem hosts—the Kaiser found time ostentatiously to promote the German Consul at Constantinople to the rank of Consul General. And upon his return home he justified all of these activities on the ground that his visit "would prove to be a lasting source of advantage to the German name and German national interests." [28]

This curious admixture of religion and diplomacy was made the more complicated when the Imperial Chancellor informed the Reichstag, on December 7, 1898, that one of the purposes of the Emperor's visit to His Ottoman

Majesty was to make it plain that the German Government did not propose to recognize anywhere "a foreign protectorate over German subjects." This served notice to France that Germany would not respect the French claim to exclusive protection of Catholic missionaries in the Ottoman Empire. "We do not lay claim," said Prince von Bülow, "to a protectorate over all Christians in the East. But only the German Emperor can protect German subjects, be they Catholics or Protestants." [29] This pronouncement was received in France with undisguisedly poor grace. One writer in a prominent fortnightly magazine frankly expressed his disgust: "Germany possesses military power; she possesses economic power; she proposes to acquire maritime power. But she needs the support of moral power. On the world's stage she aspires to play the part of Principle. To base her world-wide prestige upon the protection of Christianity, Protestant and Catholic; to centralize the divergent sources of German influence; to have all over the globe a band of followers, at once religious and economic in their interests, who will propagate the German idea, consume German products, and, while professing the gospel of Christ, will preach the gospel of the sacred person of the Emperor—these are the ultimate ends of the world policy of William II." [30]

Closely allied with the spread of German missions was the propagation of *das Deutschtum*—that is, the spread of the German language, instruction in German history and ideals, appreciation of the character of German civilization. German religious schools in the Near East were dynamos of German cultural influence. The *Jerusalems-Verein* alone, for example, maintained, in 1902, eight schools with more than 430 pupils. In these schools German was taught. This also was the case with the Catholic schools, under German influence. Even the Jews—a large number of whom had emigrated from Germany because of anti-Semitic feeling there—carried with them their German patriotism. The *Hilfsverein der deutschen Juden,* the German section of *L'Alliance Israélite Universelle,* not only taught German in its own schools, but made a strenuous effort to have German adopted as the official language of all Zionist schools in the Near East.[31]

It should be pointed out that this injection of nationalism into religious education was an obvious imitation of the French method of spreading imperial influence in Syria and Palestine. And it was frankly admitted to be an imitation. "A policy of German-Turkish culture," wrote Dr. Rohrbach, "deserves to be pressed with renewed ardor. We must endeavor to make the German language, and German science, and all the great positive values of our energetic civilization, duties faithfully fulfilled—active forces for the regeneration of Turkey by transplanting them into Turkey. To do this we need above everything else a system of German schools, which need not rival the French in magnitude, but which must be planned on a larger scale than that of the now existing schools. No lasting and secure cultural influences are possible without the connecting link of language. The intelligent and progressive young men of Turkey should have an abundant opportunity to learn German. . . . We can give the Turks an impression of our civilization and a desire to become familiar with it only when we teach them our language and thus open the door for them to all of our spiritual possessions. In doing this we are not aiming to Germanize Turkey politically or economically or to colonize it, but to introduce the German spirit into the great national process of development through which that nation, which has a great future, happens to be passing."[32] French methods were to be paid the compliment of imitation.

The sentimental appeal of the Bagdad Railway was more than a religious and cultural appeal alone. The

Great Plan was assiduously promoted by a patriotic and Pan-German press. It caught the interest of the ordinary workaday citizen, whose imagination was fired by the sweeping references to "our" trade, "our" investments, "our" religious interests in the Near East; the Bagdad Railway was the very heart of all these interests. Here was a railway which was to revive a medieval trade route to the East, which was to traverse the route of the Crusades. Here was a country which had been the much-sought-after empire of the great nations of antiquity, Assyria, Chaldea, Babylon, Persia, Greece, Rome. Here had risen and fallen the great cities of Nineveh, Babylon, and Hit. To these regions had turned the longing of the great conquerors, Sargon, Sennacherib, Nebuchadnezzar, Alexander, Saladin. With such materials some German Kipling might evolve phrases far more alluring than Fuzzy Wuzzy, and Tommy Atkins, and the White Man's Burden.[33]

Some Few Voices are Raised in Protest

Not all Germans were dazzled by the Oriental glamor of the Bagdad Railway plan. Herr Scheidemann, leader of the Social Democrats in the Reichstag, time and time again sounded warnings against the complications almost certain to result from the construction of the railway. Speaking before the Reichstag in March, 1911, for example, he said: "We are the last to misjudge the great value of this road to civilization. We know its economic significance: we know that it traverses a region which in antiquity was a fabulously fertile country, and we welcome it as a great achievement if the Bagdad Railway opens up that territory. And if, by gigantic irrigation projects, the land can be made into a granary for Europe, as well as a land to which we could look for an abundant supply of raw materials, such as cotton, that would be doubly welcome." But that is not all, continued Herr Scheidemann. German capitalists would not be able to overlook the military-strategic interests of the line, for only the establishment of a strong centralized government in Turkey "can offer European capitalism the necessary security for the realization of its great capitalistic plans." This military strengthening of Turkey would be almost certain, he pointed out, to arouse the opposition of Great Britain, Russia, and France. Particularly was he desirous of avoiding any additionally irritating relations with Great Britain, for the traditional friendship with that nation had already been seriously compromised by colonial and naval rivalries.[34] Similar warnings were uttered by other Socialists and anti-imperialists.

Quite different in character was the objection raised to the Bagdad Railway by a certain type of more conservative German. An aggressive policy in the Near East naturally would have been distasteful to the diplomatists of the old school, who were disposed to adhere to the Bismarckian principles of isolating France on the Continent and avoiding commercial and colonial conflicts overseas. According to their point of view, German ventures in the Ottoman Empire were certain to lead to two complications: first, the support of Austrian imperial ambitions in the Balkans; second, a German attempt to maintain a dominant political position at Constantinople. Under such circumstances, of course, it would not be possible to bring about a divorce of the newly married France and Russia, for Russian interests in the Near East would brook no compromise on the part of the Tsar's Government. In addition, it was feared, the establishment of German ports on the Mediterranean and on the Persian Gulf would strengthen British antipathy to Germany, already augmented by naval and commercial rivalry. The final outcome of such a situation undoubtedly would be the formation of a Franco-British-Russian coalition against the Central Powers.

During the Great War these views were given wide publicity by Prince Lichnowsky, former German ambassador to Great Britain. In a memorandum, written for a few friends but subsequently published broadcast in Europe and America,[35] the Prince vehemently denounced the *Drang nach Osten* as the greatest of German diplomatic mistakes and as one of the principal causes of the Great War. "We should have abandoned definitely the fatal tradition of pushing the Triple Alliance policies in the Near East," he said; "we should have realized that it was a mistake to make ourselves solidary with the Turks in the south and with the Austro-Magyars in the north; for the continuance of this policy . . . was bound in time, and particularly in case the requisite adroitness should be found wanting in the supreme directing agencies, to lead to the collision with Russia and the World War. Instead of coming to an understanding with Russia on the basis of the independence of the Sultan; . . . instead of renouncing military and political interference, confining ourselves to economic interests in the Near East, . . . our political ambition was directed to the attainment of a dominant position on the Bosporus. In Russia the opinion arose that the way to Constantinople ran *via* Berlin." This was the "fatal mistake, by which Russia, naturally our best friend and neighbor, was driven into the arms of France and England." Furthermore, maintained the Prince, a policy of Near Eastern expansion is contrary to the best commercial and industrial interests of the empire. "'Our future lies on the water.' Quite right"; therefore it does not lie in an overland route to the Orient. The *Drang nach Osten* "is a reversion to the Holy Roman Empire. . . . It is the policy of the Plantagenets, not that of Drake and Raleigh. . . . Berlin-Bagdad is a blind alley and not the way into the open, to unlimited possibilities, to the universal mission of the German nation." [36]

There may have been another reason for the opposition of Prince Lichnowsky to the Bagdad Railway. As the owner of large Silesian estates he was agrarian in his point of view. If it were true, as was maintained, that after the opening of Mesopotamia to cultivation, the Railway would be able to bring cheap Turkish grain to the German market, the results would not be to the liking of the agricultural interests of the empire. As Herr Scheidemann informed the Reichstag, there was something anomalous in the Conservative support of the Bagdad Railway on this score, because it was "in most violent contrast to their procedure in their own country, where they have artificially raised the cost of the necessaries of life by incredibly high protective tariffs, indirect taxation, and similar methods." [37] Perhaps Prince Lichnowsky was somewhat more intelligent and far-sighted than his land-owning associates!

There were some Germans who were not opposed to the Bagdad Railway enterprise, but who were opposed to the extravagant claims made for it by some of its friends and protagonists. A typical illustration of this is the following statement of Count zu Reventlow, shortly before the outbreak of the war: "Great Britain, Russia, and France, in order to interpose objections, made use of the expedient of identifying the *Deutsche Bank* with the German Government. To this there was added the difficult and complicating factor that in Germany itself, in many quarters, the aim and the significance of the railway plan were proclaimed to the world, partly in an inaccurate and grossly exaggerated manner. . . . In this respect great mistakes were made among us, which it was in no way necessary to make. The more quietly the Railway could have been constructed the better. . . . That it would be possible to make Turkey a dangerous threat against Egypt and India, after the development of its railway system, was correct, to be sure, but it was imperative not to say anything of that kind as long as Great Britain still had means to hinder and prevent the construction of the railway." Similar opinions were expressed from time to time on the floor of the Reichstag.[38]

The Bagdad Railway, however, was a triumphant enterprise which would brook no opposition. In the army of its followers marched the stockholders and directors of the *Deutsche Bank*—such men as Edward B. von Speyer, Wolfgang Kapp, Karl von Siemens, Karl Helfferich, Arthur von Gwinner—good patriots all, with a financial stake in the Railway. Then there came the engineers and contractors who furnished the materials and constructed the line and who shared in the profits of its subsidiary enterprises—mines, oil wells, docks, wharves, irrigation works. Next came the shipping interests—the subsidized services of Herr Ballin and the Hamburg-American Line included—which were at once the feeders and the fed of the Railway. There were also the German traders who sought in the Near East a market for their products and the German manufacturers who looked to this newly opened territory for an uninterrupted supply of raw materials. In the line of march, too, were the missionaries, Catholic and Protestant, who sought to promote a renaissance of the Holy Land through the extension of German influence there. Bringing up the rear, although by no means the least important, were the soldiers and the diplomatic and consular officers, those "parasites" of modern imperialism who almost invariably will be found in cordial support of any movement for political and economic expansion. In the reviewing stand, cheering the marchers, were the great mass of average patriotic citizens who were thrilled with "their" Bagdad Railway and "their" *Drang nach Osten.* And the chief of the reviewers was His Imperial Majesty, William II.[39]

If there was a preponderance of opinion in Germany favorable to the Bagdad Railway, there was by no means a similar favorable sentiment in the rest of Europe. Statesmen in the other imperial nations were not unaware of the potentialities of railways constructed in the backward nations of the world. They knew that "railways are the iron tentacles of latter-day expanding powers. They are stretched out caressingly at first. But once the iron has, so to say, entered the soul of the weaker nation, the tentacles swell to the dimensions of brawny arms, and the embrace tightens to a crushing grip." [40] Russia, Great Britain and France, therefore, were gradually led to obstruct the progress of the railway by political and economic means—at least until such time as they could purge the project of its political possibilities or until they could obtain for themselves a larger share of the spoils.

Thus the Bagdad Railway was an imperial enterprise. It became an important concern of the Foreign Office, a matter of national prestige. It was one of the stakes of pre-war diplomacy. Its success was associated with the national honor, to be defended, if need be, by military force and military alliances. The Railway was no longer a railway alone, but a state of mind. Professor Jastrow called it "the spectre of the twentieth century"! [41]

BIBLIOGRAPHICAL AND EXPLANATORY NOTES

[1] *Die Bagdadbahn*, p. 46.

[2] *Stenographische Berichte, XII Legislaturperiode, I Session,* Volume 231 (1908), pp. 4226a, 4253c.

[3] Wile, *op. cit.*, pp. 39-40.

[4] Riesser, *op. cit.*, p. 543; *The Quarterly Review,* Volume 235 (1921), p. 315.

[5] *Parliamentary Debates, House of Lords,* Volume 121 (1903), p. 1348.

⁸For an interesting discussion of this point see George von Siemens, "The National Importance of the Bourse," in *The Nation* (London), October 6, 1900. *Cf.*, also, W. M. Shuster, *The Strangling of Persia: a Record of European Diplomacy and Oriental Intrigue* (New York, 1912).

⁷W. M. Sombart, *Die deutsche Volkswirtschaft in neunzehnten Jahrhundert* (second edition, Berlin, 1909), p. 184.

⁸Regarding early German interest in Near Eastern colonization *cf.* K. A. Sprenger, *Babylonien, das reichste Land in der Vorzeit und das lohnendste Kolonisationsfeld für die Gegenwart* (Heidelberg, 1886); Paul Dehn, *Deutschland und die Orientbahnen* (Munich, 1883); K. Karger, *Kleinasien, ein deutsches Kolonisationsfeld* (Berlin, 1892); *Deutsche Ansprüche an das türkischen Erbe* (Munich, 1896), a symposium including an article by von Moltke.

⁹C. Nawratski, *Die jüdische Kolonisation Palästinas* (Munich, 1914); *Syria and Palestine*, p. 59; *Mesopotamia*, pp. 6-7, 11; *Anatolia*, pp. 4-7.

¹⁰*Supra*, p. 84; H. F. B. Lynch, "The Bagdad Railway," in the *Fortnightly Review*, March 1, 1911, pp. 376-377; A. Brisse, "Les intérêts de l'Allemagne dans l'Empire Ottoman," in *Revue de Géographie*, June, 1902, pp. 486-487; P. Rohrbach, *Die Bagdadbahn*, pp. 17-21, 35.

¹¹*Stenographische Berichte, XII Legislaturperiode, I Session*, Volume 231 (1908), p. 4253c; P. Rohrbach, *Die Bagdadbahn*, p. 16, and *Deutschland unter den Weltvölkern*, pp. 51-53; Von Gwinner, *loc. cit.*, p. 1090.

¹²*Die Bagdadbahn*, p. 16. *Cf.*, also, R. Henry, *Des Montes Bohèmes au Golfe Persique; l'Asie Turque et le Chemin de fer de Bagdad* (Paris, 1908), p. 509 *et seq.;* C. H. Becker, *Deutschland und der Islam* (Stuttgart and Berlin, 1914); Ernst Jäckh, *Die deutsch-türkische Waffenbrüderschaft* (Stuttgart and Berlin, 1915).

¹³H. A. Gibbons, *The Reconstruction of Poland and the Near East* (New York, 1917), pp. 109-110.

¹⁴Quoted by Marriot, *op. cit.*, p. 356.

¹⁵*Die Bagdadbahn*, pp. 18-19.

¹⁶In this connection see an important statement by Sir Thomas Barclay in the *Proceedings of the Central Asian Society* (London), March 1, 1911, pp. 21-22, and the opinion of Karl Helfferich, *Die deutsche Türkenpolitik*, p. 14.

¹⁷Von Reventlow, *op. cit.*, p. 343. Regarding the so-called *Drang nach Osten* and the coincidence of Austrian and German interests in the Near East *cf.* M. Meyer, *Balkanstaaten, Bagdadbahn* (Leipzig, 1914); J. W. Headlam, "The Balkans and Diplomacy," in the *Atlantic Monthly* (Boston), January, 1916, pp. 124

et seq.; N. and C. R. Buxton, *The War and the Balkans* (London, 1915) ; M. I. Newbigin, *Geographical Aspects of Balkan Problems* (London, 1915) ; Evans Lewin, *The German Road to the East* (New York, 1917), Chapters VIII, IX, X; P. N. Milyoukov, *The War and Balkan Politics* (Cambridge, 1917).

[18] *Stenographische Berichte, XII Legislaturperiode, 2 Session,* Volume 266 (1911), p. 5984c.

[19] *Der deutsche Imperialismus und die Arbeiterklasse* (Bremen, 1912), pp. 33, 53.

[20] *Stenographische Berichte, XII Legislaturperiode, 2 Session,* Volume 266 (1911), p. 5984c, Volume 231 (1908), p. 4253c.

[21] Charles Sarolea, *The Anglo-German Problem* (London, 1912), p. 252.

[22] A *Stiftung* is a general religious establishment, this particular one serving manifold purposes as school, hospice, home, hospital, etc.

[23] J. Richter, *A History of Protestant Missions in the Near East* (New York, 1910), pp. 258-270, 416-419; L. M. Garnett, *Turkey of the Ottomans* (London, 1911), Chapters VII-IX; H. C. Dwight, H. A. Tupper, and E. M. Bliss, *Encyclopedia of Missions* (second edition, New York, 1910), pp. 260, 263, 720; *New Schaff-Herzog Encyclopedia of Religious Knowledge* (New York, 1912), Volume XII, pp. 39-41.

[24] Cardinal M. H. Ledochowski (1822-1902). *Cf. Catholic Encyclopedia* (New York, 1912), Volume IX, pp. 111-112. French Catholics openly charged that Cardinal Ledochowski used his official position as director of all Catholic missions to promote German religious and political interests at the expense of those of France. *Cf.* an article "La Politique Allemande et le Protectorat des Missions Catholiques," in the *Revue des deux mondes,* Volume 149 (1898), pp. 11-12.

[25] On the general subject of German Catholic missions in the Near East consult W. Koehler, *Die katholische Kirchen des Morgenlandes* (Darmstadt, 1898) ; H. M. Krose, *Katholische Missionsstatistik* (Freiburg, 1908) ; L. Bréhier, article "Turkish Empire—Missions," in the *Catholic Encyclopedia,* Volume XV, pp. 101-102; L. Bertrand, "La Melée des Religions en Orient," in the *Revue des deux mondes,* Volume 53 (1909), pp. 830-861.

[26] *The Jewish Encyclopedia* (New York, 1906), Volume XII, pp. 286 *et seq.;* Sir C. W. Wilson, *Handbook for Asia Minor* (London, 1895), pp. 240 *et seq.*

[27] Etienne Lamy, "La France du Levant: le Voyage de l'Empereur Guillaume II," in *Revue des deux mondes,* Volume 151 (1899), pp. 336-337; see also Volume 150 (1898), pp. 421-440, 880-911. Further observations on the religious aspects of the Kaiser's trip to Palestine are to be found in *The Times,* Novem-

ber 23, 1898; *Annual Register*, 1898, pp. 255-257; W. von Hohenzollern, *My Memoirs, 1878-1918*, pp. 210-211.

[28] *Annual Register*, 1898, pp. 257-258.

[29] *Ibid.*, p. 261. Regarding the French protectorate of Catholics
in the Near East *cf. infra*, Chapter VII.

[30] "La Politique Allemande et le Protectorat des Missions
Catholiques," in *Revue des deux mondes*, Volume 149 (1898),
pp. 8-9.

[31] L. Bertrand, "Les Écoles d'Orient: I. Les Écoles Chrétiennes
et Israelites," in *Revue des deux mondes*, Volume 52, new series
(1909), pp. 755-794; H. M. Kallen, *Zionism and World Politics*
(Garden City, N. Y., 1921), pp. 117 *et seq.;* A. Paquet, *Die
jüdische Kolonien in Palästina* (Weimar, 1915); M. Blanckenhorn, *Syrien und die deutsche Arbeit* (Weimar, 1916), pp. 26-30;
C. Nawratzki, *Die jüdische Kolonisation Palästinas* (Munich,
1914); M. Franco, *Essai sur l'histoire des juifs de l'empire
ottoman depuis les origines jusqu'à nos jours* (Paris, 1897); G.
Corneilhan, *La judaisme en Egypte et en Syrie* (Paris, 1889).

[32] *German World Policies*, pp. 229-231. On this same general
subject consult an article by "Immanuel," entitled "Die Bagdadbahn ein Kulturwerk in Asien," in *Globus*, Volume 81 (1902),
pp. 181-185; M. Hartmann, *Islam, Mission, Politik* (Leipzig,
1912). It should be pointed out that the Anatolian Railway
itself established two schools, at Haidar Pasha and Eski Shehr,
for the instruction of its employees in German and other subjects. Bohler, *loc. cit.*, p. 275.

[33] That Germans were not unfamiliar with the spectacular history of this region is evidenced by the popularity of General von
Moltke's writings on Turkey, which were published in several
large editions, apart from his collected works, between 1900 and
1911. *Cf., e.g.*, H. K. B. (Graf von) Moltke, *Briefe über Zu-
stände und Begebenheiten in der Türkei aus den Jahren 1835 bis
1839*, seventh edition, with explanatory notes by G. Hirschfeld
(Berlin, 1911). Of this work H. S. Wilkinson, Professor of
Military History at Oxford University, wrote in the *Encyclopedia Britannica* (eleventh edition), "No other book gives so
deep an insight into the character of the Turkish Empire"
(Volume 18, p. 678). It is interesting to note, also, that Moltke
himself was a firm believer in the great military utility of all
railways. For the history of the Near East *cf.* Jastrow, *op. cit.*,
pp. 31-81; A. R. Hall, *The Ancient History of the Near East*
(fourth edition, London, 1919), Chapters V, VIII, IX, X, XII;
W. A. and E. T. A. Wigram, *The Cradle of Mankind* (London,
1914). A curious sidelight on this phase of the question is the
assertion of Baron von Hertling, in 1907, that Germany's chief
interest in the Bagdad Railway was scientific—geographic, geo-

logical, archæological—not military or economic! Quoted by Dawson, *The Evolution of Modern Germany*, p. 346.

[34] *Stenographische Berichte, XII Legislaturperiode, 2 Session,* Volume 266 (1911), p. 5980c.

[35] Karl Maximilan, sixth Prince, Lichnowsky (1860-   ) had been a member of the German diplomatic service since his youth. He was attached to the embassy at London when he was but twenty-five and later served at Constantinople, Bucharest, and Vienna and in the Foreign Office at Berlin. He resigned in 1904 to devote himself to the management of his large estates in Silesia, but he was recalled in 1912 to become German ambassador to Great Britain, succeeding Baron Marschall von Bieberstein, who had died after only a few months' service at his new post. Prince Lichnowsky's memorandum *My London Mission, 1912-1914* was written only to justify the Prince before a small circle of his acquaintances. Fugitive copies reached the press, however, and the full text was published in the Berlin *Börsen-Courier* of March 21, 1918. The quotations here given are from the translation of Munroe Smith, *The Disclosures from Germany* (New York, 1918).

[36] *The Disclosures from Germany*, pp. 37-41, 127.

[37] *Stenographische Berichte, XII Legislaturperiode, 2 Session,* Volume 226 (1911), p. 5980c. *Cf.*, also, W. H. Dawson, *The Evolution of Modern Germany*, pp. 346 *et seq.*

[38] Von Reventlow, *op. cit.*, p. 340; *Stenographische Berichte, XII Legislaturperiode, 2 Session,* Volume 226 (1911), p. 5994b.

[39] Regarding the Emperor's personal interest in the Bagdad Railway consider the following Reuter dispatch, published in *The Near East*, December 6, 1911, p. 143: "By desire of the German Emperor, Herr Gwinner, director of the *Deutsche Bank*, will give an address on the Bagdad Railway before the Emperor and a number of invited guests, in the Upper House of the Prussian Diet soon after the Emperor's return to Berlin, December 8."

[40] E. J. Dillon, quoted by Lothrop Stoddard, *The New World of Islam*, p. 98.

[41] Jastrow, *op. cit.*, p. 9.

CHAPTER VII

RUSSIA RESISTS AND FRANCE IS UNCERTAIN

RUSSIA VOICES HER DISPLEASURE

Russian objections to the Bagdad Railway were put forth as early as 1899, the year in which the Sultan announced his intention of awarding the concession to the *Deutsche Bank*. The press of Petrograd and Moscow roundly denounced the proposed railway as inimical to the vital economic interests of Russia. It was claimed that the new line would offer serious competition to the railways of the Caspian and Caucasus regions, that it would menace the success of the new Russian trans-Persian line, and that it might prove to be a rival even of the Siberian system.[1] The extension of the existing Anatolian Railway into Syria, it was asserted, would interfere with the realization of a Russian dream of a railway across Armenia to Alexandretta—a railway which would give Russian goods access to an all-year warm water port on the Mediterranean. The Mesopotamian sections of the line, with their branches, might open to German competition the markets of Persia and, later, of Afghanistan. If German capital should develop the grain-growing possibilities of the Tigris and Euphrates valleys, what would happen to the profits of the Russian landed aristocracy? And if the oil-wells of Mesopotamia were as rich as they were said to be, what would be the fate of the South Russian fields? The Tsar was urged to oppose the granting of the kilometric guarantee to the concessionaires, on the ground that the increased charges on the Ottoman

Treasury would interfere with payment of the indemnity due on account of the War of 1877.[2]

Russian objections to the Bagdad Railway did not meet with a sympathetic reception in England. *The Engineer,* of August 11, 1899, in an editorial "Railways in Asia Minor," for example, expressed its firm opinion that many of the demands for the protection of Russian economic interests in Turkey were specious. "The world has yet to learn," ran the editorial, "that Russia allows commercial considerations to play any great part in her ideas of constructing railways; the Imperial authorities are influenced mainly by the policy of political expediency. The commercial competition thus foreseen by Russia is put forward merely as a stop-gap until Russia can get time and money to repeat in Asia Minor the methods of which she has made such success in Persia and the Far East." Other British opinion was of like character.

The Russian claim for exclusive control of railway construction in northern Anatolia met with equally bitter denunciation. The London *Globe,* of August 10, 1899, characterized as "impudence" the intention of the Russian Government "to regard Asiatic Turkey as a second Manchuria, on the pretence that the whole country has been mortgaged to Russia for payment of the Turkish war indemnity. If this preposterous claim were admitted, not only the development of Asia Minor but the opening of another short-cut to the East might be delayed until the end of the next century. Russia had so many ambitious and costly projects on hand at present that her nearly bankrupt treasury could not meet any fresh drain, and especially one of such magnitude as that in question. The policy of her Government, therefore, is to preserve Asia Minor as a *tabula rasa* on which the Russian pen can write as it pleases hereafter. It is a cool project, truly, but the success which has attended similar Russian endeavors in the Far East will not, we undertake to predict, meet with repetition."

The Russian Government, meanwhile, was interposing serious objections to the Bagdad Railway. M. Zinoviev, the Tsar's minister at Constantinople, informed the Sublime Porte that the proposed extension of the Anatolian Railways from Angora across Armenia to Mosul and Bagdad would be a strategic menace to the Caucasus frontier and, as such, could not be tolerated. If Russian wishes in the matter were not respected, immediate measures would be taken to collect all arrears—amounting to over 57,000,000 francs—of the indemnity due the Tsar under the Treaty of Berlin (1878). The outcome of these demands was submission by the Sultan's Government. The proposed Angora-Kaisarieh-Diarbekr route was abandoned in favor of one extending from Konia, through the Cilician Gates of the Taurus Mountains, to Adana, Aleppo, and Mosul—the latter being the route over which the Bagdad Railway actually was constructed. The discussions between the Russian and Ottoman Governments subsequently were crystallized and confirmed by the so-called Black Sea Agreement of 1900, which pledged the Sultan to award no further concessions for railways in northern Anatolia or Armenia except to Russian nationals or to syndicates approved by the Tsar, and, furthermore, to award such Russian concessionaires terms at least as favorable as those to be granted the Bagdad Railway Company.[3]

The agreement thus reached, however, satisfied Russia only temporarily. In December, 1901, M. Witte, Imperial Minister of Finance at Petrograd, stated categorically that he considered the construction of the Bagdad Railway by any Power other than Russia a menace to the imperial interests of the Tsar. Proposals for the internationalization of the line he asserted to be chimerical; in his opinion

the nationals of one Power would be certain to control the
administration of the enterprise. The Tsar was determined that Russian capitalists should have nothing to do
with the Railway; Russian capital, for a time at least,
should be conserved for industrial development at home.
"The Government of Russia," he concluded, "is more interested in devoting its available resources to the construction of new railways within the Empire than it is in
promoting an enterprise destined to offer competition to
Russia's railways and industries." [4]   In 1902 and again
in 1903, M. Witte made similar statements, asserting that
he saw no reason for changing his point of view.[5]

Witte's words carried weight in Russia. As an erstwhile railway worker he knew the great economic importance of railways. During his régime as Minister of
Finance (1893-1903) an average of 1,400 miles of rails
was laid down annually in Russia; the Transcaspian and
Transcaucasian systems were constructed, and the Siberian
Railway was pushed almost to completion. He foresaw
that one day these railways would be powerful weapons
in the commercial and political expansion of an industrialized Russia. As an official in charge of troop movements during the Russo-Turkish War of 1877 he had
learned to understand the function of railways in offensive
and defensive warfare. Although he considered it waste-
ful to construct railways for military purposes alone, he
believed that every railway was of strategic value; in fact,
he looked upon railways as the most important single
factor in national preparedness. As the foremost protagonist of Russia's tariff war with the German Empire he
was opposed to any plan which promised to promote German commerce and to open up new resources and new
markets to German industry. As a native of the Caucasus
region and as an ardent advocate of colonial expansion
Witte looked forward to the time when Russia herself—

possessed of capital for the purpose—should dominate the transportation system of Asiatic Turkey.[6]

It is questionable, however, if the Bagdad Railway really threatened any important Russian economic interests. The railways of southern Russia, so far from being injured by competition with the proposed new railways of Turkey, would be almost certain to profit from any increase of trade in the region of the Black Sea. The Russian dream of a railway to Alexandretta was still very much of a dream; but even if the contrary had been the case, its construction for peaceful purposes would not have been hindered by the Bagdad plan. The claim that a trans-Mesopotamian railway would compete with the Far Eastern traffic of the Siberian Railways was purely fantastic; it overlooked the obvious fact that an ideal shipping route, like a straight line, is the shortest distance between two points. It would be at least a generation before Mesopotamian grain and oil could play a prominent part in the Russian market.[7]

But with Russian political interests the case was different. Ever since the days of Peter the Great, the Russian Tsars had persistently and relentlessly continued their efforts to obtain a "window" on the Mediterranean. This historical trend toward the open sea led to a well-defined intention on the part of Russia, in one way or another, to take Constantinople from the Turks. The dynastic interests of Russia were reënforced by commercial considerations. "Most of Russia's southern trade is bound to pass through the Bosporus. Her wheat and hides, her coal and oil cannot reach the European markets any other way; her manganese and petroleum are inaccessible to other nations if they cannot find an outlet from the Caucasus to the Dardanelles." During the Turco-Italian War the closing of the Straits for a few days was said to have cost Russian shipping about eight million francs.[8]

Bonds of religion and race enlisted Russian sympathy in the struggle of the Balkan states to win independence from Turkey—a cause which harmonized with the Russian ambition to bring about the disintegration of Turkey-in-Europe. The rise of German influence at Constantinople —of which the Anatolian and Bagdad Railway concessions were a tangible manifestation—had been a source of annoyance to Russia, not only because it prevented Russian domination of Turkish affairs and because it strengthened the position of Austria-Hungary in the Balkans, but also because it tended to strengthen Turkish military power. It was annoying enough to witness the rising political and economic power of Germany in the Near East; it was more annoying to realize that, under German guidance, the Turks might experience an economic and military renaissance which would end once and for all the Russian hope of possessing ancient Byzantium.

Strategically the construction of the Bagdad Railway was a real menace to Russian ambitions in the Near East. The completion of the line would enable the Ottoman Government to effect a prompt mobilization along the Armenian front. For example, the Fifth Turkish Army Corps, from Damascus, and the Sixth Corps, from Bagdad—which in the War of 1877 arrived on the field after a series of forced marches, minus a large number of its effectives, too late to save Kars or to raise the siege of Erzerum—could be brought quickly by rail from Syria and Mesopotamia to Angora for the defence of northern Anatolia. In the event of a Russo-Turkish war such a maneuver would render extremely precarious a Russian invasion of Armenia or a Russian advance on Constantinople along the south shore of the Black Sea. In a general European war in which both Russia and Turkey might be involved the existence of this railway line would make possible a Turkish stroke at the southern frontier of Russia, thus diverting troops from the European front. That the German General Staff was not ignorant of these possibilities is certain because of the presence in Turkey, during this time, of General von der Goltz.[9]

The Russian Government and the Russian press were fully aware of the menace of the Bagdad Railway to Russian imperial interests. That the Tsar did not offer serious resistance to the construction of the line was due to the rise of serious complications in the Far East, the crushing defeats of his army and navy in the War with Japan, friction with Great Britain in Persia and in Central Asia, and the outbreak of a revolutionary movement at home. But the Russian press called upon French citizens to show their loyalty to the Alliance by refusing to participate in the financing of the Railway.[10]

The plaintive call of the Russians, however, did not fall on altogether sympathetic ears in the Republic; a conflict of interests led some French citizens to invest in the Railway even though it was denounced by their Government.

The French Government Hesitates

The position of France in the Bagdad Railway controversy was anomalous. In addition to political, economic, and religious reasons for opposing the construction of the trans-Mesopotamian railway, the French had many historical and sentimental interests which influenced the Government of the Republic to resist German penetration in the Near East. French patriots recalled with pride the rôle of France in the Crusades; they remembered that Palestine itself was once a Latin kingdom; they believed that Christians in the Levant looked to France as their protector and that this protection had received formal recognition under the Capitulations, negotiated by Francis I and renewed and extended by his successors from Henry IV to Louis XV. They knew that the French language was the language not only of the educated classes in Turkey, but, also, in Syria, of the traders, so that it could be said that a traveler in Syria might almost consider himself in a French dependency. They were proud of the fact that the term "Frank" was the symbol of Western civilization in the Near East. They were aware of the far-reaching educational work of French missionaries. France, to their mind, had done a great work of Christian enlightenment in the Moslem stronghold, Turkey. Was the Government of the Republic to be backward in asserting the interests of France, when Bourbons and Bonapartes had so ably paved the way for the extension of French civilization in the Holy Land? Reasoning of this kind was popular in France during 1898 and 1899, when the Kaiser's visit to Abdul Hamid was still under discussion and when the first indications were given that a German company was to be awarded a concession for the construction of a railway from Constantinople to the Persian Gulf.

On the other hand, however, there was a considerable and a powerful group in France which urged the French Government, if not to support the project of the Bagdad Railway, at least to put no obstacles in its way. The members of this group were French financiers with investments in Turkey. They believed that the construction of the Railway would usher in a new era of prosperity in the Ottoman Empire which would materially increase the value of the Turkish securities which they owned. If the interests of these financiers were not supported by historical traditions and nationalist sentiment, they were tangible and supported by imposing facts. It was estimated, in 1903, that French investors controlled three-fifths, amounting to a billion and a half of francs, of the public obligations of the Imperial 'Ottoman Treasury. French promoters owned about 366 million francs in the securities of Turkish railroads and over 162 millions in various industrial and commercial enterprises in Asia Minor. French banks had approximately 176 million francs invested in their branches in the Near East. The total of all French investments in Turkey was more than two and a half billion francs.[11] The French-controlled Imperial Ottoman Bank, the French-owned Smyrna-Cassaba Railway, and the French-administered Ottoman Public Debt Council all favored the promotion of the Bagdad Railway idea.

For a time, the French Government decided to follow the lead of the financial interests. French bankers, in 1899, had entered into an agreement with the *Deutsche Bank* to operate the Anatolian and Smyrna-Cassaba systems under a joint rate agreement, to coöperate in the construction of the Bagdad Railway, and to attempt to secure diplomatic support for their respective enterprises.[12] At the request of the Imperial Ottoman Bank, M. Constans, the French Ambassador at Constantinople, adopted a policy of "benevolent neutrality" toward the negotiations of the *Deutsche Bank* with the Ottoman Ministry of Public Works. This course was approved by M. Delcassé, Minister of Foreign Affairs, who considered the Bagdad Railway harmless because French capitalists were to participate in its construction and operation. Just how much this diplomatic non-interference assisted the *Deutsche Bank* in obtaining the concessions of 1899 and 1903 is an open question. It is extremely doubtful if French objections could have blocked the award of the concessions, although M. Chéradame subsequently maintained that the consummation of the plans of the *Deutsche Bank* would have been impossible without the tacit coöperation of the French embassy at Constantinople.[13]

Between 1899 and 1902 the proposed Bagdad Railway was discussed occasionally by French publicists, but it could not have been considered a matter of widespread popular interest. In the spring of the latter year, however, immediately after the award of the first Bagdad concession by the Sultan, a bitter protest was voiced in the Chamber of Deputies against the policy of the French Government. M. Firmin Fauré, a deputy from Paris, introduced a resolution that "the issue of debentures, stocks, or bonds designed to permit the construction of the Bagdad Railway shall not be authorized in French territory except by vote of the Chamber of Deputies." In a few words M. Fauré denounced the Bagdad Railway plan as a menace to French prestige in the Near East and as a threat against Russian security in the Caucasus. He believed, furthermore, that Bagdad Railway bonds would be an unsafe investment: "It is a Panama that is being prepared down there. Do you choose, perchance, my dear colleagues, to allow French capital to be risked in this scheme without pronouncing it foolhardy? Do you choose to allow the great banks and the great investment syndicates to realize considerable profits at the expense of the small subscribers? If that is how you attend to the defence of French capital, well and good, but you will permit me to disagree with you." He warned the members of the Chamber that they would not dare to stand for reëlection if they thus allowed the interests of their constituents to be prejudiced.[14]

M. Delcassé, Minister of Foreign Affairs, objected to the resolution. He denied that French diplomacy had assisted the German bankers in securing the Bagdad Railway concession.[15] But the concession was a *fait accompli,* and it also was a fact that French financiers felt they could not afford to refuse the offer of participation with the German concessionaires. "I venture to ask how it can be prevented, and I inquire of the Chamber whether, when such an enterprise has been arranged and decided upon, it is not preferable that French interests, so considerable in the East, should be represented therein." He promised that every possible precaution would be taken to assure French capitalists a share in the enterprise equal to that of any other power. The Minister was upheld, the motion being defeated by a vote of 398 to 72.[16]

Less than two years later, in October, 1903, the Paris Bourse, at the instigation of the French Government, excluded all Bagdad Railway securities from the privileges of the Exchange. This change in policy was not so much the result of a *volte face* on the part of M. Rouvier and M. Delcassé as it was a consequence of a persistent clamor on the part of the French press that the construction of the Bagdad Railway, which was popularly considered a serious menace to French interests, should be obstructed by every effective method at the disposal of the Government.[17]

French Interests are Believed to be Menaced

The commercial interests of southern France were opposed to participation in the Bagdad Railway by the French Government or by French capitalists. Business men were fearful, for example, lest "the new route to India" should divert traffic between England and the East from the existing route across Europe *via* Calais to Marseilles and thence by steamer to Suez, to a new express service from Calais to Constantinople *via* Ostend, Cologne, Munich, and Vienna. Thus the importance of the port of Marseilles would be materially decreased, and French railways would lose traffic to the lines of Central Europe. Also, there was some feeling among the manufacturers of Lyons that the rise of German economic power in Turkey might interfere with the flow to France of the cheap raw silk of Syria, almost the entire output of which is consumed in French mills. The fears of the silk manufacturers were emphasized by one of the foremost French banks, the *Crédit Lyonnais,* which maintained branches in Jaffa, Jerusalem, and Beirut, for the purpose of financing silk and other shipments. This bank had experienced enough competition at the hands of the *Deutsche Palästina Bank* to assure it that further German interference was dangerous.[18]

From the political point of view there was more to be said for the French objections. Foremost among serious international complications was the strategic menace of the Railway to Russia. The Bagdad enterprise was described as the "anti-Russian maneuver *par excellence.*" To weaken Russia was to undermine the "foundation stone of French foreign policy," for it was generally conceded that "the Alliance was indispensable to the security of both nations; it assured the European equilibrium; it was the essential counterbalance to the Triple Alliance."[19] Then, too, the question of prestige was involved! In the great game of the "balance of power" an imperial advance by one nation was looked upon as a humiliation for another! Thus a German success in Turkey, whether gained at the expense of important French interests or not, would have been considered as reflecting upon the glory of France abroad! There was also a menace to France in a rejuvenated Turkey. A Sultan freed from dependence upon the Powers might effectively carry on a Pan-Islamic propaganda which would lead to serious discontent in the French colonial empire in North Africa. What would be the consequences if the Moors should answer a call to a Holy War to drive out the infidel invaders?[20]

Still more fundamental, perhaps, than any of these

reasons was the fear among far-sighted French diplomatists that the Bagdad Railway would be but the first step in a formal political alliance between Germany and Turkey. The French, more than any other European people, have been schooled in the political ramifications of foreign investments. The very foundations of the Russian Alliance, for example, were loans of French bankers to Russian industries and to the Tsar. Might not Baron Marschall von Bieberstein and Karl Helfferich, Prince von Bülow and Arthur von Gwinner, tear a leaf out of the book of French experience? Certainly the way was being paved for a Turco-German alliance, and M. Deschanel eloquently warned his colleagues in the Chamber of Deputies that there were limitless possibilities in the situation. Speaking in the Chamber on November 19, 1903, he said: "Behold a railway that can divert from the Suez Canal a part of the traffic of the Far East, so that the railways of Central Europe will become the competitors of Marseilles and of our French railways! Behold a new colonial policy which, instead of conquering territories by force of arms, makes war with funds; possesses itself of the means of communication; crushes out the life of states, little by little, by the artifices of the financiers, leaving them only a nominal existence! And we, who possess the world's greatest fund of *capital, that supreme weapon of modern conquest,* we propose to place it at the disposal of foreign interests hostile to our fundamental and permanent foreign policies! Alas, it is not the first time that our capital has gone to nourish rival, even hostile, schemes!" [21]

Religious interests supported the political and economic objections to the construction of the Bagdad Railway. French Clericals were fearful lest this railway become the very backbone of German interests in the Ottoman Empire, thus strengthening German missionary activities and jeopardizing the time-honored protectorate of France over Catholics in the Near East. As early as 1898 an anonymous writer sounded a clarion call to Catholics and nationalists alike that German economic penetration in Turkey was a matter of their common concern: "Preeminent in the Levant, thanks to the friendship of the Sultan and to the progress of the commerce of her nationals, Germany, if she gathers in, besides, our religious heritage, will crown her formidable material power with an enormous moral power; she will assume in the world the eminent place which Charlemagne, St. Louis, Francis I, Richelieu, Louis XIV, and Napoleon have assured to our country. The 'nationalization' of missions will inaugurate a period of German supremacy in the Orient, where the name of France has been so great and where it still is so loved." [22]

France occupied a unique position in the Near East. For centuries she had been recognized as shouldering a special responsibility in the protection of Catholics and of Catholic missions in the Ottoman Empire. This protectorate—which as late as 1854 had provided the occasion for a war between the empire of Napoleon III and Russia—had been acquired not by military conquest alone, but by outstanding cultural and religious services as well.[23]

Certainly at the end of the nineteenth century French missions held a preëminent position in Turkey. French Jesuits and Franciscans maintained elementary, secondary, and vocational schools in Aleppo, Damascus, Beirut, Jerusalem, and numerous smaller towns throughout Syria and Palestine. A Jesuit school established at Beirut in 1875 rapidly expanded its curricula until it obtained recognition as a university, its baccalaureate degree being accredited by the French Ministry of Public Instruction early in the decade of the eighties. The medical faculty of this Jesuit University—said to have been founded under the patronage of Jules Ferry and Léon Gambetta—was given authority to grant degrees, which were recognized officially by France in 1888 and by Turkey in 1898. In addition to the classical and medical courses, instruction was given in law, theology, philosophy, and engineering. A preparatory school, conducted in connection with the university, had an enrollment of about one thousand pupils. By 1907 it was estimated that over seventy thousand Syrian children were receiving instruction in French religious schools. In addition to these educational accomplishments mention should be made of the work of the Sisters of St. Joseph of the Apparition and the Society of St. Vincent de Paul, who made Jerusalem, Bethlehem, and other towns centers of French religious and philanthropic activity.[24]

The progress of German missions and schools was a challenge to the paramount position of France in the cultural development of the Near East. And it was not a challenge which was passed unanswered. To counteract the influence of German schools established, with the aid of the Railway Company, at a few of the more important points along the Anatolian lines, French missionary schools were established at Eski Shehr, Angora, and Konia.[25]

Furthermore, German missions seemed to bring with them an additional threat—an attempt to discredit the French claim to an exclusive protectorate over Catholics in the Ottoman Empire. As early as 1875 the German Government declared that "it recognized no exclusive right of protection of any power in behalf of Catholic establishments in the East," and that "it reserved its rights with regard to German subjects belonging to any of these establishments."[26] This position appeared to be strengthened by Article 62 of the Treaty of Berlin (1878), which affirmed that "ecclesiastics, pilgrims, and monks of all nationalities traveling in Turkey shall enjoy the same rights, advantages, and privileges. The official right of protection of the diplomatic and consular agents of the Powers in Turkey is recognized, with regard both to the above-mentioned persons and to their religious, charitable, and other establishments in the Holy Places and elsewhere." [27]

In 1885 it was proposed that the Sultan should appoint his own emissary to the Vatican, thus rendering supererogatory the time-honored procedure of transacting all affairs of the Church through the French embassy at Constantinople. French Catholics immediately charged that this proposal emanated from Berlin and did everything possible to oppose its acceptance. Italian and German influences in Rome heartily supported the idea of direct communications between the Vatican and the Porte, but Pope Leo XIII and Cardinal Rampolla finally decided against maintaining diplomatic relations with the Infidel.[28]

Largely as a result of Italian insistence that the rights of the diplomatic and consular agents of the Kingdom be given recognition, it was considered advisable for the Pope to state definitely his position on the French protectorate. This he did in an encyclical of May 22, 1888, *Aspera rerum conditio,* which informed all Catholic missionaries in the Levant that "the Protectorate of the French Nation in the countries of the East has been established for centuries and sanctioned even by treaties between the empires. Therefore there must be absolutely no innovation in this matter; this Protectorate, wherever it is in force, is to be religiously preserved, and the missionaries are warned that, if they have need of any help, they are to have recourse to the consuls and other ministers of France." [29]   In a letter dated August 1, 1898, addressed to Cardinal Langénieux, Archbishop of Rheims, Leo XIII again confirmed this opinion: "France has a special mission in the East confided to her by Providence—a noble mission consecrated not alone by ancient usage, but also by international treaties. . . . The Holy See does not wish to interfere with the glorious patrimony which France has received from its ancestors, and which beyond a doubt it means to deserve by always showing itself equal to its task." [30] No more sweeping confirmation of French rights could have been desired.

The German Government, however, was by no means willing to accept these pronouncements as final. In the name of nationalism German unification was accomplished ; in the name of nationalism German missionaries abroad must look to their own Government for protection. To admit a foreign claim to the protectorate of Germans was to stain the national honor. To accede to the French pre-tension that Catholic Germans occupied an inferior posi-tion in the East was to decrease the prestige of German citizenship. The Shantung incident was a noisy demon-stration of the intention of the German Empire to recog-nize no such distinctions. The visit of the Kaiser to the Sultan in the same year, 1898, was directly concerned with the determination of *Wilhelmstrasse* to assert the secular rights of German missionaries, Catholics as well as Protestants.[31]

French Catholics denied the German claims and worked upon national sentiment at home to add to the growing fear of German imperial aggrandizement. "Catholic missions," it was asserted, "by their very nature and pur-pose are a supra-national institution, similar to the sov-ereign majesty of the Pope." What could be the purpose of the Germans in asserting the doctrine of the "nation-alization of missions," if it were not to undermine French influence in Turkey? How great would be the national humiliation if the protectorate of the Faithful in the East should pass from the hands of Catholic France to Protestant Prussia! The Germans, too, were prejudicing the Holy See against the Republic. A notoriously pro-German party at the Vatican, supported by their political allies, the Italians, were winning the sympathies of the Pope by insinuating references to "red France," "schismatic Russia," and "heretical England"! Thus was a dark plot being hatched against France and against the unity of Christendom! [32]

This situation was not without its advantages to the French Clericals. Between the years 1899 and 1905, when the Bagdad Railway controversy was at its height, a serious domestic controversy was raging in France. In a bitter fight to extirpate Clericalism the Republican ministries of Waldeck-Rousseau and Émile Combes had put through law after law to curb the power of the Church and to break up the influence of the religious orders. The Clericals were waging a losing battle. But perhaps the last crushing blows might be warded off by resorting to a favorite maneuver of Louis Napoleon—the diversion of popular attention from domestic affairs to foreign policy. If Republicans and Monarchists, Socialists and bourgeois Liberals, Radicals and Conservatives, Free-Masons and Clericals, could be aroused against the German advance in Turkey, a common outburst of national pride might obscure, for a time at least, the domestic war on organized Catholicism. Therefore Clerical writers in France warned of the menace of the Bagdad Railway to the Russian Alliance, to the advance of French commerce, and to the ancient prerogatives in the East. "It is Germany, preëminent at Constantinople," said an anonymous writer in the *Revue des deux mondes,* "which blocks the future of Pan-Slavism in the East; it is Germany, installed in Kiao-chau, which can forestall Muscovite expansion toward the Pacific; it is Germany which, in the East and Far East, seeks to undermine our religious protectorate.

Faced by the same adversary, it is natural that France and Russia should build up a common defence." That France should not desert her ally Russia or her own prerogatives in the protectorate of Near Eastern missions is self-evident. "The protectorate over Catholics is for us, in short, a source of material advantage!" [33]

THE BAGDAD RAILWAY CLAIMS FRENCH SUPPORTERS

The Bagdad Railway was not without friends in France. The French chairman of the Ottoman Public Debt Administration was an enthusiastic supporter of the project and served on the Board of Directors of the Bagdad Railway Company, for he believed that widespread railway construction was essential to the establishment, upon a firm basis, of Turkish credit. The French-controlled Imperial Ottoman Bank, as early as 1899, had agreed to participate in the financing of the Bagdad line, and an officer of the bank had accepted the position of vice-president of the Bagdad Railway Company at the time of its incorporation in 1903. The French owners of important railways in Anatolia and Syria believed it would be suicidal for them to obstruct the plans of the *Deutsche Bank* and preferred to coöperate with the German concessionaires. Unless the French opponents of the Bagdad Railway were prepared to offer these interests material compensation for resisting its construction, it was hardly likely that, hard-headed business men as they were, they would jeopardize the security of their investments for the sake of such intangible items as international prestige and protectorates of missions.

There were two important groups of French-owned railways in Turkey-in-Asia. In Anatolia there was the important Smyrna-Cassaba system, extending east and north-east from the French-developed port of Smyrna.

At Afiun Karahissar the main line of this system from Smyrna connected with the Anatolian line from Constantinople to Konia. Therefore a route for French trade already existed to all of Asia Minor; and when the Bagdad Railway was completed, direct service could be instituted from Smyrna to Adana, Aleppo, Mosul, Bagdad, and Basra. The second group of French railways was the Syrian system, owned by *La Société Ottomane du Chemin de fer Damas-Hama et Prolongements*. This company operated railway lines from Aleppo to Damascus, from Tripoli to Homs, from Beirut to Damascus, from Jaffa to Jerusalem, and between other less important points. After the completion of the Bagdad Railway this group of railways would have direct connections, at Aleppo, with all of Europe *via* Constantinople and with the Indies *via* Basra and the Persian Gulf. Perhaps the French interests controlling these railways were chagrined at their inability to secure the trans-Mesopotamian concession for themselves. But faced with the *fait accompli* of the German concession, they realized that coöperation with the Bagdad Railway would make their lines an integral part of a greater system of rail communications within Turkey and also between Turkey and the nations of Europe and Farther Asia. Refusal to coöperate would be cutting off their noses to spite their faces.[34]

French bankers were disposed to look at the Bagdad enterprise in much the same light. The economic renaissance of Turkey, which it was hoped would be an effect of improved rail communications, would increase the value of their earlier investments in that country. But, in addition, the Bagdad Railway offered handsome profits in itself: profits of promoting the enterprise and floating the various bond issues; profits of the construction company, in which French capital was to participate; profits of the shareholders when the Railway should become a going concern. True, the Council of Ministers had requested the Bourse to outlaw the Bagdad securities. But, after all, when profits are at stake, what is a mere resolution of the Cabinet among friends? A syndicate of French financiers invested heavily in the bonds and stock of the Bagdad Railway Company, the hostility of their Government notwithstanding. And it was said that one of the bankers who participated in the syndicate was none other than M. Rouvier, Minister of Finance in the Cabinet of M. Combes, and subsequently Prime Minister.[35]

Many intelligent French students of foreign affairs felt that a merely obstructionist policy on the part of France toward the Bagdad Railway would be futile and, in the end, disastrous. In spite of the many historical and sentimental attachments of France in the Near East, she really had no vital interests which were jeopardized by the Bagdad enterprise. It was urged, therefore, that she should play the rôle of conciliator of the divergent interests of Russia, Great Britain, Germany, and Turkey. A forward-looking program, it was suggested, would be to urge these nations to reach a full and equitable agreement in the promotion of "a project unquestionably valuable in the progress of the whole human race." National material interests should be merged in "the superior interests of civilization." Mere self-interest demanded this of France, because, should a war break out over the Near Eastern question, France would most certainly become involved.[36]

As regards the claims of Russia to influence French policy in the Bagdad Railway affair, there was a considerable amount of irritability exhibited by French publicists. It was pointed out, for example, that M. Witte was unwilling to accept "internationalization" of the Railway at a time when the German and French bankers were prepared to effect a satisfactory settlement on that basis.

It was asserted, also, that Russian strategic interests were adequately safeguarded when the northern route was abandoned by the Black Sea Basin Agreement of 1900. So far from decreased difficulties of Turkish mobilization constituting a menace to Russia, "Russia still had both the power and, apparently, the inclination to be a formidable menace to Turkey." [37] How could the Colossus of the Caucasus tremble before the Sick Man!

One French writer was frank in advocating that France should pursue a course independent of Russia in this instance. "The St. Petersburg press," he wrote, "has asserted vehemently that we are unjust to support an enterprise which will injure considerably the economic interests of Russia, which will seriously prejudice its grain trade, and create a ruinous competitor to Russian railways now projected. Of what use is the Franco-Russian Alliance if our policy runs counter to Russian interests?

"We are particularly pleased to answer the question. The Franco-Russian Alliance does not imply complete servility on the part of France toward Russia, or annihilation of all free will, or perpetual agreement on matters of finance. After having furnished our ally with almost seven billion francs, we find ourselves called upon to support her policies in the Far East, although we ourselves were abandoned and isolated in the Fashoda affair. It will be well for us now to think of ourselves somewhat, although respecting scrupulously, even cordially, the clauses of the contract of alliance. . . . It is in our own interests to coöperate with Germany in the Bagdad enterprise. It is extremely regrettable that we cannot carry it out ourselves; but since it is otherwise, we should make the most of the conditions." [38]

It is said that M. Delcassé, French Minister of Foreign Affairs, certainly no friend of German imperial designs, never really was hostile to the Bagdad Railway and its affiliated enterprises. As Bismarck welcomed French colonial activities in Africa and China as a means of diverting French attention from the Rhine and the Vosges, so Delcassé hoped that the colossal Bagdad plan would absorb all German imperial inclinations, leaving Morocco an exclusive sphere of French influence. In the construction of railways in the Ottoman Empire, Germany might satisfy her "irresistible need for expansion," without menacing vital French interests. And all the while the *Quai d'Orsay,* through the French representatives on the Board of Directors of the Bagdad Railway Company, could be kept fully informed of the progress of the German concessionaires and the purpose of the German diplomatic agents interested in the success of the project.[39]

There were other ardent French nationalists who felt very much the same way about it. However, in their opinion, it would be unwise to gamble on the complete absorption of Germany in her *Bagdadbahn.* It would be wiser, perhaps, to withhold financial support until such time as the German Foreign Office was willing to execute a formal treaty conferring upon France an exclusive sphere of interest in Morocco. Bagdad was to be had for the asking—but in exchange for Morocco! It is said that in 1905, after the fall of Delcassé and on the eve of the Algeciras Conference, M. Rouvier, Prime Minister of France, approached the German ambassador in Paris with a view to negotiating a Franco-German agreement granting Germany a free hand in Turkey in return for recognition of the special interests of France in Morocco.[40]

M. André Tardieu revived this suggestion two years later. "Germany needs capital," he said. "And when one needs capital, it is to France that one comes in search of it. It is inevitable, necessary, therefore, that Germany come to us. She will be obliged to come to us sooner or later to seek our capital for the Bagdad enterprise. Germany has the concession. She has commenced the lines. But all the sections requiring the greatest engineering skill are still to be constructed, and she has not the money to construct them." If France agrees to let Germany have the necessary funds, it will be on the condition that Germany allow France important compensations. "Where will these compensations be sought? I have no hesitation in saying, in Morocco. The Act of Algeciras must be set aside, and France must have a free hand in Morocco! An agreement upon the Bagdad question would be mischievous if it concerned Bagdad alone, for, the Germans having the concession in their pockets, the positions of the negotiators would not be equal. On the other hand, if the agreement is for two purposes, if it refers to Bagdad *and* Morocco, I believe, I repeat, it would be both practicable and desirable." [41]

The proposal that French consent to the Bagdad Railway could be purchased with compensations in North Africa met with no enthusiasm in Germany. Herr Bassermann, leader of the National Liberals in the Reichstag, urged the Foreign Office to meet any such diplomatic maneuver on the part of France with a sharp rebuff. [42] At the time of the Agadir crisis, furthermore, Baron Marschall von Bieberstein is said to have warned Bethmann-Hollweg that Germany would have to stand firm on Morocco, for "if, notwithstanding Damascus and Tangier, we abandon Morocco, we lose at one blow our position in Turkey, and with it the advantages and prospects for the future which we have acquired painfully by years of toil." [43]

It was not until 1914 that an agreement was reached between France and Germany on Asiatic Turkey. For more than ten years, then, the Bagdad Railway was a stinging irritant in the relations between the Republic and the Empire. It aggravated an open wound which needed, not salt, but balm. We shall return later to consider its consequences. But in the meantime we must turn our attention to Great Britain, standing astride the Persian Gulf and blocking the way.

BIBLIOGRAPHICAL AND EXPLANATORY NOTES

[1] Regarding Russian railways in the Near East *cf.* the article "Russia—Railways," in the *Encyclopedia Britannica*, 11th edition, Volume 23, p. 891. The trans-Persian railway from Resht, a Persian port on the Caspian, to Teheran was completed in September, 1899. *Cf.* "Russia's Tightening Grip on Persia," in *The Globe* (London), August 24, 1899; also "Russian Railways in Asia," *The Financial News* (London), August 14, 1899. The Bagdad Railway frequently was referred to in the French and Russian press as the *Petit Transasiatique*.

[2] Foreign correspondence of *The Globe*, July 28, 1899; *Commerce* (London), August 2, 1899; articles quoted from the *Novoe Vremya* in *The Globe*, August 10, 1899; *The Engineer* (London), August 11, 1899; *The Observer*, August 13, 1899; R. Henry, "L'intérêt française en Asie occidentale—Le chemin de fer de Bagdad et l'alliance franco-russe," in *Questions diplomatiques et coloniales*, Volume 15 (1903), pp. 673-688.

[3] *Corps de droit ottoman*, Volume IV, pp. 64 *et seq.;* Paul Imbert, "Le chemin de fer de Bagdad," in *Revue des deux mondes*, 5 period, Volume 38 (1907), pp. 657-659.

[4] Quoted by Georges Mazel, *Le chemin de fer de Bagdad* (Montpelier, 1911), p. 324. It should be remembered that Russia at this time was experiencing the Industrial Revolution. *Cf.* James Mavor, *An Economic History of Russia*, Volume II (Toronto, 1914), Book VI.

[5] *Annual Register*, 1902, p. 323; 1903, pp. 293-294.

[6] *Memoirs of Count Witte*, edited and translated by A. Yarmolinsky (Garden City, 1921), pp. 75 *et seq.*; G. Drage, *Russian Affairs* (London, 1904), pp. 507 *et seq.*; A. Sauzède, "Le développement des voies ferrées en Russie," in *Questions diplomatiques et coloniales*, Volume 37 (1914), pp. 272-281; F. H. Skrine, *The Expansion of Russia* (Cambridge, 1904), *passim.*

[7] Bohler, *loc. cit.*, pp. 294-295; Gervais-Courtellemont, "La question du chemin de fer de Bagdad," in *Questions diplomatiques et coloniales*, Volume 23 (1907), pp. 499-507.

[8] Baron S. A. Korff, *Russia's Foreign Relations during the Last Half Century* (New York, 1922), pp. 133-134.

[9] Rohrbach, *Die Bagdadbahn,* pp. 10-13; Imbert, *loc. cit.,* p. 678. Enthusiastic Turks believed that, with adequate rail communications, Erzerum might be transformed into a Turkish Belfort. *Cf.* Mazel, *op. cit.,* p. 37. Had the Bagdad Railway and the projected railways of northern Anatolia been completed before the outbreak of the Great War, the Turks could have made a more effective defence in the Caucasus campaign of the Grand Duke Nicholas in 1916.

[10] For a general statement of the attitude of Russia and the Balkan States to the Bagdad Railway *cf.* Alexandre Ilitch, *Le chemin de fer de Bagdad, ou l'expansion de l'Allemagne en Orient* (Brussels, Paris, Leipzig, 1913), pp. 100-107, 121-123.

[11] Bohler, *loc. cit.,* pp. 273-289; *cf.,* also, P. Rohrbach, *German World Policies,* pp. 223-224.

[12] *Supra,* pp. 59-60.

[13] Chéradame, *op. cit.,* pp. 267 *et seq.; The Times,* August 10, 1899; K. Helfferich, *Die Vorgeschichte des Weltkrieges,* p. 124.

[14] *Journal Officiel, Débats parlementaires, Chambre des Députés,* March 25, 1902, p. 1468.

[15] According to M. Deschanel, this was sophistry. The French Government, if it was not guilty of an error of commission, certainly was guilty of a sin of omission. It was the opinion of M. Deschanel that the French Ambassador at Constantinople should have done something to put the French Government on record as opposed to the Bagdad Railway. M. Deschanel was not certain, however, that the French Ministry had not consented to the participation of French capital in the plan. "How can one imagine," he said, "that an institution such as the Ottoman Bank became involved in an enterprise of such great political and military importance without the approval of our Foreign Office? . . . How is it that the Ottoman Bank is a party to this enterprise, and how is it that the Board of Directors for the first section of the line has French representatives, when only a word from the Government could have prevented it?" *Ibid.,* November 20, 1903, p. 2798.

[16] *Ibid.,* March 25, 1902, pp. 1468 *et seq.*

[17] Victor Bérard, "Le Discours du Chancelier," in the *Revue de Paris,* December 15, 1906.

[18] The *Revue Bleue,* April 6, 1907, p. 429; *Syria and Palestine,* p. 126. Many of the claims that the Bagdad Railway jeopardized French prosperity were purely fantastic. It was maintained that the opening of the great Mesopotamian granary would cripple French agriculture, already seriously handicapped by the competition of the new world. To this was added the suggestion that development of cotton-growing in Turkey would stifle the infant efforts at the cultivation of cotton in the French colonies.

It is incredible that Mesopotamian grain and cotton would have interfered with the flourishing prosperity of the French peasantry; in any event, any such danger was at least a generation removed. France raised high tariff barriers against foreign competition in the home market for agricultural products; she was not an exporter of grain.

[19] *Journal Officiel, Débats parlementaires, Chambre des Députés,* March 25, 1902, pp. 1467 *et seq.*

[20] *Cf.,* M. Montbel, "Les puissances coloniales devant l'Islam," in *Questions diplomatiques et coloniales,* Volume 37 (1914), pp. 348-362.

[21] *Journal Officiel, Débats parlementaires, Chambre des Députés,* November 20, 1905, p. 2798. The italics are mine.

[22] *Revue des deux mondes,* Volume 149 (1898), p. 29.

[23] Sources of the treaties granting special privileges to France are sighted in Note 3, Chapter II. Regarding the origins and nature of the French protectorate over Roman Catholic missions see the article "Capitulations" in the *Encyclopedia Britannica,* previously cited; J. Brucker, "The Protectorate of Missionaries in the Near East," in the *Catholic Encyclopedia,* Volume XII, pp. 488-492; A. Schopoff, *Les Réformes et la Protection des Chrètiens en Turquie, 1673-1904* (Paris, 1904); *Livre de propagande de l'alliance française, 1883-1893* (Paris, 1894), especially pp. 35 *et seq.*; Viscomte Aviau de Piolant, *La défense des intérêts catholiques en Terre Sainte et en Asie Mineure* (Paris, 1886).

[24] *Syria and Palestine,* pp. 43-45, 54-55; L. Brehier, "Turkish Empire—Missions," in *Catholic Encyclopedia,* Volume XV, pp. 101-102; J. Atalla, "Les solutions de la question syrienne," in *Questions diplomatiques et coloniales,* Volume 24 (1907), p. 472.

[25] *Bulletin de la Chambre de Commerce française de Constantinople,* June 30, 1897, pp. 112-113, November 30, 1897, p. 149.

[26] Brucker, *loc. cit.,* p. 490.

[27] It should be added that the Treaty also stipulated that "the acquired rights of France are explicitly reserved, and there shall be no interference with the *statu quo* in the Holy Places." E. Hertslet, *The Map of Europe by Treaty,* Volume IV (London, 1891), p. 2797.

[28] *Revue des deux mondes,* Volume 149, (1898), pp. 24-25; Brucker, *loc. cit.,* p. 491.

[29] *Catholic Encyclopedia,* Volume XII, p. 491. The rôle of the Italians in this controversy is of considerable interest. The desire of the Italian Government to assert its right to protect its own citizens abroad was a manifestation of the Italian nationalism which brought about the establishment of the Kingdom; at the same time it was an expression of that anti-Clerical

tendency which characterized Italian politics from the days of Cavour to the outbreak of the Great War. Undoubtedly, also, there was an economic side to the question. It will be recalled that Italian trade with the Ottoman Empire grew more rapidly than that of any other power after the opening of the twentieth century. (*Supra,* pp. 105-106.) This growth was due, in no small degree, to the earlier rise of Italian missionary activity in Turkey. This growth of missions and schools, as well as of commercial establishments, was irritating to patriotic Frenchmen. *Cf.* two articles by René Pinon, "Les écoles d'Orient," in *Questions diplomatiques et coloniales,* Volume 24 (1907), pp. 415-435, 487-517. Italian missionaries, charged M. Pinon, were encouraged in every way to ignore the French protectorate, appealing only to Italian diplomatic and consular representatives. "Official Italy, Catholic and papal Italy, free-mason Italy and clerical Italy, all are working together in a common great patriotic effort for the spread of the Italian language and the rise of the national power" (p. 500). Annoying as this is, says M. Pinon, it should be "a singular lesson for certain Frenchmen!" That there was no love lost on the Italian side of the controversy may be gathered from an analysis of the Italian press comments which appeared in *Questions diplomatiques et coloniales,* Volume 37 (1914), p. 495.

[30] Brucker, *loc. cit.,* p. 491. Inasmuch as the protectorate of Catholic missions involved a considerable responsibility for France, one may ask why the French Government should have been so solicitous that no other nation be allowed to share the burden. The answer is suggested by the *Catholic Encyclopedia,* which states that the system of religious protectorates is almost invariably subject to the abuse that "the protectors will seek payment for their services by trammeling the spiritual direction of the mission or by demanding political services in return." Volume XII, p. 492.

[31] *Supra,* pp. 134-135.

[32] *Revue des deux mondes,* Volume 149 (1898), p. 39. The "pro-German party" was said to consist of Cardinals Ledochowski, Hohenlohe, Galimberti, and Kapp. *Ibid.,* pp. 11-12; Reinsch, *op. cit.,* p. 269.

[33] *Revue des deux mondes,* Volume 149 (1898), pp. 36-40. On this whole subject see, also, C. Lagier, *Byzance et Stamboul: nos droits françaises et nos missions en Orient* (Paris, 1905) ; Hilaire Capuchin, *La France Catholique en Orient durant les trois-derniers siècles* (Paris, 1902) ; A. Schopoff, *Les Réformes et la Protection des Chrétiens en Turquie* (Paris, 1904).

[34] G. Saint-Yves, *Les Chemins de fer françaises dans la Turquie d'Asie* (Paris, 1914).

[35] The French and Belgian banks principally interested were: the Imperial Ottoman Bank, the *Banque de l'Union Parisienne,* and the *Banque Internationale de Bruxelles. Cf.* article "Ou en est la question du chemin de fer de Bagdad," in *Questions diplomatiques et coloniales,* Volume 24 (1907), pp. 167-171; E. Letailleur, *Les capitalistes français contre la France* (Paris, 1916), pp. 72-110. M. Rouvier visited Turkey in 1901, at the request of the Ottoman Public Debt Administration, to suggest improvements in the fiscal system of the Empire. (*Corps de droit ottoman,* Volume IV, p. 110.) It was at this time, probably, that he learned enough of the Bagdad Railway to persuade him of the wisdom of investing in its securities.

[36] Gervais-Courtellemont, *loc. cit.,* p. 507; Imbert, *loc. cit.,* p. 682.

[37] Gervais-Courtellemont, *loc. cit.,* p. 507; Bohler, *loc. cit.,* p. 294.

[38] Bohler, *loc. cit.,* pp. 293-295.

[39] Mazel, *op. cit.,* pp. 315-322.

[40] K. Helfferich, *Die deutsche Türkenpolitik,* p. 18.

[41] "La politique extérieure de l'Allemagne," in *Questions diplomatiques et coloniales,* Volume 23 (1907), pp. 340-341.

[42] *Stenographische Berichte, XII Legislaturperiode, 1 Session,* Volume 231 (1908), pp. 4226 *et seq.*

[43] Quoted by the *Annual Register,* 1913, p. 326.

CHAPTER VIII

GREAT BRITAIN BLOCKS THE WAY

EARLY BRITISH OPINIONS ARE FAVORABLE

The idea of a trans-Mesopotamian railway was not new to informed Englishmen. As early as 1831 a young British army officer, Francis R. Chesney, who had seen service in the Near East, became impressed with the desirability of constructing a railway from the Mediterranean to the Persian Gulf. From 1835 to 1837—while Moltke was in Turkey studying military topography—Chesney was engaged in exploring the Euphrates Valley and upon his return to England brought glowing tales of the latent wealth of ancient Babylonia. It was not until twenty years later, however, that his plan for a Mesopotamian railway was taken up as a practical business proposition. In 1856 Sir William Andrew incorporated the Euphrates Valley Railway Company, appointed General Chesney as chief consulting engineer, and opened offices at Constantinople to carry on negotiations for a concession from the Imperial Ottoman Government. The plans of the Company were supported enthusiastically by Lord Palmerston, by Lord Stratford de Redcliffe, British ambassador at Constantinople, and by the Turkish ambassador in London. The following year the Sultan granted the Euphrates Valley Company a concession for a railway from the Gulf of Alexandretta to the city of Basra, with the understanding that the Ottoman Treasury would guarantee a return of six per cent upon the capital invested in the enterprise. The promoters, however, experienced difficulty in raising funds for the construction of the line, and the project had to be abandoned.[1]

Lord Palmerston, in the meantime, was busily opposing the Suez Canal project. De Lesseps was handicapped by the obstructionist policies of British diplomacy as well as by the unwillingness of British financiers to invest in his enterprise. Palmerston frankly informed the great French engineer that in the opinion of the British Government the construction of the Canal was a physical impossibility; that if it were constructed it would injure British maritime supremacy; and that, after all, it was not so much a financial and commercial venture as a political conspiracy to provide the occasion for French interference in the East![2]

Nevertheless the Suez Canal was completed in 1869, and immediately thereafter the question of a Mesopotamian railway was again brought to the fore in England. The advance of the Russians in the Near East and the control by the French of a short all-water route to the Indies gave rise to serious concern regarding the maintenance of communication with British India. In 1870 a British promoter proposed the construction of a railway from Alexandretta *via* Aleppo and Mosul to Bagdad and Basra. Such a railway, as Sir William Andrew had pointed out, would assure the undisturbed possession of India, for the "advancing standard of the barbarian Cossack would recoil before those emblems of power and progress, the electric wire and the steam engine, and his ominous tread would be restrained behind the icy barrier of the Caucasus."[3] Also it would render Great Britain independent of the French-owned Suez Canal by providing an alternative route to the East, making possible more rapid transportation of passengers, mails, and troops to India. This plan seemed desirable of execution from so many points of view that a special committee of the

House of Commons, presided over by Sir Stafford North-cote, was appointed "to examine and report upon the whole subject of railway communication between the Mediterranean, the Black Sea, and the Persian Gulf." This committee reported that the construction of a trans-Mesopotamian railway was a matter of urgent imperial concern and recommended a plan which would have involved the investment of some £10,000,000. The necessity of providing an alternative route to India was obviated, however, by Disraeli's purchase, in 1875, of a controlling interest in the Suez Canal at a cost of less than half that sum.[4]

For the forty years during which, at intervals, these projects were under discussion Germany was not even an interested spectator in Near Eastern affairs. Domestic problems of economic development and national unification were all-absorbing, and capitalistic imperialism was quite outside the scope of German policies. France and Russia, not Germany, were the disturbers of British tranquillity in the Orient.

When during the last two decades of the nineteenth century there was a marked increase of German political and economic interests in the Ottoman Empire, there was little disposition in England to resent the German advance. As late as 1899, the year in which the preliminary Bagdad Railway concession was awarded to German financiers, British opinion, on the whole, was well disposed to Teutonic peaceful penetration in the Near East. The press was delighted at the prospect that the advent of the Germans in Turkey would block Russian expansion in the Middle East. Such eminent imperialists as Joseph Chamberlain and Cecil Rhodes announced their willingness to conclude an *entente* with Germany in colonial affairs. The British Government was more suspicious of France than of Germany.[5]

During the opening years of the twentieth century, however, the situation was materially changed. Although there was a continuance of the cordial relations between the British and German Governments, there was an undercurrent of hostility to Germany in England (as well as to England in Germany) which was to be disastrous to the hopes for an Anglo-German agreement on the Near East. By 1903, the year of the definitive Bagdad concession, German diplomacy and German business were under a cloud of suspicion and unpopularity in Great Britain.

The underlying reason for the increasing estrangement between England and Germany was, as far as the British were concerned, the phenomenal rise of Germany as a world power. The commercial advance of the German Empire disturbed the complacent security and the stereotyped methods of British business. The colonial aspirations of German imperialists rudely interfered with British plans in Africa and appeared to be threatening British domination of the East. The German navy bills of 1898 and 1900 constituted a challenge to Britannia's rule of the waves. German criticism of English procedure in South Africa had aroused widespread animosity, in large part because the British themselves realized that their conduct toward the Boers had not been above reproach. This animosity was revealed in an aggravated and unreasoning form in the vigorous denunciation which greeted the Government's joint intervention with Germany in the Venezuela affair of 1902. Joseph Chamberlain, who in 1899 had advocated an Anglo-German alliance, in 1903 was preaching "tariff reform," directed, among other objectives, against the menace to the British Empire of the rising industrial prosperity of Germany. The proposal that British capital should participate in the Bagdad Railway project was introduced to the British public at a distinctly inopportune time from the point of view of those who desired some form of coöperation between England and Germany in the successful prosecution of the plan.

The British Government Yields to Pressure

The Bagdad Railway came up for discussion in Parliament on April 7, 1903. Mr. Balfour then informed the House of Commons that negotiations were being carried on between British and German capitalists, and between British capitalists and the Foreign Office, for the purpose of determining the conditions upon which British financiers might participate in the enterprise. If a satisfactory agreement could be reached by the bankers, His Majesty's Government would be asked to give its consent to a reasonable increase in the customs duties of the Ottoman Empire, to consider the utilization of the new railway for the transportation of the Indian mails, and to adopt a friendly attitude toward the establishment of the eastern terminus of the Bagdad Railway at or near Koweit.

Coöperation with the German concessionaires on any such basis was attacked vigorously from the floor of the House. One member declared it a menace to the existing British-owned Smyrna-Aidin Railway lines in Turkey, a potential competitor of British maritime supremacy, and a threat at British imperial interests in Egypt and in the region of the Persian Gulf. Another member of the House believed that "it was impossible to divorce the commercial from the political aspect of the question. What made the House take a real, live interest in it was the feeling that bound up with the future of this railway there was probably the future political control of large regions in Asia Minor, Mesopotamia, and the Persian Gulf." Another member was certain the House "knew Mesopotamia was a blessed word. They all felt it was impossible for this country to oppose the introduction of a railway through Mesopotamia. The only wonder was that the railway was not constructed forty or fifty years ago." At the same time, he felt, it would be well for Britain to be assured that her participation in the enterprise would not lead to another "Venezuela agreement"; Germany must be given to understand that Britain, by control of the Persian Gulf, held the "trump card" of the deck.

The Prime Minister made it plain, nevertheless, that he favored coöperation with the German concessionaires provided British capital were permitted to participate on a basis of equality with any other power. He believed, also, that an obstructionist policy would be futile. "I have no doubt that whatever course English financiers may take and whatever course the British Government may pursue, sooner or later this great undertaking will be carried out," said Mr. Balfour. "It is undoubtedly in the power of the British Government to hamper and impede and inconvenience any project of the kind; but that the project will ultimately be carried out, with or without our having a share in it, there is no question whatsoever."

"There are three points," continued Mr. Balfour, "which ought not to be lost sight of by the House when trying to make up their minds upon this problem in its incomplete state. They have to consider whether it is or is not desirable that what will undoubtedly be the shortest route to India should be entirely in the hands of French and German capitalists. Another question is whether they do or do not think it desirable that if there is a trade opening in the Persian Gulf, it should be within the territories of the Sheik whom we have under our special protection and with whom we have special treaties [*i.e.*, the Sheik of Koweit], or whether it should be in some other port of the Persian Gulf where we have no such preferential advantage. The House must also have in view a third consideration with regard to a railway which goes through a very rich country and which . . . is likely after a certain period of development to add greatly to the riches of Turkey, and indirectly, I suppose, greatly to the riches of any other country which is ready to take advantage of it. Whether the British producer will be able to take advantage of it is not for me to say; but the House will have to consider whether he is more likely to be able to take advantage of it if English capital is largely interested, than if it is confined to French and German capital. The House will have to calculate whether . . . it will be prudent to leave the passenger traffic in the hands of those two nations, France and Germany, with whom we are on the most friendly terms, but whose interests may not be identical with our own." [6]

Mr. Balfour's presentation of the case was hailed in Berlin as eminently lucid and fair. The *National Zeitung* and the *Vossische Zeitung* of April 8 expressed the hope that British participation in the Bagdad Railway would be approved by Parliament and the press, in order that the German promoters might have the opportunity to demonstrate that no political ambitions were connected with the enterprise. The Russian attitude of refusing even to discuss internationalization, on the other hand, was roundly denounced.

The London press, however, saw no reason for enthusiasm over the Prime Minister's proposal. *The Times,* the *Daily Mail,* the *Daily Telegraph,* the *Pall Mall Gazette,* and the *National Review* let loose a torrent of vituperation against German imperialist activities in general and the Bagdad Railway in particular. The *Spectator,* forswearing any thought of prejudice against Germany, constantly reminded its readers of German unfriendliness during the Boer War and suggested that the Bagdad negotiations offered the British Government an admirable opportunity to retaliate.

The *Manchester Guardian,* organ of the old Liberalism, likewise was opposed to British participation in the Bagdad Railway. Pleading for continued observance of Britain's time-honored policy of isolation, its leading editorial of April 15 said: "Mr. Balfour expressed his belief that 'this great international artery had better be in the hands of three great countries than in the hands of two or of one great country.' In other words, England is to be mixed up in the domestic broils of Asia Minor; every Kurdish or Arab attack on the railway will raise awkward diplomatic questions, and any disaster to the Turkish military power will place the whole enterprise in jeopardy. What is far more important, English participation in railway construction in Asia Minor will certainly strengthen the suspicions which Russia entertains regarding our policy. It is the fashion with certain English politicians to abuse Russia for building railways in Manchuria and for projecting lines across Persia. Yet Mr. Balfour seems more than half inclined to pay her policy the compliment of imitation by helping to build a railway across Mesopotamia to the Persian Gulf—and, worse still, of imperfect imitation, since the Government is certainly not prepared to occupy the territory through which the railway will pass, as Russia does in Manchuria. What vital interests of our own shall we strengthen by this sudden ardour for railways in Turkey to counterbalance the certain weakening of our friendly relations with Russia?"

Violent as was the opposition of the press to any coöperation with the Germans in the Bagdad Railway, the opposition would have been still more violent had all of the facts been public property. Mr. Balfour, however, was keeping the House and the country in complete ignorance of many of the most important aspects of the situation. Although the Prime Minister denied that there had been any negotiations between the British and German Governments regarding the Bagdad enterprise, he failed to admit that there had been such negotiations between His Majesty's Government and German financiers. He made no mention of the fact, for example, that he and Lord Lansdowne, his Secretary of State for Foreign Affairs, had attended a meeting at the home of Lord Mount Stephen at which Dr. von Gwinner, on behalf of the *Deutsche Bank,* and Lord Revelstoke, on behalf of the interested British financiers, explained the terms of the proposed participation of British capital in the Bagdad Railway.[7] The plan was to place the Railway, including the Anatolian lines, throughout its entire length from the Bosporus to the Persian Gulf, under international control. Equal participation in construction, administration, and management was to be awarded German, French, and British interests to prevent the possibility of preferential treatment for the goods or subjects of any one country.[8] To this proposal both Mr. Balfour and Lord Lansdowne gave their approval, assuring the bankers that no diplomatic obstacles would be offered by Great Britain to the construction of the Bagdad Railway. Dr. von Gwinner thereupon returned home to obtain the consent of his associates to the reapportionment of interests and, perhaps, to consult the German Foreign Office and the Ottoman minister at Berlin. This was early in April, 1903.[9]

Persistent rumors in the London press that a Bagdad Railway agreement had been negotiated brought the subject to the attention of the Cabinet, which heretofore, apparently, had not been consulted by the Prime Minister and the Secretary of State for Foreign Affairs. It was decided that the Prime Minister should make a statement to Parliament—a statement which, perhaps, might serve

as a sort of trial balloon to ascertain the opinion of the
country upon the question. Mr. Balfour's presentation
of the Bagdad Railway affair to the House of Commons,
as we have seen, however, provoked unfriendly comments
from the floor and was subjected to heavy fire from the
press. Thereupon a rebellious element in the Cabinet—
led, presumably, by Joseph Chamberlain, who now was
more interested in the development of the economic resources of the British Empire under a system of protective and preferential tariffs, than in coöperation with
other nations—persuaded Mr. Balfour not to risk the life
of his Ministry on the question of British participation
in the Bagdad enterprise. Accordingly, the agreement
with the *Deutsche Bank* was repudiated, and on April 23,
1903, Mr. Balfour informed the House of Commons that
His Majesty's Government was determined to withdraw
all support, financial and otherwise, which Great Britain
might be in a position to lend the Bagdad Railway. He
was convinced, he said, after a careful examination of the
proposals of the German promoters, that no agreement
was possible which would compensate the Empire for its
diplomatic assistance and guarantee security for British
interests.[10]

This announcement was a distinct disappointment to
the bankers in Berlin and in London. The directors of
the *Deutsche Bank* were stunned by the termination of
negotiations which they believed had been progressing
satisfactorily. The British financiers were chagrined at
the sudden decision of their Government to oppose their
participation in a promising enterprise. They were convinced that the terms offered by the German bankers met
every condition imposed by the Prime Minister. They
were agreed on the wisdom of British coöperation with
the *Deutsche Bank,* and they were not a little annoyed at
what appeared to be bad faith on the part of Downing

Street. They were convinced that only a bellicose press frustrated the attempt to make the Bagdad Railway an international highway.[11]

This, in any event, is the diagnosis of the situation furnished by Sir Clinton Dawkins, of the Morgan group, one of the British financiers interested in the project. In a letter to Dr. von Gwinner written on April 23, 1903, but not made public until six years later, he said, "As you originally introduced the Bagdad business to us, I feel that I cannot, upon its unfortunate termination, omit to express to you personally my great regret at what has occurred. After all you have done to meet the various points raised, you will naturally feel very disappointed and legitimately aggrieved. But I am glad to think, and I feel you will be convinced, that your grievance lies not against the British group but against the British Foreign Office. The fact is that the business has become involved in politics here and has been sacrificed to the very violent and bitter feeling against Germany exhibited by the majority of our newspapers, and shared in by a large number of people. This is a feeling which, as the history of recent events will show you, is not shared by the Government or reflected in official circles. But of its intensity outside these circles, for the moment, there can be no doubt; at the present moment coöperation in any enterprise which can be represented, or I might more justly say *mis*represented, as German will meet with a violent hostility which our Government has to consider."

Sir Clinton thereupon asserted that the effort of Mr. Balfour to quiet the uproar in Parliament was due to the Prime Minister's complete satisfaction with the agreement reached by the financiers. Just as success seemed assured, a bitter attack was launched on the Government "by a magazine and a newspaper [The *National Review* and *The Times*] which had made themselves conspicuous by their criticisms of the British Foreign Office on the Venezuela affair. Who instigated these papers, from whence they derived their information, is a matter upon which I cannot speak with certainty. My own impression is that the instigation proceeded from Russian sources. The clamour raised by these two organs was immediately taken up by practically the whole of the English press, London having really gone into a frenzy on the matter owing to the newspaper campaign, which it would have been quite impossible to counteract or influence. It is, I think, due to you that you should know the *histoire intime* of what has passed." [12]

There was only one London newspaper, the *St. James's Gazette*, which came out frankly in favor of British participation in the Bagdad Railway. In the issue of April 14, 1903, the editor ridiculed the suggestion of the *Spectator* that the Foreign Office was obliged to warn bankers of the financial risks involved in the enterprise. "Why our contemporary should be so anxious to save financiers, British or foreign, from making a bad investment of their money, we cannot imagine. Financiers are generally pretty wide-awake, and the City as a rule requires no advice from Fleet Street, the Strand, or Whitehall in transacting its business." In an editorial entitled "Bagdad and Bag Everything," April 22, 1903, the *Gazette* condemned *The Times* for the "curious and alarmist deductions" which that journal drew from the terms of the Bagdad Railway convention. The suggestion that this was a deliberate attempt on the part of Germany to ruin British trade was characterized "as much a figment of a fevered imagination as the mind-picture of Turkey using 'this enormous line to pour down troops to reduce the shores of the Persian Gulf to the same happy condition as Armenia and Macedonia,' about which *The Times* is so suddenly and unaccountably concerned. The concession is a monument to the German Emperor's activity, built on the ruins of the influence which we threw away, and we do not precisely see what our *locus standi* in the matter is. If the interests of the Ottoman Government and of the German concessionaires be served by the construction of the line, constructed the line will be, and there's an end. Whether it ever will, or ever can pay its way, is the affair only of capitalists who are contemplating investment in it. It is not the slightest use barking when we cannot bite, and our power of biting in the present instance is excessively small. . . . The Emperor William, like Jack Jones, has 'come into 'is little bit of splosh' in Asia Minor, and it is quite useless to be soreheaded about it. It is childish to be ever carping and nagging and 'panicking.' We question whether the Bagdad Railway—while the rule of the Sultan endures—is going to do much good or much harm to anybody. The vision which some Germans have of peaceful Hans and Gretchen swilling Löwenbrau in the Garden of Eden to the strains of a German band, is little likely of fulfilment. If trade develops, a fair share of it will come our way, provided we send good wares and such as the inhabitants want to buy." This minority opinion, however, was unheeded in the outburst of anti-German feeling which followed Mr. Balfour's first statement to the House of Commons.

As events turned out, the failure of the Balfour Government to effect the internationalization of the Bagdad Railway was a colossal diplomatic blunder. If the proposed agreement of 1903 had been consummated, the *entente* of 1904 between France and England would have taken control of the enterprise out of the hands of the Germans, who would have possessed, with their Turkish collaborators, only fourteen of the thirty votes in the Board of Directors. Sir Henry Babington Smith assures the author that there was nothing in the arrangement sug-

gested by the *Deutsche Bank* which would have prevented
eventual Franco-British domination of the line. Surely, as
Bismarck is said to have remarked, every nation must
pay sooner or later for the windows broken by its bellicose
press!

Vested Interests Come to the Fore

In addition to the pressure which was brought to bear
on the Balfour Cabinet by the newspapers, there were important vested business interests which quietly, but effectively, made themselves heard at Downing Street during
the critical days of the Bagdad negotiations of 1903.

It already has been noted that in 1888, as part of the
plans of the Public Debt Administration for the improvement of transportation facilities in Turkey, the British-
owned Smyrna-Aidin Railway Company was granted permission to construct several important branches to its main
line. For a time this new concession thoroughly satisfied
the owners and directors of the Company, and there was
no objection on their part to the extension and development of the German-owned Anatolian system. By 1903,
however, when the Bagdad concession was under discussion, the Smyrna-Aidin line demanded the protection of
the British Government against the undue extension of
German railways in the Near East. In particular, it objected to the agreement between the Anatolian Railway
and the Smyrna-Cassaba Railway, by which the latter
joined its tracks with the Anatolian system at Afiun Karahissar and accepted a schedule of tariffs satisfactory to
both lines.[18]   The Smyrna-Aidin Company feared that
the Bagdad Railway would develop the ports of Haidar
Pasha, Alexandretta, and Mersina at the expense of the
prosperity of Smyrna, thereby decreasing the relative
importance of the Smyrna-Aidin line and cutting down

the volume of its traffic. Finally, it objected to the payment of a kilometric guarantee to the German concessionaires while there was no likelihood of its being similarly favored by the custodians of the public purse. The interests of the shareholders of the railway were well represented in the House of Commons by "that watchful dragon of imperial interests", Mr. Gibson Bowles.

Mr. Bowles (Conservative member from King's Lynn, 1892-1906, and Liberal from the same constituency, 1910-1916) was a frank defender of the interests of the stockholders of the Smyrna-Aidin Railway. He believed that investors were entitled to governmental protection of their investments, whether at home or abroad. He left no doubt, however, that he took his stand on high grounds of patriotism as well. He informed the House that "he did not object to the railway, because all railways were good feeders of ships. But this was not a railway; it was a financial fraud and a political conspiracy—a fraud whereby English trade would suffer and a conspiracy whereby the political interests of England would be threatened. It amounted to a military and commercial occupation by Germany of the whole of Asia Minor." [14]

Comparable to the interests of the Smyrna-Aidin Railway were those of the Euphrates and Tigris Navigation Company, Ltd. Under this name the Lynch Brothers had been operating steamers on the Tigris and the Shatt-el-Arab since the middle of the nineteenth century. In the trade between Bagdad and Basra they enjoyed a practical monopoly. In the absence of competition they were able to render indifferent service at exorbitant rates, and there was nothing to disturb their tranquillity except an occasional complaint from a British merchant. But the old order was about to change. The Bagdad Railway concession of 1903 (articles 9 and 23) destroyed the monopoly of the Lynch Brothers by granting to the Railway

Company limited rights of navigation on the Tigris. Construction of the Mesopotamian sections of the Railway, furthermore, would be almost certain to kill, by competition, profitable navigation between Bagdad and Basra. The course of the Tigris is shallow and winding, subject to heavy rises and falls, and constantly changing with the formation and disappearance of sand shoals. The river journey from Bagdad to Basra is about five hundred miles and takes from four to five days by steamer, under favorable conditions. The distance by land is about three hundred miles and could be traversed by railway in a single day's journey, regardless of weather conditions. For passengers and most classes of freight the Bagdad Railway promised more economical transportation. The Lynch Brothers were determined, however, to resist such rude encroachment on their profitable preserves. In defence of their interests they wrapped themselves in the Union Jack and called upon their home government for protection; they were patriotic to the last degree and were determined "that the custody of a privilege highly important to British commerce would never pass to Germany except over the dead bodies of the principal partners." [15] Overcharge their countrymen they might; surrender this prerogative to a German railway they would not!

British shipping interests, also, were vigorous in their opposition to the Bagdad Railway. A trans-Mesopotamian railway, they knew, would absorb some of the through traffic to the East, and the competition of the locomotive might compel a general readjustment of freight rates. Furthermore, it was one of the avowed purposes of the Bagdad line to acquire the profitable Indian mails concession from the British Government; this would be equivalent to the withdrawal of a subsidy from the steamship lines operating to the East. It was not for their own sake, but for the sake of British commerce, however, that these shipping interests objected to the construction of the Bagdad line! They warned the British public that the proposed railway would adversely affect the traffic passing through the Suez Canal; inasmuch as the United Kingdom was a stockholder in the Canal, this was the concern of every English citizen. They pointed out that the kilometric subsidy which had been guaranteed the Railway was to be paid from an increase in the customs duties; thus, it was charged, British commerce would be obliged to contribute indirectly to the dividends of the *Deutsche Bank*. The improvement of communications between Middle Europe and the Near East would be almost certain to disturb British trade with Turkey; the feared and hated "Made in Germany" trade-mark might exert its hypnotic influence in a region where British commerce heretofore had been preëminent. If, in addition, the German owners of the Bagdad Railway should choose to grant discriminatory rates to German goods, a severe body-blow would be dealt British economic interests in the Ottoman Empire. The completion of this Railway would bring with it all sorts of German interference in the Near East and undermine British commercial and maritime interests in the region.[16]

Many of the charges brought against the Bagdad Railway by the British shipping interests could not have been substantiated. As early as 1892, Lord Curzon stated emphatically that, for most commercial purposes, a trans-Mesopotamian railway would be next to valueless. "If I were a stockholder in the P. & O. [the Peninsular and Oriental, one of the Inchcape lines touching at Indian and Persian Gulf ports], I would not," he said, "except for the possible loss of the mails, be in the least alarmed at the competition of such a railway." [17] Informed Germans, likewise, did not consider the Bagdad Railway a serious competitor to the Suez Canal. One authority, for example, wrote: "The Bagdad Railway taken as a whole is of importance only for through passenger and postal traffic (in which respect, therefore, it is of greatest value to the British in their communications with India) and occasionally for fast freight. The great bulk of the freight traffic, on the other hand, carrying the import and export trade of the East, hardly can fall to the Bagdad Railway, which, for a long time at least, must content itself with the local traffic of certain sections of the line," particularly in Cilicia, Syria, and northern Mesopotamia.[18]

The assertion that the cost of constructing and operating the line would be borne by British commerce was based upon specious reasoning. Higher customs duties would not be paid by the British merchant, but by the Turkish consumer. The only harmful effect of the increased duties would be a general increase of prices of imported commodities in Turkey, leading, perhaps, to a lesser demand for foreign goods. It was probable, on the other hand, that this slight disadvantage would be more than offset by the wider prosperity which the Railway was almost certain to bring the districts traversed. In any event, whatever burden might be saddled upon the import trade would have to be borne, in proportion to the volume of business transacted, by the competitors of British merchants as well as by British merchants themselves.

Many British business men were shrewd enough to foresee that the Bagdad Railway might prove to be far from disadvantageous to their interests. Where was the menace to British prosperity in a railway, German or otherwise, which promised improved communication with the British colonies in the Orient? The facilitation of mail service to India; the development of rapid passenger service to the East; the reduction of ocean freight rates as a result of healthy competition—all of these injured no one except the vested interests which had handicapped the expansion of British commerce by inadequate service and exorbitant rates. There was no indication that the Bagdad Railway Company proposed to discriminate against non-German shippers; in any event, such a course was specifically prohibited by the concession of 1903, which decreed that "all rates, whether they be general, special, proportional, or differential, are applicable to all travelers and consignors without distinction," and which prohibited the Company "from entering into any special contract with the object of granting reductions of the charges specified in the tariffs." [19] As the British Chamber of Commerce at Constantinople appropriately pointed out, the most certain means of avoiding discriminatory treatment was to permit and encourage the participation of British capital in the enterprise and to assure the presence of British subjects on the Board of Directors of the Company. [20]

From an economic point of view, it would appear that the British Empire had a great deal to gain from the construction of the Bagdad Railway. In proportion as improved methods of transportation shrink the earth's surface, the contacts between mother country and dependencies will become more numerous. An economic community of interest is more likely to spring up and thrive with the aid of more numerous and more rapid means of communication. True, certain interests believed that the Bagdad Railway threatened their very existence. But would the British people have been willing to sacrifice the wider economic interests of the Empire to the vested privileges of a handful of English capitalists? They would not, of course, if the issue had been put to them in such simple terms. The problem was complicated by the obvious fact that it was not alone the economic interests of the empire which were at stake. The political import of the Bagdad enterprise overshadowed all economic considerations.

Imperial Defence Becomes the Primary Concern

British journalists and statesmen, as well as the ordinary British patriot, have been accustomed to judge international questions from but one point of view—the promotion and protection of the interests of that great and benevolent institution, "the noblest fabric yet reared by the genius of a conquering nation," the British Empire.[21] Imperial considerations have been the determining factors in the formulation of diplomatic policies and of naval and military strategy. The possession of a far-flung empire has required further imperial conquests to insure the defence of those already acquired. Strategic necessities have constituted a "reason for making an empire large, and a large empire larger." [22]

India, an empire in itself, is the keystone of the British imperial system. To defend India it has been considered necessary for Great Britain to possess herself of vital strategic points along the routes of communication from the Atlantic seaboard to the Indian Ocean. The acquisition of Cape Colony from the Dutch at the conclusion of the Napoleonic Wars enabled the British fleet to dominate the old route to India, around the Cape of Good Hope. Judiciously placed naval stations at Gibraltar, Malta, and Cyprus assured the safety of British trade with the East *via* the Mediterranean. After a futile attempt to prevent the construction of the Suez Canal, which temporarily placed a new and shorter all-water route to India in the hands of the French, Great Britain proceeded to acquire the Canal for herself. To assure the protection of the Suez Canal, in turn, it was necessary to occupy Egypt and the Sudan. Control of Somaliland and Aden, together with friendly relations with Arabia, turned the Red Sea into a British lake. Menaced by the Russian advance toward India, Great Britain proceeded to dominate the entire Middle East: the foreign affairs of Afghanistan were placed under British tutelage and protection; Baluchistan was compelled to submit to the control of British agents; parts of Persia were brought within the sphere of British influence.[23]

Great Britain, apparently, was determined to control every important route to India. What, then, would be her attitude toward a trans-Mesopotamian railway, terminating at the only satisfactory deep-water port on the Persian Gulf? Was the possession of such a short-cut to India consistent with the exigencies of imperial defence?

Without a satisfactory terminus on the Persian Gulf the Bagdad Railway would lose its greatest possibilities as a great transcontinental line; with such a terminus it might become a menace to vital British interests in that region. British imperialists had been interested in control of the Persian Gulf since the seventeenth century, when the East India Company established trading posts along its shores. The British navy cleared the Gulf of pirates; it buoyed and beaconed the waters of the Gulf and the Shatt-el-Arab. A favorable treaty with the Emir of Muscat, in the latter part of the nineteenth century, provided Great Britain with a "sally port" from which to organize the defence of the entrance to the Gulf; later, Muscat became a protectorate of Great Britain. From time to time treaties were negotiated with the Arab chieftains of southern Mesopotamia, extending British influence up the Shatt-el-Arab and the Tigris and Euphrates to Bagdad. Under these circumstances, it was apparent from the very beginning that, whether or not the Balfour Government consented to British participation in the Bagdad enterprise, there would be no surrender of the privileged position enjoyed by Great Britain in the Persian Gulf. Foreign merchants might be admitted to a share in the Gulf trade, but the existence of a port under foreign control hardly could be approved.[24]

Lord Lansdowne, Secretary of State for Foreign Affairs, speaking before the House of Lords, on May 5, 1903, made the position of the Government clear: "I do not yield to the noble Lord [Lord Ellenborough] in the interest which I take in the Persian Gulf or in the feeling that this country stands, with regard to the navigation of the Persian Gulf, in a position different from that of any other power. . . . The noble Lord has asked me for a statement of our policy with regard to the Persian Gulf. I think I can give him one in a few simple words. It seems to me that our policy should be directed in the first place to protect and promote British trade in those waters. In the next place I do not think that he suggests, or that we would suggest, that those efforts should be directed towards the exclusion of the legitimate trade of other powers. In the third place—I say it without hesitation—we should regard the establishment of a naval base, or of a fortified port, in the Persian Gulf by any other power as a very grave menace to British interests, and we should certainly resist it with all the means at our disposal. I say that in no minatory spirit, because, as far as I am aware, no proposals are on foot for the establishment of a foreign naval base in the Persian Gulf." [25]

Lord Lansdowne might have reminded his hearers that, although the British Government was disposed to be friendly toward the Bagdad Railway, measures already had been taken which effectively precluded any possibility of the construction by the concessionaires, without British consent, of terminal and port works at Koweit. In 1899, when the first announcements came from Constantinople regarding the Bagdad project, Lord Curzon, then Viceroy of India, became alarmed at the construction of a railway which would link the head of the Persian Gulf with the railways of Central Europe. Lord Curzon was a trained imperialist. It was his custom to utter few words; to make no proclamations from the housetops; to act promptly —and in secret. It was at the instigation of the Indian Government that Colonel Meade, British resident in the Persian Gulf region, proceeded to Koweit and negotiated with the Sheik a clandestine agreement by which the latter accepted the "protection" of the British Government and agreed to enter into no international agreements without the consent of a British resident adviser.[26] When a German technical commission visited Koweit in 1900 to negotiate for terminal and port facilities, they found the Sheik suspiciously intractable to their wishes. Thereupon Abdul Hamid despatched an expedition to Koweit to assert his sovereignty over the Sheik's territory, but the presence of a British gunboat rendered both reason and force of no avail.[27]

"Protection" of Koweit by Great Britain served notice on both Turkey and Germany that the construction of a railway, owned and controlled by Germans, to a deepwater port on the Persian Gulf was deemed contrary to the interests of the British Empire. From first to last British officials persistently refused to accede to any arrangement which would thus jeopardize imperial communications. Control of the Persian Gulf, an outpost of Indian defence, became the keynote of British resistance to the Bagdad Railway.

During the visit of William II to England in 1907, he was informed by Lord Haldane, Sir Edward Grey, and other responsible British statesmen, that their objections to the Bagdad enterprise would be removed if the sections of the Railway from Bagdad to Basra and the Persian Gulf were under the administration of British capitalists.[28]

In March, 1911, shortly after the Kaiser and the Tsar had reached an agreement at Potsdam on the Bagdad Railway question, Lord Curzon vigorously denounced the enterprise as a blow at the heart of Britain's empire in India and called upon the Foreign Office to persist in its policy of blocking construction of the final sections of the line.[29] This was in accord with a caustic criticism of German and Russian activities in the Near East, delivered by Mr. Lloyd George to the House of Commons, during which the future Premier made it plain that, whatever course Russia might pursue, Great Britain would not compromise her vital imperial interests in the region of the Persian Gulf.[30] The German concessionaires learned, to their disappointment and chagrin, that, on this point, in any event, the British Government stood firm. Even in 1914, when an international agreement was reached permitting the construction of the Bagdad Railway, Great Britain subscribed to the arrangement with the express proviso that the terminus of the line should be Basra and that the port to be constructed at Basra should be jointly owned and controlled by German and British capitalists. Construction of the line beyond Basra was not to be undertaken without the permission of the British Government.[31]

Although fear of foreign interference in the Persian Gulf region was the chief political objection raised by Great Britain to the construction of the Bagdad Railway, it was supplemented by a number of other objections— all associated, directly or indirectly, with the defence of India. The Bagdad Railway concession of 1903 provided for the construction of a branch line from Bagdad to Khanikin, on the Turco-Persian border. This proposed railway not only would compete with the British caravan trade between these cities, amounting to about three-quarters of a million pounds sterling annually, but would, perhaps, lead to the introduction into the Persian imbroglio of the influence of another Great Power. Persia lay astride one of the natural routes of communication to India. The uncertainty of the situation in Persia already was such as to cause grave concern in Great Britain, and there were few British statesmen who would have welcomed German interference in addition to Russian intrigue.[32]

British imperialists, too, had excellent reason to fear that any increase in the power of the Sultan, such as would be certain to follow the construction of adequate rail communications in the Ottoman Empire, might be but the first step in a renaissance of Mohammedan political ambitions, and, perhaps, a Moslem uprising everywhere against Christian overlords. Such a situation— had it been sufficiently matured before the outbreak of the War of 1914—might have been disastrous to the British position in the East: a rejuvenated Turkey, supported by a powerful Germany, might have been in a position to menace the Suez Canal, "the spinal cord of the Empire," and to lend assistance to seditious uprisings in Egypt, India, and the Middle East. Why should Britain not have been disturbed at such a prospect, when prominent German publicists were boastfully announcing that this was one of the principal reasons for official espousal of the *Bagdadbahn?* [33] Why should British statesmen have closed their eyes to such a possibility, when the recognized parliamentary leader of the Social Democratic Party in Germany warned the members of the Reichstag that limits must be placed upon the political ramifications of the Bagdad enterprise, lest it lead to a disastrous war with Great Britain? [34]

Furthermore, British statesmen were too intimately acquainted with the dynamics of capitalistic imperialism to accept the assurances of Germans that the Bagdad Railway, and other German enterprises in Turkey, were business propositions only. They knew that promises to respect the sovereignty of the Sultan were courteous formalities of European diplomatists to cloak scandalous irregularities—it was in full recognition of the sacred and inviolable integrity of Turkey that Disraeli had taken possession and assumed the "defence" of Cyprus in 1878! Furthermore, experienced imperialists knew full well that economic penetration was the foundation of political control. As Mr. Lloyd George informed the House of Commons in 1911, the kilometric guarantee of the Bagdad Railway gave German bankers a firm grip on the public treasury in Turkey, and such a hold on the imperial Ottoman purse-strings might lead no one could prophesy where.[35]

British experience in Egypt, however, indicated one direction in which it might possibly lead. English control in Egypt had been acquired by the most modern and approved imperial methods. It was no old-fashioned conquest; the procedure was much more subtle than that. First, Egypt was weighted down by a great burden of debt to British capitalists; then British business men and investors acquired numerous privileges and intrenched themselves in their special position by virtue of the Anglo-French control of Egyptian finance; the "advice" of British diplomatists came to possess greater force of law than the edicts of the Khedive; "disorders" always could be counted upon to furnish an excuse for military conquest and annexation, should that crude procedure eventually become necessary.[36] Might not *Wilhelmstrasse* tear a leaf out of Downing Street's book of imperial experience?

There is a seeming inconsistency in this description of the British interests involved in the Bagdad Railway question. If British shipping might be seriously injured, if the imperial communications were to be endangered, if undisputed control of the Persian Gulf was essential to the safety of the Empire, if the defence of India was to be jeopardized, if a German protectorate might be established in Asia Minor—if all these were possibilities, how could the Balfour Government afford to temporize with the German concessionaires, holding out the hope of British assistance? Were Mr. Balfour and Lord Lansdowne less fearful for the welfare and safety of the Empire than were the newspaper editors? Rather, of course, were they convinced that the very best way of forestalling any of these developments was to permit and encourage British participation in the financing of the Bagdad Railway Company.[37] Only thus could British trade hope to share in the economic renaissance of the Ottoman Empire; only thus could there be British representatives on the Board of Directors to insist that the *Deutsche Bank* confine its efforts to the economic development of Turkey, excluding all political *arrières pensées*. And it would not have required an imperialist of the experience of Mr. Balfour to imagine that dual ownership of the Bagdad Railway might have the same ultimate outcome as the Dual Control in Egypt. But blind antagonism toward Germany prevented the average Englishman from seeing the obvious advantages of not abandoning the Bagdad Railway to the exclusive control of German and French capitalists.

British Resistance is Stiffened by the Entente

One year after the failure of the Bagdad Railway negotiations of 1903, the age-old colonial rivalry of France and Great Britain was brought to a temporary close by the *Entente Cordiale*. It is not possible, with the information now at our disposal, to estimate with any degree of accuracy the influence which the Bagdad Railway exerted upon British imperialists in the final determination to reach an agreement with France. One may agree with an eminent French authority, however, that "neither in England nor in France is the principle of the understanding to be sought. Rather was it the fear of Germany which determined England—not only her King and Government, but the whole of her people—to draw nearer France." [38] British fear and dislike of Germany were founded upon the phenomenal growth of German industry and overseas commerce, the rapid expansion of the German mercantile marine, the construction of the German navy, and the insistence of German diplomatists that Germany be not ignored in colonial matters. The Bagdad Railway did nothing to quiet those fears. It served, rather, to render precarious Britain's position in the East.

In March, 1903, when the definitive Bagdad Railway concession was granted, British imperial affairs were in a far from satisfactory state. The termination of the Boer War had ended the fear that the British Empire might lose its hold on South Africa, but the sharp criticism of British conduct toward the Boers—criticism which came not only from abroad, but from malcontents at home—had dealt a severe blow to British prestige. The relentless advance of Russia in China, Persia, and Afghanistan gave cause for anxiety as to the safety of Britain's possessions in the Middle and Far East. And although France had withdrawn gracefully from the Fashoda affair, it was by no means certain that Egypt had seen the last of French interference. Added to all of these difficulties was the proposed German-owned railway from Constantinople to the Persian Gulf, flanking the Suez Canal and reaching out to the back door of India.

Under such circumstances it was small wonder that Great Britain took stock of her foreign policies. The

Anglo-Japanese Alliance of 1902 already had ended the British policy of aloofness, and there appeared to be no sound reason against the negotiation of other treaties which similarly would strengthen the British position in the East. The Bagdad Railway negotiations collapsed, but the agreement with France—which seemed far more difficult of achievement—was consummated without further delay. Three years later, in 1907, Great Britain came to an agreement with another of her rivals in the East—Russia. The Tsar, chastened by military defeat abroad and by revolution at home, recognized a British sphere of interest in Persia, relinquished all claims in Afghanistan, and acknowledged the suzerainty of China over Tibet.[39] The understanding with France had assured the safety of the Suez Canal from an attack from the Sudan; the agreement with Russia removed the menace of an attack upon India from the north and northwest. Germany became Great Britain's only formidable rival in the Near East.

Thus the Germans found themselves facing a powerful diplomatic obstacle to the construction of the Bagdad Railway. Here was another instance, in their minds, of the "encirclement" of Germany by a hostile coalition—an "encirclement" not only on the Continent, but in a German sphere of imperial interest as well. A conspicuous German Oriental scholar said that the attitude of the other European powers toward the Bagdad Railway was the best proof of their enmity toward Germany. "Every single kilometre had to be fought for against the unyielding opposition of Great Britain, Russia, and France, who desired to frustrate any increase in the power of Turkey. Great Britain led and organized this opposition because she feared that India and Egypt were threatened by the Bagdad Railway." If one wishes to understand the diplomatic history of the War, "he needs only to study the struggle for the Bagdad Railway—he will find a laboratory full of rich materials." [40] Here was the tragedy of the Bagdad Railway—it was one of a number of imperial enterprises which together constituted a principal cause of the greatest war of modern times!

There were some ardent British imperialists who were out of sympathy with the popular opposition to the Bagdad Railway and with the policy of the *Entente* in obstructing the building of the line. Few Englishmen were more thoroughly acquainted with the Near East than Sir William Willcocks. [41] Basing his opinions upon an intimate, scientific study of conditions in Mesopotamia, he advocated full British coöperation with the *Deutsche Bank* in the construction of the Bagdad Railway, which he considered was the best means of transportation for Irak. He criticized the British Government for its shortsighted policy in the protection of the Lynch Brothers and their antiquated river service; "rivers," he said, "are for irrigation, railways for communications." Furthermore, "You cannot leave the waters of the rivers in their channels and irrigate the country with them. For navigation you may substitute railway transport; for the purpose of irrigation nothing can take the place of water." [42] He believed that adequate irrigation of the Mesopotamian Valley would result in such a wave of prosperity for the country that it would induce immigration, particularly from Egypt and British India. It was not inconceivable, under such conditions, that Britain would fall heir to ancient Mesopotamia when the Ottoman Empire should disintegrate. [43] Sir William Willcocks was neither pacifist nor visionary; he, himself, was an empire-builder.

Another British imperialist who believed that Great Britain was pursuing entirely the wrong course in obstructing German economic penetration in Turkey was Sir Harry Johnston, novelist, explorer, lecturer, former member of the consular service. He believed in "The White Man's Burden," in the inevitable overrunning of the habitable globe by the Caucasian race. But he believed that the task of spreading white civilization to the four corners of the earth was such an herculean task, that "what we white peoples ought to strive for, with speech and pen, is unity of purpose; an alliance throughout all the world in this final struggle for mastery over Nature. We ought to adjust our ambitions and eliminate causes of conflict." His program for the settlement of the Near Eastern question was: "the promotion of peace and good-will among white nations, to start with; and when the ambitions and the allotment of spheres of influence have been nicely adjusted, then to see that the educational task of the Caucasian is carried out in a right, a Christian, a practical, and sympathetic fashion towards the other races and sub-species of humanity." Sir Harry believed that Great Britain was the last country in the world which ought to oppose the legitimate colonial aspirations of any other nation. There was every reason for the recognition of the economic and moral bases of German expansion, and any dog-in-the-manger attitude on the part of British statesmen, he was sure, would defeat the highest interests of the Empire.[44]

Applying his principles to the problem of Teutonic aggrandizement in the Ottoman Empire, Sir Harry Johnston advocated that the western European nations should acknowledge the Austrian *Drang nach Osten* as a legitimate and essential part of the German plans for a Central European Federation and for the economic development of Turkey. "The Turkish Sultanate would possibly not come to an end, but would henceforth, within certain limits, be directed and dominated by German councils. Germany in fact would become the power with the principal 'say' as to the good government and economic development of Asia Minor. Syria might be constituted as a separate state under French protection, and Judea might be offered to the Jews under an international guarantee. Sinai and Egypt would pass under avowed British protection, and Arabia (except the southern portion, which already lies within the British sphere of influence) be regarded as a federation of independent Arab States. For the rest, Turkey-in-Asia—less Armenia, which might be handed over to Russia—would, in fact, become to Germany what Egypt is to England—a kingdom to be educated, regenerated, and perhaps transfused and transformed by the renewed percolation of the Aryan Caucasian. Here would be a splendid outlet for the energies of both Germany and Austria, sufficient to keep them contented, prosperous, busy, and happy, for at least a century ahead." Sir Harry believed that obstructionist tactics on the part of Great Britain would promote Prussianism within Germany, whereas, on the other hand, a frank recognition of Germany's claims in the Near East would provide Central Europe with a safety valve which would "relieve pressure on France, Belgium, and Russia, paving the way for an understanding on Continental questions. Let us—if we wish to be cynical—welcome German expansion with Kruger's metaphor of the tortoise putting out his head. Germany and Austria are dangerous to the peace of the world only so long as they are penned up in their present limits." [45]

One obvious disadvantage of the solution suggested by Sir Harry Johnston was its total indifference to the wishes of the Ottoman Turks. Apparently it was out of place to consider the welfare of Turkey in a discussion of the Bagdad Railway question! Certainly there were very few European statesmen who cared the least about the opinions of Turks in the disposition of Turkish property. Among the few was Viscount Morley, one of the old

Gladstonian Liberals. Answering Lord Curzon, in the House of Lords, March 22, 1911, Lord Morley, a member of the Asquith cabinet, asserted the right of the Turks to determine their own destinies: "A great deal of nonsense," he said, "is talked about the possible danger to British interests which may be involved some day or other when this railway is completed, and there have been whimsical apprehensions expressed. One is that it will constitute a standing menace to Egypt . . . because it would establish [by junction with the Syrian and Hedjaz railways] uninterrupted communication between the Bosporus and Western Arabia. *That would hardly be an argument for Turkey to abandon railway construction on her own soil,* whereas it overlooks the fact that the Sinai Peninsula intervenes. You cannot get over this plain cardinal fact, that this railway is made on Turkish territory by virtue of an instrument granted by the Turkish Government. . . . I see articles in newspapers every day in which it is assumed that we have the right there to do what we please. That is not so. It is not our soil, it is Turkish soil, and the Germans alone are there because the Turkish Government has given them the right to be there."[46]

BIBLIOGRAPHICAL AND EXPLANATORY NOTES

[1] Sir William Andrew, *Memoir on the Euphrates Valley Route* (London, 1857), *passim;* also *The Euphrates Valley Route to India* (London, 1882); F. R. Chesney, *Narrative of the Euphrates Expedition* (London, 1868); *The Proposed Imperial Ottoman Railway,* a prospectus issued by the promoters (London, 1857); F. von Koeppen, *Moltke in Kleinasien* (Hanover, 1883).

[2] *Cf.* article "Suez Canal" in *Encyclopedia Britannica,* Volume 26, p. 23. How similar were these objections to those subsequently advanced in opposition to the Bagdad Railway! *Cf., e. g.,* a statement by Lord Curzon, *Parliamentary Debates, House of Lords, fifth series,* Volume 7 (1911), pp. 583 *et seq.*

[3] Andrew, *Memoir on the Euphrates Valley Route,* p. 225.

⁴ *Parliamentary Debates, House of Lords,* fourth series, Volume 121 (1903), p. 1345; "The Bagdad Railway Negotiations," in *The Quarterly Review,* Volume 228 (1917), pp. 489-490; Baron Kuhn von Kuhnenfeld, *The Strategical Importance of the Euphrates Valley Railway* (English translation by Sir C. W. Wilson, London, 1873) ; V. L. Cameron, *Our Future Highway to India,* 2 volumes (London, 1880) ; A. Bérard, *La route de l'Inde par la vallée du Tigre et de l'Euphrate* (Lyons, 1887) ; F. Jones, *The Direct Highway to the East considered as the Perfection of Great Britain's duties toward British India* (London, 1873).

⁵ *Supra,* pp. 66-67.

⁶ *Parliamentary Debates, House of Commons,* Volume 120 (1903), pp. 1247-1248, 1358, 1361, 1364-1367, 1371-1374.

⁷ Lord Mount Stephen had been president of the Canadian Pacific Railway and of the Bank of Montreal. Lord Revelstoke was senior partner in the firm of Baring Brothers & Company and a director of the Bank of England.

⁸ The participation of the three Great Powers was to be on the basis of 25-25-25%, 15% was to be reserved for minor groups, and 10% for the Anatolian Railway Company. The provisions of Article 12 of the concession of 1903 were to be amended to establish a board of directors of 30, upon which each of the principal participants should be represented by 8 members. The remaining 6 members of the board were to be designated by the Ottoman Government and the Anatolian Railway Company. The directors were to be appointed by the original subscribers so that sale or transfer of shares could not alter the proportionate representation thus agreed upon.

⁹ For the facts in this and the succeeding paragraph the author is indebted to Dr. Arthur von Gwinner, managing director of the *Deutsche Bank;* and to Sir Henry Babington Smith, erstwhile chairman of the Ottoman Public Debt Administration, a partner of Sir Ernest Cassel, president of the National Bank of Turkey, and a director of the Bank of England. Dr. von Gwinner placed at the disposal of the author many of the records of the *Deutsche Bank* and of the Bagdad Railway Company, and Sir Henry Babington Smith graciously volunteered to answer many puzzling questions.

¹⁰ *Parliamentary Debates, House of Commons,* Volume 121 (1903), pp. 271-272.

¹¹ The British banking houses interested in the Bagdad enterprise were Baring Brothers, Sir Ernest Cassel, and Morgan-Grenfell Company. *Cf. The Westminster Gazette,* April 24, 1903; *Stenographische Berichte, XII Legislaturperiode, 2 Session,* Volume 260 (1910), p. 2181d. The bankers, of course, were not

bound by the decision of the Cabinet to withdraw from the negotiations; they still would have been at liberty to invest in Bagdad Railway securities, as did the French bankers. However, it has been the practice of British financiers to accept the "advice" of the Foreign Office in the case of loans which may lead to international complications. An analogous case in American experience was the decision of prominent New York financial institutions to withdraw from the Chinese consortium in 1913 because of the avowed opposition of President Wilson to the terms of the loan contract.

[12] *The Nineteenth Century,* Volume 65 (1909), pp. 1090-1091.

[13] *Supra,* pp. 30, 59-60.

[14] *Parliamentary Debates, House of Commons,* Volume 120, pp. 1360-1361; Volume 126, p. 108. The opinions of Mr. Gibson Bowles were not cordially received by *The Scotsman,* which said, April 9, 1903, "Mr. Gibson Bowles carried the House in imagination to the banks of the Euphrates and Tigris. Germany is there seeking by means of a railway to supersede our trade, and to serve herself heir to the wealth and empire of ancient Babylon and Assyria. The member for King's Lynn was, as usual, not very well posted up on his facts. On this occasion he was so entirely wrong-headed that no one on the opposition bench would agree with him. . . . The outstanding moral of the debate was, indeed, that the honorable member for King's Lynn was much in want of a holiday."

[15] Fraser, *op. cit.,* pp. 42-43. The senior member of the firm of Lynch Brothers was H. F. B. Lynch (1862-1913), who was widely known as an authority on the Near East and who, as a Liberal member of Parliament, 1906-1910, was able to call official attention to the necessity for safeguarding British interests in Persia and Mesopotamia. That he succeeded in convincing the Government of the importance of his navigation concession is evidenced by the vigorous protests filed by the British Government with the Young Turks in 1909, when the latter attempted to operate competing vessels on the Tigris and the Shatt-el-Arab. On this point see *Stenographische Berichte, XII Legislaturperiode, 2 Session,* Volume 260 (1910), pp. 2174d *et seq.* Again in 1913-1914, the British Government refused to consider any settlement of the Bagdad Railway question which did not adequately protect the interests of the Lynch Brothers. *Infra,* pp. 258-265. Mr. Lynch, however, was not an irreconcilable opponent of the *Deutsche Bank.* He took the point of view that the Germans had rendered Turkey a great service by the construction of the Anatolian Railways because of the total lack of natural means of communication in the Anatolian plateau. He urged that they were making a great mistake, however, to extend the

Anatolian system into Mesopotamia, where the Tigris and Euphrates provided natural and logical avenues of trade for the Valley of the Two Rivers. In Mesopotamia, he maintained, what was needed was a development of the river traffic, not the construction of railways. *Cf.* H. F. B. Lynch, "The Bagdad Railway," *Fortnightly Review,* March 1, 1911, pp. 384-386.

[16] It will be recalled that the Hamburg-American Line established a Persian Gulf service in 1906. *Supra,* pp. 108-109. Regarding the activities of British shipping and commercial interests in opposing the Bagdad Railway see *Diplomatic and Consular Reports,* No. 2950 (1902), pp. 25 *et seq.,* No. 3140 (1904), pp. 24 *et seq.; The Times,* April 24, 1903.

[17] G. N. Curzon, *Persia and the Persian Question* (2 volumes, London, 1892), Volume I, p. 635; a similar view was set forth by Sir Thomas Sutherland, of the P. & O., in a letter to *The Times,* April 27, 1903.

[18] E. Banse, *Auf den Spuren der Bagdadbahn* (Weimar, 1913), Chapter XI, *Die Wahrheit über die Bagdadbahn,* a critical analysis of the value of the Railway in Eastern trade, pp. 145-146. *Cf.,* also, Dr. R. Hennig, "Der verkehrsgeographische Wert des Suez- und des Bagdad-Weges," in *Georgraphische Zeitschrift,* Volume 22 (1916), pp. 649-656.

[19] *Specifications,* Articles 24-25. It might be added that the Company loyally observed this restriction; C. W. Whittall & Co., largest British merchants in Turkey so testified. *Anatolia,* p. 103; von Gwinner, *loc. cit.,* p. 1090. Sir Edward Grey said no complaints of discrimination against British goods had come to the attention of the Foreign Office. *Parliamentary Debates, House of Commons.* 5 Series, Volume 53 (1913), pp. 392-393.

[20] *Diplomatic and Consular Reports,* No. 3140, p. 30.

[21] Consider the dedication of Lord Curzon's *Persia and the Persian Question:* "To the officials, military and civil, in India, whose hands uphold the noblest fabric yet reared by the genius of a conquering nation, I dedicate this work, the unworthy tribute of the pen to a cause, which by justice or the sword, it is their high mission to defend, but whose ultimate safeguard is the spirit of the British people."

[22] Woolf, *op. cit.,* p. 24.

[23] Regarding the Anglo-Russian rivalry in the Middle East, *cf.* Rose, *op. cit.,* Part II, Chapters I-IV; Curzon, *Persia and the Persian Question,* Volume II, Chapter XXX.

[24] See a statement by Lord Lansdowne, in the House of Lords, *Parliamentary Debates,* fourth series, Volume 121 (1903), p. 1347, and a statement by Lord Curzon, *ibid.,* fifth series, Volume 7 (1911), pp. 583-587; also Curzon, *Persia and the Persian Question,* Volume II, Chapter XXVII. The strategic importance of

the Persian Gulf to the British Empire was realized by foreign observers, as well as by English statesmen. Writing in 1902, Admiral A. T. Mahan, an American, said, "The control of the Persian Gulf by a foreign state of considerable naval potentiality, a 'fleet in being' there based upon a strong military port, would reproduce the relations of Cadiz, Gibraltar, and Malta to the Mediterranean. It would flank all the routes to the farther East, to India, and to Australia, the last two actually internal to the Empire, regarded as a political system; and although at present Great Britain unquestionably could check such a fleet, so placed, by a division of her own, it might well require a detachment large enough to affect seriously the general strength of her naval position." A. T. Mahan, *Retrospect and Prospect* (New York, 1902), pp. 224-225. Lord Curzon is said to have remarked that he "would not hesitate to indict as a traitor to his country any British minister who would consent to a foreign Power establishing a station on the Persian Gulf." A. J. Dunn, *British Interests in the Persian Gulf* (London, 1907), p. 7. See also *The Persian Gulf* (No. 76 of the Foreign Office Handbooks); *Handbook of Arabia,* Volume I (Admiralty Intelligence Division, London, 1916); Lovat Fraser, *India under Curzon and After* (London, 1911).

[25] *Parliamentary Debates, House of Lords,* fourth series, Volume 121 (1903), pp. 1347-1348. Two observations should be made regarding this quotation. First, it is included in every book I have consulted on the Bagdad Railway, written since 1903, but in every instance the last sentence has been omitted— a sentence which considerably alters the spirit of the statement. Second, the German press, at the time, considered that the warning was directed, not at the Bagdad Railway, but at the rapid and alarming advance of Russia in Persia. *Cf.* an analysis of foreign press comments in an article by J. I. de La Tour, "Le chemin de fer de Bagdad et l'opinion anglaise," in *Questions diplomatiques et coloniales,* Volume 15 (1903), pp. 609-614—an excellent digest.

[26] *Cf.* a statement by Lord Cranborne, Under-Secretary of State for Foreign Affairs, in *Parliamentary Debates, House of Commons,* fourth series, Volume 101 (1902), p. 129. Although he was less than forty years of age at the time of his appointment as Governor-General of India (1898), the Right Honorable George Nathaniel Curzon, Baron Curzon of Kedleston, even at that early age, had had wide experience and training of the type so common among the masters of British imperial destiny. He was educated at Eton and Oxford, and he traveled widely in the Near East. He served as a member of Parliament from 1886 until 1898. He was Under-Secretary of State for India, 1891-

1892; Under-Secretary of State for Foreign Affairs, 1895-1898; Privy Councillor, 1895.

[27] *Supra,* p. 34; *The Annual Register,* 1901, pp. 304-305; K. Helfferich, *Die Vorgeschichte des Weltkrieges,* p. 129.

[28] Viscount Haldane, *Before the War* (London, 1920), pp. 48-51; Viscount Morley, *Recollections* (New York, 1917), p. 238.

[29] *Infra,* pp. 239-244; *Parliamentary Debates, House of Lords,* fifth series, Volume 7 (1911), pp. 583-587, 589. It is interesting to contrast this opinion of a German trans-Mesopotamian railway with that held by the same man when it was proposed that British capitalists should construct such a line. Writing in 1892, Lord Curzon had this to say regarding the project: "Its superficial attractions judiciously dressed up in a garb of patriotism, were such as to allure many minds; and I confess to having felt, without ever having succumbed to, the fascination. Closer study, however, and a visit to Syria and Mesopotamia have convinced me both that the project is unsound, and that it does not, for the present, at any rate, lie within the domain of practical politics." Lord Curzon believed that a Mesopotamian railway would be practically valueless for military purposes: "The temperature of these sandy wastes is excessively torrid and trying during the summer months and I decline to believe that during half the year any general in the world would consent to pack his soldiers into third class carriages for conveyance across those terrible thousand miles, at least if he anticipated using them in any other capacity than as hospital inmates at the end." *Persia and the Persian Question,* Volume I, pp. 633-635.

[30] *Parliamentary Debates, House of Commons,* fifth series, Volume 21 (1911), pp. 241-242.

[31] *Infra,* pp. 258-265.

[32] For the views of a typical British imperialist on the Persian situation, *cf.,* Curzon, *Persia and the Persian Question,* Volume II, Chapter XXX; a later account is that of the American, W. Morgan Shuster, *The Strangling of Persia* (New York, 1912); *cf.,* also, H. F. B. Lynch, "Railways in the Middle East," in *Proceedings of the Central Asian Society* (London), March 1, 1911.

[33] See P. Rohrbach, *Die Bagdadbahn,* p. 18; Reventlow, *op. cit.,* pp. 338-343. That Rohrbach's frank avowal of the menace of the Bagdad Railway to India and Egypt was not without influence in Great Britain is evidenced by the fact that long quotations from *Die Bagdadbahn* were read into the records of the House of Commons by the Earl of Ronaldshay, on March 23, 1911. *Parliamentary Debates,* fifth series, Volume 23, p. 628.

[34] Herr Scheidemann, in an eloquent speech to the Reichstag,

March 30, 1911, pleaded with the German Government to be sympathetic with the position in which Great Britain found herself. No nation with the imperial responsibilities of Great Britain could afford to neglect to take precautionary steps against the possibility of the Bagdad Railway being used as a weapon of offense against Egypt, the Suez Canal, and India. "Complications upon complications," he said, "are certain to arise as a result of the construction of the Bagdad Railway. But we expect of our Government, at the very least, that in the course of protecting the legitimate German economic interests which are involved in the Bagdad Railway, it will leave no stone unturned to prevent the development of Anglo-German hostility over the matter. We want to do everything possible to effect a thorough understanding with England. Only by such a policy can we hope to quiet the fears of British imperialists that the Railway is a menace to the Empire." *Stenographische Berichte, XII Legislaturperiode, 2 Session,* Volume 266 (1911), pp. 5980c-5984b.

[35] *Parliamentary Debates, House of Commons,* fifth series, Volume 21 (1911), pp. 241-242.

[36] *Cf.* H. N. Brailsford, *The War of Steel and Gold,* Chapter III, "The Egyptian Model."

[37] *Supra,* pp. 181-182.

[38] André Tardieu, *France and the Alliances* (New York, 1908), p. 46. For M. Tardieu's analysis of the causes of the growing Anglo-German hostility, *cf.* pp. 48-57. It was in the latter part of April, 1903, that the Bagdad Railway negotiations fell through. In May, Edward VII paid an official visit to Paris; in October, an arbitration agreement was signed by France and Great Britain. The following spring the treaties constituting the Entente Cordiale were executed. Sir Thomas Barclay, *Thirty Years' Reminiscences* (London, 1906), pp. 175 *et seq.* For the text of these agreements *cf. Parliamentary Papers,* Volume 103 (1905), No. Cd. 2384.

[39] For the text of the Anglo-Russian Entente, *cf. British and Foreign State Papers,* Volume 100, pp. 555 *et seq.* Regarding the nature of the Anglo-Russian rivalry in the Middle East and the effect of the Bagdad Railway in hastening a settlement of that rivalry, *cf.* Edouard Driault, *La question d'Orient depuis ses origines jusqu'à la paix de Sèvres* (Paris, 1921), Chapter VIII, and pp. 273 *et seq.*; also Tardieu, *op. cit.,* pp. 239-252, and Curzon, *op. cit.,* Volume II, Chapter XXX.

[40] Ernst Jäckh, *Die deutsch-türkische Waffenbrüderschaft* (Stuttgart, 1915), pp. 17-18.

[41] Sir William Willcocks (1852-   ) is one of the foremost

authorities on Egypt, India, and Mesopotamia. As a young man he was employed in India by the Department of Public Works and for a period of eleven years, 1872-1883, was engaged in the construction of the famous irrigation works there. From 1883-1893, he was employed in a similar capacity by the Egyptian Public Works and was largely responsible for the development of irrigation in the Nile Valley. In 1898, he planned and projected the Assuan Dam, which turned out to be the greatest irrigation work in the East. In 1909, Sir William Willcocks became consulting engineer to the Ottoman Ministry of Public Works, and was responsible for the construction, 1911-1913, by the British firm of Sir John Jackson, Ltd., of the famous Hindie barrage, the first step in the irrigation of the Valley of the Two Rivers.

[42] *Mesopotamia*, p. 54, and *The Geographical Journal*, August, 1912.

[43] *The Recreation of Chaldea* (Cairo, 1902). This suggestion led to the absurd charge by Dr. Rohrbach that Sir William Willcocks was actively promoting the establishment of a British colonial empire in southern Mesopotamia. *German World Policies*, pp. 160-161. *Cf.*, also, *Diplomatic and Consular Reports*, No. 3140 (1903), p. 27.

[44] H. H. Johnston, *Common Sense in Foreign Policy* (London, 1913), pp. v-vii. A similar opinion was expressed by Colonel A. C. Yate, at a meeting of the Central Asian Society, May 22, 1911. In answer to an alarmist paper on the Bagdad Railway which had been read to the society by André Chéradame, Colonel Yate made a spirited speech in which he warned his countrymen that M. Chéradame proposed that they should follow the same mistaken policy which had guided Lord Palmerston in resistance to the construction of the Suez Canal. "We cannot pick up every day," he said, "a Lord Beaconsfield, who will repair the errors of his blundering predecessors . . . Because the German Emperor and his instruments have adopted and put into practice the plans which Great Britain rejected [for a trans-Mesopotamian railway], we are now, forsooth, to pursue a policy which savours partly of 'sour grapes' and partly of 'dog-in-the-manger,' and which in either aspect will do nothing to strengthen British hands and promote British interests." *Proceedings of the Central Asian Society* (London), May 22, 1911, p. 19.

[45] Johnston, *op. cit.*, pp. 50-51, 61. Sir Harry Johnston made an extended lecture tour through Germany during 1912 for the purpose of promoting Anglo-German friendship. For details of this trip see Schmitt, *op. cit.*, pp. 355-356. It is interesting to note how nearly Sir Harry's proposals corresponded with the

terms of the treaties of 1913-1914. *Infra,* Chapter X. For a similar point of view, *cf.* Angus Hamilton, *Problems of the Middle East* (London, 1909), pp. 178-180.

[46] *Parliamentary Debates, House of Lords,* fifth series, Volume 7 (1911), pp. 601-602. The italics are mine.

CHAPTER IX

THE YOUNG TURKS ARE WON OVER

A GOLDEN OPPORTUNITY PRESENTS ITSELF TO THE ENTENTE POWERS

The Young Turk revolutions of 1908 and 1909, which ended the reign of Abdul Hamid in the Ottoman Empire, offered France and Great Britain an unprecedented opportunity to assume moral and political leadership in the Near East. Many members of the Committee of Union and Progress, the revolutionary party, had been educated in western European universities—chiefly in Paris—and had come to be staunch admirers of French and English institutions. "Liberty, Equality, Fraternity," the slogan of Republican France, became the watch-cry of the new era in Turkey. Parliamentary government and ministerial responsibility under a constitutional monarch, the political contribution of Britain to Western civilization, became the aim of the reformers at Constantinople. The Ottoman Empire was to be modernized politically, industrially, and socially according to the best of western European traditions.[1]

Into this scheme of things German influence fitted not at all. From the Young Turk point of view the Kaiser was an autocrat who not only had blocked democratic reform in Germany, but also had propped up the tottering régime of Abdul Hamid and thus had aided suppression of liberalism in the Ottoman Empire. As for Baron Marschall von Bieberstein, he had hobnobbed with the ex-Sultan and was considered as much a representative of the old order of things as Abdul Hamid himself. As Dr. Rohrbach described the situation, "the Young Turks, liberals of every shade, believed that Germany had been a staunch supporter of Abdul Hamid's tyrannical government and that the German influence constituted a decided danger for the era of liberalism. That thought was zealously supported by the English and French press in Constantinople. The Young Turkish liberalism showed in the beginning a decided leaning toward a certain form of Anglomania. England, the home of liberty, of parliaments, of popular government—such were the catch phrases promulgated in the daily papers." [2]

German prestige suffered still further because of the unseemly conduct of Germany's allies toward the Young Turk Government. The revolution of 1908 was less than three months old when Austria-Hungary annexed Bosnia-Herzegovina. Almost simultaneously, Ferdinand of Bulgaria—presumably at the instigation and with the connivance of Austria—declared the independence of Bulgaria from the Sultan and assumed for himself the title of tsar. To cap the climax, Italy was intriguing in Tripoli and Cyrenaica with a view to the eventual seizure of those provinces. Baron Marschall found it impossible to explain away these hostile moves of the allies of Germany, and he protested vehemently against the failure of the Foreign Office at Berlin to restrain Austria-Hungary and Italy. He warned Prince von Bülow that vigorous action must be taken if Germany's influence in the Near East were not to be totally destroyed. [3]

The decline of German prestige at Constantinople could not have been without effect upon the Bagdad Railway and the other activities of the *Deutsche Bank*. The Bagdad enterprise, in fact, was looked upon as a concrete manifestation of German hegemony at the Sublime Porte and as the crowning achievement of the friendship of those two autocrats of the autocrats, Abdul Hamid and William II. As such, it was certain to draw the fire of the reformers. The concession of 1903 had never been published in Turkey. Only fifty copies had been printed, and these had been distributed only among high officials of the Palace, the Sublime Porte, and the Ministries of War, Marine, and Public Works. It was generally supposed by the Union and Progress party, therefore, that the summaries published in the European press were limited to what the Sultan chose to make public. "The secrecy which thus enveloped the Bagdad Railway concession gave rise to the conviction that the contract contained, apart from detrimental financial and economic clauses, provisions which endangered the political independence of the State." [4] And Young Turks were determined to tolerate no such additional limitations on the sovereignty of their country.

The opening, in the autumn of 1908, of the first parliament under the constitutional régime in Turkey gave the opponents of the Bagdad Railway their chance. A bitter attack on the project—in which hardly a single provision of the contract of 1903 escaped scathing criticism—was delivered by Ismail Hakki Bey, representative from Bagdad, editor of foreign affairs for a well-known reform journal, and a prominent member of the Union and Progress party. Hakki Bey denounced the Railway as a political and economic monstrosity which could have been possible only under an autocratic and corrupt government; in any event, he believed, it could have no place in the New Turkey. He proposed complete repudiation of the existing contracts with the *Deutsche Bank*. In this proposal he received considerable support from other members of the parliament.

An equally ringing, but more reasoned, speech was delivered by the talented Djavid Bey, subsequently to become Young Turk Minister of Finance. He agreed that the concession of 1903 infringed upon the economic and administrative independence of the Ottoman Empire; he condemned the scheme of kilometric guarantees as an unwarranted and indefensible drain upon the Treasury; he denounced the preponderance of strategic over business considerations in the construction of the line; he made it plain that he had no wish to see the extension of German influence in Turkey. He believed that the Bagdad concession should be revised in the interest of Ottoman finance and Ottoman sovereignty. But there must be no repudiation. "We must accept the Bagdad Railway contract, because there should exist a continuity and a solidarity between generations and governments. If a revolutionary government remains true to the obligations of its predecessor—even if those obligations be contracted by a government of the worst and most despotic kind—it will arouse among foreigners admiration of the moral sense of the nation and will accordingly increase public confidence. Just now, more than at any other time in our history, we Turks need the confidence of the world." Everything should be done to effect a revision of the Bagdad Railway concession, however, and a firm resolve should be taken never again to commit the nation to such an engagement.

The anti-German and pro-Entente proclivities of the Young Turks were expressed in tangible ways. In 1909, for example, the Ottoman Navy was placed under the virtual command of a British admiral, and British officers continued to exercise comprehensive powers of administration over the ships and yards almost to the declaration of war in 1914. In 1909, also, Sir Ernest Cassel accepted an invitation to establish the National Bank of Turkey, for the purpose of promoting more generous investment of British capital in the Ottoman Empire. During the same year Sir William Willcocks was appointed consulting engineer to the Minister of Public Works, and his plans for the irrigation of Mesopotamia were put into immediate operation. Sir Richard Crawford, a British financier, was appointed adviser to the Minister of Finance; a British barrister was made inspector-general of the Ministry of Justice; a member of the British consular service became inspector-general of the Home Office. Later, serious consideration was given to a proposal to invite Lord Milner to head a commission to suggest reforms in the political and economic administration of Anatolia. A French officer was made inspector-general of the gendarmerie. In June, 1910, a French company was awarded a valuable concession for the construction of a railway from Soma to Panderma, and the following year the lucrative contract for the telephone service in Constantinople was granted to an Anglo-French syndicate.[5]

The Young Turk Government likewise was desirous of doing everything possible to remove French and British objections to the construction of railways in the Ottoman Empire. With this end in view they prevailed upon Dr. von Gwinner to reopen negotiations with Sir Ernest Cassel regarding British participation in the Bagdad Railway, and they secured the consent of the *Deutsche Bank* to a rearrangement of the terms of the concession of 1903. The latter was to be undertaken in accordance with British wishes and with due regard to the financial situation of Turkey. This was followed up, on November 8, 1909, by a formal request of the Ottoman ambassador at London for a statement of the terms upon which the British Government would withdraw its diplomatic objections to the Bagdad enterprise. Simultaneously negotiations were initiated for "compensations" to French interests, represented by the Imperial Ottoman Bank.

Until the end of the year 1909, then, the political situation in the Ottoman Empire under the revolutionary government had been almost altogether to the advantage of the Entente Powers. During 1910, however, German prestige began to revive in the Near East, and by the spring of 1911 German influence in Turkey had won back its former preëminent position.

The Germans Achieve a Diplomatic Triumph

The Young Turk program, in its political aspects, was not only liberal, but nationalist. In the fresh enthusiasm of the early months of the revolution, emphasis was laid upon modernizing the political institutions of the empire—parliamentary government and ministerial responsibility and equality before the law were the concern of the reformers. As time went on, however, liberalism was eclipsed by nationalism and modernizing by Ottomanizing. By the autumn of 1909 Turkish nationalist activities were in full swing. Revolts in Macedonia and Armenia were suppressed with an iron hand; there were massacres in Adana and elsewhere in Anatolia and Cilicia; restrictions were imposed upon personal liberties and upon freedom of the press; martial law was declared. Pan-Turkism and Pan-Islamism were revived as political movements.[6]

The development of an aggressive Turkish nationalism was not viewed with equanimity by the Entente nations. The newspapers of France and England roundly denounced the Adana massacres and came to adopt a hostile attitude toward the Young Turk Revolution, which only a short time previously they had extravagantly praised. Great Britain looked with apprehension upon Ottoman support of the nationalist movements in Egypt and India, and France was disturbed at the prospect of a Pan-Islamic revival in Tunis, Algeria, and Morocco. Russia demanded "reform" in Macedonia and Armenia and encouraged anti-Turk propaganda in the Balkans. English interference in Cretan affairs and British support of the insolent Sheik of Koweit still further complicated the situation.[7]

For Germany, on the other hand, Turkish nationalism held no menace. So far from desiring a weak Turkey— as did most of the other European Powers—her policy in the Near East was based upon the strengthening of Turkey. If Turkey was to be strong, she must suppress dissentient nationalist and religious minorities; therefore Germany raised no voice of protest against the Armenian and Macedonian atrocities. If Turkey sought to recover territories which formerly had acknowledged the suzerainty of the Sultan, Germany had nothing to fear; the Kaiser ruled over no such territories. If Turkey chose to arouse the Moslem world by a Pan-Islamic revival, that was no concern of Germany; the German Empire had a comparatively insignificant number of Mohammedan subjects. If the Turkish program discomfited the Entente Powers, that was to Germany's advantage in the great game of world politics; therefore Germany could afford to support the Young Turk Government. As in the days of Abdul Hamid, Germany appeared to be the only friend of the Ottomans.[8]

The improvement in the German political position at Constantinople was reflected in a changing Turkish attitude toward the Bagdad Railway. Among revolutionary leaders there was a growing realization of the great economic and political importance of railways and, particularly, of the Bagdad system. It became apparent upon examination, also, that others than Germans had obtained monopolistic concessions in the Ottoman Empire—in this respect the Lynch Brothers came in for a good deal of attention. The Ottoman General Staff—which had recalled General von der Goltz as chief military adviser—insisted that the early construction of a trans-Mesopotamian railway at whatever cost, was essential to the defence of the empire. In spite of serious financial difficulties resulting from strikes, increased cost of materials, and general economic paralysis which followed upon the heels of the revolutions of 1908 and 1909, the Anatolian and Bagdad Railway Companies advanced large sums to the Minister of Finance toward the ordinary expenses of running the Government. In addition, the concessionaires evinced a desire to meet all Turkish financial and diplomatic objections to the provisions of the concession of 1903.[9]

It was the financial needs of the Young Turk administration which enabled German diplomacy and the *Deutsche Bank* to reëstablish themselves thoroughly in the good graces of the Ottoman Government. But here again the Germans were given their chance only after England and France had turned the Turks away empty handed.

During the summer of 1910, Djavid Bey, as Ottoman Minister of Finance, went to Paris to raise a loan of $30,000,000, secured by the customs receipts of the Ottoman Empire. The negotiations with the Parisian bankers were complicated by a bitter anti-Turk campaign on the part of the press and by the frequent interference of the French Government. Nevertheless, Djavid Bey succeeded in signing a satisfactory contract with a French syndicate, and his task appeared to be accomplished. At this juncture, however, M. Pichon, French Minister of Foreign Affairs, informed the bankers that official sanction for the proposed loan would be withheld unless the Ottoman Government would consent to have its budget administered by a resident French adviser. The Young Turk ministry, determined to tolerate no further foreign intervention in the administrative affairs of the empire, flatly refused to consider any such proposal, and Djavid Bey was instructed to break off all negotiations. "As a true and loyal friend of France," wrote Djavid, "I regretted this incident as one likely to strain the future relations between the two countries."

From Paris Djavid Bey went to London. Sir Ernest Cassel appeared to be willing to negotiate a loan to Turkey of the desired amount, but, upon representations from M. Cambon, the French ambassador at London, Sir Edward Grey persuaded Cassel not to put in a bid for the bonds. This decision was reached largely, as Djavid Bey was informed by the British Foreign Office, because the Bagdad Railway was considered to be "an enterprise which under the existing concession has not been conceived in the best interests of the Ottoman Empire, while it offers, as at present controlled, an undoubted menace to the legitimate position of British trade in Mesopotamia." To the Turkish Government this statement was a piece of gratuitous impertinence, for, as Djavid Bey replied, "It was a prerogative only of the Ottoman Government to determine whether the conditions of construction and management of the Bagdad Railway were beneficial or detrimental to Turkey. England had no more right to object to the Bagdad Railway than Germany had to object to the British and French lines in operation in Turkey."

The collapse of the financial negotiations in Paris and London offered the *Deutsche Bank* an opportunity which its directors were too shrewd to overlook. Dr. Helfferich was despatched to Constantinople and within a few weeks had secured the contract for the entire issue of $30,000,-000 of the Ottoman Four Per Cent Loan of 1910, upon terms almost identical with those agreed upon with the French syndicate before M. Pichon's interference. "On this occasion," writes Djavid Bey, "the Germans handled the business with great intelligence and tact. They brought up no points which were not related directly or indirectly to the loan, and they made no conditions which would have been inconsistent with the dignity of Turkey. This attitude of Germany met with great approval on the part of the Turkish Government, which was then in a very difficult position. The result was the greatest diplomatic victory in the history of the Ottoman Empire between the revolution of 1908 and the outbreak of the Great War." [10]

The purchase of the loan of 1910 by the *Deutsche Bank,* however, did not solve the financial problems of the Young Turk Government. It was essential that measures be taken to increase the revenues of the Ottoman Empire. Accordingly, negotiations had been conducted during 1910, and were continued until midsummer of 1911, to secure the consent of the Powers to an increase of 4% in the customs duties. It was apparent from the outset that the British Government would block any project for an increase in Turkish taxes, unless it were granted important compensations of a political and economic character and unless it could determine, in large measure, the purposes for which the additional revenues would be expended. In this respect, also, it appeared that Entente policy was standing in the way of the success of the Revolution in Turkey!

British objections to the proposed increase in the Ottoman customs duties were founded in large part upon British opposition to the Bagdad Railway and, more particularly, to the sections of the Railway between Bagdad and the Persian Gulf. In the spring of 1910, the British Government proposed that a concession for a railway from Bagdad to Basra *via* Kut-el-Amara should be awarded to British financiers, in order that British economic interests in Mesopotamia might be adequately safeguarded. In May of that year Sir Edward Grey wrote the British ambassador at Constantinople, "Please explain quite clearly to the Turkish Government that the British Government will not agree to any addition to the taxes until this claim for a concession is taken into favorable consideration, and also that Great Britain's attitude towards Turkey will depend largely upon how she meets this demand of yours." Upon the refusal of the Ottoman Government to accede to this demand, Sir Edward Grey wrote to Sir Henry Babington Smith, English representative on the Ottoman Public Debt Administration, that England must be awarded at least a 55% participation in the Bagdad-Basra section of the Bagdad Railway, as well as concessions for the construction and control of port works at Koweit. In addition, Turkey should be made to understand that Great Britain could approve no agreement without the sanction of the French and Russian Governments.

When Djavid Bey was in London in July, 1910, he submitted two counterproposals to Sir Edward Grey: first, that the portion of the Bagdad Railway from Bagdad to Basra should be internationalized upon terms agreeable to Sir Ernest Cassel and Dr. Arthur von Gwinner; or, second, that the Ottoman Government itself should undertake the construction of the line beyond Bagdad. The British Foreign Office indicated that it might consent to an increase in the Ottoman customs duties until April, 1914, upon some such terms, provided the consent of the other Powers were forthcoming, and provided Turkey would surrender her right of veto over the borrowing powers of Egypt. Because of the collapse of the loan negotiations, however, nothing further came of these proposals.

On March 7, 1911, the Ottoman ministers at London and Paris presented to the British and French Governments respectively a proposition that the Bagdad-Basra section of the Bagdad Railway should be constructed by an Ottoman company, to the capital of which the Turkish Government should subscribe 40%, and German, French, and British capitalists 20% each. The Sublime Porte expressed a willingness, furthermore, to confer with representatives of France and Great Britain for the purpose of satisfying the legitimate political demands of those two nations in Syria and Mesopotamia. The following day, nevertheless, Sir Edward Grey informed the House of Commons that His Majesty's Government was not prepared to consent to an increase in the Turkish customs duties, because it was not clear that the Ottoman Government was ready to guarantee adequate protection to British commercial interests in Mesopotamia and the region of the Persian Gulf.[11]

This decision was received in Constantinople with undisguised animosity. Young Turks were as little disposed to tolerate British, as they were French, supervision of Ottoman finances and economic policies. The press roundly denounced the British and said that once again Turkey had been shown the wisdom of friendship for Germany.[12]

Entente actions were contrasted with the more conciliatory policy of the Germans. As early as November, 1910, Baron Marschall von Bieberstein had notified the Sublime Porte that Germany would place no obstacles in the way of an increase in the Ottoman customs duties and that, furthermore, his Government was prepared to urge that the Anatolian and Bagdad Railway Companies forego any additional assignment of Turkish revenues. During the first week of March, 1911, Dr. von Gwinner and Dr. Helfferich informed the Ottoman Government that the Bagdad Railway Company was willing to abandon its right to construct the sections of the line from Bagdad to Basra and the Persian Gulf, including the concessions for port and terminal facilities at Basra. The Turkish Government was to be given a free hand as to the disposition of the portion of the railway beyond Bagdad, with the single reservation that the *Deutsche Bank* should be awarded a share in the enterprise equal to that granted

any non-Ottoman group of financiers. The German proposals were accepted and incorporated in a formal convention of March 21, 1911, by which the Bagdad Railway
Company abandoned its claims to further commitments
from the Ottoman Treasury and agreed, at the pleasure
of the Turkish Government, to surrender its concession
for the Bagdad-Basra-Persian Gulf sections to an Ottoman company internationally owned and controlled.[13]

The outcome of the negotiations for an increase in the
customs duties was a keen disappointment to the Young
Turks. Desirous as they were of carrying the Bagdad
enterprise to a successful conclusion, they could not help
resenting its political implications. "We tried," writes
Djavid Bey, "to better our relations with the English; they
talked to us of the Bagdad Railway! We tried to introduce financial and economic reforms in Turkey; we found
before us the Bagdad Railway! Every time an occasion
arose, the French stirred up the Bagdad Railway question.
Even the Russians, notwithstanding the Potsdam Agreement,[14] constantly waved in their hands the Bagdad
weapon." This resentment was fortified by the knowledge
that those who opposed the Bagdad Railway were those
who believed that the Sick Man would die and were interested in the division of his inheritance. From these
Powers Turkey could accept no tutelage!

THE GERMAN RAILWAYS JUSTIFY THEIR EXISTENCE

From the Turkish point of view, the best test of the
wisdom of supporting the German railway concessions in
Turkey was an examination of the results achieved in improving political and economic conditions in the Ottoman
Empire. By 1914 the Anatolian Railways and part of the
Bagdad Railway had been in existence a sufficient length
of time to appraise their worth to Asia Minor, and the

appraisal thus arrived at would be a fair prognostication of the value of the entire system when it should be opened to operation.

Dr. von Gwinner, in justification of the Bagdad Railway enterprise, summarized what he believed to be the chief services of the Anatolian Railways to Turkey. "More than twenty years ago," he wrote in 1909, "my predecessor, the late George von Siemens, conceived the idea of restoring to civilization the great wastes of Asia Minor and Mesopotamia, once and for long the center of the history of humanity. The only means of achieving that end was by building railways; this was undertaken, slowly but persistently, and with marvelous results. Constantinople and the Turkish army at that time were eating bread made from Russian flour; they are now eating grain of their own country's growth. Security in Asia Minor at that time was hardly greater than it is to-day in Kurdistan. When the *Deutsche Bank's* engineers reached a station a little beyond Ismid (Nikomedia) on the Sea of Marmora, the neighborhood was infested by Tscherkess robbers; the chief of those robbers is now a stationmaster of the Anatolian Railway Company, drawing about £100 *per annum,* a party as respectable as the late Mr. Micawber after his conversion to thrift. The railways brought ease to the peasantry, who are obtaining for their harvest twice to four times the price formerly paid, and the railways have brought revenue to the Treasury. The Anatolian Railway's lines are in as good condition as any line in the United Kingdom, and their transportation charge is less than half the rates of any railway in England." [15]

Although this was the statement of an avowed protagonist of the Anatolian Railway, the testimony of other observers must lead to the conclusion that it was not an overestimate of the value of the Anatolian system. As early as 1903, for example, the British Consul General at Constantinople wrote: "There is no doubt that the agricultural production of the districts traversed by the Angora Railway has increased largely. Before the Angora Railway was opened there was no export of grain from that district; the annual export of wheat and barley is now from £1,500,000 to £2,000,000. The Railway has attracted a large number of immigrants from Bulgaria and Russia, who have settled in the most fertile parts. They form a hardworking and intelligent population, accustomed to more civilized methods of cultivation than the Anatolian peasantry. Population, improved communications and security are the essentials required for the development of Asia Minor. The Railway attracts the one and creates the others. All agree that the country along the Railway is much safer than elsewhere. It would be surprising, therefore, if the production of the country did not increase." [16]

The improvement in economic conditions in Anatolia became more marked as time went on. The Anatolian Railway Company established a special agricultural department for the education of the peasantry in more improved methods of farming; nurseries and experimental stations were maintained; demonstrations were given of the best systems of irrigation and drainage; attention was paid to the development of markets for surplus products of various kinds. American agricultural machinery was introduced and promised to become widely adopted. As a result of these improvements, the agricultural output of the country increased by leaps and bounds, and the cultivated areas in some districts were more than doubled. Famine, formerly a common occurrence, became a thing of the past, because irrigation eliminated the danger of recurrent droughts and floods. Increased production assured a plentiful food supply, and improved transportation enabled the surplus of one district to be transferred, in case of need, to another. All in all, the peasantry were developing qualities of industry, thrift, and adaptability which seemed to forecast great things for the future of Asia Minor.[17]

Furthermore, the German railways in Turkey, the failure of which had been freely prophesied, proved to be successful business enterprises. The directors took all possible steps to build up the earning power of the lines, rather than depend upon the minimum return guaranteed by the Ottoman Government. The railways were efficiently and intelligently administered—the operating expenses of the Anatolian and Bagdad lines never exceeded 47% of the gross receipts, although the operating expenses of the chief European railways, under much more favorable conditions, varied from 54% to 62% of gross receipts during the same period. Occasional dividends of 5% or 6% were paid by the Anatolian and Bagdad Railway Companies between 1906 and 1914, but only when the disbursements were warranted by earnings. In 1911, a notable advance was made by the introduction of oil-burning locomotives on the Bagdad lines; henceforth the German railways in Turkey were operated with fuel purchased from the Standard Oil Company of New Jersey! [18]

This scrupulously careful management eventually brought its reward. In 1911, the earnings of the Angora line exceeded the kilometric guarantee and, in accordance with the terms of the concession, the Ottoman Government received a share of the receipts. In 1912, the returns of the Eski Shehr-Konia line also exceeded the sum guaranteed by the Government, the Ottoman Treasury receiving a share of the earnings of the Anatolian system to an amount of more than $200,000. After 1913, no further payments to the Anatolian Railway Company were required under the kilometric guarantees.[19]

The results on the completed sections of the Bagdad Railway were equally promising, as will be indicated by the following table: [20]

Year	Kilometres in Operation	Passengers	Freight Tons	Gross Receipts per Kilometre (Francs)	Total Government Subsidy (Francs)
1906	200	29,629	13,693	1,368.83	624,028.21
1907	200	37,145	23,643	1,754.44	546,129.77
1908	200	52,759	15,941	1,839.86	529,443.12
1909	200	57,026	15,364	1,936.72	509,565.45
1910	200	71,665	27,756	2,571.43	381,135.58
1911	238	95,884	38,046	3,379.34	238,166.59
1912	609	288,833	57,670	5,315.67	*278,785.25*
1913	609	407,474	78,645	3,786.53	216,295.17
1914	887	597,675	116,194	8,177.97	*2,939,983.00*

Figures in italics indicate payments *to* the Turkish Government of its share of the receipts in excess of the guarantee of 4,500 francs per kilometre.

The improvement in the economic conditions of Anatolia, and the success of the German railways as business enterprises, were sources of great satisfaction and profit to the Imperial Ottoman Government. Not only was the Treasury receiving revenue from the railway lines which had formerly been a drain upon the financial resources of the empire, but the receipts from taxes in the regions traversed by the railways were constantly increasing. As early as 1893 the Ottoman Ministry of Public Works announced that the increase in tithes and the increased value of farm lands in Asia Minor had more than justified expenditures by the Sultan's Government in subsidies to the Anatolian Railway.[21] For those portions of Anatolia which were served by the Railway, the amount of the tithes had almost doubled in twenty years: in 1889, the year after the award of the Anatolian concession, $639,760 was collected; in 1898, $948,070; in 1908, $1,240,450. In certain districts the amount of the tithes collected in 1908 was five or six times as great as the yield before the construction of the Railway.[22]

The economic prospects of Turkey never were brighter than they were just before the outbreak of the Great War. The new régime had removed many of the vexatious restrictions on individual initiative which had characterized the rule of Abdul Hamid. The country's losses in men in the Italian and Balkan wars had been made up by an immigration of Moslem refugees from the ceded territories. Numerous concessions had been granted for the exploitation of mines, the construction of public utilities, and the improvement of the means of communication. "There was a feeling abroad in the land that an era of exceptional commercial and industrial activity was about to dawn upon Turkey." The Ottoman Empire was in a fair way to become modernized according to Western standards.[23]

Thus the Anatolian and Bagdad Railways achieved all that was claimed for them by their sponsors. They increased political security in Asia Minor; they brought about an economic renaissance in the homeland of the Turks; they justified the investment of public funds which was necessary to bring the system to completion. Beyond the Amanus Mountains lay the plains of Syria and the great unexploited wealth of Mesopotamia. A development of Mesopotamia, even as modest as that achieved in Anatolia, would pay the cost of the Bagdad Railway many times over. Were the Ottoman statesmen who supported this great project to be condemned for so great a service to their country? Or would they have been short-sighted had they failed to realize the great potentialities of railway construction in Asiatic Turkey? That the Bagdad Railway contributed to the causes of Turkish participation in the Great War—and to the disintegration of the Ottoman Empire—was not so much the fault of the Turks themselves as it was the blight laid upon Turkey, a "backward nation," by European imperialism.

THE YOUNG TURKS HAVE SOME MENTAL RESERVATIONS

Although the revolutionary party in Turkey had come to look with favor upon German influence in the Near East, and particularly to support the Bagdad Railway, there is little reason for accepting the too hastily drawn conclusion that the Young Turks had sold their country to the Kaiser or that they were under a definite obligation to subscribe to German diplomatic policies. They were too strongly nationalistic for that. They believed that the Ottoman Empire must eventually rid itself of foreign administrative assistance, foreign capital invested under far-reaching economic concessions, and foreign interference in Ottoman political affairs. But for a period of transition—during which Turkey could learn the secrets of Western progress and adapt them to her own purposes—it was the obvious duty of a forward-looking government to utilize European capital and European technical assistance for the welfare of the empire. Patriotism and modernism went hand in hand in the Young Turk program.[24]

The Young Turks were not unaware of the menace of the Bagdad Railway to their own best hopes. As Djavid Bey appropriately says: "The great drawback of this enterprise was its political character, which clung to it and became a source of endless toil and anxiety for the country. In a word, it poisoned the political life of Turkey. If the Bagdad concession had not been granted, the revolutionary government could have solved much more easily pending political and economic problems. But one must admire the courage of Abdul Hamid in granting the concession, no matter what the cost, because the construction of the Bagdad line was essential for the defence and the economic progress of the empire. Unfortunately for Turkey, she has always had to suffer from such politico-economic concessions.

"The Bagdad Railway did not escape the malady of politics. When one entered the meeting room of the company, one breathed the atmosphere of the ministerial chamber in *Wilhelmstrasse* and felt in both Gwinner and Helfferich the presence of undersecretaries for foreign affairs. This state of affairs, instead of simplifying the negotiations and relations between Germany and Turkey, served only to envenom them."

BIBLIOGRAPHICAL AND EXPLANATORY NOTES

[1] For accounts of the Young Turk Revolutions see René Pinon, *L'Europe et la jeune Turquie* (Paris, 1911); V. Bérard, *La rèvolution turque* (Paris, 1909); C. R. Buxton, *Turkey in Revolution* (London, 1909); Ernst Jäckh, *Der aufsteigende Halbmond* (Berlin, 1911); A. H. Lybyer, "The Turkish Parliament," in *Proceedings of the American Political Science Association*, Volume VII (1910), pp. 66 *et seq.*; S. Panaretoff, *Near Eastern Affairs and Conditions* (New York, 1922), Chapter V; A. Kutschbach, *Die türkische Revolution* (Halle, 1909); Baron C. von der Goltz, *Der jungen Türkei Niederlage und die Möglichkeit ihrer Wiedererhebung* (Berlin, 1913).

[2] Paul Rohrbach, *Germany's Isolation*, p. 50.

[3] Karl Helfferich, *Die deutsche Türkenpolitik*, p. 21.

[4] This quotation, together with many other facts in this chapter, is from a lengthy memorandum of Djavid Bey on the Bagdad Railway, prepared especially for the use of the author in the writing of this book. It is dated January 3, 1923, and was forwarded from the Lausanne Conference for Peace in the Near East. Unless otherwise specified, quotations from Djavid Bey here given are from this memorandum. There probably is no person who knows more of the Ottoman point of view on the Bagdad Railway than Djavid, who as Young Turk Minister of Finance and, later, as Turkish delegate to the Ottoman Public Debt Administration has had perhaps an unprecedented opportunity to observe the financial and economic ramifications of European imperialism in the Near East.

[5] *Diplomatic and Consular Reports*, No. 4835 (1911), p. 16; *Mesopotamia*, p. 41; *The Annual Register*, 1911, pp. 364-365; *Armenia and Kurdistan*, p. 62; *Turkey in Europe*, pp. 72-73; *Anatolia*, pp. 51-52, 81; *infra*, pp. 244-246.

[6] Pan-Turkism, or Pan-Turanianism, started as a cultural movement among Ottoman intellectuals. It assumed political aspects as a result of three important circumstances: 1. Aggressions against Turkey by foreign powers; 2. The ardent nationalism of the Balkan states bordering on Turkey; 3. The existence within Turkey of vigorous dissident nationalities, such as the Armenians and the Arabs. Pan-Turanianism and Pan-Islamism, although separate movements, had much in common. In 1911, at any rate, the Young Turks adopted Pan-Islamism as part of their program. Pinon, *op. cit.*, pp. 134 *et seq.*; *Mohammedan History*, pp. 89-96; Sir Thomas Barclay, *The Turco-Italian War and Its Problems* (London, 1912), pp. 100 *et seq.*

[7] For an excellent statement of the reaction of Turkish nationalism upon European politics see *The Quarterly Review*, Volume 228 (1917), pp. 511 *et seq.*

[8] Regarding the coincidence of German and Turkish interests during the reign of Abdul Hamid *cf. supra*, pp. 64-65, 125-130.

[9] *Report of the Anatolian Railway Company*, 1908 and 1909, pp. 8-9; *The Annual Register*, 1909, pp. 337 *et seq.*; *Stenographische Berichte, XII Legislaturperiode, I Session*, Volume 260 (1910), pp. 2174d *et seq.*

[10] From Djavid Bey's memorandum. For scattered details of these negotiations see *The Annual Register*, 1910, pp. 336-340; *Report of the Deutsche Bank*, 1910, pp. 13 *et seq.*; K. Helfferich, *Die deutsche Türkenpolitik*, pp. 23 *et seq.*; Ostrorog, *op. cit.*, pp. 60-61.

[11] *Parliamentary Debates, House of Commons*, fifth series, Volume 22 (1911), pp. 1284-1285. For further details of the negotiations of 1909-1911 *cf.* B. von Siebert, *Diplomatische Aktenstücke zur Geschichte der Ententepolitik der Vorkriegsjahre* (Berlin and Leipzig, 1921), Chapters VIII and IX. Hereinafter cited as *de Siebert* documents.

[12] *Cf.* foreign correspondence of *The Times*, March 21, 1911.

[13] *Troisième convention additionelle à la convention du 5 Mars, 1903, relative au chemin de fer de Bagdad* (Constantinople, 1911) ; *supra*, pp. 111-113.

[14] *Cf. infra*, Chapter X.

[15] *The Nineteenth Century*, Volume 65 (1909), pp. 1083-1084.

[16] *Diplomatic and Consular Reports*, No. 3140 (1903), p. 29.

[17] *Société du chemin de fer d'Anatolie—Jahresbericht des Agrikultur-Dienstes* (Berlin, 1899 *et seq.*), *passim*.

[18] *Archiv für Eisenbahnwesen,* Volume 31 (Berlin, 1908), pp. 207-211, 1485-1491; *Commerce Reports,* No. 18d (Washington, 1915), p. 9; *Diplomatic and Consular Reports,* No. 4835 (1911), p. 17; *Report of the Anatolian Railway Company,* 1910-1913, *passim.*

[19] *Report of the Anatolian Railway,* 1911-1914, *passim.*

[20] Compiled from the *Report of the Bagdad Railway Company,* 1903-1914. Figures for the years 1904 and 1905 are incomplete and have therefore been omitted. It should be kept in mind in reading this table that the years 1912-1914 were abnormal, especially as regards passenger traffic, because of the two Balkan Wars and the Great War.

[21] *The Levant Herald* (Constantinople), October 25, 1893.

[22] Caillard, *loc. cit.,* p. 439.

[23] *Commerce Reports,* No. 18d (1915), pp. 1-2.

[24] *Cf. Questions diplomatiques et coloniales,* Volume 26 (1908), pp. 475-477.

CHAPTER X

BARGAINS ARE STRUCK

THE KAISER AND THE TSAR AGREE AT POTSDAM

During the early days of November, 1910, William II entertained at the Potsdam palace his fellow sovereign Nicholas II, Tsar of all the Russias. He extended his royal hospitality, also, to the recently chosen foreign ministers of Germany and Russia respectively—Herr von Kiderlen-Waechter, next to the ambassador at Constantinople the Kaiser's most competent expert on the tortuous affairs of the Near East; and M. Sazonov, subsequently to guide Russian foreign policy during the critical days of July, 1914. It was apparent even to the untutored that there was some political significance to the conference between the German Emperor and his distinguished guests, and the press was rife with speculation as to what the outcome would be. The answer was forthcoming on November 4, when it was announced that the Kaiser and the Tsar, with the advice and assistance of their foreign ministers, had reached an agreement on the Bagdad Railway question.

A short time later the terms of this Potsdam Agreement were made public. As outlined by the German Chancellor, with some subsequent modifications, they were as follows: 1. Germany recognized the Russian sphere of interest in northern Persia, as defined by the Anglo-Russian agreement of 1907, and undertook not to seek or support concessions for railways, roads, telegraphs, or other means of communication in the region; in other words, there was to be no change in the *status quo*. 2. Russia recognized the rights of the *Deutsche Bank* in the Bagdad Railway and agreed to withdraw all diplomatic opposition to the construction of the line and to the participation of foreign capital therein. 3. Russia agreed to obtain from Persia, as soon as possible, a concession for the construction of a railway from Teheran, the capital city, to Khanikin, an important commercial city on the Turco-Persian frontier. This new railway was to be linked with a branch of the Bagdad system to be constructed in accordance with the terms of the concession of 1903 from Sadijeh, on the Tigris, to Khanikin. Both lines were to be planned for through international traffic. If, for any reason, the Russian Government should fail to build the proposed railway from Teheran to Khanikin, it was understood that German promoters might then apply for the concession. 4. The policy of the economic open door was to be observed by both nations. Russia agreed not to discriminate against German trade in Persia, and the two nations pledged reciprocal equality of treatment on the new railway lines from Sadijeh to Teheran.[1]

Russia had a great deal to gain and little to lose by the Potsdam Agreement. Whether Russia liked it or not, the Bagdad Railway had become a going concern, and there was every indication that another decade would see its completion. When finished, the Bagdad system, together with projected Persian lines, would provide Russian trade with direct communications with the Indies (*via* Bagdad and the Persian Gulf) and with the Mediterranean (*via* Mosul, Aleppo, and the Syrian coast). By the entente of 1907 with Great Britain the Tsar had renounced his imperial interests in southern Persia; therefore he had little to gain by a dog-in-the-manger attitude toward the development of Mesopotamia by the Germans. Under these circumstances continued resistance to the

Bagdad Railway appeared to be short-sighted and futile. Cheerful acquiescence, on the other hand, might bring tangible diplomatic compensations. In addition, it has been suggested, Russian reactionaries were delighted at the prospect of a *rapprochement* with Prussia, in which they saw the last strong support of a dying autocracy.[2]

From the German point of view the agreement with Russia was a diplomatic triumph. All that Germany conceded was recognition of Russia's special position in Persia, which affected no important German interests and exerted no appreciable influence on the balance of power in the Near East. In return, German trade was to be admitted to the markets of Persia, heretofore an exclusively British and Russian preserve; the sphere of the Bagdad Railway was to be considerably enlarged; Russian political obstruction of the Bagdad enterprise was to cease. Russian objections had been the first stumbling block in the way of the Railway; Russian protests had been the instigation of French opposition; now Russian recognition held out high promise for the final success of the Great Plan. The first breach had been made in the heretofore solid front presented by the Entente.[3]

Outside of Germany and Russia, however, the Potsdam Agreement met with a heated reception. The Ottoman press complained that Turkey was being politely ignored by two foreign powers in the disposition of her rights. One Constantinople daily said it was a sad commentary on Turkish "sovereignty" that in an important treaty on the Bagdad Railway "there is no mention of us, as if we had no connection with that line, and we were not masters of Bagdad and Basra and the ports of the Persian Gulf."[4] M. Hanotaux, a former French minister of foreign affairs, expressed his belief that "the negotiations at Potsdam have created a situation which, from every point of view, obliges us to ask, now, if Russia has dissolved the Triple

Entente." [5]   **Mr.** Lloyd George delivered a particularly
venomous attack upon Russia for having disregarded her
diplomatic engagements, and he announced in clarion tones
that this desertion from the ranks of the Entente—even
if condoned by France—would not cause Great Britain
to alter one iota her former policy.[6]   The "Slav peril"
appeared to be more keenly appreciated, for the moment,
in France and England than in Germany!

M. Jaurès, the brilliant French Socialist parliamentarian,
believed that the Potsdam Agreement was an admirable
instance of the menace of the Russian Alliance to the
security of France and the peace of Europe.   During the
course of a bitter debate in the Chamber of Deputies he
confronted the Minister of Foreign Affairs, M. Pichon,
with this dilemma: "What is the situation in which you
find yourself? You are going to be faced, you already are
faced, with a *fait accompli,* a Russo-German convention
on the Bagdad question. What do you propose to do?
Well, you may pursue an independent course and continue to oppose the Bagdad Railway. In that event you
will be in the unenviable position of opposing Germany
in an enterprise to which Russia—whose interests are
more directly involved—has given her support. Or, on
the other hand, you may subscribe with good grace to this
enterprise which Russia commends to you. What then
will be your situation? For some years France has successfully resisted the Bagdad Railway. If during this
time we have sulked at the enterprise, it was not of our
own choice, but out of regard for Russia, because Russia
believed her interests to be menaced. In short, we arrive
at this paradox. You have created an extremely delicate
situation between France and Germany by opposing the
Bagdad Railway, in which you had no interests other
than those of Russia. And now it is this same Russia
which, without previously consulting you, places at the

disposal of Germany the moral advantage of compelling you—you who resisted only on behalf of Russia—to accede to the Bagdad Railway." Was this the sort of ally to whom France should entrust her national safety? [7]

In the midst of the storm over the Potsdam Agreement, M. Stephen Pichon and Sir Edward Grey alone appeared to be unruffled. Both of these gentlemen, interpolated in the Chamber of Deputies and the House of Commons respectively, averred that they saw no reason for becoming disturbed or alarmed at the new Russo-German understanding. This point of view was incomprehensible to the average citizen, unskilled in the niceties of professional diplomacy, until on January 31, 1911, M. Jaurès forced M. Pichon to admit that the French Foreign Office had been informed of the character of the Potsdam negotiations before they took place. Less than a month later Mr. Lloyd George severely criticized his fellow-minister Sir Edward Grey for having taken no action against the policy of Russia at Potsdam, although, as Foreign Secretary, Sir Edward had been fully posted on the nature of the negotiations. Apparently, then, Russia had come to the agreement with Germany only after having consulted France and Great Britain and, perhaps, after having received their consent.[8]

There were a few persons who hoped that the Potsdam Agreement might be the first step in a general settlement of the Bagdad Railway entanglement. One humble member of the House of Commons, Mr. Pickersgill, said, for example, "I cannot understand the policy of continued antagonism to Germany. Ex-President Roosevelt recently gave much good advice to our Foreign Minister, and amongst other things he said that the presence of Germany on the Euphrates would strengthen the position of Great Britain on the Nile. . . . The action of Russia in the recent meeting at Potsdam has brought matters to a head, and I hope the Foreign Office will approach Turkey with a view to an arrangement for the completion of the Bagdad Railway which might be agreeable to Turkey, Germany and ourselves." [9]

The hope of Mr. Pickersgill was fulfilled, for the agreement of November 4, 1910, proved to be the first of a series of conventions regarding the Near East negotiated between 1911 and 1914 by Germany, Turkey, Great Britain and France. On the eve of the Great War the Bagdad Railway controversy had been all but settled!

FRENCH CAPITALISTS SHARE IN THE SPOILS

France, relieved of the necessity of supporting Russia's strategic objections to the Bagdad Railway, was glad to compromise with Turkey—in return for compensatory concessions to French investors. The sharp rebuff given M. Pichon by the Young Turks in the loan negotiations of the spring and summer of 1910 had convinced French diplomatists and business men alike that a policy of bullying the new administration at Constantinople would be futile.[10] Continued obstruction of Ottoman economic rehabilitation could have but two effects: to injure French prestige and prejudice the interests of French business; to drive the Young Turks into still closer association with the German Government and still greater dependence upon German capitalists. On the other hand, a conciliatory policy might be rewarded by profitable participation of French bankers in the economic development of Turkey-in-Asia and by a revival of French political influence at the Sublime Porte.

Even before the negotiation of the Potsdam Agreement the Young Turks had smiled upon French financial interests in the hope that the French Government might adopt a more friendly attitude toward the new régime in Turkey.

In June, 1910, for example, the Smyrna-Cassaba Railway was authorized to extend its existing line from Soma, in western Anatolia, to Panderma, on the Sea of Marmora. The concession carried with it the highest kilometric guarantee (18,800 francs) ever granted a railway in the Ottoman Empire, although the construction of the line offered fewer engineering and financial difficulties than other railways which had been constructed under less favorable terms. From the standpoint of the Turkish Government, however, the Soma-Panderma railway offered economic and strategic returns commensurate with the investment, for it was part of a comprehensive plan for the improvement of commercial and military communications in Asia Minor.[11]

The acceptance of this concession by French capitalists —presumably with the approval, certainly without the opposition, of their Government—was an interesting commentary on the official attitude of the French Republic toward the Bagdad Railway. If it was unprincipled for Germans to accept a guarantee for the construction and operation of their railways in Turkey, it is difficult to ascertain what dispensation exempted Frenchmen from the same stigma. If the Anatolian and Bagdad systems were anathema because of their possible utilization for military purposes, little justification can be offered for the Soma-Panderma line, which, completed in 1912, was one of the principal factors in the stubborn defence of the Dardanelles three years later.

Shortly after the promulgation of the Soma-Panderma convention additional steps were taken by the Ottoman Government toward the further extension of French railway interests in Anatolia and Syria. Negotiations were initiated with the Imperial Ottoman Bank for the award to a French-owned company, *La Société pour la Construction et l'Exploitation du Réseau de la Mer Noire,* of a concession for a comprehensive system of railways in northern Anatolia. It was proposed to construct elaborate port works at the Black Sea towns of Heraclea, Samsun, and Trebizond, and to connect the new ports by railway with the inland towns of Erzerum, Sivas, Kharput, and Van. Connections were to be established at Boli and Sivas with extensions to the Anatolian Railways, and at Arghana with a branch of the Bagdad line to Nisibin and Diarbekr. Thus adequate rail communications would be provided from the Ægean to the Persian Gulf, from the Black Sea to the Syrian shore of the Mediterranean.[12]

Simultaneously, negotiations were being carried on between the Ottoman Ministry of Public Works and the Imperial Ottoman Bank for extensive concessions to the French Syrian Railways, owned and operated by *La Société du Chemin de Fer de Damas-Hama et Prolongements*. Provision was made for the construction of port and terminal facilities at Jaffa, Haifa, and Tripoli-in-Syria; a traffic agreement was negotiated with the Ottoman-owned Hedjaz Railway, pledging both parties to abstain from discriminatory rates and other unfair competition; tentative arrangements were made for the construction of a line from Homs to the Euphrates. Provisional agreements embodying the Black Sea and Syrian railway and port concessions were signed in 1911, but technical difficulties of surveying the lines, together with the political instability occasioned by the Tripolitan and Balkan Wars, postponed the definitive contract.[13]

After the Treaty of Bucharest, August 10, 1913, the Ottoman Government was more determined than ever to do everything in its power to eliminate French opposition to railway construction in Asia Minor and to secure French aid in the further economic development of Turkey. Crushing defeats at the hands of the Italians and the Balkan states had emphasized the deficiencies of Ottoman

communications, Ottoman economic and military organization, Ottoman financial resources. The national treasury, emptied by the drain of three wars, needed replenish-
ment by an increase in the customs duties, to which French
sanction would have to be obtained, and by a foreign loan,
for which it was hoped French bankers would submit a
favorable bid. All of these questions were so closely associated with the question of political influence in the Near
East, however, that it was obviously desirable to arrive at
some *modus vivendi* between French and German interests in Ottoman railways and in Ottoman financial affairs.
Accordingly, the Young Turk Government prevailed upon
the Imperial Ottoman Bank and the *Deutsche Bank* to
discuss a basis for a Franco-German agreement, and
Djavid Bey was despatched to Paris to conduct whatever negotiations might be necessary with the French
Government.

On August 19 and 20 and September 24, 25, 26, 1913,
a series of important meetings was held in Berlin to ascertain upon what terms French and German investments in
Turkey might be apportioned with the least possibility of
conflict. German interests were represented by Dr. von
Gwinner and Dr. Helfferich; the chief of the French
negotiators were Baron de Neuflize, a Regent of the Bank
of France, and M. de Klapka, Secretary-General of the
Imperial Ottoman Bank. Supposedly the conferences were
conducted only between the interested financiers, but the
discussions were participated in by representatives of the
French, German, and Ottoman foreign offices. Obstacles
which, at the start, seemed insurmountable were overcome
at the Berlin meetings and a series of minor conferences
which followed. The result was one of the most important international agreements of the years immediately
preceding the Great War—the secret Franco-German convention of February 15, 1914. The terms of this agree-

ment, heretofore unpublished, may be summarized as
follows: [14]

1. Northern Anatolia was recognized as a sphere of French
influence for purposes of railway development. Arrangements
were concluded for linking the Anatolian and Bagdad systems
with the proposed Black Sea Railways, and traffic agreements
satisfactory to all of the companies were ratified and appended
to the convention. It was agreed that the port and terminal
facilities at Heraclea should be constructed by a Franco-German
company.

2. Syria, likewise, was recognized as a French sphere of influence. In particular, the right of the Syrian Railways to construct a line from Tripoli-in-Syria to Deir es Zor, on the
Euphrates, was confirmed. A traffic agreement between the
Bagdad and Syrian companies was ratified and appended to
the convention.

3. The regions traversed by the Anatolian and Bagdad Railways were defined as a German sphere of influence. A neutral
zone was established in Northern Syria to avoid infringement
upon German or French rights in that region.

4. The *Deutsche Bank* and the Imperial Ottoman Bank each
pledged itself to respect the concessions of the other, to seek no
railway concessions within the sphere of influence of the other,
and to do nothing, directly or indirectly, to hinder the construction or exploitation of the railway lines of the other in Asiatic
Turkey.

5. It was agreed that appropriate diplomatic and financial
measures should be taken to bring about an increase in the
revenues of the Ottoman Empire, sufficient, at least, to finance
all of the projected railways, both French and German. Construction of the lines already authorized, or to be authorized,
should be pursued, as far as possible, *pari passu,* each group to
receive subsidies from the Ottoman Treasury in about the same
proportion.

6. The *Deutsche Bank* agreed to repurchase from the Imperial
Ottoman Bank all of the latter's shares and debentures of the
Bagdad Railway and its subsidiary enterprises, amounting to
Fr. 69,400,000. Payment was to be made in like value of Imperial
Ottoman bonds of the Customs Loan of 1911, Second Series,
which had been underwritten by a German syndicate.

Certain observations should be made regarding the character of this convention, if its full significance is to be

appreciated. It was an agreement between two great financial groups in France and Germany; as such it was signed by M. Sergent, Sub-Governor of the Bank of France; M. de Klapka, Secretary-General of the Imperial Ottoman Bank; and Dr. Karl Helfferich, Managing Director of the *Deutsche Bank*. In addition, it was an understanding between the Governments of France and Germany; as such it was signed by M. Ponsot, of the French Embassy in Berlin, and by Herr von Rosenberg, of the German Foreign Office. A speech of Chancellor von Bethmann-Hollweg to the Reichstag, December 9, 1913, acknowledged the official character of the negotiations being conducted by the French and German bankers. That the French Government considered the convention a binding international agreement is made perfectly clear by a despatch of Baron Beyens, Belgian Minister in Berlin, to M. Davignon, Belgian Minister of Foreign Affairs, February 20, 1914, in which the attention of the Belgian Government is officially called to the existence of the convention.[15] The agreement, furthermore, was acceptable to the Ottoman Government, for the Sultan promptly confirmed the concessions for the new Black Sea and Syrian lines and for the necessary extensions to the Anatolian Railways. Much has been written about governmental support of investors in foreign countries, but, so far as the author has been able to ascertain, this is the first instance in which a financial pact and an international agreement have been combined in one document. No longer are treaties negotiated by diplomatists alone, but by diplomatists and bankers!

From the standpoint of the French interests involved, the February convention of 1914 was an eminently satisfactory settlement of the Bagdad Railway controversy. French capitalists secured concessions for more than 2,000 miles of railways in Asiatic Turkey, thus eliminating the danger of eventual German control of all communications in the Ottoman Empire. The Imperial Ottoman Bank was relieved of the risk of carrying an investment of almost seventy million francs in the Bagdad enterprise—an investment which had been a "frozen asset" because of the persistent refusal of the French Government to admit the Bagdad securities to the Bourse. In return, the Bank received a large block of Imperial Ottoman bonds, which were readily negotiable and which materially increased French influence in the Ottoman Public Debt Administration. Furthermore, as a result of a tacit agreement with the *Deutsche Bank,* the Imperial Ottoman Bank was awarded the Imperial Ottoman Five Per Cent Loan of 1914, amounting to $100,000,000, upon terms affording a handsome profit to the underwriters.[16] As for the French Government, it was enabled to emerge gracefully from the difficult situation in which it found itself after the Potsdam Agreement. France no longer was obliged to pursue a purely Russian policy in the Near East, for the Tsar's Government—in addition to withdrawing its objections to German railways in Asiatic Turkey—gave its consent to the construction of the French Black Sea Railways with the sole proviso that the system should not be completed in its entirety until Russia had constructed certain strategic railways necessary to assure the safety of the Caucasus frontier.[17]

German diplomacy, on the other hand, had strengthened its position in the Near East by securing definite recognition of central and southern Anatolia, northern Syria and Mesopotamia as German spheres of interest. German financiers acquired exclusive control of the Bagdad enterprise and were assured that there would be no further obstruction of their plans by the French Government. The French promise to coöperate in improving the financial situation in Turkey meant that funds would be forthcoming for continued construction of uncompleted sections of the Bagdad Railway. The Young Turks were delighted at the prospect that the Powers might finally consent to the much-needed increase in the customs duties. They were no less delighted to know that railway construction in Asia Minor—which held out so much promise for the economic development and the political stability of the country—was to go on unimpeded by Franco-German rivalry and antagonism.[18]

There was some harsh criticism in Great Britain, however, of the advantages which France had obtained for herself in the Ottoman Empire. Sir Mark Sykes, an eminent student of Near Eastern affairs, believed that the new state of affairs was worse than the old. Speaking in the House of Commons, March 18, 1914, he warned the Foreign Office that "the policy of French financiers will produce eventually the collapse of the Ottoman Empire. . . . Take the proposed loan arranged with the French Government, for something over £20,000,000. In order to get this there are concessions which I cannot help feeling are more brazen and more fatal than any I have seen. The existing railways in Syria meander for miles to avoid legitimate profits in order to extort a guarantee. Alongside these railways you can see the merchants' merchandise and the peasants' produce rotting because the railway people do not trouble to warehouse the stuff or to shift it. They have got their guarantee, and they do not care. These concessions, which have been extracted from Turkey, mean a monopoly of all Syrian transit; and, further, a native press is to be subventioned practically in the interest of these particular monopolies. . . . In practice, loans, kilometric guarantees, monopolies, and a financed native press must, whether the financiers desire it or not, pave the way to annexation. I submit that this is not the spirit of the *entente*. The British people did not stand by the

French people at Agadir to fill the pockets of financiers whose names are unknown outside Constantinople or the Paris Bourse. . . . The Ottoman Empire is shaken, and the cosmopolitan financier is now staking out the land into spheres of interest. An empire may survive disaster, but it cannot survive exploitation. A country like Turkey, without legislative capacity, without understanding what the economics of Europe mean and at the same time rich, is a lamb for the slaughter." [19]

This trenchant criticism of French policy might have been taken more seriously had Great Britain herself been actuated by magnanimous impulses. Instead, British financiers were joining the common scramble for concessions, and British statesmen were pursuing with ruthless avidity every means of protecting British imperial interests.

The Young Turks Conciliate Great Britain

The Bagdad negotiations of 1910-1911 between Sir Ernest Cassel and Dr. von Gwinner, on the one hand, and the British and Ottoman Governments, on the other, came to naught, it will be recalled, because of the refusal of Sir Edward Grey to consent to an increase in the Turkish customs duties. The Sublime Porte was unwilling to grant the economic concessions demanded by Great Britain as the price of her assistance in Ottoman financial stabilization. But the Young Turks were shrewd enough to keep the door open for further negotiations by removing the chief political objection of England to the Bagdad enterprise—namely, that it menaced British imperial interests in the region of the Persian Gulf. In the convention of March 21, 1911, with the Bagdad Railway Company, the Ottoman Government reserved to itself considerable latitude in the disposition of the sections of the line beyond Bagdad.[20]

Conversations were resumed in July, 1911, when the Turkish minister in London solicited of the Foreign Office a further statement of the conditions upon which British objections to the Bagdad Railway might be waived. He was informed that English acquiescence might be forthcoming if the Bagdad-Basra section of the railway were constructed by a company in which British, French, German, Russian, and Turkish capital should share equally; if adequate guarantees were obtained regarding the protection of British imperial interests in southern Mesopotamia and Persia; if English capital were granted important navigation rights on the Shatt-el-Arab, including complete exemption of British ships and British goods from Ottoman tolls; if safeguards were provided against discriminatory and differential tariffs on the Bagdad system.

These proposals met with only partial acceptance by the Ottoman Government. Turkey was willing to internationalize the southernmost sections of the Bagdad Railway, but under no circumstances would she permit Russian participation in an enterprise which was so vital to the defence of the Sultan's Empire. Turkey was prepared to discuss with England measures for the protection of legitimate British interests in the Middle East, provided there be no further infringement on the sovereign rights of the Sultan in southern Mesopotamia. Turkey agreed that the principle of the economic open door should be scrupulously observed throughout the Ottoman Empire; therefore she could not agree to discriminatory treatment in favor of British commerce on the Shatt-el-Arab, the Tigris, and the Euphrates. Upon these conditions the Ottoman minister at London was authorized to continue negotiations in the most friendly spirit.[21]

The Agadir crisis, which threatened war between England and Germany, and the Tripolitan War, which diverted

Turkish attention from domestic reform to defence of the Empire, unfortunately led to a suspension of the Anglo-Turkish conversations. They were not resumed until 1913, when Turkey found a breathing spell between the first and second phases of the First Balkan War.

During the interim, however, steps were taken to remove the obstacles which stood in the way of an Anglo-German understanding. In February, 1912, Lord Haldane visited Berlin as the guest of the Kaiser to discuss curtailment of the naval programs of the two Powers and to agree upon other measures which would effect a *rapprochement* between *Wilhelmstrasse* and Downing Street. As regards the Bagdad Railway, Lord Haldane informed the German Government that he stood upon the position he had taken in 1907—that Great Britain was prepared to grant its consent to the enterprise if British political interests in Mesopotamia were adequately safeguarded[22] A few months later, Baron Marschall von Bieberstein—who for fifteen years had guided Germany's destiny in the Near East—was transferred from Constantinople to the embassy at London, as the first step in an attempt to reconcile British imperial interests with German diplomatic hegemony in Turkey. Almost simultaneously, Sir Harry Johnston, whose enthusiasm for German ventures in Asia Minor has already been mentioned,[23] began a quasi-official lecture tour in Germany to urge a sane settlement of the Near Eastern tangle. Another important development was the appointment as German Minister of Foreign Affairs, in January, 1913, of Herr von Jagow, who believed that a great European war was inevitable unless England and Germany could come to terms on the Turkish question.[24]

In this manner the stage was set for a resumption of Anglo-Turkish conversations on the Bagdad Railway. In February, 1913, Hakki Pasha, minister plenipotentiary and extraordinary of the Ottoman Government, arrived in London with instructions to leave no stone unturned to settle outstanding differences with Great Britain. For almost four months Hakki Pasha and Sir Edward Grey discussed the problems of the Near East and conferred with Herr von Kühlmann and Prince Lichnowsky, of the German embassy at London, regarding the general terms of a tripartite settlement of the economic and political questions at issue. In May, 1913, a full agreement was reached upon the following wide range of subjects: regularization of the legal position in Turkey of British religious, educational, and medical institutions; pecuniary claims of Great Britain against the Ottoman Empire; the Turkish veto on the borrowing powers of Egypt; Turco-Persian boundary disputes, particularly in so far as they affected oil lands; navigation of the Tigris, Euphrates, and Shatt-el-Arab; irrigation of the Mesopotamian valley; the status of Koweit. The settlements agreed upon were ratified by a series of treaties between Great Britain and Turkey, notably those of July 29, and October 21, 1913, and of June, 1914. Reconciliation of British and German interests was reserved for discussion between London and Berlin.[25]

In so far as concerned the Bagdad Railway, the substance of the Anglo-Turkish agreements of 1913 is as follows:

1. Turkey recognized the special position of Great Britain in the region of the Persian Gulf. Therefore, although Great Britain acknowledged the suzerainty of the Sultan over Koweit, the Ottoman Government pledged a policy of non-interference in the affairs of the principality. The existing treaties between the Sheik and Great Britain were confirmed.

2. The terminus of the Bagdad Railway was to be Basra, unless and until Great Britain should give consent to an extension of the line to the Persian Gulf.

3. In order to assure equality of treatment for all, regardless of nationality or other considerations, the Ottoman Government

agreed that two British citizens should be elected to the Board of Directors of the Bagdad Railway Company.

4. Exclusive rights of navigation by steamers and barges on the Tigris, Euphrates, and Shatt-el-Arab were granted to the Ottoman River Navigation Company, to be formed by Baron Inchcape, chairman of the Peninsular and Oriental and the British India Steam Navigation Companies. The Navigation Company, in which Turkish capital was to be offered a fifty per cent participation, was to have wide powers for the improvement and regulation of all navigable streams in Mesopotamia, in co-operation with a commission to be appointed by the Ottoman Government. Lord Inchcape's concession was for a period of sixty years, with optional renewals for ten-year periods.

5. It was agreed, however, that the Bagdad Railway and Inchcape concessions were without prejudice to the rights of the Lynch Brothers, which were specifically reaffirmed. The Lynch Brothers, in fact, were granted the privilege of adding another steamer to their equipment, with the single restriction that it fly the Turkish flag.

6. The British Government agreed that no navigation rights of its nationals would be construed as permitting interference with the development of Mesopotamia by irrigation, and the Ottoman Government guaranteed that no irrigation works would be permitted to divert navigable streams from their course.

7. In return for these, and other, assurances and concessions, Great Britain consented to support an increase of 4% in the customs duties of the Ottoman Empire.

The terms of this settlement were hailed by the English press as an admirable solution of the Mesopotamian imbroglio. *The Times* of May 17, 1913, for example, said: "Great Britain will have no further reason for looking askance at a project which should do much for the development of Asiatic Turkey. Our interests will be safeguarded; we have always said that a terminus at Basra offered no menace to specific British interests in the Persian Gulf; and the German promoters will be free to complete their great project with the benevolent acquiescence of Great Britain. There will be no official participation in the construction of the line, but there will also be nothing to deter British capital from being associated with the scheme. We believe that if some such solution is adopted, a fertile source of international misunderstanding will disappear. It is a solution which should receive the approval of France and Russia and should give gratification to Germany. It appears to leave no room for subsequent differences of opinion, while it wipes out a whole series of obscure disputes. It will be a further demonstration of that spirit of coöperation among the Great Powers which has done so much of late to preserve the peace of Europe. It should convince Germany that Great Britain does not oppose the essential elements of the Bagdad Railway scheme provided her own special interests are protected. Above all, it will relieve the financial disabilities of Turkey and will enable her to press forward the great task of binding with bonds of steel the great Asiatic territories in which her future chiefly lies." Other press opinion was in accord with Sir Edward Grey that the agreement "justifies us in saying that it is no longer in British interests to oppose the line." [26]

In Germany, likewise, the Anglo-Turkish agreement was favorably received. The *Berliner Tageblatt* of December 29, 1913, hailed it as a triumph of German diplomacy. "For years," it said, "this undertaking has threatened to become a bone of contention between Russia, England, and Germany. The German Government has now, through its cleverness and tenacity, succeeded in removing all differences and in bringing the line altogether into German possession." In the Reichstag, as well, the general tenor of the comments was favorable, although Herr Bassermann and other National Liberals were somewhat vociferous about the great "sacrifices" which Germany had made to propitiate Great Britain. Among the Social Democrats and the Centrists, however, the sentiment was obviously in accord with one member who

said, "We share the general satisfaction at this *rapprochement,* which is an aid to world peace, but we also
are of the opinion that there is no occasion for over-
exuberance or patriotic bombast."[27]

As usual, the rôle of the Turks themselves was slighted.
A casual observer might have remarked that whatever
"benevolent acquiescence" was included in the settlement
originated in Constantinople rather than in London, and
that the "sacrifices" involved were much more painful to
Turkey than to Germany!

BRITISH IMPERIAL INTERESTS ARE FURTHER SAFEGUARDED

In the Speech from the Throne, February 10, 1914,
King George V informed Parliament that the Near Eastern question was approaching a solution. "My relations
with foreign Powers continue to be friendly," he said. "I
am happy to say that my negotiations, both with the German Government and the Ottoman Government as regards
matters of importance to the commercial and industrial
interests of this country in Mesopotamia are rapidly approaching a satisfactory issue." Nothing was said to
indicate the character of the negotiations or to identify the
"commercial and industrial interests" which were the
objects of royal solicitude.

Before the British Government would give its consent
to a final agreement with Turkey and Germany regarding the Bagdad Railway, the King might have added, it
was determined to acquire for certain worthy Britons a
share in some of the choicest economic plums in the
Ottoman Empire. Heading the interests which were thus
to be favored was the Right Honorable James Lyle
Mackay, Baron Inchcape of Strathnaver, who had been the
beneficiary of the aforementioned Mesopotamian naviga-

tion concession of July, 1913. Lord Inchcape is perhaps the foremost shipping magnate in the British Empire. He is chairman and managing director of the Peninsular and Oriental and the British India Steam Navigation Companies ; chairman and director of the Australasian United Steam Navigation Company and the Eastern and Australian Steamship Company; a director of the Steamship Owners' Coal Association, the Australasia and China Telegraph Company, the Marine Insurance Company, the Central Queensland Meat Export Company, and various other commercial enterprises. He is a vice-president of the Suez Canal Company. He has extensive interests in the petroleum industry as a director of the Anglo-Persian Oil Company, Scottish Oils, Ltd., and the D'Arcy Exploration Company.

Lord Inchcape's interests were given ample consideration in the Anglo-German negotiations of 1914. On February 23, a contract was signed at London between the Bagdad Railway Company and Lord Inchcape, the signatures to which were witnessed by Herr von Kühlmann, of the German embassy, and Sir Eyre Crowe, of the British Foreign Office. Under the terms of this contract the Bagdad Railway Company acknowledged the monopolistic privileges in Mesopotamian river navigation conferred upon Lord Inchcape's interests by the Ottoman Government ; agreed to cancel its outstanding engagements with the Lynch Brothers for the transportation of railway materials between Basra and points along the Tigris ; and guaranteed Lord Inchcape a minimum amount of 100,000 tons of freight, at a figure of 22½ shillings per ton, in the transportation on the Tigris of supplies for the construction of the Bagdad Railway and its subsidiary enterprises.[28]

This contract was so obviously in contravention of earlier rights of the Lynch Brothers, which had been specifically reaffirmed by the negotiations with Turkey, that it was amended by an agreement of March 27, 1914, between Lord Inchcape, Mr. John F. Lynch, and the Bagdad Railway Company. The latter arrangement provided: 1. That Lord Inchcape should immediately organize the Ottoman Navigation Company to take over the concession of July, 1913, and the rights conferred upon Lord Inchcape by his agreement of February 23, 1914, with the Bagdad Railway Company; 2. That the Lynch Brothers should be admitted to participation in the new Navigation Company and that Mr. John F. Lynch should be elected a director thereof; 3. That the Bagdad Railway should assign to a new Ottoman Ports Company—in which Mr. Lynch and Lord Inchcape should be granted a 40% participation—all of the rights of the Railway to the construction of port and terminal facilities at Bagdad and Basra; 4. That the Bagdad Railway Company should be granted a 20% participation in the new Ottoman Navigation Company. Thus were Lord Inchcape's powerful interests further propitiated! Thus did the Lynch Brothers cease to be big fish in a small pond, to become small fish in a big lake!

Measures were now taken to protect another vested interest, the British-owned Smyrna-Aidin Railway Company. On March 26, a draft agreement, subsequently confirmed as part of the Anglo-German convention of June 15, was executed by Dr. Carl Bergmann, of the Bagdad Railway Company, and Lord Rathmore, of the Smyrna-Aidin Company. It provided for important extensions of over 200 miles to the existing Smyrna-Aidin line (including a junction with the Anatolian-Bagdad system at Afiun Karahissar), granted to British interests valuable navigation rights on the lakes of Asia Minor, and protected each railway from discriminatory treatment at the hands of the other. This settlement was approved by Herr von Kühlmann, on behalf of the German Government; Mr. Alwyn Parker, of the British Foreign Office; and Hakki Pasha, minister plenipotentiary of the Sultan to the Court of St. James.[29]

Oil—the magic word which has become the open sesame of so many diplomatic mysteries—was of no inconsiderable importance in 1914. Early in that eventful year the British Government—in order to insure an uninterrupted supply of fuel to the fleet—had purchased a controlling interest in the Anglo-Persian Oil Company. As a necessary step in the negotiations regarding Turkish oilfields the German Government was obliged, in March, 1914, to recognize southern Mesopotamia, as well as central and southern Persia, as the exclusive field of operations of the Anglo-Persian Company, and, in addition, to agree to the construction of a railway from Kut-el-Amara to Mendeli for the purpose of facilitating petroleum shipments. Thereupon an Anglo-German syndicate organized the Turkish Petroleum Company for the acquisition and exploitation of the oil resources of the vilayets of Mosul and Bagdad. Half of the stock of the new company was assigned to the National Bank of Turkey (controlled by Sir Ernest Cassel) and the D'Arcy group (in which Lord Inchcape was interested); one quarter was assigned to the Royal Dutch Company, and the remainder was reserved for the *Deutsche Bank*. Upon joint representations by the British and German ambassadors at the Sublime Porte, the Sultan, in June, 1914, conferred upon the Turkish Petroleum Company exclusive rights of exploitation of the oil resources of the Mesopotamian valley from Mosul to Bagdad.[30]

The vested interests of certain of its citizens having thus been amply protected, the British Government proceeded to complete its negotiations with the German ambassador in London. On June 15, 1914, Sir Edward Grey and

Prince Lichnowsky initialed an important convention regarding the delimitation of English and German interests in Asiatic Turkey. The following day *The Times* announced that the terms of an Anglo-German agreement had been incorporated in a draft treaty, and on June 29, Sir Edward Grey informed the House of Commons that formal ratification of the convention was being postponed only "until Turkey and Germany have completed their own separate negotiations." By mid-July all was in readiness for the definitive signing of the treaty, but the widening importance of the Austro-Serbian dispute and the outbreak of the Great War put an end to the Bagdad Railway conversations.[31]

The terms of the convention of June 15, 1914—which might have meant so much to the future of Anglo-German relations—constituted a complete settlement of the controversy which had waged for more than ten years over German railway construction in the Mesopotamian valley. The reconciliation of the divergent interests of the two Powers was based upon the following considerations:[32]

1. "In recognition of the general importance of the Bagdad Railway in international trade" the British Government bound itself not "to adopt or to support any measures which might render more difficult the construction or management of the Bagdad Railway by the Bagdad Railway Company or to prevent the participation of capital in the enterprise." Great Britain further agreed that under no circumstances would it "undertake railway construction on Ottoman territory in direct competition with lines of the Bagdad Railway Company or in contravention of existing rights of the Company or support the efforts of any persons or companies directed to this end," unless in accord with the expressed wishes of the German Government.

2. His Britannic Majesty's Government pledged itself to support an increase in the customs duties of the Ottoman Empire from 11% to 15% *ad valorem* and, furthermore, to "raise no objection to the assignment to the Bagdad Railway Company of already existing Turkish State revenues, or of revenues from the

intended increase in tariff duties, or of the proposed monopolies or taxes on the consumption of alcohol, petroleum, matches, tinder, cigarette-paper, playing cards, and sugar to the extent necessary for the completion of the Railway."

3. The terminus of the Bagdad Railway was to be Basra. Both of the signatory Powers declared that under no circumstances would they "support the construction of a branch from Basra or any other point on the main line of the Bagdad Railway to the Persian Gulf, unless a complete understanding be previously arrived at between the Imperial Ottoman, the Imperial German, and His Britannic Majesty's Governments." The German Government furthermore pledged itself under no circumstances to "undertake the construction of a harbor or a railway station on the Persian Gulf or support efforts of any persons or companies directed toward that end, unless a complete agreement be previously arrived at with His Britannic Majesty's Government."

4. The German Government undertook to see that "on the lines of the Bagdad Railway Company, as hitherto, no direct or indirect discrimination in transit facilities or freight rates shall be made in the transportation of goods of the same kind between the same places, either on account of ownership or on account of origin or destination of the goods or because of any other consideration." In other words, the German Government agreed to enforce Articles 24 and 25 of the Specifications of March 5, 1903, which provided that "all rates, whether they be general, special, proportional, or differential, shall be applicable to all shippers and passengers without distinction," and which prohibited the Company to enter into any agreement for the purpose of granting reductions in the rates announced in its published tariffs.

5. In order further to protect British interests the German Government assumed responsibility for the election to the Board of Directors of the Bagdad Railway Company of "two English members acceptable to His Britannic Majesty's Government."

6. Both Powers pledged themselves unreservedly to observe the principle of the economic open door in the operation of railway, ports, irrigation, and navigation enterprises in Turkey-in-Asia.

7. Great Britain recognized German interests in the irrigation of the Cilician plain, and Germany recognized British interests in the irrigation of the lower Mesopotamian valley.

8. Both signatory Powers took cognizance of and agreed to observe the Anglo-Turkish agreement of July, 1913, conferring important navigation rights in Mesopotamia upon British sub-

jects; the agreements between Lord Inchcape and the Bagdad Railway Company, regarding navigation and port and terminal facilities on the Tigris and Euphrates; the agreement between the Smyrna-Aidin Railway and the Bagdad Railway regarding important extensions to the former line.

9. Great Britain and Germany agreed to "use their good offices with the Imperial Ottoman Government to the end that the Shatt-el-Arab shall be brought into a satisfactory navigable condition and permanently maintained in such condition, so that ocean-going ships may always be assured of free and easy access to the port of Basra, and, further, that the shipping on the Shatt-el-Arab shall always be open to ocean-going ships under the same conditions to ships of all nations, regardless of the nationality of the ships or their cargo."

10. It was agreed, finally, that any differences of opinion resulting from the convention or its appended documents should be subject to arbitration. If the signatory Powers were unable to agree upon an arbitrator or a special court of arbitration, the case was to be submitted to the Permanent Court of Arbitration at the Hague.

From both the German and the British points of view the foregoing convention was an admirable solution of the Turkish problem. Had the agreement been reached ten years earlier, it might have avoided estrangement between the two nations. Had it come at almost any other time than on the eve of the Great War, it would have been a powerful stimulus to an Anglo-German *rapprochement*.

Germany, it is true, was obliged to abandon any hope of establishing a port on the Persian Gulf. But there were grave uncertainties that Koweit could ever be developed as a commercially profitable terminus for the Bagdad Railway, whereas its very possession by a German company would have been a constant source of irritation to Great Britain. Basra, on the other hand, had obvious advantages. Like many of the great harbors of the world —Hamburg, Bremen, Antwerp, London, New York—it was on a river, rather than the open sea; and inasmuch as Great Britain had agreed that the freedom of the open sea should be applied to the Shatt-el-Arab, German ships were assured unrestricted access to the southern terminus of the Bagdad Railway. In return for surrendering the Basra-Persian Gulf section of the Bagdad system and for admitting British capitalists to participation in the Bagdad and Basra ports company, Germany received full recognition of her economic rights in Anatolia, Syria, and northern Mesopotamia, together with a minor share in Lord Inchcape's navigation enterprises and in the newly formed Turkish Petroleum Company. Above all, British opposition to the Bagdad Railway, which had been so stubbornly maintained since 1903, was to be a thing of the past. For these considerations Germany could well afford to accept a subordinate place in southern Mesopotamia and to recognize British interests in the Persian Gulf.

Great Britain gained even more than Germany. She abandoned her policy of obstruction of the Bagdad Railway and consented to an increase in the customs duties of the Ottoman Empire. These considerations had never been ends in themselves, but rather pawns in the great game of diplomacy, to be surrendered in return for other valuable considerations. For them England secured guarantees of equality of treatment for British citizens and British goods on the German railway lines in Turkey. In addition, English capitalists received a monopoly of navigation on the Tigris and Euphrates, a 40% interest in port and terminal facilities at Bagdad and Basra, control of the oil resources of the Mesopotamian valley, extensions to British-owned railways in southern Anatolia, and other valuable economic concessions. British political control was recognized as dominant in southern Mesopotamia; therefore the Bagdad Railway no longer could be said to be a menace to the safety of India. As for Britain's new position in the Persian Gulf, one of her own publicists said, "England has virtually annexed another sea, one of the world's highways." [33]

DIPLOMATIC BARGAINING FAILS TO PRESERVE PEACE

It is one of the tragedies of pre-War diplomacy that the negotiations of 1910-1914 failed to preserve peace in the Near East or, at least, to prevent the entry of Turkey into the Great War. But the failure of the treaties between Germany and the Entente Powers regarding the Ottoman Empire can be traced, in general, to the same reasons that contributed to the collapse of all diplomacy in the crisis of 1914. Imperialism, nationalism, militarism—these were the causes of the Great War; these were the causes of Ottoman participation in the Great War.

One obvious defect of the Potsdam Agreement, the Franco-German agreement regarding Anatolian railways, the Anglo-Turkish settlement of 1913, and the Anglo-German convention regarding Mesopotamia, was the fact that they were founded upon the principle of imperial compensations. Each of the Great Powers involved made "sacrifices"—but in return for important considerations. And throughout all of the bargaining the rights of Turkey, a "backward nation," were completely ignored. As the German ambassador in London wrote: "The real purpose of these treaties was to divide Asia Minor into spheres of interest, although this expression was anxiously avoided, out of regard for the rights of the Sultan. . . . By virtue of the treaties all Mesopotamia as far as Basra became our sphere of interest, without prejudice to older British rights in the navigation of the Tigris and in the Willcocks irrigation works. Our sphere further included the whole region of the Bagdad and Anatolian Railways. The British economic domain was to include the coasts of the Persian Gulf and the Smyrna-Aidin line; the French, Syria; the Russian, Armenia." [34]

In the scramble for concessions in Asia Minor, Italy had been overlooked. The proposed extension of the

Smyrna-Aidin Railway met with vehement denunciation on the part of patriotic Italians who looked forward to the further development of Italian economic influence in the hinterland of the port of Adalia. The Italian press loudly demanded that energetic action be taken by the Government to secure from Turkey compensatory concessions or, in default of that, to announce to the Sublime Porte that Italy would not return to Turkey the Dodecanese Islands, of which Italy was in temporary occupation under the terms of the Treaty of Lausanne (1912). A formal demand of this character was made by King Victor Emmanuel's ambassador at Constantinople, but was met with a curt refusal on the part of the Turks to bargain for the return of their own property.[35]

The Young Turks were not unaware of the true character of the agreements they had entered into with the respective European Powers, but they considered themselves impotent to act otherwise at the time. They knew full well that there was grave danger in an extension of British influence in Mesopotamia, French interests in Syria, and Franco-Russian enterprise in northern Anatolia. They had not forgotten the spoliation of their empire by Austria-Hungary and Italy. They were not altogether unsuspicious about the intentions of Germany. But they believed they could never emancipate their country from foreign domination until they had modernized it. They needed foreign capital and foreign technical assistance, and they had to pay the price. In order to throw off the yoke of European imperialism they had to consent temporarily to be victimized by it.[36]

Nationalistic fervor added to the difficulties created by imperialist rivalry. M. André Tardieu, political editor at the time of *Le Temps,* did not let a single opportunity pass during February and March, 1914, to denounce the French Government for its pro-German policy in the Bagdad Railway question. When M. Cambon, French ambassador at Berlin, was asked whether the Franco-German agreement on Turkish railways would improve the relations between his country and the German Empire, he said: "Official relations, yes, perhaps to some extent, but I do not think that the agreement will affect the great body of public opinion on both sides of the Vosges. It will not, unfortunately, change the tone of the French press towards the Germans. . . . There is no doubt whatever that the majority, both of Germans and Frenchmen, desire to live at peace; but there is a powerful minority in each country that dreams of nothing but battles and wars, either of conquest or revenge. That is the peril that is always with us; it is like living alongside a barrel of gunpowder which may explode on the slightest provocation." Herr von Jagow, German Minister of Foreign Affairs, expressed a similar opinion when he said that he was watching for a favorable moment for the publication of the Anglo-German convention of June 15, 1914—"an appropriate moment when the danger of adverse criticism was no longer so acute." [37] Hatred, suspicion, fear, and other unbridled passions were the stock-in-trade of the Continental press during the months preceding the outbreak of the Great War. Patriotic bombast, not international conciliation, was demanded by the imperialist and nationalist minorities, who exerted only too much influence upon the Governments and made politicians fear lest their efforts at peace be misconstrued as treason!

A situation which was made bad by imperial rivalries and national antagonisms was made intolerable by militarism. During the year 1913-1914, when the diplomatists were working for peace, preparations were being made for war. In the month of August, 1913, while conversations were being held in Berlin to reconcile French and German interests in the Near East, General Joffre was on his way to Russia to confer with the Tsar's general staff regarding the reorganization of the Russian army. In October of the same year, while tripartite negotiations were being conducted by England, Turkey, and Germany regarding Mesopotamia, General Liman von Sanders was despatched to Constantinople by the Kaiser as head of a German military mission to rebuild the Ottoman army and improve the Ottoman system of defence. Considerations of military strategy were vitiating the efforts of conciliatory diplomacy.

The mission of Liman von Sanders created a crisis at Constantinople. The Russian, French, and British ambassadors protested against such an obvious menace to the interests of the Entente. Russia, in particular, objected to the announced intention of the German general to strengthen the defences of the Straits. All three of the Powers expressed opposition to the further proposal that Field Marshal von Sanders be placed in command of the First Army Corps, with headquarters at Constantinople. The Ottoman Government replied that it meant no offence to England or France, but that it could not allow its military policy to be determined by Russia. It called attention to the fact that the improvement of the navy was in the hands of a British mission and that the reorganization of the gendarmerie was going on under the direction of a French general. German officers were being asked to perform similar services for the army because the great majority of Turkish officers had completed their training in Germany, and the rest, since the days of General von der Goltz Pasha, had been educated and experienced in German methods. To change from German to French or British technique appeared to the Ottoman Minister of War an extremely inadvisable procedure.[38]

Although the storm over Liman von Sanders cleared by February, 1914, it left behind it certain permanent effects. It strengthened German influence at Constantinople, indirectly because of the increased Turkish hostility to Russia and suspicion of France and England, directly because of the presence of hundreds of German staff and regimental officers who used every opportunity to increase German prestige in the army and the civil services. The German ambassador at the Sublime Porte, Baron von Wangenheim, readily capitalized this prestige in the interest of German diplomacy. A formal Turco-German alliance was rapidly passing from the realm of the possible to the realm of the probable.

In the meantime feverish efforts were being made to complete Turkey's military preparations. In March, 1914, at the request of the Minister of War, a conference was held of representatives of all railways in Asiatic Turkey to discuss the utilization of Ottoman rail communications for mobilization in the event of war. Under the guidance of German and Turkish staff officers a plan was adopted by which the respective railways agreed to merge their services into a unified national system for the transportation of troops. Throughout the spring of 1914 the defences of the Dardanelles were being strengthened, schools were being conducted for junior officers and non-commissioned officers, the General Staff was reorganized, new plans for mobilization were in process of completion. On July 23, 1914, the handiwork of Field Marshal Liman von Sanders Pasha was exhibited in a great national military review. On that occasion Baron von Wangenheim said to the Ottoman Minister of Marine: "Djemal Pasha, just look at the amazing results achieved by German officers in a short time. You have now a Turkish army which can be compared with the best organized armies in the world! All German officers are at one in praising the moral strength of the Turkish soldier, and indeed it has proved itself beyond all expectation. We could claim we have won a great victory if we could call ourselves the ally of a Government which has such an army at its disposal!" [39]

A few days later the Ottoman Empire was admitted to the Triple Alliance—with the consent of Austria, but without even the knowledge of Italy. The die was cast for Turkey's participation in the War of the Nations! [40]

BIBLIOGRAPHICAL AND EXPLANATORY NOTES

[1] Statement of Chancellor von Bethmann Hollweg to the Reichstag, December 10, 1910, in *Stenographische Berichte, XII Legislaturperiode, 2 Session,* Volume 262, pp. 3561b *et seq. Cf.,* also, *The Annual Register,* 1910, pp. 314-315, 335-336; Shuster, *op. cit.,* pp. 225 *et seq.* The informal agreement reached at Potsdam was confirmed by a treaty of August 19, 1911. *The Annual Register,* 1911, pp. 357-358. For the diplomatic correspondence arising out of the Potsdam Agreement *cf.* de Siebert, *op. cit.,* Chapter IX.

[2] Korff, *op. cit.,* pp. 163-164. Baron Korff believes, also, that the Potsdam Agreement was forced upon the weak and vacillating Nicholas II by the unscrupulous and bullying William II.

[3] *Supra,* pp. 65-66, 147-153. For German estimates of the importance of the Potsdam Agreement see a reasoned and temperate speech by Dr. Spahn, of the Catholic Centre, and an impassioned and boisterous speech by Herr Bassermann, of the National Liberals. *Stenographische Berichte, XII Legislaturperiode, 2 Session,* Volume 266 (1911), pp. 5973 *et seq.,* 5984 *et seq.*

[4] *The Times,* January 18, 1911.

[5] Quoted by W. M. Fullerton, *Problems of Power* (new and revised edition, New York, 1915), p. 171.

[6] *Parliamentary Debates, House of Commons,* fifth series, Volume 21 (1911), pp. 241-244.

[7] *Journal Officiel, Débats parlementaires, Chambre des Députés,* January 13, 1911, pp. 33-34. M. Jaurès was one of the Frenchmen who felt that their Government never should have opposed the Bagdad Railway in the first instance.

[8] *Ibid.,* January 16, pp. 64 *et seq.; Parliamentary Debates, House of Commons,* Volume 21 (1911), pp. 82 *et seq.,* 243-244; *The Times,* January 17 and 19, 1911.

[9] *Parliamentary Debates, House of Commons,* Volume 21 (1911), p. 82.

[10] *Cf. supra,* pp. 224-225.

[11] *Cf.* G. Saint-Yves, "Les chemins de fer français dans la Turquie d'Asie," in *Questions diplomatiques et coloniales,* Volume 37 (1914), pp. 526-531; *Anatolia,* pp. 51-52.

[12] It was proposed that the Anatolian Railways should construct three branches: one from a point east of Bulgurlu north and northeast to Kaisarieh and Sivas; a second from Angora east to the aforementioned branch, joining it near Kaisarieh; a third from Adabazar to Boli. The branch of the Bagdad Railway from Nisibin to Diarbekr and Arghana was authorized by the concession of 1903.

[13] Much of the present account of the negotiations of the years 1910-1914 is based upon documentary material furnished by Dr. von Gwinner and upon additional information supplied by Sir Henry Babington Smith and Djavid Bey. Almost everything heretofore published has been very general in character, but one may find some illuminating details in the following: R. de Caix, "La France et les chemins de fer de l'Asie turque," in *Questions diplomatiques et coloniales,* Volume 36 (1913), pp. 386-387; *Armenia and Kurdistan,* p. 36; *Commerce Reports,* No. 18a (1915), pp. 2-3; *Stenographische Berichte, XIII Legislaturperiode, I Session,* Volume 291 (1913), pp. 6274c *et seq.; American Journal of International Law,* April, 1918; Commandant de Thomasson, "Les négociations franco-allemandes," in *Questions diplomatiques et coloniales,* Volume 37 (1914), pp. 257 *et seq.*

[14] For certified copies of the minutes of the meetings of August 19-20 and September 24-26, 1913, and for the text of the convention of February 15, 1914, the author is indebted to Dr. von Gwinner.

[15] *Stenographische Berichte, XIII Legislaturperiode, I Session,* Volume 291 (1913), p. 6274c. No. 111 of a series of despatches published by the German Foreign Office (Berlin, 1915), an English translation of which is to be found in E. D. Morel's *Diplomacy Revealed* (London, 1921), pp. 282-283.

[16] *Parliamentary Papers,* No. Cmd. 964 (1920).

[17] *Cf.* de Caix, *op. cit.,* pp. 386-387.

[18] It should be made clear that not all the terms of the Franco-German agreement were carried out before the beginning of the Great War. Because of the delay in the negotiations with Great Britain (*cf. infra*) the exchange of Bagdad Railway securities for Imperial Ottoman Bonds was not completed, with the result that, when the War came, French bankers still held an interest in the Bagdad Railway Company.

[19] *Parliamentary Debates, House of Commons,* fifth series, Volume 59 (1914), pp. 2179-2189. Sir Mark Sykes (1879-1919) had traveled extensively in the Near and Far East and was the author of many books on the political and economic problems of those regions. During the Great War he was commissioned by the British Government to negotiate with France regarding the

delimitation of the Allies' interests in Mesopotamia and Syria. He was one of the authors of the Sykes-Picot Treaty of 1916.

[20] *Supra*, pp. 111-112, 228-229.

[21] Memorandum of Djavid Bey, cited in Chapter IX, *supra*.

[22] Haldane, *op. cit., passim;* W. von Hohenzollern, *My Memoirs, 1878-1918*, pp. 142-156; *supra*, pp. 198-199; *The Annual Register*, 1912, pp. 16, 332; Count de Lalaing, Belgian Minister in London, to M. Davignon, Belgian Minister of Foreign Affairs, February 9 and 16, 1912, despatches Nos. 88 and 90, translated in Morel, *op. cit.*, pp. 228-230.

[23] *Supra*, pp. 205-207.

[24] Baron Marschall died in September, 1912, after only a few weeks of service at his new post. He was succeeded by Prince Lichnowsky, who took up his duties in London in November. Regarding the lecture tour of Sir Harry Johnston see the authentic account by Bernadotte Schmitt, *England and Germany, 1740-1914*, pp. 355-356. Herr von Jagow's opinion of the importance of an Anglo-German understanding on the Near East is to be found in his reply to Prince Lichnowsky, in the *Norddeutsche Allgemeine Zeitung* of March 23, 1918, translated by Munroe Smith, *The Disclosures from Germany*, pp. 130-131.

[25] Regarding the Anglo-Turkish negotiations *cf. Parliamentary Debates, House of Commons*, Volume 53 (1913), pp. 392-395; *Stenographische Berichte, XIII Legislaturperiode, 1 Session*, Volume 291 (1913), pp. 6274c-6294d; Karl Helfferich, *Die Vorgeschichte des Weltkrieges*, pp. 143 *et seq.; Mesopotamia*, pp. 97-98; *The Times* (London), May 17 and May 31, 1913; *The Quarterly Review*, Volume 228 (1917), pp. 517-521; de Siebert, *op. cit.*, Chapter XX.

[26] *Parliamentary Debates, House of Commons*, Volume 53 (1913), p. 393.

[27] *Stenographische Berichte, XIII Legislaturperiode, 1 Session*, Volume 289 (1913), p. 4744d. *Cf.*, also, *ibid.*, pp. 4744c-4746c; Volume 290 (1913), p. 5326a-c.

[28] For copies of this and other agreements the author is indebted to Dr. von Gwinner, of the *Deutsche Bank*.

[29] For the text of the agreement *cf.* E. M. Earle, "The Secret Anglo-German Convention of 1914 regarding Asiatic Turkey," in the *Political Science Quarterly* (New York), Volume XXXVIII (1923), pp. 41-44.

[30] "Correspondence between His Majesty's Government and the United States Ambassador respecting Economic Rights in Mandated Territories," *Parliamentary Papers*, No. Cmd. 675 (1921); *The Daily News* (London), June 26, 1920; G. Slocombe, "The Oil Behind the War Scare," in *The Daily Herald* (Lon-

don), October 12 and 13, 1922; *The Disclosures from Germany,* p. 238.

[21] *Parliamentary Debates, House of Commons,* Volume 64 (1914), pp. 116-117.

[22] For the complete text of the convention, cf. E. M. Earle, "The Secret Anglo-German Convention of 1914 regarding Asiatic Turkey," *loc. cit.,* pp. 24-44.

[23] Fullerton, *op. cit.,* p. 307.

[24] Prince Lichnowsky, quoted from *The Disclosures from Germany,* pp. 71-72.

[25] Saint-Yves, *loc. cit.,* pp. 526-531; *Anatolia,* pp. 49 *et seq.* Regarding the earlier development of Italian economic interests in Turkey cf. *supra,* pp. 105-107.

[26] For an interesting discussion of this point see Ahmed Djemal Pasha, *Erinnerungen eines türkischen Staatsmannes* (Munich, 1922), translated into English under the title, *Memories of a Turkish Statesman, 1913-1919* (New York, 1923), pp. 107-115 of the translation, pp. 113-122 of the German text. (Hereafter page references are given for the translation only.)

[27] Baron Beyens, Belgian minister in Berlin, to M. Davignon, Belgian Minister of Foreign Affairs, No. 111 of the Belgian documents, translated in Morel's *Diplomacy Revealed,* p. 283. The quotation from von Jagow is from *The Disclosures from Germany,* p. 251.

[28] Regarding the German military mission to Turkey cf. Djemal Pasha, *op. cit.,* pp. 65-70, 101-102; Liman von Sanders, *Fünf Jahre Türkei* (Berlin, 1919); Field Marshal von der Goltz, *Die Militärische Lage der Türkei nach dem Balkankriege* (Berlin, 1913); *The Disclosures from Germany,* pp. 57 *et seq.*

[29] Djemal Pasha, *op. cit.,* p. 108.

[40] *Ibid.,* pp. 107-115. Regarding other aspects of German military and diplomatic successes in Turkey during 1914, cf. *Anatolia,* pp. 44-45; Henry Morgenthau, *Ambassador Morgenthau's Story* (New York, 1918); Karl Helfferich, *Die deutsche Türkenpolitik,* pp. 28 *et seq.,* and *Die Vorgeschichte des Weltkrieges, passim;* André Chéradame, *The Pan German Plot Unmasked* (New York, 1917)—all representing widely divergent points of view.

CHAPTER XI

TURKEY, CRUSHED TO EARTH, RISES AGAIN

Nationalism and Militarism Triumph at Constantinople

The outbreak of the Great War precipitated a serious political crisis at Constantinople. Decisions of the utmost moment to the future of the Ottoman Empire had to be taken. Chief among these was the choice between neutrality and entry into the war in coöperation with the Central Powers. Pacifists and Entente sympathizers, of whom Djavid Bey was perhaps the foremost, counseled non-intervention in the struggle. Militarists and Germanophiles, headed by Enver Pasha, the distinguished Minister of War, advocated early and complete observance of the alliance with Germany, which called for active military measures against the Entente. In support of the pacifists were the great mass of the people, overburdened with taxes, worn out with military service, and weary of the sacrifices occasioned by the Tripolitan and Balkan Wars. In support of the militarists were German economic power, German military prestige, and the powerful emotion of Turkish nationalism.

The case of the pacifists, like that of their opponents, was based frankly upon national self-interest. A great European war seemed to them to offer an unprecedented opportunity for setting Ottoman affairs in order without the perennial menace of foreign interference. Ottoman neutrality would be solicited by some of the belligerents, Ottoman intervention by others; during the war, however, no nation could afford to bully Turkey. By clever diplomatic bargaining economic and political privileges of the greatest importance might be obtained—the Capitulations, for example, might be abolished. Neutral Turkey might grow prosperous by a thriving commerce with the belligerents. After the peace both victor and vanquished would be too exhausted to think of aggression against a revivified Ottoman Empire. To remain neutral was to assure peace, security, and prosperity. To intervene was to invite defeat and dismemberment.

Militarists, however, appraised the situation differently. National honor demanded that Turkey go to the assistance of her allies. But, more than that, national security demanded the decisive defeat of the Entente Powers. As contrasted with the firm friendship of Germany for Turkey, it was pointed out, there was the traditional policy of Russia to dismember the Ottoman Empire and of France and Great Britain to infringe upon Ottoman sovereignty whenever opportunity presented itself. A victorious Russia would certainly appropriate Constantinople, and as "compensations" France would take Syria and England Mesopotamia. By closing the Dardanelles and declaring war, Turkey could deal Russian economic and military power a blow from which the empire of the Tsars might never recover. By associating herself with the seemingly irresistible military forces of Germany, Turkey might once and for all eliminate Russia—the feared and hated enemy of both Turks and Germans—from Near Eastern affairs. In addition, British security in Egypt might be shaken, and the French colonial empire in North Africa might be menaced by a Pan-Islamic revival. In these circumstances the war might be for Turkey a war of liberation, from which only the craven-hearted would shrink.

For a time, however, practical considerations led to the

maintenance of Ottoman neutrality. "To Germany the 'sphere of influence' in Turkey was of far greater economic and political importance than all her 'colonies' in Africa and in the South Seas put together. The latter, under the German flag, were an obvious and quick prey to Great Britain's naval superiority, but so long as Turkey remained out of the war the German sphere of influence in Anatolia and Mesopotamia was protected by the neutral Crescent flag. As soon as Turkey entered the war, however, Great Britain's naval superiority could be brought to bear upon Germany's interests in the Near East as well as upon her interests in Africa and Oceanica. If German imperialists were devoted to a Berlin-to-Bagdad *Mittel-Europa* project, there were British imperialists whose hearts and minds were set upon a Suez-to-Singapore South-Asia project. The Ottoman Empire occupied a strategic position in both schemes. A neutral Turkey, on the whole, was favorable to German imperialism. A Turkey in armed alliance with Germany presented a splendid opportunity for British imperialism." [1]

Turkish mobilization, furthermore, was a tediously slow process. The construction of the Bagdad Railway, as we have seen, had not been completed before the outbreak of the Great War.[2] There were wide gaps in northern Mesopotamia and in the Amanus mountains which made difficult the transportation of troops for the defence of Irak, an attack on the Suez, an offensive in the Caucasus, or the fortification of the Dardanelles. The entry of Turkey into the war before the completion of mobilization would have been of no material advantage to Germany and would almost certainly have brought disaster to the Ottoman Empire. Therefore, while the war went well for Germany on the French and Russian fronts, German influence at Constantinople was more concerned with creating sentiment for war and with speeding up mobilization than with encouraging premature intervention. After the Teutonic defeats at the Marne and in Galicia, however, active Turkish support was needed for the purpose of menacing Russian security in the Caucasus and British security in Egypt, as well as for bolstering up German morale. During the latter part of September and the month of October, Marshal Liman von Sanders, Baron von Wangenheim, the commanders of the *Goeben* and the *Breslau,* and other German influences at Constantinople exerted the strongest possible pressure on the Ottoman Government to bring Turkey into the war on the side of her Teutonic allies.

On October 31, 1914, the Turkish Government took the fatal step of precipitating war with the Entente Powers, after Enver Pasha, Minister of War, and Djemal Pasha, Minister of Marine, were satisfied that Ottoman preparations were sufficiently advanced to warrant the beginning of hostilities. The outcome of the Bagdad Railway concession of 1903 was the entry of Turkey into the War of 1914![3]

Discouraged by their failure to maintain the peace, and fearful of impending disaster to their country, Djavid Bey and three other members of the Ottoman ministry resigned their posts. There were other indications, also, that intelligent public opinion at Constantinople was not whole-hearted in support of war. But the nationalists—playing upon the "traditional enmity" toward Russia—had their way, and with an outburst of patriotic fervor Turkey began hostilities. In a proclamation to the army and navy the Sultan affirmed that the war was being waged for the defence of the Caliphate and the "emancipation" of the Fatherland: "During the last three hundred years," he said, "the Russian Empire has caused our country to suffer many losses in territory. And when we finally arose to a sentiment of awakening and regeneration which was to increase our national welfare and our power, the Russian Empire made every effort to destroy our attempts, either with war or with numerous machinations and intrigues. Russia, England, and France never for a moment ceased harboring ill-will against our Caliphate, to which millions of Mussulmans, suffering under the tyranny of foreign domination, are religiously and whole-heartedly devoted. And it was always these powers that started every misfortune that came upon us. Therefore, in this mighty struggle which we are undertaking, we once and for all will put an end to the attacks made from one side against the Caliphate and from the other against the existence of our country." [4]

Turcophiles in Germany were enthusiastic over Otto-man participation in the Great War. The Turkish mili-tary contribution to a Teutonic victory might not be decisive, but neither would it be insignificant. And Ger-man coöperation in Ottoman military ventures would certainly strengthen German economic penetration in the Near East, even though Turkish arms might not drive Britain out of Egypt or Russia out of the Caucasus. "Over there in Turkey," wrote Dr. Ernest Jäckh, "stretch Anatolia and Mesopotamia—Anatolia, the 'land of sun-rise,' Mesopotamia, an ancient paradise. Let these names be to us a symbol. May this world war bring to Germany and Turkey the sunrise and the paradise of a new era. May it confer upon a strengthened Turkey and a greater Germany the blessings of fruitful Turco-Teutonic co-operation in peace after victorious Turco-Teutonic col-laboration in war." [5]

ASIATIC TURKEY BECOMES ONE OF THE STAKES OF THE WAR

Whatever may have been the European origins of the Great War, there was no disposition on the part of the belligerents to overlook its imperial possibilities. A war which was fought for the protection of France against German aggression, for the defence of Belgian neutrality, for the recovery of Alsace-Lorraine, for the democratizing of a bureaucratic German Empire—this war was fought not only in Flanders and Picardy and the Vosges, but in Africa and Asia and the South Seas; not only in Poland and Galicia and East Prussia, but in Mesopotamia and Syria and the Dardanelles. Anatolia, Palestine, and the region of the Persian Gulf were as much the stakes of the war as *Italia irredenta,* the lost provinces of France, or the Serbian "outlet" to the Adriatic.

Of all the spoils of the war, Turkey was among the richest. Her undeveloped wealth in minerals and fuel; her potentialities as a producer of foodstuffs, cotton, and other agricultural products; her possibilities as a market —these were alluring as war-time necessities and peace-time assets. Her strategic position was of inestimable importance to any nation which hoped to establish colonial power in the eastern Mediterranean. Her future as a sphere of influence promised unusual opportunities for the investment of capital and the acquisition of exclusive economic rights. It was no accident, therefore, that brought men from Berlin and Bombay, Stuttgart and Sydney, Munich and Marseilles, to fight bitterly for possession of the cliffs of Gallipoli, the deserts of Mesopotamia, and the coast of Syria. Turkey-in-Asia was a rich prize upon which imperialists in Berlin and Vienna, London and Paris and Petrograd, had set their hearts.

No sooner had Turkey entered the war than the imperial aspects of the struggle became apparent. Germany was deluged with literature designed to show that Ottoman participation in the war would assure Germany and Austria their legitimate "place in the sun." Business men and diplomatists, missionaries and Oriental scholars [6] combined in prophesying that the Turco-German brother-hood-in-arms would fortify the Teutonic economic posi-tion in the Near East, disturb Russian equanimity in the Caucasus, menace Britain's communications with India, and end once and for all French pretensions in Syria. Moslem sympathizers predicted that the Holy War would shake the Entente empires to their foundations. Pan-Germans frankly avowed that the war offered an oppor-tunity to make Berlin-to-Bagdad a reality rather than a dream—some went so far as to believe that German domi-nation could be 'extended from the North Cape to the Persian Gulf! Mercantilists foresaw the possibility of creating a politically unified and an economically self-sufficient Middle Europe.[7]

As a means of promoting closer relationships with Turkey numerous societies were established in Germany for the purpose of disseminating information on the Near East and its importance in the war. For example, Dr. Hugo Grothe conducted at Leipzig the work of the *Deutsches Vorderasienkomitee—Vereinigung zur För-derung deutscher Kulturarbeit im islamischen Orient.* This organization published and distributed hundreds of thousands of books, pamphlets, and maps regarding Asiatic Turkey; conducted a Near East Institute, at which lectures and courses of instruction were given; maintained an information bureau for business men in-terested in commercial and industrial opportunities in the Ottoman Empire; and established German libraries in Constantinople, Aleppo, Bagdad, Konia, and elsewhere along the line of the Bagdad Railway. A similar organ-ization, the *Deutsch-türkische Vereinigung,* was main-tained at Berlin under the honorary presidency of Dr. von Gwinner of the *Deutsche Bank* and the active super-vision of Dr. Ernest Jäckh. The two societies numbered among their members and patrons Herr Ballin, of the

Hamburg-American Line, General von der Goltz, Baron von Wangenheim, and the Ottoman ambassador at Berlin.[8]

The watchdogs of British imperial welfare, however, were not asleep. Lord Crewe, the Secretary of State for India, was busily engaged in plans for safeguarding British economic and strategic interests in Mesopotamia. Early in September, 1914, General Sir Edmund Barrow, Military Secretary of the India Office, prepared a memorandum, "The Rôle of India in a Turkish War," which proposed the immediate occupation of Basra on the grounds that it was "the psychological moment to take action" and that "so unexpected a stroke at this moment would have a startling effect" in checkmating Turkish intrigues, encouraging the Arabs to revolt and thus forestalling an Ottoman attack on the Suez, and in protecting the oil installations at the head of the Persian Gulf.[9] Supporters of a pro-Balkan policy, in the meantime, were urging an attack on Turkey from the Mediterranean. Winston Churchill, Chief Lord of the Admiralty, for example, in a memorandum of August 19, 1914, to Sir Edward Grey, advocated an alliance with Greece against Turkey; by September 4 he had completed plans for a military and naval attack on the Dardanelles; on September 21 he telegraphed Admiral Carden, at Malta, to "sink the *Goeben* and *Breslau,* no matter what flag they fly, if they come out of the Straits." Mr. Churchill, with whose name will ever be associated the disastrous expedition to the Dardanelles, believed that, whatever the outcome of the war on the Western Front, the success or failure of Germany would be measured in terms of her power in the Near East after the termination of hostilities. To destroy German economic and political domination of Turkey it was necessary to have an expedition at the head of the Persian Gulf and, possibly, another in Syria, but the commanding strategic position was the Straits. The capture of Constantinople would win the war.[10]

There were others who considered that a purely defensive policy should be followed in the Near East. Lord Kitchener, for example, believed in concentrating the maximum possible man power in France and advocated restricting Eastern operations to the protection of the Suez Canal and other essential communications. Influential military critics, like Colonel Repington, were firmly opposed to "side shows" in Mesopotamia, at the Dardanelles, or elsewhere, which would divert men, matériel, and popular attention from the Western Front. Sir Edward Grey appeared to be more interested in Continental than in colonial questions. Lord Curzon was swayed between fear of a Moslem uprising in India and the hope that British prestige in the East might be materially enhanced by outstanding military successes at the expense of the Turks.[11]

The Near Eastern imperialists, however, had their way. During September, 1914, the Government of India was ordered to prepare an expeditionary force for service in the region of the Persian Gulf. Early in October, almost four weeks before Turkey entered the war, Indian Expeditionary Force "D," under General Delamain, sailed from Bombay under sealed orders. It next appeared on October 23, at Bahrein Island, in the Persian Gulf, where General Delamain learned the purposes of the expedition which he commanded. His army was to occupy Adaban Island, at the mouth of the Shatt-el-Arab, "with the object of protecting the oil refineries, tanks and pipe lines [of the Anglo-Persian Company], covering the landing of reënforcements should these be required, and assuring the local Arabs of support against Turkey." For the last-named purpose Sir Percy Cox, subsequently British High Commissioner in Irak, was attached to the army as "political officer." In addition, General Delamain was to "take such military and political action as he should consider feasible to strengthen his position and, if necessary, occupy Basra." Nevertheless, he was warned that the rôle of his force was "that of demonstrating at the head of the Persian Gulf" and that on no account was he "to take any hostile action against the Turks without orders from the Government of India, *except in the case of absolute military necessity*"! [12]

Meanwhile, Sir Arthur Henry McMahon, subsequently first High Commissioner in Egypt under the Protectorate, entered into an agreement, dated October 23, 1914, with the Sherif of Mecca, assuring the latter that Great Britain was prepared "to recognize and support the independence of the Arabs within territories in which Great Britain is free to act without detriment to the interests of her ally, France," it being understood that "the districts of Mersina and Alexandretta and portions of Syria lying to the west of the districts of Damascus, Homs, Hama and Aleppo cannot be said to be purely Arab." In other words, an independent Arab state was considered to be feasible insofar as it did not conflict with the sphere of interest in Syria developed by French railway-builders and recognized by the Franco-German agreement of February 15, 1914. [13]

Even before Turkey formally entered the war, therefore, a British army was "demonstrating" in the Shatt-el-Arab; Sir Percy Cox was coöperating with the Sheik of Koweit for the purpose of precipitating a rebellion among the Arabs of Mesopotamia, and a British representative had sown the seeds of a separatist movement in the Hedjaz. It was a short step from this, after the declaration of hostilities, to the occupation of Basra, on November 22, and of Kurna, on December 9. The close of the year 1914 saw Turkey in the unenviable position of having to choose between increasing German economic and political domination, on the one hand, and dismemberment by the Entente Allies, on the other.

The political and military situation of Turkey did not improve during the year 1915. By mid-January, the rigors of a Caucasian winter and the absence of adequate means of communication and supply brought to a standstill Enver Pasha's drive against the Russians. Early in February, Djemal Pasha's army, which had crossed the Sinai Peninsula in the face of seemingly insuperable obstacles, attacked the Suez Canal only to be decisively defeated by its British and French defenders. During March a secret agreement was reached between Great Britain, France, and Russia for the partition of the Ottoman Empire, including the assignment of Constantinople to the Tsar. On April 26, by the Treaty of London which brought Italy into the war, the Entente Powers bound themselves to "preserve the political balance in the Mediterranean" by recognizing the right of Italy "to receive on the division of Turkey an equal share with Great Britain, France and Russia in the basin of the Mediterranean, and more specifically in that part of it contiguous to the province of Adalia, where Italy already had obtained special rights and developed certain interests"; likewise the Allies agreed to protect the interests of Italy "in the event that the territorial inviolability of Asiatic Turkey should be sustained by the Powers" or that "only a redistribution of spheres of interest should take place." [14] To give greater effect to these secret imperialistic agreements British troops were landed at the Dardanelles on April 28. The bargains were sealed with the blood of those heroic Britons and immortal Anzacs who went through the tortures of hell—and worse—at Gallipoli! [15]

In the meantime, British activities were resumed in

Mesopotamia.   In March, 1915, General J. E. Nixon was ordered to Basra with renewed instructions "to secure the safety of the oilfields, pipe line and refineries of the Anglo-Persian Oil Company," as well as with orders to consolidate his position for the purpose of "retaining complete control of lower Mesopotamia" and of making possible a subsequent advance on Bagdad.   On May 29, in accordance with these instructions, the Sixth Division, under General Sir Charles Townshend, occupied Amara, a town of 12,000 lying about fifty miles north of Basra on the Tigris, seat of the Turkish provincial administration and one of the principal entrepôts of Mesopotamian trade.   Beyond this point General Nixon refused to extend his operations unless assured adequate reënforcements, which were not forthcoming.   Nevertheless, because of the insistence of Sir Percy Cox that some outstanding success was necessary to retain support of the Arabs, another advance was ordered in the early autumn. On September 29, General Townshend occupied Kut-el-Amara, 180 miles north of his former position.

Then followed the decision to advance on Bagdad—a move which will go down in history as one of the chief blunders of the war, as well as a conspicuous instance of the manner in which political desiderata were allowed to outweigh military considerations.   The soldiers on the ground were opposed to the move.   General Nixon believed it would be disastrous to advance farther than Kut without substantial reënforcements.   General Townshend was convinced that "Mesopotamia was a secondary theatre of war, and on principle should be held on the defensive with a minimum force," and he warned his superiors that his troops "were tired, and their tails were not up, but slightly down," that they were fearful of the distance from the sea and "were going down, in consequence, with every imaginable disease."   But the statesmen at London were thinking not only of winning the war but of eliminating Germany from all future political and economic competition in the backward areas of the world. "Because of the great political and military advantages to be derived from the capture of Bagdad," and because the "uncertainty" of the situation at the Dardanelles made apparent "the great need of a striking success in the East," Austen Chamberlain, Secretary of State for India, telegraphed the Viceroy on October 23, 1915, that an immediate advance should be begun. Fearful of the consequences, but faithful to his trust, General Townshend began the hundred-mile march to Bagdad. Worn out, but heroic beyond words, his troops drove the Turkish forces back and, on November 22, occupied Ctesiphon, only eighteen miles from their goal. This, however, marked the high tide of Allied success in the Near East during 1915, for General Townshend was destined to reach Bagdad only as a prisoner of war.[16]

GERMANY WINS TEMPORARY DOMINATION OF THE NEAR EAST

Allied military successes in Turkey were not looked upon with equanimity in Germany. There was a realization in Berlin, as well as London and Paris and Petrograd, that the stakes of the war were as much imperial as Continental. Nothing had as yet occurred which had lessened the importance of establishing an economically self-sufficient Middle European *bloc* of nations. In the event that the German oversea colonies could not be recovered, Asiatic Turkey—because of its favorable geographical position, its natural resources, and its potentialities as a market—would be almost indispensable in the German imperial scheme of things. As Paul Rohrbach wrote in *Das grössere Deutschland* in August, 1915,

"After a year of war almost everybody in Germany is of the opinion that victory or defeat—at least political victory or defeat—depends upon the preservation of Turkey and the maintenance of our communications with her."

The dogged defence of the Dardanelles had convinced Germany that, granted proper support, Turkey could be depended upon to give a good account of herself. The problem was one of supplementing Ottoman man power with Teutonic military genius, technical skill, and organizing ability. The enlistment of Bulgaria and the obliteration of Serbia made possible more active German assistance to Turkey, and during the latter months of 1915 and the early months of 1916 strenuous efforts were made to bring the Turkish military machine to a high point of efficiency. Large numbers of German staff officers were despatched to Mesopotamia, Syria, and Anatolia, and Turkish officers were brought to the French and Russian fronts to learn the methods of modern warfare. The Prussian system of military service was adopted throughout the Ottoman Empire, and exemptions were reduced to a minimum. Liberal credits were established with German banks for the purchase of supplies for the new levies of troops. Field Marshal von der Goltz was sent to Mesopotamia as commander-in-chief of the Turkish troops in that region.[17]

Perhaps the chief handicap of the Turks in all their campaigns was inadequate means of transportation. The Ottoman armies operating in the vicinity of Gaza and of Bagdad were dependent upon lines of communication more than twelve hundred miles long; and had the Bagdad Railway been non-existent, it is doubtful if any military operations at all could have been conducted in those regions. But the Bagdad Railway was uncompleted. Troops and supplies being despatched from or to Anatolia had to be transported across the Taurus and Amanus mountains by mule-back, wagon, or automobile, and then reloaded on cars south or north of the unfinished tunnels. To remedy these deficiencies, herculean efforts were made by Germans and Turks during 1915 to improve the service on existing lines and to hurry the completion of the Bagdad Railway. Locomotives and other rolling stock were shipped to Turkey, and German railway experts coöperated with the military authorities in utilizing transportation facilities to the best advantage. In September, 1915, the Bagtché tunnel was pierced; and although through service to Aleppo was not inaugurated until October, 1918, a temporary narrow-gauge line was used, during the interim, to transport troops and matériel through the tunnel. Commenting on the importance of the Bagtché tunnel, the American Consul General at Constantinople wrote: "With its completion the most serious difficulties connected with the construction of the Bagdad Railway have been overcome, and the work of connecting up many of the isolated stretches of track may be expected to be completed with reasonable rapidity. In spite of delays occasioned by the war, this most important undertaking in railway construction in Turkey has passed the problematical stage and is now certain to become an accomplished fact in the near future." [18]

The effects of German assistance to Turkey soon made themselves apparent. Field Marshal von der Goltz, commanding a reënforced and reinvigorated Ottoman army, supported by German artillery, compelled General Townshend to abandon hope of occupying Bagdad and to fall back toward Basra. By December 5, 1915, Townshend's army was besieged in Kut-el-Amara; and although the Turks failed to take the town by storm, they did not fail to 'beat off every Russian and British force sent to the relief of the beleaguered troops. About the same time, December 10, evacuation of the Dardanelles was begun, and the last of the British troops were withdrawn during the first week of January, 1916. On April 29, Townshend's famished garrison surrendered. Shortly thereafter the offensive of the Grand Duke Nicholas in Turkish Armenia was brought to a standstill. During July and August a second Ottoman attack was launched against the Suez Canal; and although it was unsuccessful, the expedition reminded the British that Egypt was by no means immune from danger. By the end of the year 1916 Turkey, with German assistance, had completely cleared her soil of enemy troops, except for a retreating Russian army in northern Anatolia and a defeated British expedition at the head of the Persian Gulf.[19]

As for Germany, she "was unopposed in her mastery of that whole vast region of southeastern Europe and southwestern Asia which goes by the name of the Near East. . . . She now enjoyed uninterrupted and unmenaced communication and commerce with Constantinople not only, but far away, over the great arteries of Asiatic Turkey [the Bagdad and Hedjaz railways], with Damascus, Jerusalem, and Mecca, and with Bagdad likewise. . . . If military exploits had been as conclusive as they had been spectacular, Germany would have won the Great War in 1916 and imposed a *Pax Germanica* upon the world. . . . With the adherence of Turkey and Bulgaria to the Teutonic Alliance, and the triumphs of those states, a Germanized *Mittel-Europa* could be said to stretch from the North Sea to the Persian Gulf, from the Baltic to the Red Sea, from Lithuania and Ukrainia to Picardy and Champagne. It was the greatest achievement in empire-building on the continent of Europe since the days of Napoleon Bonaparte." [20]

If Germany had been alarmed during the summer of 1915 at the prospect that she might lose her preponderant position in Turkey, the world was now alarmed at the prospect that she might maintain that position. Nor was that alarm easily dispelled, for the Bagdad Railway and the power and prestige it gave Germany in the Near East were pointed to by statesmen as additional evidence of the manner in which the Kaiser and his cohorts had plotted in secret against the peace of an unsuspecting and unprepared world. In fact, the Bagdad Railway came to be considered one of the fundamental causes of the war, as well as one of the chief prizes for which the war was being fought. President Wilson, for example, in his Flag Day speech, June 14, 1917, stated the case in the following terms: [21]

"The rulers of Germany . . . were glad to go forward unmolested, filling the thrones of Balkan states with German princes, putting German officers at the service of Turkey to drill her armies and make interest with her government, developing plans of sedition and rebellion in India and Egypt, setting their fires in Persia. The demands made by Austria upon Serbia were a mere single step in a plan which compassed Europe and Asia, from Berlin to Bagdad. . . .

"The plan was to throw a broad belt of German military power and political control across the very centre of Europe and beyond the Mediterranean into the heart of Asia; and Austria-Hungary was to be as much their tool and pawn as Serbia or Bulgaria or Turkey or the ponderous states of the East. . . . The dream had its heart at Berlin. It could have had a heart nowhere else! . . .

"And they have actually carried the greater part of that amazing plan into execution. . . . The so-called Central Powers are in fact but a single Power. Serbia is at its mercy, should its hands be but for a moment freed. Bulgaria has consented to its will, and Roumania is overrun. The Turkish armies, which Germans trained, are serving Germany, certainly not themselves, and the guns of German warships lying in the harbor at Constantinople remind Turkish statesmen every day that they have no choice but to take their orders from Berlin. From Hamburg to the Persian Gulf the net is spread!"

As late as November 12, 1917, after some spectacular victories by the Allies in Mesopotamia and Syria, President Wilson made it plain that no peace was possible which did not destroy German military power in the Near East. Addressing the American Federation of Labor, at Buffalo, N. Y., he said: [22]

"Look at the map of Europe now. Germany, in thrusting upon us again and again the discussion of peace, talks about what? Talks about Belgium—talks about Alsace-Lorraine. Well, these are deeply interesting subjects to us and to them, but they are not talking about the heart of the matter. Take the map and look at it. Germany has absolute control of Austria-Hungary, practical control of the Balkan States, control of Turkey, control of Asia Minor. I saw a map the other day in which the whole thing was printed in appropriate black, and the black stretched all the way from Hamburg to Bagdad—the bulk of the German power inserted into the heart of the world. If she can keep that, she has kept all that her dreams contemplated when the war began. If she can keep that, her power can disturb the world as long as she keeps it, always provided . . . the present influences that control the German Government continue to control it."

In the light of all the facts, this diagnosis of the situation is incomplete, to say the least. Had President Wilson been cognizant of the contemporaneous counter-activities of the Allied Powers, he might not have been prepared to offer so simple an explanation of a many-sided problem. For it was not German imperialism alone which menaced the peace of the Near East and of the world, but *all* imperialism.

"Berlin to Bagdad" Becomes But a Memory

Germany may have been determined to dominate the Ottoman Empire by military force. But from the Turkish point of view domination by Germany was hardly more objectionable than the dismemberment which was certain to be the result of an Allied victory.

Indeed, confident that they would eventually win the war, the Entente Powers had proceeded far in their plans for the division of the Ottoman Empire. During the spring of 1915, as has been indicated,[23] Russia had been promised Constantinople, and Italy had been assigned a share of the spoils equal to that of Great Britain, France, or Russia. To give full effect to these understandings, further negotiations were conducted during the autumn of 1915 and the spring of 1916, looking toward a more specific delimitation of interests.

Accordingly, on April 26, 1916—the first anniversary of the Treaty of London with Italy—France and Russia signed the secret Sazonov-Paléologue Treaty concerning their respective territorial rights in Asiatic Turkey. Russia was awarded full sovereignty over the vilayets of Trebizond, Erzerum, Bitlis, and Van—a vast area of 60,000 square miles (about one and one-fifth times the size of the State of New York), containing valuable mineral and petroleum resources. This handsome prize put Russia well on the road to Constantinople and in a fair way to turn the Black Sea into a Russian lake. And at the moment the treaty was signed the armies of the Grand Duke Nicholas were actually overrunning the territory which Russia had staked out for herself! For her part, France was to receive adequate compensations in the region to the south and southwest of the Russian acquisitions, the actual delimitation of boundaries and other details to be the result of direct negotiation with Great Britain.[24]

Thus came into existence the famous Sykes-Picot Treaty of May 9, 1916, defining British and French political and economic interests in the hoped-for dismemberment of the Ottoman Empire. The Syrian coast from Tyre to Alexandretta, the province of Cilicia, and southern Armenia (from Sivas on the north and west to Diarbekr on the south and east) were allocated to France in full sovereignty. In addition, a French "zone of in-

fluence" was established over a vast area including the
provinces of Aleppo, Damascus, Deir, and Mosul. Administration of this stretch of coast and its hinterland
would give French imperialists what they most wanted in
the Near East—actual possession of a country in which
France had many religious and cultural interests, control
of the silk production of Syria and the potential cotton
production of Cilicia, ownership of the Arghana copper
mines, and acquisition of that portion of the Bagdad
Railway lying between Mosul and the Cilician Gates of the
Taurus.[25] Aside from its satisfaction of French imperial ambitions, however, "the French area defied every
known law of geographic, ethnographic, and linguistic
unity which one might cite who would attempt to justify
it." [26]

Great Britain, by way of "compensation," was to receive complete control over lower Mesopotamia from
Tekrit to the Persian Gulf and from the Arabian boundary to the Persian frontier. In addition, she was recognized as having special political and economic interests—
particularly the right "to furnish such advisers as the
Arabs might desire"—in a vast territory lying south of
the French "zone of influence" and extending from the
Sinai Peninsula to the Persian border. Palestine was
to be internationalized, but was subsequently established
as a homeland for the Jews. In this manner Britain,
also, had adequately protected her imperial interests—
she had secured possession of the Bagdad Railway in
southern Mesopotamia; she had gained complete control
of the head of the Persian Gulf, thus fortifying her
strategic position in the Indian Ocean; she was assured
the Mesopotamian cotton supply for the mills of Manchester and the Mesopotamian oil supply for the dread-
noughts of the Grand Fleet; she had erected in Palestine
a buffer state which would block any future Ottoman

attacks on the Suez Canal. All in all, Sir Mark Sykes had driven a satisfactory bargain.[27]

Italian ambitions now had to be propitiated. For a whole year before the United States entered the war—while the Allied governments were professing unselfish war aims—secret negotiations were being conducted by representatives of France, Great Britain and Italy to determine what advantages and territories, equivalent to those gained by the other Allies, might be awarded Italy. In April, 1917, by the so-called St. Jean de Maurienne Agreement, Italy was granted complete possession of almost the entire southern half of Anatolia—including the important cities of Adalia, Konia, and Smyrna—together with an extensive "zone of influence" northeast of Smyrna. With such a hold on the coast of Asia Minor, Italian imperialists might realize their dream of dominating the trade of the Ægean and of reëstablishing the ancient power of Venice in the commerce of the Near East.[28]

These inter-Allied agreements for the disposal of Asiatic Turkey were instructive instances of the "old diplomacy" in coöperation with the "new imperialism." The treaties were secret covenants, secretly arrived at; they bartered territories and peoples in the most approved manner of Metternich and Richelieu. But they were less concerned with narrowly political claims than with the exclusive economic privileges which sovereignty carried with it; they determined boundaries with recognition of their strategic importance, but with greater regard for the location of oilfields, mineral deposits, railways and ports of commercial importance. They left no doubt as to what were the real stakes of the war in the Near East.

It is difficult, if not impossible, to reconcile the secret treaties with the pronouncements of Allied statesmen regarding the origins and purposes of the Great War.

Certainly they were no part of the American program for peace, which promised to "the Turkish portions of the Ottoman Empire a secure sovereignty"; which demanded "a free, open-minded, and absolutely impartial adjustment of all colonial claims, based upon a strict observance of the principle that in determining all such questions of sovereignty the interests of the populations concerned must have equal weight with the equitable claims of the government whose title is to be determined"; and which announced in no uncertain terms that "the day of conquest and aggrandizement is gone by" as is also "the day of secret covenants entered into in the interest of particular governments and likely at some unlooked-for moment to upset the peace of the world." [29]

Allied diplomacy was to have its way in the Near East, however, for the goddess of victory finally smiled upon the Allied armies and frowned upon both Turks and Germans. As 1916 had been a year of Turco-German triumphs at the Dardanelles and in Mesopotamia, 1917 brought conspicuous Allied victories along the Tigris and in Syria, and 1918 saw the complete collapse of the Ottoman Empire. On February 24, 1917, General Sir Stanley Maude, in command of reënforced and rejuvenated British forces in Mesopotamia, captured Kut-el-Amara, retrieving the disaster which had befallen Townshend's army a year before. Deprived of the services of Field Marshal von der Goltz, who died during the Caucasus campaign, the Turks retired in disorder, and on March 11 British troops entered Bagdad—the ancient city which had bulked so large in the German scheme of things in the Near East. Although the capture of Bagdad was not in itself of great strategic importance, its effect on morale in the belligerent countries was considerable. British imperialists were in possession of the ancient capital of the Arabian Caliphs, as well as the chief entrepôt of caravan trade in the Middle East; therefore their prestige with both Arabs and Turks was certain to rise. At home, pictures of British troops in the Bagdad of the Arabian Nights appealed to the imagination of the war-weary, as well as the optimistic, patriot. In the Central Powers, on the other hand, the loss of Bagdad created scepticism as to whether the German dream of "Hamburg to the Persian Gulf" was not now beyond realization. This scepticism became more confirmed when, on April 24, General Maude captured Samarra, northern railhead of the uncompleted Bagdad line in Mesopotamia.[30]

Scepticism would have turned to alarm, however, had Germans been fully aware of the significance of the British advance in the Land of the Two Rivers. For behind the armies of General Maude came civil officials by the hundreds to consolidate the victory and to lay the foundations of permanent occupation. An Irrigation Department was established to deal with the menace of floods, to drain marshes, and to economize in the use of water. An Agricultural Department undertook the cultivation of irrigated lands and conducted elaborate experiments in the growing of cotton—the commodity which means so much in the British imperial system. A railway was constructed from Basra to Bagdad which, when opened to commerce in 1919, became an integral part of the Constantinople-Basra system. There was every indication that the British were in Mesopotamia to stay.[31]

Germans and Turks were sufficiently aroused, however, to take strenuous measures to counteract General Maude's successes. In April, 1917, Field Marshal von Mackensen, hero of the Balkan and Rumanian campaigns and strong man of the Near East, was sent to Constantinople to confer with Enver Pasha regarding the military situation. It was decided, apparently, that Bagdad must be

retaken at all costs, for throughout the summer quantities
of rolling stock for the Bagdad Railway were shipped to
Turkey, enormous supplies of munitions were accumulated at Haidar Pasha, and a division of picked German
troops (including machine-gun and artillery units) made
its appearance in Anatolia. Command of all the Turkish
armies in Mesopotamia was conferred upon General von
Falkenhayn, former German Chief of Staff. Germany
was not yet prepared to surrender her sphere of interest
in Turkey.

The great expedition against Bagdad, however, had to
be abandoned. In the first place, Turkish officers were
loath to serve under von Falkenhayn. Turkish nationalism was beginning to assert itself, and German supervision of Ottoman military affairs was resented—Mustapha Kemal Pasha, for example, refused to accept orders
from German generals and resigned his commission.
Von Falkenhayn himself was disliked because of his
dictatorial methods and was held in light esteem because
of his responsibility for the disastrous Verdun offensive.
Furthermore, many Turks deemed it inadvisable to dis-
sipate energy in a Mesopotamian campaign, the avowed
purpose of which was a recovery of German prestige,
when all available man power was required for the defence of Syria. Djemal Pasha was so insistent on this
point that he received from the Kaiser an "invitation" to
visit the Western Front! In the second place, Providence or, perhaps, an Allied spy intervened to thwart
the German plans, for a great fire and a series of explo-
sions (September 23-26, 1917) destroyed the entire port
and terminal of Haidar Pasha, together with all the munitions and supplies which had been accumulated there
by months of patient effort. And finally, the spectacular
campaign of Field Marshal Allenby in Palestine, which
opened with the capture of Beersheba, on October 31,

convinced even von Falkenhayn that an expedition in Mesopotamia, while Aleppo was in danger, would be the height of folly. German energies were thereupon diverted to the defence of the Holy Land.[32]

During the autumn of 1917, Great Britain and France, to assure their possession of the territories assigned them by the Sykes-Picot Treaty, began a Syrian campaign which was not to terminate until Turkey had been put out of the war. Under Field Marshal Sir E. H. H. Allenby, British troops, reënforced by French units and assisted by the rebellious Arabs of the Hedjaz, captured Gaza (November 7), Jaffa (November 16), and Jerusalem (December 9). The triumphal entry of General Allenby into Jerusalem was hailed throughout Christendom as marking the success of a modern crusade to rid Palestine of Ottoman domination forever. Jericho was occupied, February 21, 1918, but Turkish resistance, under Marshal Liman von Sanders, stiffened for a time, and it was not until the autumn that large-scale operations were resumed. On October 1, Damascus was occupied by a combined Arab and British army; a week later Beirut was taken; and on October 25, Aleppo, the most important junction point on the Bagdad Railway, capitulated. Five days afterward, Turkey gave up the hopeless fight by signing the Mudros armistice, terminating hostilities.[33]

Thus ended a Great Adventure for both Turkey and Germany. Germany lost all hope of retaining any economic or political influence in the Ottoman Empire; the dream of Berlin-to-Bagdad became a nightmare. Turkey faced dismemberment. "The Bagdad Railway had proved to be the backbone of Turkish utility and power in the War. Were it not for its existence, the Ottoman resistance in Mesopotamia and in Syria could have been discounted as a practical consideration in the War, and the sending of Turkish reënforcements to the Caucasus would have been even more materially delayed than was in fact the case." [34] For Turkey, then, the war had come at a most inappropriate time. Had hostilities begun ten years later, after the completion of the Bagdad system, military operations in the Near East might have had an entirely different result. As it was, the Bagdad Railway—and the international complications arising from it—proved to be the ruination of the Ottoman Empire.

To the Victors Belong the Spoils

During 1919, the Allied Governments set about possessing themselves of the spoils which were theirs by virtue of the secret treaties and by right of conquest. In April, Italian troops occupied Adalia and rapidly extended their lines into the interior as far as Konia. In November, French armies replaced the British forces in Syria and Cilicia. Great Britain began the "pacification" of the tribesmen of Mesopotamia and Kurdistan. And in the meantime there was plentiful evidence that German rights in the Near East would be speedily liquidated in the interest of the victorious Powers. For example, on March 26, the Interallied Commission on Ports, Waterways, and Railways announced at Paris the adoption of "a new transportation agreement designed to secure a route to the Orient by railway without passing through the territories of the Central Empires." Accordingly, a fast train, the "Simplon-Orient Express," was to be run regularly from Calais to Constantinople via Paris, Lausanne, Milan, Venice, Trieste, Agram, and Vinkovce. Later this service was to be extended into Asiatic Turkey, over the lines of the Anatolian, Bagdad, and Syrian railways. To meet a changed situation one must provide new paths of imperial expansion, and the

French press spoke glowingly of the prospect that the slogans "Hamburg to the Persian Gulf" and "Berlin to Bagdad" would be speedily replaced by "Calais to Cairo" and "Bordeaux to Bagdad"![35]

All German rights in the Bagdad Railway and other economic enterprises in the Near East were abrogated by the Treaty of Versailles, signed June 28, 1919. The German Government was obligated to obtain and to turn over to the Reparation Commission "any rights and interests of German nationals in any public utility undertaking or in any concession operating in . . . Turkey, Austria, Hungary, and Bulgaria" and agreed, as well, "to recognize and accept all arrangements which the Allied and Associated Powers may make with Turkey and Bulgaria with reference to any rights, interests and privileges whatever which might be claimed by Germany or her nationals in Turkey and Bulgaria."[36]

The Treaty of Sèvres, August 10, 1920—together with the accompanying secret Tripartite Agreement of the same date between Great Britain, France, and Italy—carried still further the liquidation of German interests in the Near East. The Turkish Government was required to dispose of all property rights in Turkey of Germany, Austria, Hungary, Bulgaria, or their respective nationals and to turn over the proceeds of all purchases and sales to the Reparation Commission established under the treaties of peace with those Powers. The Anatolian and Bagdad Railways were to be expropriated by Turkey and all of their rights, privileges, and properties to be assigned— at a valuation to be determined by an arbitrator appointed by the Council of the League of Nations—to a Franco-British-Italian corporation to be designated by the representatives of the Allied Powers. German stockholders were to be compensated for their holdings, but the amount of their compensation was to be turned over to the Reparation Commission; compensation due the Turkish Government was to be assigned to the Allied Governments toward the costs of maintaining their armies of occupation on Turkish soil. German and Turkish property in ceded territories of the Ottoman Empire was to be similarly liquidated. The Treaty of Versailles and the Treaty of Sèvres left hardly a vestige of German influence in the Near East.[37]

The Sèvres settlement, furthermore, destroyed the Ottoman Empire and sought to give the Allies a stranglehold upon the economic life of Turkey. Great Britain and France received essentially the same territorial privileges as they had laid out for themselves in the Sykes-Picot Treaty, with the vague restrictions that they should exercise in Mesopotamia and Palestine and in Syria and Cilicia respectively only the rights of mandatory powers. Great Britain was confirmed in her oil and navigation concessions in Mesopotamia, France in her railway rights in Syria; in addition, the Hedjaz Railway was turned over outright to their joint ownership and administration. Italy received only a "sphere of influence" in southern Anatolia, including the port of Adalia, but, as a consequence of one of the most sordid of the transactions of the Paris Conference, she was deprived of the bulk of the privileges guaranteed her under the Treaty of London and the St. Jean de Maurienne Agreement.[38] Greece was installed in Smyrna—the most important harbor in Asia Minor, a harbor the control of which was vital to the peasantry of Anatolia for the free export of their produce and for the unimpeded importation of farm machinery and other wares of western industry. Constantinople was put under the jurisdiction of an international commission for control of the Straits, and the balance of the former Russian sphere of interest was assigned to the ill-fated Armenian Republic. The Hedjaz was declared to be an independent Arab state. The Ottoman Empire was no more.

Even the Turkey that remained—a portion of Anatolia—enjoyed sovereignty in name only. The Capitulations, which the Sultan had terminated in the autumn of 1914, were reëstablished and extended. Concessions to Allied nationals were confirmed in all the rights which they enjoyed before Ottoman entry into the Great War. Because of the reparations, and because of the high cost of the Allied armies of occupation, the country was being loaded down with a still further burden of debt from which there appeared to be no escape—and debts not only mortgaged Turkish revenues but impaired Turkish administrative integrity. To assure prompt payment of both old and new financial obligations of the Turkish Government, an Interallied Financial Commission was superimposed upon the Ottoman Public Debt Administration. The Financial Commission had full supervision over taxation, customs, loans, and currency; exercised final control over the Turkish budget; and had the right to veto any proposed concession. In control of its domestic affairs the new Turkey was tied hand and foot. Here, indeed, was a Carthaginian peace! And all of this was done in order "to help Turkey, to develop her resources, and to avoid the international rivalries which have obstructed these objects in the past!" [39]

"THE OTTOMAN EMPIRE IS DEAD. LONG LIVE TURKEY!"

In the meantime, however, while the Sèvres Treaty was still in the making, there was a small handful of Turkish patriots who were determined at all costs to win that complete independence for which Turkey had entered the war. These Nationalists were outraged by the Greek occupation of Smyrna, in May, 1919, which they considered a forecast of the kind of peace to be dictated to Turkey. During the summer of 1919 they held two conferences at Erzerum and Sivas and agreed to reject any treaty which handed over Turkish populations to foreign domination, which would reduce Turkey to economic servitude to the victorious Powers, or which would impair the sovereignty of their country. Upon this program they won a sweeping victory in the parliamentary elections of 1919-1920. For leadership they depended largely upon that brilliant soldier and staunch Turk, Mustapha Kemal Pasha, who had distinguished himself by his quarrel with Liman von Sanders at the Dardanelles and his defiance of von Falkenhayn in Syria. Mustapha Kemal Pasha, who had bitterly contested the growth of German influence in Turkey during the war, was not likely to accept without a struggle the extension of Allied control over Turkish affairs.[40]

In Constantinople, January 28, 1920, the Nationalist members of the Turkish Parliament signed the celebrated "National Pact"—frequently referred to as a Declaration of Independence of the New Turkey. "The Pact was something more than a statement of war-aims or a party programme. It was the first adequate expression of a sentiment which had been growing up in the minds of Western-educated Turks for three or four generations, which in a half-conscious way had inspired the reforms of the Revolution of 1908, and which may dominate Turkey and influence the rest of the Middle East for many generations to come. It was an emphatic adoption of the Western national idea." [41] It was based upon principles which had received wide acceptance among peoples of the Allied nations during the war: self-determination of peoples, to be expressed by plebiscite; protection of the rights of minorities, but no further limitations of national sovereignty. As regards the Capitulations and the Ottoman Public Debt Administration, the Pact is explicit: "With a view to assuring our national and economic development," it reads, "and with the end of securing to the country a more regular and more modern administration, the signatories of the present pact consider the possession of complete independence and liberty as the *sine qua non* of our national existence. In consequence, we oppose all juridical or financial restrictions of any nature which would arrest our national development." Rather that Turkey should die free than live in slavery! Foreswearing any intention of recovering the Sultan's former Arab possessions, the Pact proceeded to serve notice, however, that Cilicia, Mosul, and the Turkish portions of Thrace must be reunited with the fatherland. "The Ottoman Empire is dead! Long live Turkey!" [42]

With this amazing program Mustapha Kemal Pasha undertook to liberate Turkey. In April, 1920, the government of the Grand National Assembly was instituted in Angora and proceeded to administer those portions of Anatolia which were not under Allied or Greek occupation. The proposed Treaty of Sèvres—which was handed to the Turkish delegates at Paris on May 11—was condemned as inconsistent with the legitimate national aspirations of the Turkish people. The Allies and the Constantinople Government were denounced—the former as invaders of the sacred soil of Turkey, the latter as tools of European imperialists. Then followed a series of successful military campaigns: by October, 1920, the French position in Cilicia had been rendered untenable, the Armenian Republic had been obliterated, the British forces of occupation had been forced back into the Ismid peninsula, and the Italians had withdrawn their troops to Adalia. In the spring of 1921 separate treaties were negotiated with Russia, Italy, and France, providing for a cessation of military operations and for the evacuation of certain Turkish territories.[43] Then came the long, bitter struggle against the Greeks, terminating with the Mudania armistice of October 10, 1922, which assured to the Turks the return of Smyrna and portions of Thrace. On November 1, the Sultanate was abolished, and Turkey became a republic. Four days later the Turkish Nationalists entered Constantinople in triumph. The struggle for the territorial and administrative integrity of a New Turkey seemed to be won.

The victory of the Nationalists scrapped the Treaty of Sèvres and called for a complete readjustment of the Near Eastern situation. When the first Lausanne Conference for Peace in the Near East assembled on November 20, 1922, there were high hopes that a just and lasting settlement might be arrived at. The conference was only a few days old, however, when the time-honored obstacles to peace in the Levant made their appearance: the rival diplomatic policies of the Great Powers; the desire of the West, by means of the Capitulations, to maintain a firm hold upon its vested interests in the East; the imperialistic struggle of rival concessionaires, supported by their respective governments, for possession of the raw materials, the markets, and the communications of Asiatic Turkey. Once more the Bagdad Railway, with its tributary lines in Anatolia and Syria, became one of the stakes of diplomacy!

BIBLIOGRAPHICAL AND EXPLANATORY NOTES

[1] C. J. H. Hayes, *A Brief History of the Great War* (New York, 1920), pp. 71-72; "A Rival to the Bagdad Line," in *The Near East*, May 25, 1917.

[2] *Supra*, Chapter V.

[3] Regarding the diplomatic situation at Constantinople during the critical months of July to November, 1914, *cf.* "Correspondence respecting events leading to the rupture of relations with Turkey," *Parliamentary Papers*, No. Cd. 7628 (1914); C.

Mehrmann, *Der diplomatische Krieg in Vorderasien* (Dresden, 1916); J. Aulneau, *La Turquie et la Guerre* (Paris, 1916); C. Strupp, *Diplomatische Aktenstücke zur orientalischen Frage* (Berlin, 1916); Historicus, "Origines de l'alliance turco-germanique," in *Revue,* 7 series, Volume III (Paris, 1915), pp. 267 *et seq.;* Ostrorog, *op. cit.,* Chapters XII-XVI; footnote 40, Chapter X, *supra.*

⁴ Quoted from *Current History,* Volume I (New York, 1915), p. 1032.

⁵ *Die deutsch-türkische Waffenbrüderschaft,* p. 30.

⁶ Notably Dr. Ernst Jäckh and Dr. Hugo Grothe.

⁷ The following list of books is given without any pretence that it is a complete bibliography of German publications on the Near Eastern question during the year 1914-1915: A. Ritter, *Berlin-Bagdad, neue Ziele mitteleuropäischer Politik* (Munich, 1915) and *Nordkap-Bagdad, das politische Programm des Krieges* (Frankfort a. M., 1914); Hugo Grothe, *Die Türken und ihre gegnerkriegsgeographische Betrachtungen* (Frankfurt a. M., 1915), *Deutsch-türkische wirtschaftliche Interessengemeinschaft* (Munich, 1915), and *Deutschland, die Türkei und der Islam* (Leipzig, 1915); C. A. Schäfer, *Deutsch-türkische Freundschaft* (Stuttgart, 1915); Carl H. Becker, *Deutschland und der Islam* (Leipzig, 1914); J. Ritter von Riba, *Der türkische Bundesgenosse* (Berlin, 1915); J. Hall, *Der Islam und die abendländische Kultur* (Weimar, 1915); Ernst Marré, *Die Türken und wir nach dem Kriege* (Leipzig, 1916); Tekin Alp, *Türkismus und Pantürkismus* (Weimar, 1915); R. Schäfer, *Der deutsche Krieg, die Türkei, Islam und Christentum* (Leipzig, 1915); W. T. Vela, *Die Zukunft der Türkei in Bundnis mit Deutschland* (Berlin, 1915); W. Blanckenburg, *Die Zukunftsarbeit der deutschen Schule in der Türkei* (Berlin, 1915); H. Schmidt, *Das Eisenbahnwesen in der asiatischen Türkei* (Berlin, 1914); H. Margulies, *Der Kampf zwischen Bagdad und Suez in Altertums* (Weimar, 1915); M. Horten, *Die islamische Geisteskultur* (Leipzig, 1915); Fritz Regel, *Die deutsche Forschung in türkische Vordasien* (Leipzig, 1915); M. Roloff, *Arabien und seine Bedeutung für die Erstärkung des Osmanenreiches* (Leipzig, 1915); A. Paquet, *Die jüdische Kolonien in Palästina* (Weimar, 1915); C. Nawratzki, *Die jüdische Kolonisation Palästinas* (Munich, 1914); D. Trietsch, *Die Juden der Türkei* (Leipzig, 1915). Two notable magazine articles are: R. Hennig, "Der verkehrsgeographische Wert des Suez—und des Bagdad-Weges," in *Geographische Zeitschrift,* 1916, pp. 649-656; A. Tschawisch, "Der Islam und Deutschland—Wie soll man sich die Zukunft des Islams denken?", in *Deutsche Revue,* 1915, Volume III, pp. 249 *et seq.*

[8] See advertisements regarding the society and its work in a series of pamphlets *Länder und Völker der Turkei*, edited by Dr. Hugo Grothe (Leipzig, 1915, *et seq.*), and descriptions of similar organizations in a series *Orientbücherei*, edited by Dr. Ernst Jäckh (Stuttgart and Berlin, 1914, *et seq.*).

[9] "Report of the Commission Appointed by Act of Parliament to Enquire into the Operations of War in Mesopotamia," *Parliamentary Papers*, 1917, No. Cd. 8610.

[10] W. S. Churchill, *The World Crisis, 1910-1915* (New York, 1923), pp. 529-535; A. MacCallum Scott, *Winston Churchill in Peace and War* (London, 1916), Chapter X.

[11] C. C. Repington, *The First World War, 1914-1918* (2 volumes, London, 1920), Volume I, pp. 42, 51, etc. *ad lib.;* Churchill, *op. cit.,* pp. 537-538.

[12] The italics are mine. The proposed debarkation of troops, however, was certain to involve a breach of Persian neutrality. *Cf. Parliamentary Papers,* 1917, No. Cd. 8610.

[13] *Ibid.* Regarding the Franco-German agreement of February 15, 1914, *cf. supra*, pp. 246-250.

[14] The text of the agreement between England, France and Russia regarding the disposition of Constantinople and other portions of Turkey is to be found in *Full Texts of the Secret Treaties as Revealed at Petrograd* (New York, *The Evening Post,* 1918); *cf.,* also, R. S. Baker, *Woodrow Wilson and World Settlement* (3 volumes, Garden City, 1922), Volume I, Chapter III. The text of the Treaty of London between Italy and the Allies is to be found in *Parliamentary Papers,* 1920, No. Cmd. 671, Miscellaneous No. 7.

[15] The best single work on military operations in Turkey during the Great War is Edmund Dane's *British Campaigns in the Nearer East, 1914-1918* (2 volumes, London, 1919). Regarding the Caucasus campaigns of 1914-1915 *cf.* M. P. Price, *War and Revolution in Asiatic Russia* (London, 1918), Chapter I; R. Machray, "The Campaign in the Caucasus," in the *Fortnightly Review,* Volume 97 (1915), pp. 458-471. Excellent accounts of the first Turkish offensive against the Suez Canal are to be found in G. Douin, *Un épisode de la guerre mondiale: l'attaque du canal de Suez, 3 Fevrier, 1915* (Paris, 1922); C. Stiénon, "Sur le chemin de fer de Bagdad," in *Revue des deux mondes,* 6 series, Volume 5 (1916), pp. 148-174; T. Wiegand, *Sinai* (Berlin, 1920); N. Moutran, *La Syrie de demain: France et Syrie* (Paris, 1916); R. Hennig, *Der Kampf um den Suezkanal* (Stuttgart, 1915); E. Serman, *Mit den Türken an der Front* (Berlin, 1915); J. Walther, *Zum Kampf in der Wüste am Sinai und Nil* (Leipzig, 1916); P. Schweder, *Im türkischen Hauptquartier* (Leipzig, 1916); *Eine Geschichte der Türkei im Weltkriege* (Munich,

1919). For the Mesopotamian expedition of 1914-1915 consult *Despatches Regarding Operations in the Persian Gulf and Mesopotamia* (London, the War Office, 1915); G. M. Chesney, "The Mesopotamian Breakdown," in the *Fortnightly Review*, Volume 102 (1917), pp. 247-256; H. B. Reynardson, *Mesopotamia, 1914-1915* (London, 1919); C. H. Barber, *Besieged in Kut and After* (Edinburgh, 1917). Of the great quantity of material available on the Dardanelles campaign, *cf.*, in particular, the following: *Gallipoli: der Kampf um den Orient, von einem Offizier aus dem Stab des Marschalls Liman von Sanders* (Berlin, 1916); General Sir Ian Hamilton, *Gallipoli Diary* (London, 1920); H. W. Nevinson, *The Dardanelles Campaign* (London, 1918); S. A. Moseley, *The Truth About the Dardanelles* (London, 1916); John Masefield, *Gallipoli* (London, 1916).

[16] *Parliamentary Papers*, 1917, No. Cd. 8610; C. V. F. Townshend, *My Campaign in Mesopotamia* (London, 1920).

[17] Regarding renewed German activity and interest in the Near East after the elimination of Serbia from the war seemed to bring the *Drang nach Osten* within the realm of practical politics, *cf.*: R. Zabel, *Im Kampfe um Konstantinopel und die wirtschaftliche Lage der Türkei während des Weltkrieges* (Leipzig, 1916); C. H. Müller, *Die wirtschaftliche Bedeutung der Bagdadbahn* (Hamburg, 1917); R. Junge, *Die deutsch-türkischen Wirtschaftsbeziehungen* (Weimar, 1916); E. Marré, *Die Türken und wir nach dem Kriege: ein praktisches Wirtschaftsprogramm* (Berlin, 1916); H. Rohde, *Deutschland in Vorderasien* (Berlin, 1916); H. W. Schmidt, *Auskunftsbuch für den Handel mit der Türkei* (Leipzig, 1917); E. Mygind, *Anatolien und seine wirtschaftliche Bedeutung* (Berlin, 1916); C. V. Bichtligen, "Die Bagdadbahn, eine Hochstrasse des Weltverkehrs in ihrer wirtschaftliche Bedeutung," in *Soziale Revue*, 16 year (1916), pp. 1-11, 123-139; F. C. Endres, *Die Türkei* (Munich, 1916); A. Philippsohn, *Das türkische Reich* (Weimar, 1916); H. Kettner, *Vom Goldenen Tor zum Goldenen Horn und nach Bagdad* (Berlin, 1917). For the point of view of Allied sympathizers, *cf.*: E. F. Benson, *Deutschland über Allah* (London, 1917), and *Crescent and Iron Cross* (New York, 1918); E. A. Martel, *L'emprise austro-allemande sur la Turquie et l'Asie Mineure* (Paris, 1918); H. C. Woods, *The Cradle of the War* (New York, 1919), and an article, "The Bagdad Railway in the War," in the *Fortnightly Review*, Volume 102 (1917), pp. 235-247; J. Thureau, "La pénétration allemande en Asie Mineure," in *Revue politique et parlementaire*, Volume 86 (1916), pp. 19-44; R. Lane, "Turkey under Germany's Tutelage," in *Unpopular Review*, Volume 9 (1918), pp. 328 *et seq.;* N. Markovitch, *Le pangermanisme en Orient* (Nice, 1916); A. J. Toynbee, *Turkey, a Past and a Future* (New York, 1917).

[18] Quoted in *The Near East,* November 12, 1915. For other material regarding construction of the Bagdad Railway during the war and its utilization for military purposes, *cf.: Report of the Bagdad Railway Company,* 1914, pp. 6-7; 1915, pp. 3-6; *The Engineer,* February 4, 1915; "Transportation in the War—The Railways of Mesopotamia," in *Modern Transport* (London), November, 1919; D. G. Heslop, "The Bagdad Railway," in *The Engineer* (London), November 12 and 26 and December 3 and 17, 1920; "Railways of Mesopotamia," in the *Railway Gazette* (London), War Transportation Number, September 21, 1920, pp. 129-140; "Die Bagdadbahn und der Durchschlag des letzten grossen Tunnels," in *Asien,* 14 year (1917), pp. 97-101.

[19] Dane, *op. cit.,* Volume I, Chapters VIII-XII, inclusive; "The German-Turkish Expedition Against the Suez Canal in 1916," in *Journal of the United Service Institution,* Volume 65 (London, 1920), pp. 353-357.

[20] Hayes, *op. cit.,* pp. 142-143.

[21] Quoted from the official text as given in E. E. Robinson and V. J. West, *The Foreign Policy of Woodrow Wilson, 1913-1917* (New York, 1917), pp. 403-405.

[22] *The New York Times,* November 13, 1917.

[23] *Supra,* p. 285.

[24] Baker, *op. cit.,* Volume I, Chapter IV, contains an excellent account of the inter-Allied negotiations of 1916-1917 regarding Asiatic Turkey, based upon the private papers of Woodrow Wilson. *Cf.,* also, *Full Texts of the Secret Treaties as Revealed at Petrograd.*

[25] The Treaty provided that the Bagdad Railway should not be extended southward from Mosul or northward from Samarra without the express consent of both France and Great Britain and in no case before the construction of a railway from Bagdad to Aleppo *via* the Euphrates Valley—the purpose being, as far as possible, to develop southern Mesopotamia and the Syrian coast rather than Kurdistan. By a subsequent agreement of December, 1918, between Messrs. Lloyd George and Clémenceau, Mosul was transferred to Great Britain.

[26] W. L. Westermann, "The Armenian Problem and the Disruption of Turkey," in *What Really Happened at Paris—The Story of the Peace Conference, 1918-1919, by American Delegates,* edited by E. M. House and C. Seymour (New York, 1921), pp. 176-203. *Cf.* p. 183.

[27] The text of the Sykes-Picot Treaty was first published by *The Manchester Guardian,* January 8, 1920, and was reprinted in *Current History,* Volume XI (1920), pp. 339-341. *Cf.,* also, Bowman, *The New World,* pp. 100-104; Baker, *op. cit.,* pp. 67-69.

[28] Baker, *op. cit.,* pp. 68-70. The negotiations concerning the

St. Jean de Maurienne Agreement extended from the autumn of 1916 to August, 1917. The agreement appears to have been negotiated with the Italians by Mr. Lloyd George, in April, 1917, while Mr. Balfour was in America with the British Mission. It was amended in August, as a result of the insistence of the Italians that they had not received an adequate share of the spoils.

[29] President Wilson's address to a joint session of the Congress of the United States, January 8, 1918, setting forth the famous Fourteen Points of a durable peace. Quoted from James Brown Scott, *President Wilson's Foreign Policy* (New York, 1918), pp. 354-363.

[30] Regarding General Maude's brilliant campaign in Mesopotamia, *cf.:* Dane, *op. cit.,* Volume II, Chapters II, III, XII; E. F. Eagan, *The War in the Cradle of the World* (London, 1918); Kermit Roosevelt, *War in the Garden of Eden* (New York, 1919); Sir Charles Collwell, *Life of Sir Stanley Maude* (London, 1920); E. Betts, *The Bagging of Bagdad* (London, 1920); E. Candler, *The Long Road to Bagdad* (London, 1920); C. Cato (pseudonym), *The Navy in Mesopotamia* (London, 1917); F. Maurice, "The Mesopotamian Campaign," in *Asia,* Volume 18 (New York, 1918), pp. 933-936.

[31] British intrenchment in Mesopotamia, 1917-1920, is described in the following: "Review of the Civil Administration of Mesopotamia," *Parliamentary Papers,* No. Cmd. 1061 (1920); R. Thomas, *Report on Cotton Experimental Work in Mesopotamia* (Bagdad, 1919); "Cotton Growing in Mesopotamia," *Bulletin of the Imperial Institute,* Volume 18 (London, 1920), pp. 73-82; *Mesopotamia as a Country for Future Development* (Cairo, Ministry of Public Works, 1919); "Transportation and Irrigation in Mesopotamia," *Commerce Reports,* No. 50 (Washington, 1919), pp. 948-954; Sir H. P. Hewett, *Some Impressions of Mesopotamia* (London, 1919); C. R. Wimshurst, *The Wheats and Barleys of Mesopotamia* (Basra, 1920); *Review of the Civil Administration of the Occupied Territories of Irak* (Bagdad, 1918); L. J. Hall, *Inland Water Transport in Mesopotamia* (London, 1921); Sir Mark Sykes, *The Commercial Future of Bagdad* (London, 1917); "Turkish Rule and British Administration in Mesopotamia," in The Quarterly *Review,* Volume 232 (1919), pp. 401 *et seq.;* W. Ormsby Gore, "The Organization of British Responsibilities in the Middle East," in *Journal of the Central Asian Society,* Volume 7 (1920), pp. 83-105; I. A. Shah, "The Colonization of Mesopotamia," in *United Service Magazine,* Volume 179 (1919), pp. 350 *et seq.*

[32] Townshend, *op. cit.,* pp. 375 *et seq.;* Djemal Pasha, *op. cit.,* Chapter VII; *Current History,* Volume XII (1920), pp. 117-118;

A. D. C. Russell, *loc. cit.*, pp. 325 *et seq.*; F. C. Endres, *Der Weltkrieg der Türkei* (Berlin, 1919).

[33] Regarding General Allenby's campaigns in Palestine and Syria, see: H. Pirie-Gordon, *A Brief Record of the Advance of the Egyptian Expeditionary Force* (London, 1919); W. T. Massey, *Allenby's Final Triumph* (London, 1920); C. C. R. Murphy, *Soldiers of the Prophet* (London, 1921); H. O. Lock, *The Conquerors of Palestine Through Forty Centuries* (New York, 1921); R. E. C. Adams, *The Modern Crusaders* (London, 1920); H. Dinning, *Nile to Aleppo: With the Light Horse in the Near East* (London, 1920); P. E. White, *The Disintegration of the Turkish Empire* (London, 1920); C. T. Atkinson, "General Liman von Sanders and His Experiences in Palestine," *Army Quarterly*, Volume 3 (London, 1922), pp. 257-275; A. Aaronsohn, *Mit der türkischen Armee in Palästina* (Berne, 1918); J. Bourelly, *Campagne d'Égypte et de Syrie contre les Turcs* (Paris, 1919); G. Gautherot, *La France en Syrie et en Cilicie* (Paris, 1920); C. Stiénon, *Les campagnes d'Orient et les intérêts de l'entente* (Paris, 1918), and *La défense de l'Orient et le rôle de l'Angleterre* (Paris, 1918); A. Mandelstamm, *Le sort de l'Empire Ottoman* (Paris, 1917); G. A. Schreiner, *From Berlin to Bagdad: Behind the Scenes in the Near East* (New York, 1918).

[34] H. Charles Woods, *The Cradle of the War*, p. 271.

[35] See a suggestive article by Hilaire Belloc, "Europe's New Paths of Empire," in *Our World* (New York), October, 1922, pp. 41-46; *The Evening Post* (New York), January 3 and March 27, 1919.

[36] *The Treaty of Peace with Germany*, Articles 155, 258, 260, 261, 297.

[37] "Treaty of Peace with Turkey, Signed at Sèvres August 10, 1920," *Parliamentary Papers*, No. Cmd. 964, Treaty Series No. 11, 1920; "Tripartite Agreement Between the British Empire, France, and Italy, Respecting Anatolia, Signed at Sèvres, August 10, 1920," *Parliamentary Papers*, No. Cmd. 963, Treaty Series No. 12, 1920. An official summary of the Sèvres treaty was published in *The Nation* (New York), International Relations Section, Volume 111 (1920), pp. 21-28, and in *Current History*, Volume XIII (1921), pp. 164-184. An excellent discussion of the main provisions of the treaty and its probable effects is to be found in Bowman's *The New World*, Chapters XXIV and XXVI.

[38] Regarding the negotiations at the Paris Conference by which the claims of Italy were disregarded in favor of those of Greece, *cf.* Baker, *op. cit.*, Volume II, Chapter XXXII, and Volume III, Documents Nos. 1, 31-41.

[39] Preamble to the Tripartite Agreement of August 10, 1920.

[40] Regarding the Turkish Nationalist movement, see: Major

General James G. Harbord, "Mustapha Kemal Pasha and His Party," in the *World's Work*, Volume 36 (London, 1920), pp. 470-482; M. Paillarès *La kémalisme devant les Alliés* (Paris, 1922); "The Recovery of the Sick Man of Europe," an excellent review, with a colored map, in the *Literary Digest*, November 11, 1922, pp. 17 *et seq.*; M. K. Zia Bey, "How the Turks Feel," in *Asia*, Volume XXII (1922), pp. 857 *et seq.*, and "The New Turkish Democracy," in *The Nation*, Volume 115 (New York, 1922), pp. 546-548; Major General Sir Charles Townshend, "Great Britain and the Turks," in *Asia*, Volume XXII (1922), pp. 949-953; Clair Price, "Mustapha Kemal and the Angora Government," in *Current History*, Volume XVI (1922), pp. 790-800; Ludwell Denny, "The Turk Comes Back," in *The Nation*, Volume 115 (1922), pp. 575-577; "The New Epoch in Turkey," in the *Muslim Standard* (London), November 9, 1922.

⁴¹ A. J. Toynbee, *The Western Question in Greece and Turkey: A Study in the Contact of Civilizations* (New York, 1922), p. 190. Professor Toynbee's book is the most noteworthy of recent contributions to the history of Turkey since the Great War.

⁴² The text of the National Pact, as translated from the French, is to be found in *The Nation*, Volume 115 (1922), pp. 447-448, in *Current History*, Volume XVII (1922), pp. 280-281, and in Toynbee, *op. cit.*, pp. 207-211 (in both French and English).

⁴³ *Infra.*, pp. 316-317, 323-324.

CHAPTER XII

THE STRUGGLE FOR THE BAGDAD RAILWAY IS RESUMED

GERMANY IS ELIMINATED AND RUSSIA WITHDRAWS

The Great War has completely destroyed German influence in the Near East. In the way of any resumption of German enterprise in Turkey are formidable obstacles which are not likely to be removed for some time. To begin with, the Turks themselves will not encourage German attempts to recover the Bagdad Railway or other property rights which were liquidated by the Treaty of Versailles. Among Turkish Nationalists there is satisfaction that Turkey has "shaken off the yoke of the ambitious leaders who dragged the country into the general war on the side of Germany" and has got rid of the "arrogance" of the Germans who infested the Near East during the last years of the war. Resentment at German military domination of Turkey during 1917 and 1918 will not soon disappear.[1]

Furthermore, Germany possesses neither the disposition nor the power to regain her former preëminence in the Near East. The confiscation by the Treaty of Versailles of private property in foreign investments has set a precedent which will make German investors—as well as prudent investors everywhere—extremely chary of utilizing their funds for the promotion of such enterprises as the Bagdad Railway. The surplus production and surplus capital of Germany may be absorbed by reparations payments or attracted to such enterprises as the reconstruction of the German merchant marine. But the *Drang nach Osten* has become a thing of the past. The dismemberment of the Austrian Empire and the erection of the Jugoslav Kingdom have shut off German access, through friendly states, to the Balkan Peninsula and Asiatic Turkey. Formidable customs barriers will stand in the way of overland trade with the Near East and render railway traffic from "Berlin to Bagdad" unprofitable. Defeat and disarmament have destroyed German prestige in the Moslem world. Democratization of both Germany and Turkey, it is hoped, will render increasingly difficult the kind of secret intrigue that characterized Turco-German relations during the régime of William II and of Abdul Hamid. If Germany returns to the Near East in the next generation or two, it is not likely to be in the rôle of an Imperial Germany promoting railway enterprises of great economic and strategic importance.

Russian diplomatic policy toward Turkey has likewise undergone important changes. Imperial Russia had been a bitter opponent of Imperial Germany in the Bagdad Railway project. Imperial Russia had conspired with Great Britain and France to bring about the collapse and dismemberment of the Ottoman Empire. Imperial Russia was the "traditional enemy" of the Turk. But Imperial Russia was destroyed in 1917 by military defeat and social revolution. Regardless of the pronunciamentos of bourgeois imperialists like Professor Milyukov, revolutionary Russia was certain to look upon the Near Eastern question in a new light. Political and economic disorganization incidental to the war and the revolution would have made it imperative for any government in Russia to curtail its imperialistic pretensions. And with the advent of Bolshevism the outcome was certain. A government which was anti-capitalist and anti-imperialist could not sanction Russian "spheres of interest" or Russian territorial aggrandizement at the expense of Turkey. A government which preached "self-determination of peoples" and "no annexations" could not confirm the secret treaties of 1915-1916. A government which was engaged in repelling foreign invasion and in resisting counter-revolutionary insurrections had to keep within strict limits its military liabilities. Therefore, Soviet Russia speedily foreswore any intention of occupying Constantinople, declared unreservedly for a free Armenia, and proceeded forthwith to withdraw its troops from Persia. These measures were considered "a complete break with the barbarous policy of bourgeois civilization which built the prosperity of the exploiters among the few chosen nations upon the enslavement of the laboring population in Asia," as well as an expression of Bolshevist Russia's "inflexible determination to wrest humanity from the talons of financial capital and imperialism, which have drenched the earth with blood in this most criminal of wars." [2]

Turkish Nationalist resistance to the Treaty of Sèvres met with a sympathetic response on the part of Bolshevist Russia, and on March 16, 1921, the Government of the Grand National Assembly and the Government of the Russian Socialist Federated Soviet Republic signed at Moscow a treaty to confirm "the solidarity which unites them in the struggle against imperialism." By the terms of this treaty Russia refused to recognize the validity of the Treaty of Sèvres or of any other "international acts which are imposed by force." Russia ceded to Turkey the territories of Kars and Ardahan, in the Caucasus region, as a manifestation of full accord with the principles of the National Pact. The Soviet Republic, "recognizing that the régime of the capitulations is incompatible with the national development of Turkey, as well as with the full exercise of its sovereign rights, considers null and void the exercise in Turkey of all functions and all rights under the capitulatory régime." In particular, Russia freed Turkey "from any financial or other obligations based on international treaties concluded between Turkey and the Government of the Tsar." As regards the construction of railways in Anatolia, the Soviet Government completely reversed the former policy of Imperial Russia, which was to oppose all such railways as a strategic menace.[3] It was now provided that, "with the object of facilitating intercourse between their respective countries, both Governments agree to take in concert with each other all measures to develop and maintain within the shortest possible time, railway, telegraphic, and other means of communication," as well as measures "to secure the free and unhampered traffic of passengers and commodities between the two countries." Finally, both countries agreed to stand together in resisting all foreign interference in their domestic affairs: "Recognizing that the nationalist movements in the East," reads the treaty, "are similar to and in harmony with the struggle of the Russian proletariat to establish a new social order, the two contracting parties assert solemnly the rights of these peoples to freedom, independence, and free choice of the forms of government under which they shall live." [4]

No more complete disavowal of Russian imperialism could be desired by the New Turkey. It is by no means certain, however, that Russia will continue indefinitely to pursue so magnanimous a policy in the Near East. With the development of her natural resources and the extension of industrialism, it is not improbable that Russia—in common with the other Great Powers—will once again feel the urge to imperialism. Raw materials, markets, the maintenance of unimpeded routes of commercial

communication, and opportunities for profitable investment of capital are likely to be considered—in the present
anarchic state of international relations—as essential to
an industrial state under working-class government as
to an industrial state under bourgeois administration. If
such be the case, Russian economic penetration in Turkey
and Persia may be resumed, and Russian eyes may once
more be cast covetously at Constantinople. "In Mongolia
and Tibet, in Persia and Afghanistan, in Caucasia and at
Constantinople, the Russian has been pressing forward
for three hundred years," writes an eminent American
geographer, "and no system of government can stand that
denies him proper commercial outlets." [5]

Nevertheless, whatever be the future policy of Russia in the Near East, for the present the Russian Republic has no economic or strategic interests which are
inconsistent with the national development of the Turkish people. Certainly Russia has neither the economic
nor the political resources to demand a share in the Bagdad Railway or to seek for herself other railway concessions in Anatolia. And the Western Powers are little
likely to heed the wishes of the Soviet Government until
such time as those wishes are rendered articulate in a
language the Western Powers understand—the language
of power.

FRANCE STEALS A MARCH AND IS ACCOMPANIED BY ITALY

Those who believed that the defeat of Germany and
the withdrawal of Russia would solve all problems of
competitive imperialism in the Near East were destined
to be disillusioned. For no sooner was the war over than
France and Great Britain took to pursuing divergent
policies regarding Turkey. The rivalry between these
two powers—which had been terminated for a time by

the Entente of 1904—was resumed in all its former intensity. The Entente, in fact, had been formed because of common fear of Germany, rather than because of coincidence of colonial interests; and with that fear removed, the foundation of effective coöperation had been undermined.[6] The Great War may be said to have terminated the first episode of the great Bagdad Railway drama—the rise and fall of German power in the Near East; it opened a second episode, which promises to be equally portentous—an Anglo-French struggle for the right of accession to the exalted position which Germany formerly occupied in the realm of the Turks.

Anglo-French rivalry in the Near East will not be an unprecedented phenomenon. "Since the Congress of Vienna in 1814, France and Great Britain have never fought in the Levant with naval and military weapons (though they have several times been on the verge of open war), but their struggle has been real and bitter for all that, and though it has not here gone the length of empire-building, it has not been confined to trade. Its characteristic fields have been diplomacy and culture, its entrenchments embassies, consulates, religious missions, and schools. It has flared up on the Upper Nile, in Egypt, on the Isthmus of Suez, in Palestine, in the Lebanon, at Mosul, at the Dardanelles, at Salonica, in Constantinople. The crises of 1839-41 and 1882 over Egypt and of 1898 over the Egyptian Sudan are landmarks on a road that has never been smooth, for conflicts [of one sort or another] have perpetually kept alive the combative instinct in French and English missionaries, schoolmasters, consuls, diplomatists, civil servants, ministers of state, and journalists. One cannot understand—or make allowances for—the post-war relations of the French and British Governments over the 'Eastern Question' unless one realizes this tradition of rivalry and its accumulated inheritance of suspicion and resentment. It is a bad mental background for the individuals who have to represent the two countries. The French are perhaps more affected by it than the English, because on the whole they have had the worst of the struggle in the Levant as well as in India, and failure cuts deeper memories than success." [7]

French statesmen were dissatisfied with the division of the spoils of war in the Near East. They had a feeling that here, as elsewhere, Britain had obtained the lion's share. They believed that Mr. Lloyd George had been guilty of sharp practice in his agreement of December, 1918, with M. Clémenceau, by the terms of which Mosul and Palestine were to be turned over to Great Britain. [8] Frenchmen were suspicious of British solicitude for the Arabs, which they believed was not based upon disinterested benevolence; in fact, self-determination for the Arabs came to be considered a political move to render precarious the French mandate for Syria. French patriots chafed at British emphasis upon the fact that "the British had done the fighting in Turkey almost without French help" and that "there would have been no question of Syria but for England and the million soldiers the British Empire had put in the field against the Turks." French pride was hurt by the rapid rise of British prestige in a region where France had so many interests. And prestige—diplomatic, military, religious, cultural, and economic—has always been an important desideratum in Near Eastern diplomacy. [9]

French dissatisfaction with the Turkish settlement was one of the issues of the San Remo Conference of April, 1920, at which were assigned the mandates for the territories of the former Ottoman Empire. Exclusive control by Great Britain of the oilfields of the Mosul district was so vigorously contested that M. Philippe Berthelot, of the French Foreign Office, and Professor Sir John Cadman, Director of His Majesty's Petroleum Department, were instructed to work out a compromise. Thus came into existence the San Remo Oil Agreement of April 24, 1920, by which Great Britain, in effect, assigned to France the former German interest in the Turkish Petroleum Company's concession for exploitation of the oilfields in the vilayets of Mosul and Bagdad.[10] But the British drove a shrewd bargain, for it was provided, in consideration, that the French Government should agree, "as soon as application is made, to the construction of two separate pipe-lines and railways necessary for their construction and maintenance and for the transport of oil from Mesopotamia and Persia through French spheres of influence to a port or ports on the Mediterranean." The oil thus transported was to be free of all French taxes.[11]

French imperialists likewise were dissatisfied with the disposition of the Bagdad Railway as provided for by the unratified Sèvres Treaty. French bankers had held a thirty per cent interest in the Bagdad line while it was under German control, [12] and they believed, for this reason, that they were entitled to a controlling voice in the enterprise when it should be reorganized by the Allies. Although the settlement at Sèvres—the Treaty of Peace with Turkey and the Tripartite Agreement between Great Britain, France, and Italy—recognized the special interests of France in the Bagdad Railway, and particularly in the Mersina-Adana branch, it provided, as has been seen, for international ownership, control, and operation.[13] Now, Frenchmen were suspicious of internationalization, particularly where British participation was involved. Had not the condominium in Egypt proved to be a step in the direction of an eventual British protectorate? Might not the history of the Suez Canal be repeated in the history of the Bagdad Railway? Would Great Britain look with any greater equanimity upon French, than upon German, interests in one of the great highways to India? To answer these questions was but to increase the French feeling of insecurity.

French dissatisfaction with the distribution of the spoils in the Near East and French fear of British imperial power and prestige—these were factors in a new alignment of the diplomatic forces in Turkey during 1920-1922. British imperialists were desirous of keeping Turkey weak. A weak Turkey could never again menace Britain's communications in the Persian Gulf and at Suez; a weak Turkey could be of no moral or material assistance to restless Moslems in Egypt and India. To keep Turkey weak the Treaty of Sèvres had loaded down the Ottoman Treasury with an enormous burden of reparations and occupation costs (to which France could not object without repudiating the principle of reparations); had taken away Turkish administration of Smyrna and Constantinople, the two ports essential to the commercial life of Anatolia; and had made possible a Greek war of devastation and extermination in the homeland of the Turks. France, on the other hand, would have preferred to see Turkey reasonably strong. A strong, prosperous Turkey would the more readily pay off its pre-War debt, of which French investors held approximately sixty per cent; payment of this debt was more important to France than payment of Turkish reparations. A strong Turkey, furthermore, might fortify the French position in the Near East. As Germany had utilized Ottoman strength against Russia and Great Britain, so France might utilize Nationalist Turkey against a Bolshevist Russia which would not pay its debts or an imperial Britain which might prove unfaithful to the Entente.[14]

Anglo-French differences in the Near East were brought to a head by the rapid rise of the military power of the Angora Government, for it was against France that Mustapha Kemal's troops launched their principal early attacks. General Gouraud—his hands tied by an Arab rebellion which had necessitated a considerable extension of his lines in Syria—was unable to repulse the Turkish invasion of Cilicia, which reached really serious proportions in the autumn of 1920. Time and again French units were defeated and French garrisons massacred by the victorious Nationalists. In these circumstances, France "had to choose between the two following alternatives: either to maintain her effectives and to continue the war in Cilicia, or to negotiate with the *de facto* authority which was in command of the Turkish troops in that region." The French armies in Syria and Cilicia already numbered more than 100,000 men; to reenforce them would have been to flout the opinion of the nation and the Chamber, "which had vigorously expressed their determination to put an end to cruel bloodshed and to expenditure which it was particularly difficult to bear." To negotiate with Mustapha Kemal was, to all intents and purposes, to scrap the unratified Treaty of Sèvres. The French Government chose the latter alternative. It is said that during the London Conference of February-March, 1921, "M. Briand declared to Mr. Lloyd George on several occasions, without the British Prime Minister making the slightest observation, that he would not leave England without having concluded an agreement with the Angora delegation. M. Briand pointed out that neither the Chamber nor French public opinion would agree to the prolongation of hostilities, involving as they did losses which were both heavy and useless." [15]

Accordingly, on March 9, 1921, there was signed at

London a Franco-Turkish agreement terminating hostilities in Cilicia. The Turkish Nationalists recognized the special religious and cultural interests of France in Turkey and granted priority to French capitalists in the awarding of concessions in Cilicia and southern Armenia. French interests in the Bagdad Railway were confirmed. In return, France was to evacuate Cilicia, to readjust the boundary between Turkey and Syria, and to adopt a more friendly attitude toward the Government of the Grand National Assembly.[16]

The Italian Government was only too glad to have so excellent an excuse for throwing over the Treaty of Sèvres, which had thoroughly frustrated Italian hopes in Asia Minor to the advantage of Greece. Italian troops, furthermore, had been driven out of Konia and were finding their hold in Adalia increasingly precarious; the Italian Government had neither the disposition nor the resources to wage war. Therefore, on March 13, 1921, the Italian and Turkish ministers of foreign affairs signed at London a separate treaty, providing for "economic collaboration" between Turkey and Italy in the hinterland of Adalia, including part of the sanjaks of Konia, Aidin, and Afiun Karahissar, as well as for the award to an Italian group of the concession for the Heraclea coal mines.[17] The Royal Italian Government pledged itself to "support effectively all the demands of the Turkish delegation relative to the peace treaty," more especially the demands of Turkey for complete sovereignty and for the restitution of Thrace and Smyrna. Italian troops were to be withdrawn from Ottoman soil.[18]

During the summer of 1921 further negotiations were conducted between France and Turkey for the purpose of elaborating and confirming their March agreement. The outcome was the so-called Angora Treaty, signed October 20, 1921, by M. Henri Franklin-Bouillon, a

special agent of the French Government, and Yussuf
Kemal Bey, Minister of Foreign Affairs in the Government of the Grand National Assembly. This treaty
formally brought to an end the state of war between the
two countries, provided for the repatriation of all pris-
oners, defined new boundaries between Turkey and Syria,
and awarded valuable economic privileges to French
capitalists. It obligated the French Government "to make
every effort to settle in a spirit of cordial agreement all
questions relating to the independence and sovereignty of
Turkey." [19]

The Bagdad Railway was given a great deal of consideration in the Angora Treaty. The Turks wanted
possession of the line because of its great political and
strategic value; French capitalists sought full recognition of their previous investments in the railway, together
with a controlling interest in its operation. A solution was
reached which fully satisfied both Turkish Nationalists
and French imperialists. The Turco-Syrian boundary
was so "rectified" that the Bagdad Railway from Haidar
Pasha to Nisibin was to lie within Turkish territory,
whereas formerly the sections from the Cilician Gates
to Nisibin lay within the French mandate for Cilicia and
Syria.[20] In return for these territorial readjustments the
Turkish Government assigned to a French group (to be
nominated by the French Government) the *Deutsche
Bank's* concession for those sections of the railway, including branches, between Bozanti and Nisibin, "together
with all the rights, privileges, and advantages attached to
that concession." The Government of the Grand National Assembly, furthermore, declared itself "ready to
examine in the most favorable spirit all other desires
that may be expressed by French groups relative to mine,
railway, harbor and river concessions, on condition that
such desires shall conform to the reciprocal interest of

Turkey and France." In particular, the Turkish Government agreed to take under advisement the award to French capitalists of concessions for the exploitation of the Arghana copper mines and for the development of cotton-growing in Cilicia.[21]

Thus France sought to make herself heir to the former German estate in Asiatic Turkey. Her capitalists became the recipients of the kilometric guarantee for which German concessionaires had been so freely criticized. And in some respects the conditions of French tenancy were questionable. The old Bagdad Railway concession had prohibited the Germans, under any and all circumstances to grant discriminatory rates or service to any passenger or shipper.[22] The conditions of French control of the line, however, recognized only a limited application of the principle of the "open door": "Over this section and its branches," reads Article 10 of the Angora Treaty, "no preferential tariff shall be established *in principle*. Each Government, however, *reserves the right to study in concert with the other any exception to this rule which may become necessary. In case agreement proves impossible, each party will be free to act as he thinks best.*"[23]

During the spring of 1922 the concession for the operation of the French sections of the Bagdad Railway, as defined by the Angora Treaty, was assigned to the Cilician-Syrian Railway Company (*La société d'exploitation des chemins de fers de Cilicie-Nord Syrie.*) The Mesopotamian sections of the line, from Basra to Bagdad and Samarra, were under the jurisdiction of the British Civil Administration for Irak. From Haidar Pasha to the Cilician Gates the Railway was being operated by the Turkish Nationalist Government, although its utilization for commercial purposes was seriously curtailed by the Greco-Turkish War.[24]

British Interests Acquire a Claim to the Bagdad Railway

The Angora Treaty met with a distinctly heated reception from the British Government. During November and December, 1921, Lord Curzon carried on a lengthy correspondence with the French Embassy at London, in which he made it perfectly plain that the British Government considered the Franklin-Bouillon treaty a breach of good faith on the part of France, in the light of which Great Britain must possess greater freedom of action than would otherwise be the case.[25]

Lord Curzon called into question the moral right of the French Government to enter into separate understandings with Turkey or to recognize the Angora Assembly as the *de jure* government of the country. He insisted that a revision of the frontier of northern Syria "could not be regarded as the concern of France alone":

"It hands back to Turkey a large and fertile extent of territory which had been conquered from her by British forces and which constituted a common gage of allied victory, although by an arrangement between the Allies the mandate has been awarded to France. The mandate is now under consideration by the League of Nations, and this important and far-reaching modification of the territory to which it applies altogether ignores the League of Nations, while the return to Turkey of territory handed over to the Allies in common without previous notification to Great Britain and Italy is inconsistent with both the spirit and the letter of the treaties which all three have signed.

"Further, the revision provides for handing back to Turkey the localities of Nisibin and Jezirit-ibn-Omar, both of which are of great strategic importance in relation to Mosul and Mesopotamia; the same consideration applies to the handing back to Turkey of the track of the Bagdad Railway between Tchoban Bey and Nisibin. . . . His Majesty's Government cannot remain indifferent to the manifest strategic importance to their position in Irak of the return to Turkey of the Bagdad Railway or of the transfer to that power of the localities of Jezirit-ibn-Omar and Nisibin."

In addition to disputing the territorial readjustments
contemplated by the Angora Treaty, the British Government challenged the transfer to French capitalists of the
former German concession for the Bozanti-Nisibin sections of the Bagdad Railway. Lord Curzon pointed out
that Great Britain would not recognize the Franco-
Turkish treaty as overriding the Treaty of Sèvres,
"whereby Turkey was herself to liquidate the whole
Bagdad Railway on the demand of the principal Allies";
neither would the British Government assent to the award
to France of "a large portion of the railway without regard to the claims of her other allies upon a concern
which both under the Treaty of Versailles and the Treaty
of Sèvres is the Allies' common asset." [26]

"Apart from the immediate and premature advantage gained
by France by this transfer of a large portion of the Bagdad line
to a French company in advance—and therefore possibly to the
prejudice—of the reciprocal allied arrangements contemplated by
Article 294 of the Treaty of Sèvres and Article 4 of the Tripartite Agreement, it is necessary to point out that these stretches
of the railway which were previously in Syria, but are now
surrendered to Turkey, although placed in the French zone of
economic interest, ought naturally to be divided among the Allies
in accordance with the above mentioned treaties. . . . The transfer
to a French company of that part of the railway which still
remains in Syria does not in itself fulfil the provisions of the
Treaty of Sèvres, which stipulates for liquidation by the manda-
tary and the assignment of the proceeds to the Financial Commission as an allied asset."

The correspondence was concluded by Lord Curzon
with emphatic statements that "when peace is finally concluded the different agreements which have been negotiated up to date, including the Angora Agreement, will
require to be adjusted with a view to taking their place
in a general settlement"; that he was obliged "explicitly
to reserve the attitude of His Majesty's Government with
regard to the Angora Agreement"; and that there must

especially be reserved for further discussion "all articles of the Agreement which appear to infringe the provisions of the Treaty of Sèvres and the Tripartite Agreement.

Subsequent events did nothing to restore Anglo-French unity in the Near East. At the Washington Conference in December, 1921, Lord Lee and M. Briand engaged in a verbal war over submarines which created no little hard feeling and suspicion in both Great Britain and France. Differences of opinion regarding Russia and other questions discussed at the Genoa Conference, together with a clash over reparations in midsummer, 1922, strained relations still further. Charges by Greeks and Englishmen that France and Italy were supplying munitions to the Turkish Nationalists were received with counter-charges that British officers were aboard Greek warships and that British "observers" were directing Greek military operations in Asia Minor.[27] Feeling ran high in September, 1922, when—seeking to avoid a Near Eastern war—the French and Italian Governments withdrew their troops from the Neutral Zone of the Straits, leaving the British forces to face, alone, the victorious Nationalist army of Mustapha Kemal Pasha. British patriots were further irritated by the mysterious activities of M. Henri Franklin-Bouillon in the negotiations preceding the Mudania armistice and by the claims of the Paris press to a great victory thereby for French prestige at Angora and Constantinople. Fundamental differences of opinion regarding reparations—culminating in the French invasion of the Ruhr in January, 1923— made still more difficult coöperation by the former Allies in the Near East. In fact, it might be questioned whether the Entente Cordiale any longer existed.

This situation was brought into sharp relief at the first Lausanne Conference for Peace in the East.[28] Great Britain's interests were chiefly territorial. She had abandoned all hope of destroying Turkish power by creating a Greek empire in Asia Minor; Greece was gone from Smyrna for good. But England was determined to maintain her hold in Mesopotamia—particularly in the oilfields of Mosul—and to hold out for neutralization of the Straits. These territorial questions occupied the major part of the first six weeks of the Conference. France had no interest in the decisions regarding the Straits and Mosul; therefore she supported the Turks and placed Lord Curzon in the position of appearing to be the real opponent of Turkish Nationalist ambitions and the principal obstacle in the way of an equitable settlement. Lord Curzon himself strengthened this impression, for many of his utterances were provocative and bombastic in the extreme—apparently he would not give up the idea that the Turks could be bluffed and bullied into submission.

While the conference as a whole was debating territorial questions and problems concerning the rights of minorities, a member of the French delegation was presiding over the sessions of the all-important Committee on Financial and Economic Issues. It was in this committee that questions of the Ottoman Public Debt and of concessions were to be threshed out; therefore it was in this committee that French imperialists hoped to achieve real successes. And while France was framing the economic sections of the treaty, her co-worker Italy was supervising the work of the Committee on the Status of Foreigners in Turkey, to determine the conditions upon which French and Italian schools and missions should continue their activities in Asia Minor. In this manner France hoped to protect adequately her economic and cultural interests in the Near East.

As the work of these committees progressed, the Turks became more and more suspicious of French aims. The

Nationalist delegates—including Djavid Bey—were mindful of the price which their country had had to pay because of its economic exploitation by Germany, and they were determined not to permit another European Power to succeed to the position which Germany had left vacant. Friction developed, therefore, as soon as concessions came up for consideration. The French delegation asked for the incorporation in the treaty of provisions confirming all concessions to Allied nationals whether granted by the old Ottoman Government before the War, or by the Constantinople Government after the armistice, or by mandatory powers in territory subsequently evacuated (as in Cilicia, Smyrna, and Adalia). The Turks objected that they were not aware of the nature, the number and extent, or the beneficiaries of the concessions coming within the last two categories; confirmation of such would have to be the subject of independent investigation and negotiation, for the Turks would not sign any blank checks at Lausanne. They doubted whether they could accept the financial burden which would be involved in validating concessions granted by the Sultan's Government before the War, especially if the National Assembly was to be obliged to honor Ottoman pre-War debts in full. In any case, the Turkish delegates insisted, no concessions would be confirmed if they in any way limited the sovereignty of Turkey or infringed upon its financial and administrative integrity. Between the French and Turkish views was a chasm which it would be difficult, indeed, to bridge. The French stood upon the rock of the old imperialism; the Turks were fortified in their new nationalism. The French were seeking to intrench certain important vested interests; the Turks were striving to preserve a precious independence, recently won at great price.

In these circumstances, it was to be expected that the

British and the Turks should seek to effect an understanding. The claims of Great Britain, it appeared, were
more easily reconcilable with the Turkish program than
were the claims of France. Concessions obtained by
British nationals between 1910 and 1914 were largely in
areas detached from Turkey during the War—chiefly in
Mesopotamia—whereas many of the most important
French concessions were in Anatolia, the stronghold of
the Turkish Nationalists.[29] To Great Britain, therefore,
it was a matter of comparative indifference whether all
concessions within Turkey were specifically confirmed;
to France it was a matter of the utmost importance. According to the proposed Lausanne treaty the Turkish
Government was to expropriate the former German railways in Turkey, with a view to incorporating them into a
state-owned system, and was to pay therefor to the
Financial Commission, on reparations account, a sum to
be fixed by an arbitrator appointed by the League of
Nations.[30] It suited British interests thus to prevent a
rival Power from obtaining control of the former Bagdad line; it suited French interests not at all to be deprived of a considerable share in a highly important
enterprise. In the settlement of questions regarding the
Ottoman Public Debt, likewise, the French were more
obdurate than the British.

In the closing days of the conference, the question of
Mosul and its oilfields—the last question which stood in
the way of an Anglo-Turkish agreement—was temporarily settled by a decision to make it the subject of
"direct and friendly negotiations between the two interested Powers." But no agreement was possible between
Turkey and France on concessions and capitulations.
When the first Lausanne Conference broke up, therefore,
it was because of the determination of the Turks not to
accept economic, financial, and judicial clauses which they

believed menaced their independence. "The treaty," said Ismet Pasha, head of the Turkish delegation, "would strangle Turkey economically. I refuse to accept economic slavery for my country, and the demands of the Allies remove all possibility of economic rehabilitation and kill all our hopes." On the other hand, the refusal of the Turks to sign was characterized by the chief of the French delegates as "a crime." [31]

During the interim between the first and second Lausanne conferences French prestige in the Near East was dealt some severe blows. The Turkish press attacked the French Government for having insisted upon concessions and capitulations which were designed to keep Turkey under foreign domination in the interest of bondholders and promoters. Such conduct, it was pointed out, was altogether inconsistent with the terms of the Angora Treaty by which France agreed "to make every effort to settle in a spirit of cordial agreement all questions relating to the independence and sovereignty of Turkey." [32] In the National Assembly hostility to French claims was so pronounced that no further action was taken toward the ratification of the Angora Treaty— and without such ratification the French title to certain sections of the Bagdad Railway would be invalid. The Turkish army on the Syrian frontier was reënforced for the purpose of bringing home to France the determination of the Angora Government to tolerate no foreign interference in its domestic affairs. The situation in Syria became so serious that M. Poincaré saw fit to despatch to Beirut one of Marshal Foch's right-hand men, General Weygand, as commander-in-chief in Syria.

The breach between France and Turkey was widened when, on April 10, 1923, the Angora Government awarded to an American syndicate headed by Admiral Colby M. Chester, a retired officer of the United States

Navy, concessions for almost three thousand miles of railway, together with valuable rights to the exploitation of the mineral resources of Anatolia.[33] The Chester concessions conflicted with certain French claims which had been under discussion at the first Lausanne Conference: the concession for a Black Sea railway system, which had been conferred upon French capitalists in 1913; and rights to the Arghana copper mines, to which a French group had been given a kind of priority under the Angora Treaty of 1921.[34] In part, at least, the award of the Chester concessions at this particular time was a shrewd political move on the part of the Nationalist Government. It was designed to serve notice on France that no treaty would be acceptable to Turkey which would require complete confirmation of pre-War concessions; from this decision there could be no departure without infringing upon American rights and without recognizing the acts of a former Sultan as superior to acts of the new government of Turkey. It was intended, also, to win for the Turks a measure of American diplomatic support. That the French Government understood the implications of the Chester concessions is evidenced by the fact that the Foreign Office despatched to Angora a note which characterized the award as "a deliberately unfriendly act, of a nature to influence adversely the coming negotiations at Lausanne." [35]

When the second Lausanne Conference convened on April 22, 1923, therefore, it was France, not Great Britain, which was on the defensive. And the French position became steadily worse, rather than better. On May 15, it was announced that a syndicate of British banks had purchased a controlling interest in the *Bank für orientalischen Eisenbahnen,* of Zurich, the *Deutsche Bank's* holding company for the Anatolian and Bagdad Railway Companies. Ismet Pasha, it was said, was kept fully informed of the British plans and expressed his pleasure at the consummation of the transaction. Thus, after twenty years of diplomatic bargaining, British imperialists had won possession of the "short cut to India"![36] Should Great Britain succeed in establishing her point that the *Bank für orientalischen Eisenbahnen* is a neutral Swiss, rather than enemy German, corporation and therefore exempt from seizure under the reparations provisions of the Treaty of Versailles; and should the Chester concessions be recognized as superseding the rights of the Black Sea Railways, French interests in the Levant will face a powerful Anglo-American competition which it will be very difficult for them to combat with any degree of success.[37] And the power of the French Government is so heavily invested in the Ruhr occupation that it is doubtful if it can do anything at all to coerce the Turks into full recognition of French claims.

Kaleidoscopic indeed have been the changes in the Near East since the outbreak of the Great War in 1914. The economic and political power of Germany in Anatolia, Syria, and Mesopotamia has been completely destroyed. The Ottoman Empire has disappeared, and in its place has risen a republican Nationalist Turkey. Tsarist Russia, with its consuming desire for aggrandizement in the Caucasus, in Asia Minor, and at the Straits, has given way to a proletarian Russia which foreswears imperialist ambition. Italy, which sought to transform the Adriatic and the Ægean into Italian lakes, has finally been compelled to recognize that she assumed imperial liabilities out of all proportion to her economic resources. France, after achieving a temporary victory in the New Turkey, has had to surrender her position to more powerful competitors. But Great Britain has emerged from the conflict in all her glory. She has obtained possession of another highway to the East. Alongside the Suez Canal, in the collection of British imperial jewels, will be placed the Bagdad Railway; alongside of Malta and Gibraltar and Cyprus must be placed Jerusalem and Basra and Bagdad.

No less remarkable than all these changes, however, is the entry of American interests into the tangled problem of the Near East.

America Embarks upon an Uncharted Sea

The Great War was accompanied by a definite growth of American prestige in the Near East. After the entry of Turkey into the war against the Allied Powers, American schools and missions were left practically a free hand in the Ottoman Empire; and inasmuch as the United States did not declare war against Turkey, American institutions were not disturbed even after 1917. Carrying on their work under the most trying circumstances, these educational and philanthropic enterprises established a still greater reputation than they formerly possessed for efficient and disinterested service. In consequence, an American official mission to the Near East in 1919 was able to report that the moral influence of the United States in that region of the world was greater than that of any other Power. President Wilson was looked upon as the champion of small nations and oppressed peoples. Americans were considered to be charitable and generous to a fault. The United States was hailed as the only nation which had entered the war for unselfish purposes.[38]

Since the armistice of 1918 events have not materially decreased the prestige which the War built up. "From Adrianople to Amritsar, and from Tiflis to Aden, America is considered a friend. It has become a tradition in the Near East to interpret every action of the

European Powers as an attempt at political domination. America is the only power considered strong enough to provide the Orient with the capital and expert knowledge for its industrial development, without aiming at more than a legitimate profit. The Oriental feels that he needs coöperation with the West; but he is anxious to restrict that coöperation to the economic field. And he considers the United States the only power which would replace Europe's political ambitions by a sound, matter-of-fact, and sincere economic policy." [39]

During the Great War the economic situation of the United States underwent certain fundamental changes which seem to forecast increasing American interest in imperialism. Before the War, America was practically self-sufficient in raw materials; its export trade was composed very largely of foodstuffs and raw materials which found a ready market in the great industrial nations of Europe; financially, it was a debtor, not a creditor, nation. The enormous industrial expansion of the United States during the Great War, however, has changed these conditions. Raw materials have become an increasingly greater proportion of the nation's import trade, and American business men are becoming concerned about foreign control of certain essential commodities such as rubber, nitrates, chrome, and petroleum. American export trade has experienced an unparalleled period of expansion, and American manufactured articles are competing in world markets which formerly were the exclusive preserves of European nations. Furthermore, the export of American capital has almost kept pace with the export of American goods, so that by 1920 the United States had taken its place alongside Great Britain and France as one of the great creditor nations of the world. As time goes on American business will be reaching out over the world for a fair share of the earth's resources in raw materials, for new markets capable of development, and for opportunities for the profitable investment of capital.[40]

These new tendencies were quickly reflected in American relations with the Near East. As early as the spring of 1920 the Government of the United States was engaged in a lengthy correspondence with His Britannic Majesty's Government regarding the right of American capital to participate in the exploitation of the oil resources of Mesopotamia.[41] About the same time the Guaranty Trust Company of New York—the second largest bank in the United States—established a branch in Constantinople and proceeded to inform American business men regarding the opportunities for commercial expansion in the Near East. In a booklet entitled *Trading with the Near East—Present Conditions and Future Prospects,* the bank had this to say:

"The establishing of a Constantinople branch of the Guaranty Trust Company of New York brings forcibly to mind the growing importance of the Near East to American foreign trade. Up to the present time American business in Constantinople has been seriously handicapped by the absence of American banking facilities. Our traders were forced to rely on British, French, or other foreign banks for their financial transactions. This was not only inconvenient, but it was devoid of that business secrecy which is so necessary in exploiting new fields.

"Before the war merchandise from the United States was a negligible factor in the business life of Constantinople, and a vessel flying the Stars and Stripes was a rare sight. Today one will find four or five American liners in the Golden Horn at all times. . . . Today a dozen important American corporations have permanent offices there, and many other American concerns are represented by local agents.

"The future possibilities of imports from and exports to the Eastern Mediterranean, the Sea of Marmora, and the Black Sea ports from the United States are of almost unbelievable proportions. These entire sections must be fed, clothed, and largely rehabilitated. Roads, ports, railways, and public works of all kinds are needed everywhere. The merchants of the Near East have valuable raw products to send us in exchange for the manufactured goods which they so urgently need."

This estimate of the situation was confirmed by the American Chamber of Commerce for the Levant when, in urging upon the Department of State the vigorous defence of the "open door" in Turkey, it said: "The opportunities for the expansion of American interests in the Near East are practically unlimited, provided there is a fair field open for individual enterprise. . . . In fact, with the conclusion of peace, there is the economic structure of an empire to be developed." [42]

The rapid development of American economic interests in Turkey can be most effectively presented by reference to the trade statistics. American exports to Turkey at the opening of the twentieth century amounted to only $50,000. In 1913 they had risen to $3,500,000. But between 1913 and 1920 they showed a phenomenal increase of over twelve hundred per cent, reaching the sum of $42,200,000. Nor 'was this trade one sided, for during the period 1913-1920, American imports from Turkey increased from $22,100,000 to $39,600,000.[43]

The Chester concessions are another important step in the development of a new American policy in the Near East. They provide for the construction by the Ottoman-American Development Company—a Turkish corporation owned and administered by Americans—of approximately 2800 miles of railways, of which the following are the most important:

1. An extension of the old Anatolian Railway from Angora to Sivas, with a branch to the port of Samsun, on the Black Sea.

2. A line from Sivas to Erzerum and on to the Persian and Russian frontiers, with branches to the Black Sea ports of Tireboli and Trebizond.

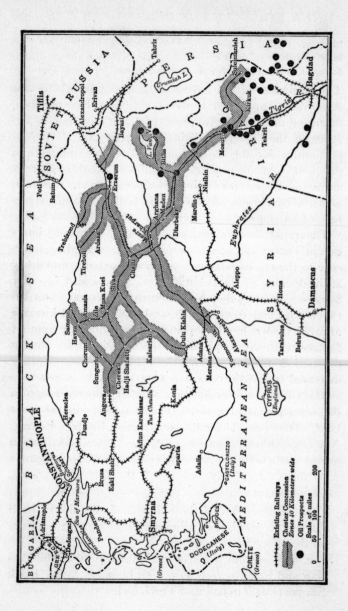

3. A line from Oulu Kishla, on the Bagdad Railway, to Sivas *via* Kaisarieh.

4. A trans-Armenian railway from Sivas to Kharput, Arghana, Diarbekr, Mosul, and Suleimanieh, including branches to Bitlis and Van.

5. A railway from Kharput to Youmourtalik, a port on the Gulf of Alexandretta.

No more elaborate project for railway construction in Asiatic Turkey has ever been incorporated in a definitive concession. That it should be entrusted to American promoters and American engineers is one of the most significant developments in the long and involved history of the Eastern Question.

But the Chester concessions do not stop at railway construction alone. As in the case of the Bagdad Railway, the Turkish Government is obliged to offer the financiers powerful inducements to the investment of capital in railway enterprises which, in themselves, may be unremunerative for a time. The German promoters of the Bagdad Railway obtained a kilometric guarantee, or subsidy; the American promoters of the Chester lines are granted exclusive rights to the exploitation of all mineral resources, including oil, lying within a zone of twenty kilometres on each side of the railway lines. The Bagdad Railway mortgaged the revenues of Imperial Turkey; the Chester concessions mortgage the natural resources of Nationalist Turkey. The Ottoman-American Development Company, furthermore, is authorized to carry out important enterprises subsidiary to the construction of the railway lines and the exploitation of the mines aforementioned. It may, for example, lay such pipe lines as are necessary to the proper development of the petroleum wells lying within its zone of operations. It is permitted to utilize water-power along the line of its railways and to instal hydro-electric stations for the service of its mines, ports, or railways. It is required to construct elaborate port and terminal facilities at Samsun, on the Black Sea, and at Youmour-talik, on the Gulf of Alexandretta.

There are other respects in which the terms of the Chester grant are strikingly similar to those of the Bagdad Railway concession of March 5, 1903.[44] Lands owned by the Turkish Government and needed for right-of-way, terminal facilities, or exploitation of mineral resources are transferred to the Ottoman-American Development Company, free of charge, for the period of the concession (ninety-nine years). Public lands required for construction purposes—including sand-pits, gravel-pits, and quarries—may be utilized without rental, and wood and timber may be cut from State-owned forests without compensation. As public utilities, the Chester enterprises are granted full rights of expropriation of such privately owned land as may be necessary for purposes of construction or operation. Like the *Deutsche Bank,* the Ottoman-American Development Company is granted sweeping exemption from taxation, as follows: "The materials, machines, coal, and other commodities required for the construction operations of the Company, whether purchased in Turkey or imported from abroad, shall be exempt from all customs duties or other tax. The coal imported for the operation of the [railway] lines shall be exempt from customs duties for a period of twenty years, dating from the ratification of the present agreement. For the entire duration of the concession the lines and ports constructed by the Company, as well as its capital and revenues, shall be exempt from all imposts." [45]

From the Turkish point of view, the Chester concessions may be justified on the grounds that the new railways will bring political stability to Anatolia [46] and will initiate an era of unprecedented economic progress. From the point of view of those American interests which believe in the stimulation of foreign trade, likewise, the Chester project has much to commend it. Exploitation of the oilfields of the vilayets of Erzerum, Bitlis, Van, and Mosul, and the development of the mineral resources of Armenia—including the valuable Arghana copper mines—will provide rich sources of supply of raw materials. In the construction of railways, ports, and pipe lines there will be a considerable demand for American steel products. Economic development of the vast region through which the new railways will pass promises to furnish a market for American products, such as agricultural machinery, and to offer ample opportunity for the profitable investment of American capital. The Chester project may well become an imperial enterprise of the first rank.

With the exception of the temporary advantage which they hoped to gain at the second Lausanne Conference, the Turkish Government wished no political importance to be attached to the Chester concessions. As Abdul Hamid had awarded the Anatolian and Bagdad Railway concessions to a German company because he believed Germans would be less likely to associate political aims with their economic privileges, so the Government of the National Assembly has awarded the Chester concessions to an American syndicate because Turkish Nationalists are convinced that Americans have no political interests in Turkey. This was made clear by Dr. I. Fouad Bey, a member of the National Assembly, in a semi-official visit to the United States during April, 1923. "We Turks wish to develop our country," he said. "We need foreign coöperation to develop it. We cannot do without this coöperation. Now, there are two kinds of foreign coöperation. There is the foreign coöperation that is coupled with foreign political domination—coöperation that brings profit only to the foreign investor. We have had enough of that kind.

There is another kind of coöperation—the kind we conceive the Chester project and other American enterprises to be. This kind of coöperation is a business enterprise and has no imperialistic aim. It is a form of coöperation designed to profit both America and Turkey, and not to invade Turkish sovereignty and Turkish political interests in any way. That is why we prefer American coöperation. That is why the Grand National Assembly at Angora is prepared to welcome American capital with open arms and secure it in all its rights." [47]

These sentiments found a ready echo among American merchants. At a dinner given in honor of Dr. Fouad Bey by the American Federated Chambers of Commerce for the Near East, one of the speakers said: "Turkey, in our opinion, is destined to have a magnificent future. It is on the threshold of a new and great era. Its extraordinary resources, amazingly rich, are practically untouched. Although in remote ages of antiquity these vast regions played a great rôle in history, they have for many centuries lain practically fallow. The tools, appliances, machinery and methods which have been so highly perfected in the United States are appropriate to and will be needed for the development of this marvelous latent wealth. Our capital likewise can be very helpful. The members of our Chamber of Commerce have a keen interest in the furtherance of trade relations between Turkey and the United States. We want both to increase the imports of its raw materials into our country and to stimulate the export of our manufactured articles to Turkey. We are inspired by no political aims. We seek no annexation of territory. We desire no exclusive privileges. Our motto, if we had one, would be 'A fair field and no favors.' In the development of commercial relations with Turkey, in seeking the investment of our capital there, we ask for nothing more than an open door." [48]

The American press, likewise, is in accord with a policy of governmental non-intervention in the ramifications of the Chester project. The following editorial from the new York *World* of April 23, 1923, is perhaps representative:

"There is no reason why the State Department should make itself the attorney for or the promoter of the Chester business enterprises. If the Angora Government has granted privileges to the Admiral's company, then the Admiral's business is with Angora and not with Washington.

"Certainly the American people have no more interest in taking up the Chester concessions diplomatically than they would have if the Admiral were proposing to open a candy store in Piccadilly, a dressmaking establishment in the Rue de la Paix, or a beauty parlor on the Riviera. If the Admiral and his friends wish to invest money in Turkey, they no doubt know what they are doing. They will expect profits commensurate with the risks, and they should not expect the United States Government, which will enjoy none of the profits, to insure them against the risks."

It is difficult, nevertheless, to see how the Chester concessions, and their affiliated enterprises can be kept scrupulously free from political complications. The French Government, in defence of the interests of its nationals, has announced semi-officially that American support of the concessions might lead to "a diplomatic incident of the first importance." [49] Furthermore, the United States Navy is said to be vitally interested in the Chester project. The oilfields to which Admiral Chester's Ottoman-American Development Company obtain rights of exploitation may prove to be important sources of fuel supply to American destroyers operating in the Mediterranean— Mr. Denby, Secretary of the Navy, said apropos of the concessions that the Navy "is always concerned with the possibility of oil supplies." [50] Furthermore, an American-built port at Youmourtalik, on the Gulf of Alexandretta, might conceivably be utilized as an American naval base.

Such a station, less than 150 miles from Cyprus and less than 400 miles from the Suez Canal, could hardly be expected to increase the British sense of security in the Eastern Mediterranean.

The American Navy has already been very active in the Near East. "Soon after the armistice, Rear Admiral Bristol was sent to Constantinople to command the small American naval forces there. A large part of his efforts was immediately devoted to the promotion of American business in that unsettled region, including the countries bordering on the Black Sea. He soon established for himself such an influential position by sheer force of character and by his intelligent grasp of both the political and economic situations that he was appointed high commissioner by the State Department.

"Early in 1919 several American destroyers were ordered to Constantinople for duty in the Near East. Although these destroyers are good fighting ships, it costs some $4,000,000 a year to maintain them on this particular duty, which does not train the crews for use in battle. . . . The possible development of the economic resources of this part of the world was carefully investigated by representatives of American commercial interests. These representatives were given every assistance by the Navy, transportation furnished them to various places, and all information of commercial activities obtained by naval officers in their frequent trips around the Black Sea given them. The competition for trade in this part of the world is very keen, the various European countries using every means at their disposal to obtain preferential rates. The Navy not only assists our commercial firms to obtain business, but when business opportunities present themselves, American firms are notified and given full information on the subject. One destroyer is kept continuously at Samsun, Turkey, to look after the American tobacco interests at that port.

. . . The present opportunities for development of American commerce in the Near East are very great, and its permanent success will depend largely upon the continued influence of the Navy in that region." [51] This is the situation as diagnosed by the Navy Department itself.

"With the assistance of a small force of destroyers based on Constantinople," according to an instructor in the United States Naval Academy, "our commercial representatives are establishing themselves firmly in a trade which means millions of dollars to the farmers of the American Middle West. By utilizing the wireless of destroyers in Turkish ports, at Durazzo, and elsewhere, commercial messages have been put through without delay. . . . Destroyers are entering Turkish ports with 'drummers' as regular passengers, and their fantails piled high with American samples. An American destroyer has made a special trip at thirty knots to get American oil prospectors into a newly opened field." Here is "dollar diplomacy" with a vengeance! "If this continues, we shall cease to take a purely academic interest in the naval problems of the Near East. These problems are concerned with the protection of commerce, the control of narrow places in the Mediterranean waterways, and the naval forces which the interested nations can bring to bear. They cannot be discussed without constant reference to political and commercial aims." [52]

Americans would do well to take stock of this Near Eastern situation. Mustapha Kemal Pasha invites the participation of American capital in railway construction in Anatolia for substantially the same reasons which prompted Abdul Hamid to award the Bagdad Railway concession to German bankers. In 1888, Abdul Hamid considered Germany economically powerful but politically disinterested. Today, Mustapha Kemal Pasha believes that American promoters, engineers, and industrialists possess the resources and the technical skill which are required to develop and modernize Asia Minor. And, from the Turkish point of view, the political record of the United States in the Near East is a good record. America never has annexed Ottoman territory or staked out spheres of interest on Turkish soil; America has not participated in the Ottoman Public Debt Administration; America has few Mohammedan subjects and therefore is not fearful of the political strength of Pan-Islamism; America did not declare war on Turkey during the European struggle; America was not a party to the hated treaty of Sèvres. America alone among the Western Powers seems capable of becoming a sincere and disinterested friend of Turkey.[53] The avowed foreign policies of the United States appear to confirm the opinion of the Turks that Americans can be depended upon not to infringe upon Turkish sovereignty. America must be kept scrupulously free from all "foreign entanglements"; therefore an American mandate for Armenia has been firmly declined. Splendid isolation is declared to be the fundamental American principle in international affairs.

The political theory of isolation, however, is not altogether in harmony with the economic fact of American world power. The enormous expansion of American commercial and financial interests during and since the Great War brings the United States face to face with new, difficult, and complicated international problems. American business men will be increasingly interested in the backward countries of the world, in which they can purchase raw materials, to which they can sell their finished products, and in which they can invest their capital. American financiers, manufacturers, and merchants will look to their government for assistance in the extension of foreign markets and for protection in their foreign investments. Already there is grave danger that the United

States may "plunge into national competitive imperialism, with all its profits and dangers, following its financiers wherever they may lead." [54]

The situation is not unlike that which faced the German Empire in 1888. When the *Deutsche Bank* initiated its Anatolian railway enterprises, it inquired of the German Government whether it might expect protection for its investments in Turkey. Bismarck—who desired to avoid imperialistic entanglements and to limit German political interests, as far as possible, to the continent of Europe— replied with a warning that the risk involved "must be assumed exclusively by the entrepreneurs" and that the Bank must not count upon the support of the German Government in "precarious enterprises in foreign countries." But Bismarck's policy did not take full cognizance of the phenomenal industrial and commercial expansion of the German Empire, whose nationals were acquiring economic interests in Asia and in Africa and on the Seven Seas. William II was more sensitive than Bismarck to the demands of German industrial, commercial, and financial interests that they be granted active governmental support and protection abroad. Bismarck tolerated German enterprises in Turkey; William II sponsored them. It was under William II, not under Bismarck, that Germany definitely entered the arena of imperial competition.[55]

The development of American interests in Turkey puts the Government of the United States to a test of statesmanship. The temptations will be numerous to lend governmental assistance to American business men against their European competitors; to utilize the new American economic position in Turkey for the acquisition of political influence; to use diplomatic pressure in securing additional commercial and financial opportunities; to emphasize the economic, at the expense of the moral, factors in Near Eastern affairs. To yield to these temptations will be to destroy the great prestige which America now possesses in the Levant by reason of disinterested social and educational service. To yield will be to forfeit the trust which Turkish nationalists have put in American hands. To yield will be to intrench the system of economic imperialism which has been the curse of the Near East for half a century. To yield will be to involve the United States in foreign entanglements more portentous than those connected with the League of Nations, or the International Court of Justice, or any other plan which has yet been suggested for American participation in the reconstruction of a devastated Europe and a turbulent Asia.

The Chester concessions may be either promise or menace. They will give promise of a new era in the Near East insofar as they contribute to the development and the prosperity of Asia Minor, without infringing upon the integrity and sovereignty of democratic Turkey, and without involving the Government of the United States in serious diplomatic controversies with other Great Powers. They will be a menace—to Turkey, to the United States, and to the peace of the world—if, unhappily, they should lead republican America in the footsteps of imperial Germany.

BIBLIOGRAPHICAL AND EXPLANATORY NOTES

[1] Mufty-Zade Zia Bey, "How the Turks Feel," in *Asia*, Volume XXII (1922), p. 857.

[2] "Declaration of the Rights of the Toiling and Exploited People," Article III. Available in English translation in *International Conciliation*, No. 136 (New York, 1919).

[3] *Supra*, Chapter VII.

[4] The text of the Russo-Turkish Treaty of March 16, 1921, is given as an appendix to an article by A. Nazaroff, "Russia's Treaty with Turkey," in *Current History*, Volume XVII (1922), pp. 276-279.

[5] Bowman, *op. cit.*, p. 398.

[6] *Cf. supra*, pp. 202-203. Professor Toynbee now speaks of this feature of the Entente in terms of contempt: "Its direct motive

was covetousness, and it rested locally on nothing more substantial than the precarious honor among thieves who find their business threatened by a vigorous and talented competitor. Some of the thieves, at any rate, never got out of the habit of picking their temporary partners' pockets." *Op. cit.*, p. 46.

[7] *Ibid.*, pp. 45-46.

[8] It seems to be established that Mr. Lloyd George compelled a readjustment of the terms of the Sykes-Picot Treaty by threatening M. Clémenceau with a complete exposure and repudiation of all of the secret treaties. *Cf.* Baker, *op. cit.*, Volume I, pp. 70-72.

[9] See Minutes of the Council of Four, March 20, 1919, reported in full by Baker, *op. cit.*, Volume III, Document No. 1.

[10] Regarding the claims of the Turkish Petroleum Company, *cf. supra*, p. 261.

[11] *Parliamentary Papers*, No. Cmd. 675 (1920). *Cf.*, also, the "Franco-British Convention of December 23, 1920, on Certain Points Connected with the Mandates for Syria, the Lebanon, Palestine, and Mesopotamia," *Parliamentary Papers*, No. Cmd. 1195 (1921). For a general discussion of the oil situation, see: H. Bérenger, *La politique du pétrole* (Paris, 1920) ; F. Delaisi, *Le pétrole—La politique de la production* (Paris, 1921) ; A. Apostol and A. Michelson, *La lutte pour le pétrole* (Paris, 1922).

[12] *Cf. supra*, Chapter X, Note 18.

[13] *Supra*, pp. 301-302.

[14] Interesting sidelights on these points will be found in the correspondence between the French and British Governments regarding the Angora Treaty of October 20, 1921, *Parliamentary Papers*, No. Cmd. 1571, Turkey No. 1 (1922). *Cf.*, also, Toynbee, *op. cit.*, Chapter III, "Greece and Turkey in the Vicious Circle"; Jean Lescure, "Faut-il détruire la Turquie?" in *Revue politique et parlementaire*, Volume 103 (1920), pp. 42-48; "Where Diplomacy Failed," *The Daily Telegraph* (London), September 19, 1922.

[15] M. de Montille to the Marquess Curzon of Kedleston, November 17, 1921, in the official correspondence cited in Note 14.

[16] *Cf.* a statement by M. Briand regarding the purposes and the scope of the agreement, *Journal officiel, Débats parlementaires, Chambre des députés*, March 16, 1921, pp. 1272-1273. The text of the agreement is available in *Current History*, Volume XIV (1921), pp. 203-204, and in the *Contemporary Review*, Volume 119 (1921), pp. 677-679.

[17] Regarding the Heraclea coal mines *cf. supra*, p. 14. During the War the mines were operated by Hugo Stinnes.

[18] For the text of the Turco-Italian treaty see *L'Europe Nouvelle* (Paris), May 28, 1921, or *The Nation*, Volume 113 (New York, 1921), p. 214. *The New York Times*, April 13, 1921, con-

tains a good summary of the treaty and the circumstances of its negotiation.

[19] The text of the Angora Treaty is given in *Parliamentary Papers,* No. Cmd. 1556, Turkey No. 2 (1921). It has been reprinted in Current History, January, 1922. For a statement by M. Briand regarding the purposes and scope of the treaty, *cf. Journal officiel, Débats parlementaires, Sénat,* October 28, 1921, pp. 818-819.

[20] Aleppo remained within the French mandate for Syria, so that for a time—until the Turks construct a substitute line—through trains will have to pass through French territory for a short distance. Guarantees against interruption of either military or commercial traffic were exacted by the Turks, however. In addition, Turkey was guaranteed full use of the port of Alexandretta on a basis of absolute equality with Syria.

[21] Most of the supplementary economic concessions are provided for in a covering letter of Yussuf Kemal Bey and in an exchange of notes which coincided with the signature of the treaty. These were kept absolutely secret until December, when their contents were made known to the British Government.

[22] *Supra,* p. 83.

[23] The italics are mine. Discrimination against British trade from Mosul to Alexandretta, for example, might be used to force Great Britain to abandon many of her claims in northern Mesopotamia.

[24] *The Times* (London), August 2, 1922; *Manchester Guardian Commercial,* August 31, 1922; *Chicago Tribune,* Paris edition, August 21, 1922.

[25] For the text of the correspondence, *cf. Parliamentary Papers,* No. Cmd. 1571, Turkey No. 1 (1922).

[26] *Cf. supra,* pp. 301-302.

[27] A not unrepresentative Greek view is the following: "Nationalist Turkey became, in a military sense, French territory. Political missions, military missions, propaganda missions, financial missions, found their way from Paris to Angora. The entire credit of the French Republic was placed behind Kemal. The warships of France and the liners of the *Messageries Maritimes* became Turkish transports, and the French arsenals were placed at the disposal of the Turks. Once the ally of Kemal, France supported him to the fullest extent of its ability and its resources." A. T. Polyzoides, "The Greek Collapse in Asia Minor," in *Current History,* Volume XVII (1923), p. 35.

[28] Material regarding the Lausanne Conference is scattered and fragmentary. The text of the proposed treaty is to be found in *L'Europe Nouvelle* (Paris), February 24 and March 10, 1923; a summary is given in *The Times* (London), February 1, 1923. The

newspaper accounts which I have used are those of *The New York Times, The Times* (London), *The Manchester Guardian, The World* (New York), and the *Christian Science Monitor* (Boston). For reports and editorial comment in weekly periodicals I have consulted *The Near East, L'Europe Nouvelle, Journal des Débats, The New Statesman* (London), *The Nation* (New York). The following magazine articles have proved useful: "The Lausanne Conference," in *Current History,* Volume XVII (1923), pp. 531-537, 743-748, 929-930; Saint-Brice, "De la Ruhr à Lausanne," in *Correspondance d'Orient* (Paris), February, 1923; "The Oriental Labyrinth at Lausanne," in the *Literary Digest,* April 21, 1923, pp. 19-20; H. Froidevaux, "Les négociations de Lausanne et leur suspension," in *L'Asie Française,* 33 year, No. 208 (Paris, 1923), pp. 8-10; J. C. Powell, "Italy at Lausanne," in *The New Statesman,* Volume XX (1922), pp. 291-292; A. J. Toynbee, "The New Status of Turkey," in the *Contemporary Review,* Volume 123 (1923), pp. 281-289; P. Bruneau, "La question de Mossoul," in *L'Europe Nouvelle,* February 3, 1923, pp. 138-140. For some of my information regarding the Lausanne Conference I am indebted to Djavid Bey.

[29] *Cf. supra,* Chapters IX and X, *ad lib.*

[30] Compare with the provisions of the Treaty of Sèvres, *supra,* pp. 301-302.

[31] *The New York Times,* February 5, 1923.

[32] *Cf. supra,* pp. 324-325.

[33] The Chester concessions will be treated more fully in the succeeding pages.

[34] *Supra,* pp. 245-249, 325-326. It was the Turkish contention that the Black Sea concessions were invalid for the following reasons: they were negotiated by a government for the acts of which the National Assembly assumed no responsibility; they never had been ratified by the Turkish Parliament; the French bankers had not fulfilled all the conditions upon which the concessions were predicated.

[35] *The New York Times,* April 12, 1923.

[36] Regarding the *Bank für orientalischen Eisenbahnen, cf. supra,* p. 32. Accounts of the purchase by British interests are to be found in *The New York Times,* April 28, May 15 and 16, 1923, and *The Times* (London), May 18, 1923.

[37] The Chester concessions conflict, to a degree, with the rights of the British-owned Turkish Petroleum Company (*cf. supra,* Chapter X) in the vilayet of Mosul. The area in conflict is so small, compared to the total of the two concessions, however, that it is extremely doubtful if there will be any serious difficulty in reaching a satisfactory adjustment.

[38] "Report of the King-Crane Mission to the Near East," pub-

lished as a supplement to the *Editor and Publisher,* Volume 55 (New York, 1922), pp. I-XXVIII. *Cf.,* also, "Report of the American Military Mission to Armenia," Senate Document No. 266, Sixty-sixth Congress, First Session (Washington, 1920).

[39] E. J. Bing, "Chester and Turkey, Inc.," in *The New Republic,* Volume XXXIV (New York, 1923), pp. 290-292.

[40] *Cf.* E. M. Earle, "The Outlook for American Imperialism," in the *Annals of the American Academy of Political and Social Science,* Volume CVIII (Philadelphia, 1923).

[41] For the text of this correspondence, *cf. Parliamentary Papers,* No. Cmd. 675 (1921).

[42] *The New York Times,* October 29, 1922.

[43] *Statistical Abstract of the United States,* 1921, *passim*; "The Trade of Turkey During 1920," *Commerce Reports,* Special Supplement (Washington, 1921).

[44] Compare with the terms of the Bagdad Railway concession, *supra,* pp. 70-71, 77-84.

[45] The text of the Chester concessions—in an English translation which leaves much to be desired—is to be found in *Current History,* Volume XVIII (1923), pp. 485-489. For an official copy of the concessions, with a map, I am indebted to Mr. M. Zekeria, Secretary of the Turkish Information Service in New York.

[46] The Chester concessions contain the usual provisions for the utilization of the railways by the gendarmerie and the military, both in time of peace and in time of war.

[47] *The World* (New York), April 10, 1923.

[48] The remarks are those of Mr. Ernest Filsinger, of the firm of Lawrence & Company, exporters. Mr. Filsinger has been good enough to supply me with a copy of his speech.

[49] *The New York Times,* April 12, 1923.

[50] *Ibid.,* April 23, 1923.

[51] *The United States Navy as an Industrial Asset* (Washington, Office of Naval Intelligence, 1923). *Cf.,* also, C. Merz, "Bristol, Quarterdeck Diplomat," in *Our World,* December, 1922.

[52] Allen Westcott, "The Struggle for the Mediterranean," in *Our World,* February, 1923, pp. 11-17.

[53] *Cf., supra,* pp. 63-65.

[54] *Cf.* W. E. Weyl, *American World Policies* (New York, 1917), Chapter V; A. Demangeon, *America and the Race for World Dominion* (Garden City, 1921), a translation of *Le Déclin de l'Europe* (Paris, 1920).

[55] *Supra,* pp. 40-42.

INDEX

Abdul Hamid, Sultan, 5, 23, 198; problems of, 9; interest in railway construction, 20, 30; deposition of, 97.

Adaban Island, 283.

Adalia, 267, 285, 302, 324.

Adana, 22, 72. (*See also* Mersina-Adana Railway.)

Adrianople, 29.

Afiun Karahissar, 34, 53, 324.

Agadir crisis, 170, 253.

Agriculture in Turkey. (*See* Turkey, agricultural conditions.)

Aidin, 324. (*See also* Smyrna-Aidin Railway.)

Alashehr, 34.

Aleppo, 2, 22, 62, 71, 73, 281, 299.

Alexandretta, 19, 62, 73, 110, 112, 151.

Allenby, Field Marshal Sir E. H. H., 298-299.

Alliance Israélite Universelle, 133.

Amanus Mountains, 22, 72, 94, 234, 277, 289; Bagdad Railway tunnels through, 113, 119, 289.

Amara, 286.

America. (*See* United States of America.)

American Federated Chambers of Commerce for the Near East, 344.

Anatolia, 280, 302, 305; geography of, 10; natural resources of, 13-14; railways of, 29-30. (*See also* Anatolian Railway, Smyrna-Cassaba Railway, Smyrna-Aidin Railway, Black Sea Railways, etc.)

Anatolian Railway, 34, 53, 61, 63, 224, 248, 339; concession of 1888, 32; concession of 1893, 33; agreement with Smyrna-Cassaba Railway, 59-60; board of directors, 85; irrigation enterprises, 98, 117; economic achievements of, 230-232; concessions of 1914, 248-249, 272.

Andrew, Sir William, 176-177.

Anglo-French Entente. (*See* Entente Cordiale.)

Anglo-French rivalry in the Near East, 318-329.

Anglo-German Agreement of June 15, 1914, 261-265.

Anglo-German rivalry, 138, 179-180, 203.

Anglo-Japanese Alliance, 204.

Anglo-Persian Oil Company, 259, 261, 283, 286.

Anglo-Russian Agreement (1907), 204.

Anglo-Turkish Agreements (1913), 254-258, 263-264.

Angora, 31, 32, 33, 34, 305, 339.

Angora Government. (*See* Grand National Assembly.)

Angora Treaty (October 20, 1921), 324-325, 333, 352.

Arabs, 9-10, 15, 87, 196, 207, 282-284, 294, 297, 299, 302, 305, 320.

Ardahan, 316.

Arghana, 246, 340; copper mines of, 326, 334, 343.

Armenia, 2, 9, 44; republic of, 302, 305; proposed American mandate, 348.

Asia Minor. (*See* Anatolia.)

Atlas Line, 107.

Auguste Victoria, Kaiserin, 132.